D1481704

ial

Library

MACROBIUS

I

LCL 510

MACROBIUS

SATURNALIA

BOOKS 1–2

EDITED AND TRANSLATED BY

ROBERT A. KASTER

HARVARD UNIVERSITY PRESS
CAMBRIDGE, MASSACHUSETTS
LONDON, ENGLAND
2011

50 YBP ¹⁄₁₁   24.00

First published 2011

LOEB CLASSICAL LIBRARY® is a registered trademark
of the President and Fellows of Harvard College

Library of Congress Control Number 2010924777
CIP data available from the Library of Congress

ISBN 978-0-674-99649-6

*Composed in ZephGreek and ZephText by
Technologies 'N Typography, Merrimac, Massachusetts.
Printed on acid-free paper and bound by
The Maple-Vail Book Manufacturing Group*

CONTENTS

For Paul and Emily, Anna and Thomas

"Nature has formed many different attachments
for us in this life, Eustathius my child,
but she has forged no bond of affection stronger than
the one that binds us to our offspring."

PREFACE

Not least among the pleasures of sitting down to complete this project by writing the preface is having the chance to thank the individuals and institutions that have helped to bring me to this day.

To start with the latter, I am indebted once again to Princeton University for a sabbatical semester, and to the university's Humanities Council, which allowed me to extend that semester to a full academic year by naming me an Old Dominion Professor for 2008–2009: without the chance to sit in my small, quiet office above J. Crew on Palmer Square and commune with Macrobius, I would not have finished this project for many months, perhaps years. I am also very grateful to the institutions that provided the microfilms and digitized images without which my edition would have been impossible: Bayerische Staatsbibliothek, Munich; Biblioteca Apostolica Vaticana; Biblioteca Medicea Laurentiana, Florence; Biblioteca Nacional de España, Madrid; Biblioteca Nazionale di Napoli; Bibliothèque Interuniversitaire—Section Médecine, Montpellier; Bibliothèque Nationale de France, Paris; Bibliothèque Royale de Belgique, Brussels; Bodleian Library, Oxford; British Library, London; Burgerbibliothek, Bern; Cambridge University Library; Herzog August Bibliothek, Wolfenbüttel; Institut de Recherche et d'Histoire des

Textes, Paris; Parker Library, Corpus Christi College, Cambridge; Staatsbibliothek, Bamberg; Universitätsbibliothek, Salzburg; Universiteitsbibliotheek, Leiden; Yale Medical Library. The cost of those images was largely borne by the Magie Fund of the Department of Classics in Princeton University, which has been repeatedly generous in supporting my work.

Among individuals, thanks go first to Jeff Henderson, series editor of the Loeb Classical Library: he was warmly receptive when—on a back staircase at the meetings of the American Philological Association in San Diego—I first raised the possibility of contributing to the series, and he has been consistently supportive since then. I also want to thank Jennifer Snodgrass, formerly of Harvard University Press, who worked with me at an early stage, and Ian Stevenson, who has seen the project through the Press. Bruce Barker-Benfield and Michael Reeve very kindly and helpfully pointed me toward some manuscript resources, and curators at several libraries responded to queries concerning books in their collections: my thanks for that go to Patrick Andrist (Bern), Justin Clegg (British Library), Wolfgang-Valentin Ikas (Munich), Alexandra Ilginus (Wolfenbüttel), Martin Germann (Bern), and Jayne Ringrose (Cambridge University Library), as also to Nathalie Picque of the IRHT, who was both patient and helpful.

Then there are the scholars who responded with unfailing kindness when I disturbed their peace, often out of the blue, with questions on any number of odd subjects: warms thanks, then, to Markus Asper, Alan Bowen, Ted Champlin, Elaine Fantham, Chris Faraone, Denis Feeney, Matt Fox, Tom Hare, Alex Jones, Joshua Katz,

PREFACE

Chris Kraus, Bob Lamberton, Pauline LeVen, John D. Morgan, Charles Murgia, Chris Pelling, Don Skemer, Katharina Volk, Heinrich Von Staden, Peter White, and Christian Wildberg; Leofranc Holford-Strevens and Michele Salzman deserve special thanks for reviewing my notes on the calendar. In the later stages of the project Alan Cameron and Mike Fontaine let me see some of their work in advance of publication, and Alan and Chris Kraus were constructive readers of a draft of the introduction. Finally, Peter White, bless his heart, not only was responsible for suggesting that a Loeb edition of the *Saturnalia* would be more useful than several other possibilities I had in mind but then—bearing out the principle that no good deed goes unpunished—took on the job of meticulously vetting a draft of the translation, improving it in countless ways.

Whatever else might be said about Macrobius (and opinions have certainly varied), there's surely no doubt that in the *Saturnalia*'s first sentence he hit the nail squarely on the head. I can think of no work more appropriate to dedicate to my dear children and their dear spouses.

Princeton, New Jersey
20 July 2009

ix

INTRODUCTION

1. MACROBIUS AMBROSIUS THEODOSIUS

A learned man "born under an alien sky," Macrobius Ambrosius Theodosius is known today as the author of three very different works.[1] First, and probably earliest, there is a treatise on the similarities and differences of the Greek and Latin verbal systems (his command of Greek was unusually strong for a Latin-speaker of his day), which survives only in excerpts.[2] Then there is the work that caused Macrobius to be counted a great philosopher in the High Middle Ages and later, his commentary, in two books, on the "Dream of Scipio" that concludes Cicero's *On the Commonwealth*: written by Cicero to present a view of the

---

[1] "Alien sky" (*Praef.* 11): Africa is the conventional guess, reasonable but no more; his misunderstandings of Greek (Wissowa 1880, 15, cf. e.g. 7.6.5n.) and his use of "we" when referring to Latin-speakers (e.g., *Comm.* 1.14.21), rule out the eastern Roman Empire. All citations are of the *Saturnalia*, and all dates are CE, unless otherwise indicated.

[2] Edition: Paolis 1990. Its relative date is deduced from the fact that this work lacks the titles, *vir clarissimus et inlustris*, found in the inscriptions to the other two, though their absence is possibly due to the fact that we have only excerpts.

soul and the afterlife that would encourage just and vigorous participation in civic life, the "Dream" serves Macrobius as the point of departure for a thoroughly Neoplatonic treatment of (especially) cosmology and the soul's ascent to the One.[3]

Finally, there is the work that is the chief reason Macrobius is still read today: the *Saturnalia*, an encyclopedic compilation quarried from mostly unnamed sources (see §4 below) and cast as a dialogue that gathers together members of the Roman aristocracy prominent in the late fourth century, along with their learned entourage, to discuss matters ridiculous and sublime, and above all the poetry of Virgil. Set ca. 383 (see §2 below), the discussion presents Virgil as the master of all human knowledge, from diction and rhetoric through philosophy and religion, making explicit a view long implied by the scholarship gathered around the poems and anticipating the miraculous figure of "Virgil the magician" known to the Middle Ages.

About Macrobius as author of the *Saturnalia* two different but not entirely incompatible stories used to be told, both of them straightforward and tidy. In the first, Macrobius was a pedant and plagiarist writing at a time of cultural decline, a man of doubtful honesty and intelligence whom we should nonetheless grudgingly thank for pre-

---

[3] Besides Willis' Teubner (1963; 3rd ed. 1994), recent editions include Regali 1983–90, Armisen-Marchetti 2001–3, and Neri 2007. That *Comm.* antedates *Sat.* is inferred from the fact that subjects treated in both works are handled more fully, and in a way more appropriate to the context, in the former (Wissowa 1880, 12).

serving much precious ancient lore that would otherwise be lost.[4] In the second, Macrobius was a celebrant of the cultural and religious ideals of Vettius Agorius Praetextatus, Quintus Aurelius Symmachus, and Virius Nicomachus Flavianus, the most prominent of the aristocrats in the dialogue, who were also the most prominent champions of the traditional religious views and practices that an increasingly aggressive Christianity contemptuously labeled "pagan."[5]

In both versions it was assumed that he was a contemporary of the men and events portrayed, and a public career was duly stitched together for him from the offices known to have been held by one or more men named Macrobius in the late fourth and early fifth centuries, culminating in the post of imperial chamberlain (*praepositus sacri cubiculi*) in 422 (this despite the fact that the post was regularly held by a eunuch, while Macrobius' two major works are dedicated to his son). In the case of the story's second version, this assumption made Macrobius not simply a front-line observer of but an active combatant in the culture wars of the fourth century's last two decades, which saw the emperor Gratian remove the four-hundred-year-old altar of Victory from the Roman senate chamber in 382 and withdraw state subsidy for traditional civic cults; Symmachus fail to persuade Valentinian to restore

[4] This is the view that pervades Wissowa 1880, on Macrobius' sources, though it is still found, e.g., in Williams 1966–67, 50 ("interest in learning for its own sake . . . at a time when pedantry was unusually pervasive").

[5] This is the view developed most fully and sympathetically by Bloch 1945 and 1963.

the altar, when he was urban prefect in 384, and Praetextatus die late the same year; Theodosius the Great issue a law closing all temples and banning all forms of traditional cult in 391; and Flavianus kill himself when the usurper Eugenius, whom he supported, was defeated by Theodosius at the battle of the Frigidus in 394. In the aftermath, Flavianus' memory was "condemned"—his name stricken from the public records and eradicated from public inscriptions—and his homonymous son was forced to convert to Christianity. But Macrobius (the story had it) kept the memory of Flavianus, of Praetextatus, and of their religious commitments alive by creating the *Saturnalia* around 395[6]—and refusing to allow the name of Christianity even to appear in the text.

A straightforward and tidy story; but its foundations were radically undermined when Alan Cameron published "The Date and Identity of Macrobius" in 1966.[7] Macrobius, it emerged, was not a contemporary of the events described above, in fact was almost certainly not born until some years after the *Saturnalia*'s dramatic date; not only that, Macrobius was not the name he commonly went by. Rather, Theodosius is the name he used when referring to himself in the dedication of his grammatical

[6] The date conventionally accepted after Georgii 1912.

[7] Cameron 1966 brilliantly developed a suggestion made in passing a generation earlier by Santo Mazzarino (1938, 256–59). Cameron has refined and elaborated the several converging arguments in Cameron 2011, Chapter 7, which the following account accepts in most significant respects and on which it gratefully draws.

work;[8] and that is only what we should expect, since some-one called Macrobius Ambrosius Theodosius would al-most invariably have been called by the third of his names in contexts that called for only one name.[9]

In trying to reconstruct his career, Cameron taught us, we must look not for a Macrobius, but for a Theodosius who had a public career leading to the rank—*vir clarissimus et inlustris*—that the manuscripts of his two major works attest. If we do, we find only one candidate: a Theodosius who was praetorian prefect of Italy—one of the five most important posts in the imperial administration—in 430. A man who was praetorian prefect at that date would

---

[8] "Theodosius to his friend Symmachus" (*Theodosius Symmacho suo*: in light of the revised chronology, Symmachus cannot be Quintus Aurelius Symmachus, who died in 402, when Macrobius was still a child, but must be his son or grandson). The dedicatee of Avianus' (or Avienus') fables, called "excellent Theodosius" (*Theodosi optime*) and described in terms that strikingly tally with Macrobius' traits (cf. Cameron 1967, 386–87), is generally taken to be our author.

[9] Macrobius Ambrosius Theodosius is the form of the name that appears in the inscription to the *Commentary* and in the explicit to *Comm.* 1 that accompanies the subscription attesting the collaborative corrections performed by Aurelius Memmius Symmachus (cos. 485) and the author's grandson, Macrobius Plotinus Eudoxius. In the manuscripts of the *Saturnalia* he is called Macrobius Theodosius, the form also used by Boethius (son-in-law of the Symmachus just mentioned: *In Isagog. Porph.* p. 31.22 Brandt) and Cassiodorus (*Expos. Psalm.* p. 116.125 Adriaen). On Roman naming practices in late antiquity, see Cameron 2011, Chapter 7, §2. Of course I agree with Cameron (1966, 28) that it would be pedantic now to drop the medieval habit of referring to the man by his first name.

in the normal course have been born ca. 390; and that fact
in turn fits snugly with the following family tree:

Macrobius Ambrosius Theodosius,
praetorian prefect 430 (PLRE 2:1102–3)

Macrobius Plotinus Eustathius,
urban prefect 461/465 (PLRE 2:43610)[10]

Macrobius Plotinus Eudoxius,
vir clarissimus before 485 (PLRE 2:41311)[11]

The third name of the son in this stemma is the name by
which his father addresses him in the prefaces to the *Commentary* and *Saturnalia*; his first name is his father's; and
his second name, while vanishingly rare in the Roman aris-

---

[10] Attested by two inscriptions: *CIL* 15.7109a = *ILS* 813 and
CIL 6.41394 = *AE* 1984, no. 34; the latter, published after *PLRE* 2,
establishes the name Macrobius. The dedication of the *Commentary* speaks of him as having read Plato and Cicero with his father
(*Comm.* 1.1.1), that of the *Saturnalia* as studying diligently on his
own (*Praef.* 2): not an infant or small child, then, but a young man,
perhaps born ca. 420 or a few years earlier, which meshes nicely
with the date of his prefecture.

[11] Attested by the subscription to *Comm.* 1, n. 9 above; "before
485" because Aurelius Memmius Symmachus is himself only *vir
clarissimus* in the subscription, which shows that he had not yet
held his consulship.

tocracy, is utterly appropriate for the son of a Neoplatonist like our author. The first two names are then repeated in the next generation, adorning the young man who joined a future consul in the pious labor of correcting a manuscript of his grandfather's work.

If Macrobius did not gain the rank of *inlustris* until 430, his two major works must belong to the years that followed, with the *Commentary* preceding the *Saturnalia*. Fifty years or more, then, stand between the dialogue's creation and the gathering it purports to describe; and in that time the world had changed, more than an ordinary fifty years' worth. By the time Macrobius was composing the *Saturnalia*, nearly a generation had passed since the sack of Rome in 410, and in the interval much of Spain had passed into the control of the Suebi, the Goths had settled in Gaul, and the Vandals had seized North Africa. The western empire was a much smaller, fragile-seeming place, and it was possible to look back longingly to the richer and more robust polity of two generations earlier. In fact "richer commonwealth" (*locupletior res publica*) is the very phrase used to characterize the age of Praetextatus, Symmachus, and Flavianus in the inscription (*CIL* 6.1782) that accompanies the statue raised in the forum of Trajan in 431 to mark the rehabilitation—the bringing-back-to-memory by selective forgetting—of none other than Flavianus himself.[12] In the same year, thirty-seven years after

[12] Flavianus is said to have come to grief not because he sided with a usurper against the emperor, but because of the "blind slander" and "malice" of "wicked men"; for a translation of the complete inscription, see Hedrick, 2000, 2 and 4.

his conversion, Flavianus' son (now in his seventies) followed Macrobius as praetorian prefect of Italy.

That is the context in which we must set the *Saturnalia*, and the celebratory, backward-looking impulses that animate it. "The leading members of the Roman nobility and other learned men" (1.1.1) whom it brings together represent a highly idealized and highly stylized republic of learning. In their interactions, the individuals spontaneously sort themselves according to their social rank (see §§2–3), and social rank is roughly coordinated with the dignity of the field in which each person is represented as being an expert—while at the same time the virtuous fiction is maintained that all are equally expert in every field. As one of the participants says, when called on to contribute early in the work (1.3.1):

> Those of you drawing me into this conversation have learned, and well remember, all that the ancients developed to perfection, so I see no point in telling the knowledgeable what they already know. But lest anyone suppose that I find disagreeable the honor of being asked, I'll briefly review whatever my slender recollection might suggest on this topic.

And so the dialogue proceeds, as each person contributes from his store of knowledge a small portion of "all that the ancients developed to perfection." The perfection of the ancients is absolutely central to the sentimental antiquarianism that is the dialogue's beating heart: "We must always revere the days gone by, if we have any sense" (3.14.2). The simple fact that a thought or datum is ancient

guarantees that it is good and worth knowing; and so each datum is produced, held up, and admired as a jewel.

This is nowhere more true than in the centerpiece of Book 1 that is regularly cited as the prime (and often the only) piece of evidence of Macrobius' own theological commitments: the discourse on solar theology placed in the mouth of Praetextatus, who seeks to show that most gods of the Greco-Roman pantheon—and of Egypt, Syria, Phoenicia, Thrace, and Phrygia too—are but particular manifestations of the Sun (1.17–23).[13] Now it is true that the data offered up seem to be derived in large part from Neoplatonist sources (see §4); it is also true that solar syncretism and the supreme divinity of the Sun played important roles in Neoplatonic theology, as the emperor Julian's *Hymn to the Sun* vividly attests. Yet it cannot be stressed too strongly that Praetextatus' discourse is not it-self an exercise in Neoplatonic theology. As Wolf Liebeschuetz has put it:

[13] See Wissowa 1880, 42–44, Wessner 1928, 194–96, Courcelle 1969, 26–31, Flamant 1977, 652–80 (with 655–68 on the sources), Mastandrea 1979, 169–92 (esp. 174–75), Liebeschuetz 1999. Praetextatus was priest of the Sun (*pontifex solis*), but there is no reason to assume that the speech reflects his actual beliefs (or that Macrobius knew what those beliefs were), especially given the striking omission of the solar deity Mithras, in whose cult Praetextatus held the highest rank as celebrant (Liebeschuetz ibid., 200 n. 78). It is also plainly arbitrary to assume that this segment must reflect "la religion de Macrobe" (the subtitle of Flamant's chapter cited above): the author of a dialogue featuring the American founding fathers might well have one or more of them speak learnedly, even feelingly, about deism or freemasonry, yet not be a deist or freemason himself.

The arguments Macrobius has put into the mouth of Praetextatus are not based on Neoplatonic cosmogony. In Neoplatonic systems the traditional gods represent . . . stages in the chain of emanation from the primeval intelligible One to the infinite diversity of the material world. The ultimate unity of the Neoplatonic gods lies in the fact that they all are emanations of the One, and thus can be shown to form the constituent parts of an essentially monotheistic scheme. This line of thought does not occur in Praetextatus' speech.[14]

In fact, it could be said that Praetextatus' speech does not so much develop a "line of thought" as take a single premise—that the individual gods can be identified with the Sun—and assemble a highly selective catalogue of disparate data—allegorizing etymologies, iconographic details, myths, historical anecdotes, and a few mere fictions—that can be taken to support or exemplify the premise, provided one is already inclined to think it valid. That element of circularity, however, is secondary. The crucial point is that the manner of proceeding is not theological at all—not concerned with establishing basic principles of divinity and exploring the systematic relationship of those principles with one another—but is more nearly, and more sim-

---

[14] Liebescheutz 1999, 198, subsequently remarking (201), "The pagan material expounded by Praetextatus was part of the Roman cultural tradition and as such still tolerated by all but the most fanatical Christians. . . . The fact that Praetextatus' speech avoids Neoplatonic metaphysics helps to keep it uncontroversial. . . . In other words by omitting Neoplatonic cosmogony Macrobius avoided a clash with Genesis and Christian theology."

ply, philological, concerned with accumulating data to support a series of definitions that have the general form "God X is the Sun because . . ." And that character is consistent with the reaction that the speech elicits at its conclusion, and with the qualities of mind that are praised (1.24.1): "Then this one began to praise his memory, that one his learning, all of them his piety." Piety (*religio*), no doubt, but first *memoria* and *doctrina*: "The hearers recognized an astonishing feat of learning and intelligence, and received it not unlike the way an academic audience might receive a stimulating and original lecture on Roman religion today."[15]

The sensibility that pervades the *Saturnalia* is fully comparable with the sentiments expressed by a contemporary of Macrobius, the grammarian Phocas, who (like Macrobius) calls the *Aeneid* a "sacred poem" and speaks of the schools of the traditional literary culture as "wisdom's gymnasium, where one finds marked out the pathway to a blessed life"[16]—and Phocas was probably a Christian, and was certainly writing for a Christian audience. In fact there is nothing in the *Saturnalia* that a Christian with antiquarian tastes and an elegiac cast of mind could not have written; and I am persuaded that Macrobius, like Phocas, was

15 Liebeschuetz 1999, 196–97.

16 Respectively, *Life of Virgil* praef. 24 (with Praetextatus at 1.24.13 "Let's not allow this sacred poem's inner sancta to be concealed," and similarly 1.7.8 "the sacred study of literature") and *GL* 5.411.2ff. (with the narrator Postumianus at 1.2.13 "As I listened, I thought to myself that I was entering on the kind of life enjoyed by those whom sages call 'blessed'"): cf. Kaster 1988, 340–41.

probably a Christian and was certainly writing for an audience he assumed to be Christian. Consider the following:[17]

- The name Theodosius is hardly found among the Roman elite before the reign of Theodosius the Great: since Macrobius was given the name around the same time that the latter was closing the temples and forbidding the cult of the traditional religion, the parents who named him after the emperor are very unlikely to have been "pagans."

- As already noted, Macrobius held one of the very highest positions in what was, by 430, a thoroughly Christianized imperial administration, a very unlikely achievement had he been a known adherent of the traditional religion.

- Macrobius at one point has a character say, "I too once snatched my hand out from under the teacher's rod, I too have heard lectures on pontifical law" (3.10.2): ineptly, for while the speaker certainly could have attended the grammarian's school (the point of the "teacher's rod," alluding to Juvenal 1.15), he certainly could not have heard "lectures on pontifical law," since no such things were ever given. The man who wrote those words had no personal experience of the ways in which the lore and practices of the traditional religion were transmitted but simply used the analogy of the literary culture's institutions—or the analogy of Christian catechistic practice.

[17] The following points are made also in Cameron 2011, Chapter 7 ad fin.

- Another speaker, referring to the cycle of market days, is made to say, "The festivals held every ninth day provide the opportunities for the *pagani* and *rustici* to gather for purposes of trade or to see to their personal affairs" (1.16.6). In their original senses, the terms *pagani* and *rustici* were essentially synonyms ("people of the countryside," "peasants"): Macrobius here used the second to gloss the first because he anticipated that his Christian audience would understand *pagani* in the pejorative, sectarian sense it had come to have.

- Among the witticisms attributed to Augustus early in Book 2 is the following: "On hearing that the son of Herod, king of the Jews, had been slain when Herod ordered that all boys in Syria under the age of two be killed, Augustus said, 'It's better to be Herod's pig than his son'" (2.4.11). Herod the Great did kill his oldest son and heir apparent shortly before his own death in 4 BCE, which could easily have prompted Augustus' remark. But that murder had nothing to do with the event it is tied to here, the Slaughter of the Innocents, which Matthew alone of the Evangelists recounts (2:16–18) and—as has long been noted—Macrobius alone of secular authors mentions. The witticism in its present form can derive only from a Christian source, and Macrobius assumes that his Christian audience will need no explanation.

Some will no doubt try to explain all this away, but the accumulated burden of special pleading entailed in so doing should make them pause for thought. The picture that Macrobius holds up to us simply will not come into focus if

we insist on viewing it through a lens ground to see matters only in terms of a sharp "pagan" vs. Christian divide.

2. DRAMATIC DATE AND
DRAMATIS PERSONAE

The *Saturnalia's* action begins on 16 December, the eve of the holiday that gives the dialogue its name, and continues for the next three days, 17–19 December. But of which year? Clearly not after the death of Praetextatus, who passed away sometime between 9 September 384 and 1 January 385; and apparently not December of 384 itself—even if one were to grant that Praetextatus could have died in the brief interval between the holiday and the new year—because at the start of the dialogue the man who will be its narrator, Postumianus, looks back at the gathering from the second week in January and refers to Praetextatus' role as host without referring to his subsequent death (1.2.5). December 383, then? Or December 382, perhaps the last Saturnalia before Gratian withdrew the state's subsidy of civic cults? So Alan Cameron has attractively suggested, while acknowledging that we do not know exactly when Gratian took that step.[18]

In making such calculations, however, what we know is less important than what we know Macrobius knew; and here we must admit that we know too little. Certainly Macrobius knew that Cicero's *On the Commonwealth* is set just before the younger Scipio Africanus' death (129 BCE), and he probably knew the similar pattern followed in

[18] Cameron 2011, Chapter 7, §5. Gratian ruled in the West from 375 until his death in August 383.

On the Orator (set just before Crassus' death in 91 BCE) and *On Old Age* (set a year before Cato's death in 149 BCE).[19] It is therefore highly likely that he imagined the dialogue's taking place not very long before the death of its most distinguished character. But that Macrobius knew exactly when Praetextatus died, or just when Gratian issued his law, seems to me more doubtful; we are further hampered by the fact that we do not have the dialogue's end, where any foreshadowing of Praetextatus' death is most likely to have occurred. Best, then, to say that the dialogue takes place over the December holiday ca. 383 and leave it at that.

Now to introduce the men who populate the work. After bringing on the two characters who appear in the scene that leads to the dialogue proper, I briefly take up each of the actors in turn, following the order that the group spontaneously assumes when they take turns recalling ancient jokes at the start of Book 2 (see §3 below)—save that the boorish and aggressive Evangelus will be put in his place, with the other two uninvited guests at the end, and not ceded the earlier position that he claims for himself. I give references to the relevant entries in the *Prosopography of the Later Roman Empire*, where more detail can in most cases be found.[20]

[19] Cameron (ibid.) draws out the implications of 1.1.4 "... men like Cotta and Laelius and Scipio . . . hold[ing] forth on the most substantial topics in the books of the ancients" (see the note in the translation ad loc.) and notes other parallels in Plato's *Phaedo* and Tacitus' *Dialogue on Orators*.

[20] For detailed discussion of Macrobius' characters, see also Schmidt 2008.

DECIUS (*PLRE* 1: 35–36): Caecina Decius Albinus Iunior, son of the interlocutor Caecina Albinus and father of Caecina Decius Aginatius Albinus, prefect of Rome in 414 and 426[21] and dedicatee of one of Servius' scholarly works (see below). Still a young man ca. 383, he held (among other offices) the governorship of Campania ca. 397/98 and prefecture of Rome in 402 and was a correspondent of Symmachus.

POSTUMIANUS (*PLRE* 1: 718–19): known by this name only, though if he is the recipient of Libanius *Ep.* 1036, his grandfather was probably Gaius Ceionius Rufius Volusianus (cos. 314), and he was therefore a kinsman of the interlocutor Rufius Albinus (see below).[22] He is represented as an advocate with a forensic practice so active that his labors prevent him from accepting Praetextatus' invitation to the banquet (1.2.6, 1.6.20); presumably we are to think of him as being in his prime. He is not known to have held any offices, but if he is the subject of Symmachus' commendation in *Ep.* 3.48 (so *PLRE*), he was "from one of the best families" (*de summatibus*).

PRAETEXTATUS (*PLRE* 1: 722–24): one of the most distinguished men of his generation (born by 310), Vettius Agorius Praetextatus (Macrobius uses only the first or last

---

[21] I accept the identification of Albinus 7 and Albinus 10 in *PLRE* 2:50–51, 53.

[22] Libanius' letter, dated to 392, is assigned to this Postumianus by *PLRE*, but a homonymous contemporary who was praetorian prefect (East?) in 383 seems equally possible; note that in writing to the latter, Gregory Nazianzen stresses the man's learning in both Greek and Latin, an emphasis that appears in Libanius' letter also.

name) held the governorship of Achaea (362–64), the prefecture of Rome (367–68), and the praetorian prefecture of Illyricum and Africa (384), among other offices; he was consul designate for 385 but died before assuming office (see above). A strong supporter of traditional religious ways, he held many priesthoods, including an augurship, pontificates of Vesta and of the Sun, and membership on the Board of Fifteen (cf. 1.6.13n.); he was also an initiate in the Eleusinian mysteries and held the supreme rank of "father of fathers" (*pater patrum*) in the worship of Mithras. He was a friend and correspondent of Symmachus. Beyond the discourse on solar theology given to him at 1.17–23 (cf. §1), he also speaks on the origin of his name (1.6), on the origin of the Saturnalia (1.7.18–10. 24), on the humanity of slaves (1.11), and on the Roman calendar (1.12.1–16.37); part of his speech showing Virgil to be the "supreme pontiff" survives at the beginning of Book 3 (3.1–12, cf. §4 below).

FLAVIANUS (*PLRE* 1: 347–49): Virius Nicomachus Flavianus (Macrobius uses the middle name once, otherwise the last name) was a generation younger than Praetextatus (born ca. 334): he was (among other titles) vicar of Africa (377), the emperor's quaestor (*quaestor sacri palatii*, an influential position at court: 389/90), and praetorian prefect of Illyricum and Italy (390–92). When he sided with the usurper Eugenius in 393, he was reappointed praetorian prefect and made sole consul for 394 but committed suicide when Eugenius was defeated in September 394. His memory was officially "condemned" (cf. §1 above) but later rehabilitated, in 431, through the efforts of his son and grandson. A man of literary attainments, as a historian and a translator of the *Life of Apol-*

lonius of Tyana, he was also a correspondent and close friend of Symmachus, whose son married Flavianus' granddaughter and whose daughter married Flavianus' son. In a segment of the *Saturnalia* now lost, he spoke on Virgil's mastery of augural lore (1.24.17, cf. §4 below).

SYMMACHUS (*PLRE* 1: 865–70): Quintus Aurelius Symmachus (Macrobius calls him Quintus Aurelius and Aurelius Symmachus, but usually just Symmachus) was probably born ca. 340: his offices included the governorship of Africa (373), the prefecture of Rome (384–85), and a consulship (391); in 382 he went on a fruitless embassy to ask Gratian to restore the altar of Victory to the senate house (cf. §1 above), and as prefect he petitioned Valentinian II for the same purpose (*Relatio* 3), again fruitlessly, when Ambrose of Milan opposed him (*Ep.* 18). Having delivered a panegyric of the usurper Magnus Maximus (r. 383–88), he suffered disgrace after Maximus was killed but apologized to Theodosius and was forgiven. Macrobius had Symmachus, a noted orator, speak on Virgil's rhetorical skill, though that segment too is now lost (1.24.14, cf. §4 below). The communiqués (*relationes*) that he sent to Valentinian as urban prefect survive as the tenth book of his correspondence, which was organized and published by his son after Symmachus died ca. 402; his great-grandson, with Macrobius' own grandson, corrected a copy of the *Commentary* sometime before 485.

CAECINA ALBINUS (*PLRE* 1: 34–35): Publilius Ceionius Caecina Albinus (Macrobius use only the last two names) is known to have held only one office, the governorship of Numidia in the mid-360s. He is introduced in the dialogue as Symmachus' companion, "very close both in age and in their characters and pursuits" (1.2.15), but he

INTRODUCTION

does not appear in Symmachus' surviving correspondence. As noted above, his son Decius appears in the prelude to the narrative proper and his grandson was a prominent contemporary of Macrobius. He was perhaps a brother of the next interlocutor, Rufius Albinus (*PLRE* 1: 1138, stemma 13); if he was, Macrobius does not register that fact. He is presented as an expert in Roman antiquities and speaks on the demarcation of the Roman day (1.3), the luxury of the ancients (3.13, a fragmentary text), and Virgil's diction (6.4–5, cf. 1.24.19 and §4 below).

Rufius Albinus (*PLRE* 1: 37–38): Ceionius Rufius Albinus (again, Macrobius uses only the last two names) was the governor of an unknown province before holding the prefecture of Rome (389–91); his son, Rufius Antonius Agrypnius Volusianus, was Macrobius' predecessor as praetorian prefect of Italy in 429. Like Caecina Albinus, he serves as an expert in Roman antiquities, continuing Caecina's discourse on Roman luxury in Book 3 (3.14–17) and preceding Caecina's contribution in Book 6 with a lecture on Virgil's borrowings from earlier Latin poetry (6.1–3, cf. 1.24.19 and §4 below).

Eustathius (*PLRE* 1: 311): a Greek philosopher said to be a friend of Flavianus (1.6.4), represented as equally adept in the doctrines of Plato, Aristotle, and the Stoa and said to be fluent in both Latin and Greek (1.5.13, 16). Beyond playing the expert in treating Virgil's knowledge of astrology and "all of philosophy" (cf. 1.24.18; the segment is lost), and his uses of Greek literature (5.2–22), Eustathius' main interventions concern the proper attitude toward sensual pleasure (2.8.5–16, fragmentary) and the proper place of philosophy and raillery in sympotic settings (7.1.5–3.24), and include a series of debates with the phy-

sician Dysarius in Book 7 (7.5, on the virtues of a varied vs. a simple diet; 7.13.21–7.14.21, on seawater and optics; and esp. 7.15, on the paths of ingestion and breathing). No indication of his age is given, and he is not otherwise attested.

AVIENUS (cf. *PLRE* 2:191–92): In his introduction Macrobius says (1.1.5), "And let no one fault me if one or two of those whom this gathering has brought together did not reach their maturity until after the age of Praetextatus": Avienus is the first of these (the other is Servius), and he is represented as an impulsive, even obstreperous adolescent who becomes progressively more attuned to the ways of the gathering (see section §3). That he is meant to be a young aristocrat is shown by a guest's reference to "your own Messala": his family evidently claimed descent from Messala Corvinus (cos. 31 BCE), as did the family of the homonymous consul of 450, Gennadius Avienus.[23] In line with his age he claims no particular expertise but promises that "if anything occurs to me while I hear you speak on your chosen topics, or if I've spotted something noteworthy in my reading before now, I'll produce it as the occasion prompts" (1.24.20); he also takes an extended turn recounting jokes in 2.4–7. He is probably to be identified with the Avianus (or Avienus: both forms of the name are found in the manuscripts) who dedicated a collection of fables to Macrobius.[24]

[23] De Rossi *ICUR* 1: 328 (cited by Cameron 2011, Chapter 7, §4), noting that the consul of 450 belonged to the Corvini (Sidon. Ap. 1.9.4); his grandson was Fl. Ennodius Messala (cos. 506: *PLRE* 2:759–60).

[24] The argument, first made in Cameron 1967, is restated

EUSEBIUS (*PLRE* 1: 304): a Greek teacher of rhetoric, invited at the last minute to occupy the place vacated by Postumianus (above) and therefore absent from the proceedings on the eve of the holiday (1.2.15–1.5.16), Eusebius is the participant who provides the account that Postumianus in turn relates to Decius. He serves as the expert on Virgil's oratorical skill, though only part of his discourse survives (4.1.1–5.1.20).[25] He describes himself (and the physician Dysarius) as nearing old age (7.10.1); he is not otherwise attested.

SERVIUS (*PLRE* 1:827):[26] with Avienus (clearly the younger of the two), the grammarian Servius is the other participant who did not reach full maturity until after the time of the dialogue: since he is presented as having only "recently" set himself up as a grammarian (1.2.15), yet is repeatedly said to be a scholar and teacher of the greatest distinction (1.24.8, 20, 6.4.4, 7.11.2), the anachronism should lie in granting him his later reputation at the very outset of his career, and his birth should be placed ca. 360.[27] He might be the recipient of one letter of Symmachus (*Ep.* 8.60: the contents are rather general, but Servius is a rare name). His authentic surviving works include sev-

---

to meet criticisms in Cameron 2011, Chapter 7, §4; cf. 7.8.6n; see also the very detailed discussion in Schmidt 2008, 56–76.

[25] His identification as the speaker in Book 4 assumes that there is no lacuna between that book and Book 5: see 4.6.24n.

[26] See also Kaster 1988, 356–59; on the very uncertain evidence for the additional names Honoratus and Maurus (or Marius), ibid., 356–57.

[27] So Cameron 2011, Chapter 7, §4. I abandon my earlier view (Kaster 1988, 358) that he was not born until the 370s.

eral short technical treatises (*On Final Syllables, On One Hundred Meters, On the Meters of Horace*), a commentary on the grammatical handbook of Aelius Donatus (mid-fourth century), and a commentary on the poems of Virgil. *On One Hundred Meters*—dedicated to an aristocratic pupil named Albinus = Caecina Decius Aginatius Albinus, son of the Decius and grandson of the Caecina Albinus discussed above—should be dated to the first years of the fifth century; there is reason to think that he wrote the commentary on Virgil—which Macrobius did not use—before the sack of Rome in 410.[28] Besides speaking as an expert on Virgil's figurative speech (6.6) and defending him from criticism or solving linguistic puzzles (6.7–9), Servius leads a discussion of some archaic usages (1.4.4–25) and lectures on the names of fruits, nuts, and olives (3.18–20).

EVANGELUS (cf. *PLRE* 1: 286): the only aristocrat among the three uninvited guests (cf. §4), with an estate at Tibur (7.16.15), Evangelus plays the role usually assigned to the Cynic philosopher in the tradition of sympotic dialogues, opposing the views of the majority and thereby compelling their defense: it is his scorn for the group's exalted view of Virgil, at the end of the first morning's proceedings (1.24.2–9), that sets the agenda for the second and third days, when the poet's vast skill and learning are the main topics of discussion. Because of his name and his

---

[28] Cf. Murgia 2003, 61–64. Macrobius used the commentary of Aelius Donatus, which was Servius' own main source (cf. §4 below and the notes to the translation passim), and puts in Servius' mouth grammatical doctrine that contradicts some central principles of the historical Servius' work: see Kaster 1988, 171–74.

stance as an oppositional figure, it has often been thought that Evangelus should be understood to be a Christian outsider; but this is simply incorrect. There is nothing distinctively Christian about the name (the only other Evangelus in *PLRE* 1 is a man who collaborated in building a temple of Apollo), and so far from opposing the views and ways of the old religion, he presents himself as an expert in them. *He* is the man who says that he has attended lectures on pontifical lore (3.10.2, cf. §1 above), and he carries out an extended critique of Virgil on that basis (3.10.3–12.10), without in the least suggesting that the subject itself is unimportant or the beliefs wrong: if anything, his point is that the matter is too profound to expect a simple versifier to get it right. And something very much like that is his position in the confrontation that brings Virgil to the fore in the first place. When Praetextatus finishes his syncretistic discourse on the Sun, Evangelus expresses neither the revulsion nor the contempt we might expect if he were a Christian outsider; rather, he quite soberly says, "I for my part am impressed that *the power of such great divinities* could be thus comprehended" (1.24.2), making plain that he does in fact regard them as divinities.[29] What he *does* strongly condemn, however, is the notion that a mere poet could have anything worthwhile to say about such impor-

---

[29] Similarly, he is outraged at the thought that "divinities care for slaves" (1.11.1), implying that they are in fact divinities and certainly too grand to care for slaves. Cf. also his use of the same term, "god the craftsman" (*deus opifex*), that Macrobius employs a number of times to refer to the Demiurge handed down from Plato's *Timaeus*: 5.2.1n.

tant matters: "That you call our friend from Mantua as witness to this detail and that, when matters divine are the subject—that should be thought more a display of favoritism than of good judgment" (ibid.). It is that remark, received as the merest philistinism, that sets the others off, but there is nothing remotely Christian about it. It is just part of the boorish character that Evangelus wears from beginning to end: expressing contempt for slaves (1.11.1), bullying the weakest member of the group (2.2.12, cf. §3), calling intemperately for wine (2.8.4), ridiculing the notion that Virgil—the son of "peasants" from Mantua—was learned in Greek (5.2.1), trying to provoke a quarrel between two other guests (7.5.1–2), aggressively questioning the physician, Dysarius, not in order to learn but in the attempt to trip him up (7.9), and asking the physician—with only mockery intended—which came first, the chicken or the egg (7.16). There is good reason to think that Macrobius elaborated the character of Evangelus, as he probably did that of the other two uninvited guests, from reading the correspondence of Symmachus, who refers to a certain Evangelus as a man given to backbiting (*obtrectatio*) and thoughtlessness (*incautus animus*: *Ep.* 6.7): that does sound like the character who was "given to sharply cutting remarks, with a bold tongue that left wounds, . . . aggressive and careless of offense, which he gave to friend and foe alike with words that rankled" (1.7.2).

DYSARIUS (*PLRE* 1: 275): a man approaching old age (cf. above, on Eusebius) and "then reputed to be the foremost physician in Rome" (1.7.1), Dysarius fills one of the roles required by the sympotic tradition (§3), but the extant text gives him very little to say before Book 7, which he dominates as the guests take turns asking him ques-

tions (7.4–16).[30] He is probably based upon the Dysarius who appears in Symmachus' correspondence as one "who rightly holds pride of place among those who profess the art of medicine" (*Ep.* 3.37, cf. 9.44).

Horus (*PLRE* 1: 445): a man of Egyptian origin (1.15.4), Horus is introduced as a former boxing champion who had turned to philosophy and gained a reputation as a Cynic (1.7.3); he is said to be on especially familiar terms with young Avienus (1.7.13), whom he gently reproves at one point (2.3.15). As an Egyptian, he plays the part of an outsider asking questions about Roman institutions (1.7.14–16, on the origin of the Saturnalia; 1.15.1–3, on intercalation) or providing information about Egyptian culture (7.13.9–10); as a Cynic who owns no property beyond a single cloak (7.13.17), he denounces the luxury of the day, drawing a response from Caecina Albinus (implied by 3.13.16 and 3.14.4, though the denunciation is lost in a lacuna after 3.12). Horus is probably based upon the homonymous philosopher commended to Flavianus in a letter of Symmachus (*Ep.* 2.39), with his standing as a Cynic determined by the demands of the genre, and his ethnicity easily inferred from his name (cf. 1.21.13). How Macrobius came to cast him as a former boxer is less clear.[31]

---

[30] He does take his turn telling a joke in Book 2, though the joke happens to be lost in a brief lacuna (2.2.14).

[31] *PLRE* ibid. assumes that the friend of Symmachus is to be identified with the homonymous Olympic victor of 364 commended by Libanius (*Ep.* 1278–79): conceivable, but the man is not said to be have been, specifically, a victor in boxing, and in any case it is highly unlikely that Macrobius knew Libanius' correspondence.

Beyond the three most distinguished figures—Prae-textatus, Flavianus, Symmachus—we can see that the other participants came to be included in the dialogue by various paths: two aristocrats (the Albini) who were kin of distinguished men among Macrobius' own circle of acquaintance in the higher reaches of the imperial administration; a young aristocrat who later probably dedicated a literary work to Macrobius (Avienus); the foremost Virgilian scholar of the generation immediately past (Servius); and the three uninvited guests (Evangelus, Dysarius, Horus), probably based on figures who appear in Symmachus' correspondence. But despite this diversity, they all shared one characteristic: in line with another common feature of the dialogue tradition, they were all very likely dead by the time Macrobius wrote.[32]

3. THE *SATURNALIA* AS DIALOGUE

We have already glanced several times in passing at elements of the *Saturnalia* belonging to the tradition of sympotic dialogues that extends back to Plato, and Macrobius registers his debt to the tradition very self-consciously. In his introduction, he says that the topics to be discussed will range from the serious to the less austere, taking the tradition as his warrant (1.1.3):

> For not only in the works of others who have described banquets, but especially in the great symposium of Plato, the banqueters did not converse about some more serious subject but described Love in various witty ways.

[32] See Cameron 2011, Chapter 7, §6.

Then, after again appealing to Plato to authorize his introducing "one or two [interlocutors who] did not reach their maturity until after the age of Praetextatus" (1.1.5), he begins his narrative some weeks after the gathering by having one man—Decius—approach another—Postumianus—to learn what was said, only to discover that his would-be informant has himself had to rely on a third party—Eusebius—for an account: that is, he follows the pattern of Plato's *Symposium*, in which a friend of Apollodorus receives the account that Apollodorus himself received from Aristodemus (*Symp.* 172A–173B). The arrival of one or more uninvited guests when the banquet is already under way is another element already found in the *Symposium* (1.7.1–3 ~ *Symp.* 212D), and in both cases the arrival—of Alcibiades and, still more decisively, of Evangelus—causes events to take a turn they would not otherwise have taken (cf. §2 above, on Evangelus). Thanks to Eryximachus in the *Symposium*, too, a physician, like Macrobius' Dysarius, would become a fixture. That standard character was later joined (for example, in Lucian's *Symposium* and Athenaeus' *Scholars' Banquet*) by the Cynic philosopher —although here Macrobius worked something of a variation on the traditional forms, for while his Horus does perform one of the roles expected of a Cynic, in denouncing the luxury of the times (cf. §2), the figure who most deeply challenges the values of the group is the most prominent of the uninvited guests, Evangelus, a peer of the other aristocrats and (therefore) a man whose challenge must receive a full response.[33]

[33] For a survey of the tropes and motifs that Macrobius drew from this tradition, see Martin 1931, 64–79, with Flamant 1968.

But beyond importing such motifs, what does Macrobius make of the dialogue form? In answering that question one cannot help but acknowledge, first, that the subtlety and suppleness of his conceptions need not cause Plato to look to his laurels. Macrobius does not use dialogue as a medium in which ideas are defined, developed, or discarded through continuous give-and-take: the typical passage more closely resembles the extended myths that close the *Gorgias* and *Republic* than dialogue properly so called. The guests take turns delivering their party pieces and generally recede into the background while it is someone else's turn. The effect, overall, is rather stiff.

Yet the work's literary shortcomings should not be overstated, for there are many signs that Macrobius approached his job seriously and with some imagination.[34] The variation on the roles of Cynic and uninvited guest already noted is one example; his attention to characterization is another. Take, for example, the point early in Book 2 when it becomes Servius' turn to tell a joke (2.2.12). Consistent with his behavior throughout—at his first entrance he is described as "both marvelously learned and likably modest [*amabilis verecundia*], with his eyes upon the ground and looking as though he were trying to hide" (1.2.15)—he hesitates momentarily out of *verecundia* and receives as thanks the harshest of Evangelus' personal attacks:

For a fresh discussion of sympotic dialogue in the first to fifth centuries CE, including Macrobius, see König 2008.

[34] For a more detailed discussion of the points that follow, cf. Kaster 1980, on which I draw here; on Macrobius' "didactic project," see also Goldlust 2007.

You declare us all shameless, schoolteacher (*grammatice*), if you want to appear to keep silent as a way of safeguarding your own sense of shame: neither your haughtiness nor that of Dysarius or Horus will escape being branded as arrogance if you do not choose to imitate Praetextatus and the rest of us.

The outburst is an extraordinary breach of etiquette, made particularly ugly by Evangelus' choice of target, the man least likely to defend himself. With its several distortions, it vividly conveys the mean and sardonic cast of his mind: he willfully misinterprets Servius' *verecundia* as arrogance (*superbia*), gratuitously includes in his broadside the innocent Dysarius and Horus, who were simply waiting to follow Servius before taking their turns (see further below), and demands that Servius imitate his betters, although his own consistent refusal to imitate the attitudes and behavior of the group is his most distinctive trait. But the most pointed detail is the use of *grammatice*: the title that would, in another man's mouth, straightforwardly acknowledge the grammarian's special craft—the thing that makes a place for him in this exalted company—is twisted by Evangelus into a sneer at something he regards as a low trade. The bare vocative is the taunt of a bully, an insult comparable in its force to another of Evangelus' terms of abuse, "little Greek" (*Graeculus*: 7.9.26). It tells Servius— and of course the reader—that this is a man who will pay no heed to any claim of social position derived from his skill.

Consider, too, the subtle treatment of Avienus, who emerges as a kind of anti-Evangelus over the course of the dialogue. Avienus begins the dialogue as a young man on

the threshold of culture—he has already read his Virgil (implied at 6.7.1–4) but is still pondering the course of proper rhetorical training (5.1.2)—and both his age and his relative ignorance are at issue in the episode that introduces Avienus to the reader. When Caecina Albinus has finished discussing the actual starting point of the holiday (1.4.1), Avienus expresses polite puzzlement at certain apparently novel expressions Caecina had used, and Servius, prompted by Symmachus to explain, replies that Caecina's expressions involved not "novelty" but "antiquity." With an obliqueness corresponding to Avienus' politeness, Servius thus lets the young man know that the fault was his own: Avienus' ignorance has led him to mistake the ancient and respectable for the untoward and flawed. Avienus immediately responds by denouncing Servius for "call[ing] back into service words that disappeared from use many centuries ago—just as though you were talking with Evander's mother—and goad[ing] even these excellent men, whose memory is well furnished by continuous reading, to heap them up."[35] It is a rude blast worthy of Evangelus, and appropriately rebuked by Praetextatus; it is also the baseline against which Avienus' subsequent development is to be measured. For he soon makes plain that he is basically a decent sort, knowing his place and his limits (cf. 1.7.17, 1.24.20), and though he retains a certain youthful exuberance in the early books—interrupting the conversations (1.6.3, 2.3.14) or, with excessive enthusiasm, equating Praetextatus with Socrates (2.1.2)—this exuberance melts away, or rather is more properly channeled, in the

---

[35] 1.5.1–2, largely drawn from Gell. 1.10, where they are, by contrast, the words of an older, respected figure scolding a pretentious young man.

later books. There, with perfect docility, he successively places himself at the feet of Eusebius (5.1.2ff), Servius (6.7.1ff), Eustathius (7.2.1ff), and Dysarius (7.12.1ff), in the last instance asking the physician as many questions (fourteen) as all seven of the preceding guests combined.[36] In this exercise of modesty and keen engagement, his assimilation to the values of the gathering is complete. The change in his behavior is epitomized in his adoption of a new and lower place in the group's self-ranking (see just below), and the last words we hear him speak in the work are the simple and affecting "Since I'm ignorant of the reason, I want to know" (7.12.28).

Avienus' willingness to take on the values of the group is the counter to Evangelus' defiance of the group, and it is in his conception of the group that Macrobius perhaps makes particularly clear why he chose the dialogue form. There are two places where the proceedings shift from random conversation or the continuous exposition of an individual to a different form: early in Book 2, where each of the company takes his turn in telling a joke handed down from antiquity (2.2.1–5), and again in Book 7, where each member has the opportunity to consult the physician, Dysarius (7.4.1ff.). In each place, the existence of a fixed order (*ordo*) is noted specifically; in each place, the gathering falls into the *ordo* spontaneously;[37] and in each place, the *ordo* is essentially the same (with two interesting varia-

---

[36] Note the comment of Eustathius (7.3.23), "It is right that I shape your young mind, which is so readily taught that it anticipates the lessons it should learn."

[37] At 7.4.1 Praetextatus suggests that the order be determined by lot (*sortiamur*), but all then urge him to go first, and the order unfolds from there.

tions) and clearly hierarchical, determined by a combination of social status and the dignity of one's learning:

2.2.1 Praetextatus	7.4.1 Praetextatus
2.2.4 Flavianus	7.6.1 Flavianus
2.2.5 Symmachus	7.7.1 Symmachus
2.2.6 Caecina Albinus	7.8.1 Rufius Albinus
2.2.7 Rufius Albinus	7.8.7 Caecina Albinus
2.2.8 Eustathius	7.9.1 Evangelus
2.2.9 Avienus	7.9.26 Eustathius
2.2.10 Evangelus	7. 10.1 Eusebius
2.2.11 Eusebius	7.11.1 Servius
2.2.12 Servius	7.12.1 Avienus
2.2.14 Dysarius	7. 13.1 Horus
2.2.15 Horus	(Dysarius serves as *consultus*)

In the first series the *ordo* proceeds from Praetextatus through the remainder of the nobles to the philosopher Eustathius; the young man Avienus and the uninvited noble Evangelus follow, succeeded by the two remaining representatives of the literary culture, the rhetor and the grammarian, and finally the two other uninvited guests, the physician and the Cynic. The second series mirrors the first, with two significant changes:[38] Avienus places himself farther down in the *ordo*, as the last of the invited, an act consistent with the alteration of his behavior over the course the dialogue; and Evangelus characteristically and self-consciously (7.9.27) thrusts himself ahead of the philosopher, Eustathius, to follow the other nobles. The ability of each member (save Evangelus) instinctively and au-

[38] The reversal of the two Albini is insignificant, since they are treated as interchangeable throughout the work.

tomatically to define and assume his proper place is the essence of the ethos that dominates the dialogue.

That ethos, in particular, facilitates the communal effort of the symposium. The properly animated guests make repeated displays of a modest selflessness that is inspired by each man's confidence in the group as a whole: they know individually when to yield to others' expertise, when to assert their own, how to combine becomingly the two kinds of behavior—and Virgil himself is presumed to have exhibited precisely the same qualities in his own sphere, delicately coordinating deference and self-assertion in his treatment of the literary tradition.[39] That is why, in introducing the topic of Virgil's literary borrowings, Rufius Albinus adduces the anecdote of the comic poet Afranius (6.1.4–5):

> When Afranius . . . was being accused of taking too much material over from Menander, he made the following very becoming [*non inverecunde*] reply . . . : "I admit," he said, "I've borrowed not only from him but as any author had something that met my needs, something I thought I couldn't improve upon, even when the other wrote in Latin." But if it's granted that writers of prose and poetry ought to enjoy this common partnership in their shared material [*societas et rerum communio*], who would blame Virgil if he borrowed some things from older writers to augment his work's refinement?

This defense of borrowing evidently looks as much to Macrobius' own time—and beyond literature, to the context of the dialogue—as it does to Virgil's literary practice. It is

[39] See 1.16.44 with Kaster 1980, 231ff.

noteworthy that in the treatment of literary imitation that
extends over two whole books, the competitive element—
the writer's contest (ἀγών) or rivalry (*aemulatio*) with his
peers or predecessors, emphasized by both ancient and
modern readers—is entirely absent. Instead, all stress is
placed on literary borrowing as a means of preserving and
showing respect for the culture's "common partnership" as
it extends into the past, just as the intellectual borrowing
among the participants in the symposium is a means of rec-
ognizing and affirming the order, the "common partnership," of the present.

The idea of literary borrowing found in the *Saturnalia*
is thus not just a principle of composition but a moral im-
perative, forming a major link between the dialogue's substance and its form: the harmony and continuity that result
when a Virgil or an Afranius turns his "modest regard"
(*verecundia*) to the past mirror the harmonious workings
of the dialogue. "In every area of life," says the philosopher Eustathius (7.1.13), "and especially in the jovial setting of a banquet, anything that seems out of tune should—
provided proper means are used—be reduced to a single harmony." The metaphor of harmony proceeds from
the metaphor that opens Book 7 (the whole is borrowed
from Plutarch: see 7.1.2n.). There Symmachus, respond-
ing to a suggestion that the group consider philosophical questions, doubts that philosophy's "modest restraint"
(*verecundia*) could tolerate the possible "dissonance"
(*strepitus*) of such a discussion (7.1.2), but he is assured by
Eustathius that, like the "partnership" (*societas*) of a chorus, the *societas* of their group will provide the harmony
demanded by philosophy's *verecundia* (7.1.9). The metaphor of the chorus, with the key and melody set by the
whole—drowning out the discordant voices or influencing

them for the better—and with individuals now and again offering solos that resonate with the harmony of the whole, is evidently suited not only to the gathering but also to the relationship between past and present. The "common partnership" of the past culture against which the poet, for example, defines himself both sets limits that are freely acknowledged and finds preservation in his work. Just so, the "partnership" of dialogue enjoys a reciprocal relationship with "modest restraint," on the one hand encouraging and rewarding it, on the other governed and preserved by it. Both the "partnership" and the individual are well served.

4. THE PLAN OF THE WORK AND ITS SOURCES

Cultural "borrowing," of course, has a special resonance for the *Saturnalia* in another respect: it is the means by which the text is very largely constituted. As Macrobius says at the outset, addressing his son (*Praef.* 4):

> Please do not fault me if I often set forth the accounts I draw from my varied reading in the very words that the authors themselves used; the work before you promises not a display of eloquence but an accumulation of things worth knowing.

As authorial statements go, this one wins fair points for veracity, not least for its last six words: it is worth pausing to acknowledge that any reader who mastered the contents even of the remnant that survives[40] and followed out the ramifications suggested by each datum would

---

[40] As much as 40 percent of the original text has been lost: see n. 57 below.

in fact emerge with a much richer understanding of ancient Greek and especially Roman culture. It is true, too, that the authors from whom Macrobius borrows are often quoted verbatim, if not typically by name: because Macrobius nowhere names Aulus Gellius, whom he quarried extensively, and names another certain source, Plutarch, only in a very general way (7.3.24), it has been an article of faith among those who trace Macrobius' sources that any author he names was actually quoted by an author whose name he suppresses.[41] And yet this is only what we should expect. The interlocutors whom Macrobius is constructing are citizens of his idealized republic of learning, the sort of men who *would* have all that learning on the tips of their tongues: were they to say "as Gellius reports" or "according to Plutarch" at every turn, the effect would be very different. To catch the flavor, imagine Ovid footnoting Varro every dozen lines in the *Fasti*.

At the same time, the adverb "often" in the phrase "often quoted verbatim" should be given full weight, because comparison with the authors who survive plainly shows that Macrobius tends not just to copy but also to rephrase, edit, supplement, and elide, fitting the source to his framework.[42] That framework is first described metaphorically, as "an orderly system of limbs" (*Praef.* 3), then in terms

[41] This happens to be certainly untrue in the case of Cornelius Labeo and probably untrue in the case of Serenus Sammonicus: see §4 below.

[42] Macrobius' treatment of Gellius has been analyzed most minutely: see Lögdberg 1936, 1–74.

that more plainly let the reader know what to expect (1.1.1–4): the three days of the holiday will each be spent in continuous conversation that is "learned and beguiling" (and "morally unimpeachable"), with the mornings given over to "more vigorous" discussion of weightier topics and the talk becoming "less austere" as the day wears on. It has in fact sometimes been suggested that Macrobius originally composed the work in three large units— three "days"—that were only secondarily divided into "books"; but however that might be—the evidence is no better than ambiguous—it is clear that the day-by-day progression provides the "orderly system of limbs" that Macrobius first advertises.[43] First, the conversation be-

---

[43] The inscription before the preface in the archetype certainly had "Conviviorum primi diei Saturnaliorum," but in only three manuscripts (DPX) is that phrase followed by *liber* and only one of those (the highly idiosyncratic P) has a book number, *primus*; at the end of Book 3, which coincides with the end of Day 2, MLRFC (i.e., presumably, β: see §5) have "Conviviorum secundi explicit." Beyond that all is unclear, because the end of Day 1, beginning of Day 2, and both beginning and end of Day 3 are all lost in lacunae: this rather casts doubt on the authenticity of (e.g.) the explicit to Book 2 shared by most β-manuscripts ("Conviviorum primi diei Saturnaliorum explicit"). The division into seven books first appears in some Italian manuscripts of the 15th century (a five-book format is found in some other manuscripts of the same period), and it came to be the norm in the printed editions: see Dorfbauer 2010, where an attractive case is also made for supposing that Macrobius himself chose a six-book format (cf. Cic. *Rep.*), with two books for each day of the festival.

tween Decius and Postumianus sets the scene (1.2.1–14, cf. §3): we learn that what follows is the latter's narrative, based on his written record of the oral report he received from Eusebius, as supplemented by Avienus for the holiday's eve, before Eusebius was present (1.2.13). There follows a relatively brief account of the proceedings on the eve, then the three days, each comprising three segments —morning, afternoon, and evening—with each day unfolding at the home of a different aristocratic host. It is a sad irony of transmission that in two of the three cases, the main discourse of the host has been lost.

The following table is intended to orient the reader to the proceedings. It is organized by day and, within each day, by segment; for each segment I indicate the chief topics of discussion, the lead speaker on each topic, and (where possible) the certain or probable sources. For extant sources I give only a general indication—e.g., "Gellius"—reserving detailed references for the notes to the translation; an asterisk (*) indicates that the source is not extant, its contribution having been inferred more or less probably; "et al." indicates that an identifiable source is significantly supplemented by one or more unknown sources.[44]

[44] The most important general discussions of Macrobius' sources (all at various points displaying unwarranted certainty about their premises and inferences) are Linke 1880, Wissowa 1880 and 1913, and Wessner 1928, 182–96. In his preface, not included here, Macrobius drew on Gellius, the younger Seneca, and Athenaeus; see the nn. ad loc.

INTRODUCTION

The eve of the Saturnalia, 16 December:
The house of Praetextatus

Day 1, 17 December: The house of Praetextatus

[45] Gellius, the one securely identifiable source, plays a relatively minor role.

[46] The background of 1.17–23 is too complex for us to elucidate fully, given the state of our knowledge. Much of it plainly depends on one or more Greek sources, where Porphyry's influence must be present (cf. esp. Flamant cited in n. 13 above), and there must also be a debt to the Latin Neoplatonist Cornelius Labeo (cf. 1.18.1n.); other influences are also present (e.g., 1.17.7–65

Day 2, 18 December: The house of Flavianus

---

has been plausibly traced to Apollodorus of Athens by way of Cornutus; see 1.17.7n.).

[47] The jokes told in 2.2–5 are derived from (probably) more than one older collection, of which there were many: see 2.1.8n.

[48] 1.24.16–21 and 24 allow us to identify Eustathius' and Flavianus' topics and the order in which they spoke.

Day 3, 19 December: The house of Symmachus

[49] Because the comments of Macrobius, Servius, and (especially) Servius Danielis repeatedly overlap in this segment, it is highly likely that all three draw on a common source, the variorum commentary of Aelius Donatus (see Marinone 1946, Santoro 1946); the debt would probably be still more evident if the contributions of Eustathius and (especially) Flavianus survived. The segment is incomplete at its beginning and end.

[50] Implied by 3.13.16 and 3.14.4.

[51] Though Macrobius cites him twice by name (3.16.6, 3.17.4), contrary to his treatment of (e.g.) Gellius, I suspect that Serenus was the direct source of lore derived from the elder Pliny (cf. 3.16.6, where Serenus is quoted quoting Pliny, with the nn. in that segment passim) and of one augmented chapter of Gellius (see 3.17.5n., on Gell. 2.24).

[52] Symmachus' discourse, promised at 1.24.14, is lost. Identification of Eusebius as the speaker depends on the end of Book 4 being continuous with the start of Book 5 (see 4.6.24n.); his speech as it survives probably draws on at least two sources (see 4.1.1 and 4.5.1nn).

[53] Virgil's imitations of Homer were catalogued starting in the first century CE, especially with a view to convicting him of "thefts" (Donatus *Life of Virgil* 46). We cannot say which of the earlier catalogues Macrobius drew on here and in the following segments.

[54] 6.1–2 (on Virgil's smaller and larger imitations) and 6.3 (on Virgil's imitation of Latin poets who preceded him in imitating

Homer) probably derive from two earlier collections and are to be distinguished in turn from the source of 6.4–5 (on Virgil's use of archaic diction and figures); see Jocelyn 1964. Note that several passages cited in 6.3 are also cited as examples of Virgil's direct imitation of Homer in Book 5 (see the nn. passim).

[55] Dysarius in this segment is consulted by each of the guests in turn, with two interruptions engineered by Evangelus (7.5, 7.9). The main sources, here and in the balance of the book, are Plutarch and at least one collection of "problems" like those falsely ascribed to Aristotle and Alexander of Aphrodisias; since Macrobius' text resembles the latter especially (see the nn. passim) yet does not draw directly upon that collection, the two must derive their material from a common source.

5. TEXT AND TRANSLATION

Between the 430s and the Carolingian age there are only a
few certain signs that the *Saturnalia* found an audience:
sometime around the middle of the sixth century Cassiodorus cited 5.21.18 in passing while commenting on Psalm
10; in the following century a much condensed version of
1.12–15, on the Roman calendar, was produced in Ire-
land.[56] Beyond that, all our extant manuscripts clearly de-
scend from a single ancestor, which for five of the *Saturnalia*'s seven books preserved a text that had suffered losses
ranging from the serious to the catastrophic.[57] From this

[56] This is the so-called *Disputatio Chori* [i.e., *Hori*] *et Praetextati*; see Arweiler 2000. Selections from the same epitome also
appear in another seventh-century Irish tract, the anonymous
De ratione conputandi (edited by D. Ó Cróinín in Walsh and Ó
Cróinín 1988, 115–213). Isidore of Seville is sometimes thought to
have used the *Saturnalia*, but the evidence suggests a debt to one
or more common sources.

[57] The segment comprising preliminaries and the account of
Day 1 (= Books 1–2, ca. 31,600 words) is lacunose at the end; the
account of Day 2 (= Book 3, ca. 10,600 words) is (catastrophically)
lacunose at its start and has a substantial gap in the middle (between 3.12 and 3.13); and Day 3 (Books 4–7, ca. 46,000 words) is
lacunose at both beginning and end. Given that the contributions
of Praetextatus (pontifical lore, Day 2) and Eusebius (oratory,
Day 3) are only partially preserved, and that the contributions of
Eustathius (philosophy and astrology, Day 2), Flavianus (augural
lore, Day 2), Horus (critique of contemporary mores, Day 2), and
Symmachus (rhetoric, Day 3) are entirely missing, it is not unrea-
sonable to suppose that as much as 300 modern pages of text have
been lost.

archetype there were derived three distinct families, two of which are more closely related to each other than either is to the third. The basic structure of the tradition can therefore be represented thus:

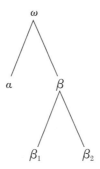

The families α and β_1 include one or more manuscripts that date to the ninth century, while the earliest representative of β_2 that has all seven books dates to ca. 990–1015 (one β_2-manuscript that has only Book 7 was written in the tenth century). All the descendants of β_1 have only the first three books.

In his edition of 1852—a landmark in the modern reception of the *Saturnalia*—Ludwig von Jan was the first to draw on a broad sampling of the prehumanist manuscripts and to use the early printed editions systematically. Yet Jan's text was yoked to an astoundingly inaccurate critical apparatus, and before the end of the century his edition had been eclipsed by Franz Eyssenhardt's Teubner, which set the clock back four centuries by effectively relying on only two manuscripts for the first three books and only one

for the last four. Antonio La Penna made the next large advance in 1953, when he published a systematic survey of many of the manuscripts Jan had used, together with a number of others, identifying for the first time the three manuscript families that define the medieval tradition.[58] James Willis soon refined La Penna's findings by making plain the relation between β_1 and β_2,[59] and his new Teubner, first published in 1963, offered an improved text. Nino Marinone's important bilingual edition, prepared for the *Classici Latini* series (2nd ed. 1977), was based on Willis' text; though it shed no new light on the manuscript tradition, it did depart from Willis' judgment in over ninety places, incorporating both Marinone's own corrections and those noted by Willis' early reviewers.[60]

In laying the groundwork for my edition, I have extensively checked Willis' (often unreliable) reports of the manuscripts, confirming (or not) every instance of a shared error in his apparatus; drawn on the collations of two important manuscripts published by M. J. Carton after Willis'

[58] La Penna 1953, 226–35.

[59] Willis 1957, 153–57; Willis's correction was accepted by La Penna in his review of Willis's edition (1963, 453–54). For an overview, see also the summary in Marshall 1983, with remarks by B. C. Barker-Benfield on the manuscripts (1983, 222–24).

[60] Marinone 1977, 61–77; I differ from Marinone in only a relative handful of these cases. Besides Marinone's Italian version there is Percival Davies' highly readable English translation of Eyssenhardt's text (New York 1969)—out of print but now available online as an "ACLS Humanities e-Book"—along with recent translations in French, of Books 1–3 (Guittard 2008; Books 4–7 in preparation by Guittard and Benjamin Goldlust), and in German, of the whole work (Schönberger 2008).

edition appeared;[61] attempted a census of all other pre-thirteenth-century witnesses; and on the basis of that census collated twenty-one additional prehumanist manuscripts wholly or in part. As a result, I have discarded two of the manuscripts that Willis used and recruited eight others. The report of these results is published elsewhere;[62] the stemma that I use in reconstructing the archetype is implied in the table of sigla given below.

A note on the translation: Macrobius writes in what is sometimes called the "chancellery style" typical of the period (except, of course, where he is transcribing a Gellius or a Seneca more or less verbatim)—highly elaborate and verbose, with a passion for adjectives and adverbs, the passive voice, and abstract nouns used in place of verbs (it is, in fact, very much like bad English style). To attempt to reproduce the general effect in translation would be no favor to the reader, and I have not done so. I have aimed above all to produce a readable version, retaining some of the Macrobian pomp and formality, especially in the preface, while incorporating features of spoken English (e.g., contractions) to make the dialogue sound more like speech that might actually be spoken. One specialized point: I use Latinized forms of Greek names (e.g., Achilles, Hercules) when translating Macrobius' Latin, transliterated Greek forms (e.g., Akhilleus, Hêraklês) when translating the extensive passages of Greek that Macrobius quotes.

The critical apparatus appended to the Latin text is very limited, in keeping with the Loeb Classical Library format. I have generally included a note only where the ar-

61 Carton 1966.
62 Kaster 2010.

chetype was corrupt and emendation (medieval, Renaissance, or modern) has been needed, or where the archetype offered a text different from the standard modern text of an author being quoted.[63] The sigla used in the apparatus are as follows:

ω archetype of α and β
  α hyparchetype of λPG
    λ hyparchetype of ND

N Naples V.B.10	s. IX med-¾ (lacking Sat. 7.5.2ff)
D Oxford Bodl. Auct. T.2.27	s. XI in. (lacking Sat. 3.4.9ff)
P Paris lat. 6371	s. XI (complete)
G Strasbourg BNU 14	s. XI (complete)

  β hyparchetype of $β_1$ and $β_2$[64]
    $β_1$ hyparchetype of Mπs

M Montpellier Médecine 225	s. IX$^{3/3}$ (*Sat.* 1.12.21–3 fin)[65]

      π hyparchetype of BV

[63] A more detailed apparatus will be included in the edition that is to follow for the Oxford Classical Texts series.

[64] The oldest member of this family, K (= Vat. Pal. lat. 886, s. IX$^{in.}$ Lorsch), contains only excerpts (1. 11. 2–1. 11. 43, 2.1.7–2.7.11, 3.13.11–3.20.8): I do not generally cite it, although it uniquely has the correct reading *Hercules* (vs. *Herculis*) at 3.15.7 and joins M in reading *Tiberinus* (vs. *Tiberinos*) at 3.16.18.

[65] Where M is unavailable down to *Sat.* 1.12.21, its place can be held by Paris lat. 16676 (X), a descendant or twin dating to s. XII.

B Bamberg Class. 37 (M.V.5)	s. IX$^{3/3}$ (lacking 3.19.5– fin)[66]
V Vatican Reg. lat. 1650	s. IX$^{2/2}$ (*Sat.* 1–3)
ς hyparchetype of OL	
O London BL Cotton Vit. C.III	s. IX$^{3/4}$ (*Sat.* 1–3)
L Vatican lat. 5207	s. X$^{1/4}$ (*Sat.* 1–3)
β_2 hyparchetype of Fδ in *Sat.* 1–6	
F Florence Laur. Plut. 90 sup. 25	s. XII (complete)
δ hyparchetype of Rε	
R Vatican Reg. lat. 2043	s. X ex./XI in. (lacking *Sat.* 7.14.11ff)[67]
ε hyparchetype of AC	
A Cambridge Univ. Library Ff.3.5	s. XII (complete)[68]
C Cambridge Corpus Christi Coll. 71	s. XII (complete)

[66] After its departure B's place can be filled by E (see below), a closely related manuscript that is otherwise the source of some good conjectures.

[67] Where R is lacking after *Sat.* 7.14.11, it can be represented by the agreement of Florence Laur. Plut. 51.8 (W), a direct copy dating to s. XI, and London BL Harl. 3859 (H), a copy of a copy dating to ca. 1100.

[68] An ancestor of A lacked 3.18.9 *Plautus in* through 3.20.8 *discessio est*, a segment of text—the equivalent of one folium— that is misplaced to follow 3.17.18 *monstruosae* in A's twin, C.

hyparchetype of Fγ in *Sat.* 7

F Florence Laur. Plut. 90 sup. 25	s. XII (complete)

γ hyparchetype of Qδ

Q Bern, Burgerbibl. 514	s. X (*Sat.* 7)
δ as above	

Also worth occasional citation, as sources of good conjectural readings, are:

J Vatican lat. 3417	s.XI (*Sat.* 1–4, 7)[69]
E Naples Bibl. naz. V.B.12	s. XII (*Sat.* 1–3)[70]
U Wolfenbüttel 4619 (*olim* Gudianus 312)	s. XIII (*Sat.* 1–3)[71]
S Munich clm 15738 (*olim* Salisburg. 38)	s. XV (complete)

Printed editions cited in the critical apparatus include:

ed. Ven. 1472	*In Somnium Scipionis expositio; Saturnalia.* Nicolas Jenson. Venice 1472.
ed. Ven. 1500	*In somnium Scipionis; Saturnalia.* Philippus Pincius. Venice 1500.
ed. Ven. 1513	*En tibi lector candidissime. Macrobius etc.* Joannes Rivius. Venice 1513.
ed. Colon. 1521	*Macrobii Aurelii Theodosii viri consularis In Somnium Scipionis libri duo: et septem eiusdem libri Saturnaliorum.* Arnoldus Vesaliensis. Cologne 1521.

[69] J is an apograph of R in Books 1–4 and of Q in Book 7; Panormita was among its correctors.

[70] E is very closely related to B: see Kaster 2010, 12 n. 44.

[71] U is a member of the β_1 family; both U and S were used by Jan.

ed. Ven. 1528	*Macrobii In Somnivm Scipionis Ex Ciceronis. VI. Libro de Rep. Ervditissima Explanatio. Eivsdem Saturnaliorum Libri VII.* Aedes Aldi [Manutii] Et Andreae Asulani Soceri. Venice 1528.
ed. Lugd. 1532	*Macrobii Avrelii Theodosii . . . In Somnium Scipionis Libri II. Saturnaliorum Libri VII.* Seb. Gryphivs. Lyon 1532.
ed. Basil. 1535	*In Somnium Scipionis libri II. Eiusdem Saturnaliorum libri VII.* Ioachim Camerarius. Basel 1535.
ed. Lugd. 1538	*Macrobii Avrelii Theodosii . . . In Somnium Scipionis Libri II. Saturnaliorum Libri VII.* Seb. Gryphivs. Lyon 1538.
ed. Lugd. 1550	*Macrobii Avrelii Theodosii . . . In Somnium Scipionis Libri II. Saturnaliorum Libri VII.* Seb. Gryphivs. Lyon 1550.
ed. Paris. 1585	*Aurelii Macrobii Ambrosii Theodosii . . . In Somnium Scipionis libri 2: eiusdem Conviviorum Saturnaliorum libri VII.* Henricus Stephanus. Paris 1585.
ed. Lugd. Bat. 1597	*Opera.* Johannes Isacius Pontanus. Leiden 1597.
ed. Lugd. Bat. 1670	*Aur. Theodosii Macrobii . . . Opera.* Jacobus Gronovius. Leiden 1670.
ed. Lips. 1774	*Aur. Theodosii Macrobii . . . opera.* Johann Karl Zeune. Leipzig 1774.
ed. Bipont. 1788	*Aur. Theodosii Macrobii . . . opera.* Societas Bipontina. Zweibrücken 1788.

Jan	*Macrobii Ambrosii Theodosii . . .* *Saturnaliorum libri VII.* Ludwig von Jan. Quedlinburg and Leipzig 1852.
Eyssenhardt	*Macrobius.* Franz Eyssenhardt. 2nd ed. Leipzig 1893.
Willis	*Macrobius*, vol. 1. James Willis. Leipzig 1963 (3rd ed. 1994).
Marinone[2]	*I Saturnali di Macrobio Teodosio.* Nino Marinone. 2nd ed. Turin 1977.

References to the texts that Macrobius expressly cites or quotes are embedded in the translation; references to Virgil (*E(clogues)*, *G(eorgics)*, *A(eneid)*) and Homer (*Il(iad)*, *Od(yssey)*) are designated by the abbreviation of the work cited. An asterisk (*) joined to a citation of Virgil signals a comment in the vulgate Servius (Serv.) parallel to M.'s remarks; an obelus (†), a parallel comment in Servius Danielis (DServ.); references are given in the notes when parallel comments occur in Serv., DServ., or both ((D)Serv.) on lines that M. does not cite. Most such parallels are probably derived from a common source, the commentary of Aelius Donatus: see §4 above. Where appropriate, editions used are identified either in the table of abbreviations or in the Index Locorum (by editor and year of publication). Historical persons mentioned in the text are generally identified in the Index of Names.

ABBREVIATIONS

CA	J. U. Powell, ed. *Collectanea Alexandrina*. Oxford, 1925
CAG	*Commentaria in Aristotelem Graeca*. 23 vols. Berlin, 1882–1909
CCAG	*Catalogus Codicum Astrologorum Graecorum*. 12 vols. Brussels, 1898–1924
CGF	G. Kaibel, ed. *Comicorum Graecorum Fragmenta*. Vol. 1, fasc. 1. Berlin, 1899
CIL	*Corpus Inscriptionum Latinarum*. 17 vols. Berlin, 1862–
CPG	F. G. Schneidewin and E. L. von Leutsch, ed. *Corpus paroemiographorum Graecorum*. Vol. 1. Göttingen, 1839
EGM	R. Fowler, ed. *Early Greek Mythography*. Vol. 1. Oxford, 2000
FCRR	H. Scullard. *Festivals and Ceremonies of the Roman Republic*. Ithaca, NY, 1981
FGrH	F. Jacoby, ed. *Die Fragmente der griechischen Historiker*. 4 parts. Leiden, 1957–
FHG	C. and T. Müller, ed. *Fragmenta Historicorum Graecorum*. 5 vols. Paris, 1878–1885
FLP²	E. Courtney, ed. *The Fragmentary Latin Poets*. 2nd ed. Oxford, 2003

FPL[3]	J. Blänsdorf, ed. *Fragmenta Poetarum Latinorum.* 3rd ed. Stuttgart, 1995
GG	*Grammatici Graeci.* Leipzig, 1867–
GL	H. Keil, ed. *Grammatici Latini.* 7 vols. (with a supplement edited by H. Hagen). Leipzig, 1855–1880
GRF 1	H. Funaioli, ed. *Grammaticae Romanae Fragmenta.* Leipzig, 1907
GRF 2	A. Mazarino, ed. *Grammaticae Romanae Fragmenta Aetatis Caesareae.* Turin, 1955
HRR	H. Peter, ed. *Historicorum romanorum reliquiae.* 2nd ed. 2 vols. Leipzig, 1914
IAH	F. P. Bremer, ed. *Iurisprudentiae Antehadrianae.* 2 vols. Leipzig, 1898–1901
IAR[6]	P. E. Huschke, ed. *Iurisprudentiae Anteiustinianae Reliquiae.* 6th ed. E. Seckel and B. Kübler. 2 vols. Leipzig, 1908–1911
ICUR	J. B. de Rossi, ed. *Inscriptiones Christianae Urbis Romae.* 2 vols. Rome, 1861–1888
IG	*Inscriptiones Graecae.* 14 vols. Berlin, 1873–
IGBulg	G. Mikhailov, ed. *Inscriptiones Graecae in Bulgaria repertae.* Serdica, 1956–
ILS	H. Dessau, ed. *Inscriptiones Latinae Selectae.* 3 vols. Berlin, 1892–1916
Inscr. It.	*Inscriptiones Italiae.* 13 vols. Rome, 1931–
ISmyrna	*Die Inschriften von Smyrna.* 2 vols. Bonn, 1982–1900
LALE	R. Maltby. *Lexicon of Ancient Latin Etymologies.* Leeds, 1981

Lausberg   H. Lausberg. *Handbook of Literary Rhetoric*. Trans. M. T. Bliss, A. Jansen, D. E. Orton. Ed. D. E. Orton and R. D. Anderson. Leiden, 1998

LIMC   *Lexicon Iconographicum Mythologiae Classicae*. 8 vols. Zürich, 1981–

*LSJ*⁹   H. G. Liddell and R. Scott. *Greek-English Lexicon*, 9th ed. Rev. by H. S. Jones, with a revised supplement. Oxford, 1996

LTUR   E. M. Steinby, ed. *Lexicon Topographicum Urbis Romae*. 6 vols. Rome, 1993–2000

LTUR Sub.   A. La Regina, ed. *Lexicon Topographicum Urbis Romae: Suburbium*. 5 vols. Rome, 2001–

MRR   T. R. S. Broughton. *Magistrates of the Roman Republic*. Vols. 1–2: New York, 1951; Vol. 3 (supplement): Atlanta, 1986

OGIS   W. Dittenberger, ed. *Orientis Graeci Inscriptiones Selectae*. 2 vols. Leipzig, 1903–1905

*ORF*²   E. Malcovati, ed. *Oratorum Romanorum Fragmenta*. 2nd ed. Turin, 1955

Otto   A. Otto. *Die Sprichwörter und sprichwörtlichen Redensarten der Römer*. Leipzig, 1890

PCG   R. Kassel and C. Austin, ed. *Poetae Comici Graeci*. 8 vols. Berlin, 1983–

PEGr   A. Bernabé, ed. *Poetae Epici Graeci*. Stuttgart, 1996–

ABBREVIATIONS

PLRE	A. H. M. Jones, J. R. Martindale, and J. Morris, ed. *Prosopography of the Later Roman Empire*. 3 vols. Cambridge, 1971–1992
PMGr	D. Page, ed. *Poetae Melici Graeci*. Oxford, 1962
RS	M. Crawford, ed. *Roman Statutes*. 2 vols. London, 1996
SRPF[3]	O. Ribbeck, ed. *Scaenicae Romanorum poesis fragmenta*. 3rd ed. 2 vols. Leipzig, 1897–1898
SRRR	F. Speranza, ed. *Scriptorum Romanorum de re rustica reliquiae*. Messina, 1974–
SVF	J. von Arnim, ed. *Stoicorum veterum fragmenta*. 4 vols. Leipzig, 1903–1924
TLL	*Thesaurus Linguae Latinae*. Leipzig, 1900–
TrGF	B. Snell and R. Kannicht, ed. *Tragicorum Graecorum Fragmenta*. 5 vols. Göttingen, 1971–2004

BIBLIOGRAPHY

Armisen-Marchetti, M., ed. 2001–2003. *Commentaire au Songe de Scipion*. 2 vols. Paris.

Arweiler, A. 2000. "Zu Text und Überlieferung einer gekürzten Fassung von Macrobius *Saturnalia* 1,12,2–1, 15,20." *ZPE* 131: 45–57.

Barker-Benfield, B. C. 1983. "Macrobius: Introduction/ Commentary on Cicero's *Somnium Scipionis*." In L. D. Reynolds, ed., *Texts and Transmission: A Survey of the Latin Classics*. Oxford. 222–32.

Bloch, H. 1945. "A New Document of the Last Pagan Revival in the West." *HTR* 38: 199–244.

———. 1963. "The Pagan Revival in the West at the End of the Fourth Century." In A. Momigliano, ed., *The Conflict between Paganism and Christianity in the Fourth Century*. Oxford. 193–218.

Brind'Amour, P. 1983. *Le calendrier romain: recherches chronologiques*. Ottawa.

Brown, M. K. *The "Narratives" of Konon*. Munich.

Cameron, A. 1966. "The Date and Identity of Macrobius." *JRS* 56: 25–38.

———. 1967. "Macrobius, Avienus, and Avianus." *CQ* 17: 385–99.

———. 2011. *The Last Pagans of Rome*. Oxford.

Carton, M. J. 1966. *Three Unstudied Manuscripts of*

Macrobius' "Saturnalia." PhD dissertation. St. Louis University.

Coarelli, F. 2007. *Rome and Environs: An Archaeological Guide*. Trans. by J. J. Clauss and D. P. Harmon; illustrations adapted by J. A. Clauss and P. A. MacKay. Berkeley.

Coulter, J. A. *The Literary Microcosm: Theories of Interpretation of the Later Neoplatonists*. Columbia Studies in the Classical Tradition, 2. Leiden.

Courcelle, P. 1969. *Latin Writers and Their Greek Sources*. Trans. by H. E. Wedeck. Cambridge, MA.

Criniti, N, ed. 1981. *Granii Liciniani Historiarum reliquiae*. Leipzig.

Dean-Jones, L. A. 1994. *Women's Bodies in Classical Greek Science*. Oxford.

Dorfbauer, L. J. 2010. "Die Bucheinteilung der *Saturnalia* des Macrobius." *MH* 67: 43–63.

Douglas, A. E., ed. 1966. *M. Tulli Ciceronis "Brutus."* Oxford.

Flamant, J. 1968. "La technique du banquet dans les Saturnales de Macrobe." *REL* 46: 303–19.

———. 1977. *Macrobe et le néo-platonisme latin a la fin du IVe siècle*. Études préliminaires aux religions orientales dans l'empire romain, Vol. 58. Leiden.

Flower, H. 2006. *The Art of Forgetting: Disgrace and Oblivion in Roman Political Culture*. Chapel Hill, NC.

Fontaine, M. 2009. *Funny Words in Plautine Comedy*. Oxford.

Georgii, H. 1912. "Zur Bestimmung der Zeit des Servius." *Phililogus* 71: 518–26.

Goldlust, B. 2007. "Une orchestration littéraire du sa-

voir: le projet didactique de Macrobe dans les *Saturnales*." In B. Goldlust and J.-B. Guillaumin, eds., *Schedae* (Colloque « Héritages et traditions encyclopédiques », Université de Caen, 2 février 2007). Fasc. 1. Caen. 27–44.

Guittard, C. 2004. *Les Saturnales, Livres I-III*. 2nd ed. Paris.

Hajjar, J. N. 1977. *La triade d'Héliopolis-Baalbek*. Vol. 1–2: *Son culte et sa diffusion à travers les textes littéraires et les documents iconographiques et épigraphiques*. Études préliminaires aux religions orientales dans l'empire romain, Vol. 59. Leiden.

———. 1985. *La triade d'Héliopolis-Baalbek*. Vol. 3: *Iconographie, théologie, culte et sanctuaires*. Leiden.

Hedrick, C. 2000. *History and Silence: Purge and Rehabilitation of Memory in Late Antiquity*. Austin, TX.

Heitsch, E. 1961–1964. *Die griechischen Dichterfragmente der römischen Kaiserzeit*. 2 vols. Göttingen.

Herzog, R., and P. L. Schmidt. 1989. *Handbuch der lateinischen Literatur der Antike*, Vol. 5. Munich.

Jocelyn, H. D. 1964. "Ancient Scholarship and Virgil's Use of Republican Latin Poetry. I." *CQ* 14: 280–95.

———, ed. 1967. *The Tragedies of Ennius: The Fragments*. Cambridge.

Kaster, R. A. 1980. "Macrobius and Servius: *Verecundia* and the Grammarian's Function." *HSCP* 84: 219–62.

———. 1988. *Guardians of Language: The Grammarian and Society in Late Antiquity*. Berkeley.

———, ed. 1995. *Suetonius: De grammaticis et rhetoribus*. Oxford.

———. 2010. *Studies on the Text of Macrobius's "Saturna-*

lia." American Philological Association Monographs. New York.

König, J. 2008. "Sympotic Dialogue in the First to Fifth Centuries CE." In S. Goldhill, ed., *The End of Dialogue in Antiquity*. Cambridge. 85–113.

Lamberton, R. 1986. *Homer the Theologian: Neoplatonist Allegorical Reading and the Growth of the Epic Tradition*. Berkeley.

———, and J. J. Keaney, eds. 1992. *Homer's Ancient Readers: The Hermeneutics of Greek Epic's Earliest Exegetes*. Princeton.

Lange, K., and M. Hirmer. 1968. *Egypt: Architecture, Sculpture, Painting in Three Thousand Years*. Trans. by R. H. Boothroyd. London.

La Penna, A. 1953. "Studi sulla tradizione dei Saturnali di Macrobio." *ASNP* 22: 225–52.

———. 1964. Review of Willis 1963. *RFIC* 92: 452–61.

Liebeschuetz, W. 1999. "The Significance of the Speech of Praetextatus." In P. Athanassiadi and M. Frede, eds., *Pagan Monotheism in Late Antiquity*. Oxford. 185–205.

Lightfoot, J. L., ed. 2003. *Lucian: On the Syrian Goddess*. Oxford.

Lindberg, D. C. 1976. *Theories of Vision from al-Kindi to Kepler*. Chicago.

Linke, H. 1880. *Quaestiones de Macrobii Saturnaliorum fontibus*. Breslau.

Lipìnski, E. 1995. *Dieux et déesses de l'univers phénicien et punique*. Orientalia Lovaniensia analecta, 64. Leuven.

Lögdberg, G. 1936. *In Macrobii Saturnalia adnotationes*. Uppsala.

Marinone, N. 1946. *Elio Donato, Macrobio e Servio, commentatori di Vergilio*. Vercelli.

———. 1970. "Il banchetto dei pontefici in Macrobio." *Maia* 23: 271–78.

———, ed. 1977. *I Saturnali di Macrobio Theodosio*. 2nd ed. Turin.

Marshall, P. K. 1983. "Macrobius: *Saturnalia*." In L. D. Reynolds, ed., *Texts and Transmission: A Survey of the Latin Classics*. Oxford. 233–35.

Martin, J. 1931. *Symposion: Die Geschichte einer literarischen Form*. Studien zur Geschichte und Kultur des Alterums 17.1–2. Paderborn.

Mastandrea, P. 1979. *Un neoplatonico latino Cornelio Labeone*. Leiden.

Mazzarino, S. 1938. "La politica religiosa di Stilico." *RIL* 71: 235–62.

Michalowski, K. 1969. *Art of Ancient Egypt*. Trans. and adapted by N. Guterman. New York.

Michels, A. K. 1967. *The Calendar of the Roman Republic*. Princeton.

Murgia, C. E. 2003. "The Dating of Servius Revisited." *CP* 98: 45–69.

Neri, M., ed. 2007. *Commento al Sogno di Scipione*. Milan.

Paolis, P. de, ed. 1990. *Macrobii Theodosii De uerborum Graeci et Latini differentiis uel societatibus excerpta*. Urbino.

Piankoff, A., ed. 1964. *The Litany of Re*. Bollingen Series XL.4. New York.

Regali, M., ed. 1983–1990. *Commento al Somnium Scipionis*. 2 vols. Pisa.

Roullet, A. 1972. *The Egyptian and Egyptianizing Monu-*

ments of Imperial Rome. Études préliminares aux religions orientales dans l'empire romain, Vol. 20. Leiden.

Rüpke, J. 2008. *Fasti sacerdotum: A Prosopography of Pagan, Jewish, and Christian Religious Officials in the City of Rome, 300 BC to AD 499*. Trans. by D. Richardson. Oxford.

Salzman, M. R. 1990. *On Roman Time: The Codex-Calendar of 354 and the Rhythms of Urban Life in Late Antiquity*. Berkeley.

Santoro, A. 1946. *Esegeti virgiliani antichi: Donato, Macrobio, Servio*. Bari.

Schmidt, P. L. 2008. "(Macrobius) Theodosius und das Personal der Saturnalia." *RFIC* 136: 47–83.

Schönberger, O. and E. 2008. *Tischgespräche am Saturnalienfest: Ambrosius Theodosius Macrobius*. Würzburg.

Spiegelberg, W. 1901. "Buchis, der heilige Stier von Hermonthis: Zu Macrobius Sat. I, XXI, 20." *APF* 1: 339–42.

Syme, R. 1986. *The Augustan Aristocracy*. Oxford.

Treggiari, S. 1991. *Roman Marriage: Iusti Coniuges from the Time of Cicero to the Time of Ulpian*. Oxford.

Walsh, M., and D. Ó Cróinín, eds. 1988. *Cummian's Letter "De controversia Paschali" and the "De ratione conputandi."* Toronto.

Wessner, P. 1928. "Macrobius." *RE* 14,1: 170–98.

Williams, R. D. 1966–1967. "Servius, Commentator and Guide." *PVS* 6: 50–56.

Willis, J. 1957. "De codicibus aliquot manuscriptis Macrobii *Saturnalia* continentibus." *RhM* 100: 152–64.

———, ed. 1963. *Ambrosii Theodosii Macrobii Saturnalia*, Vol. 1; *Ambrosii Theodosii Macrobii. Commentarii in Somnium Scipionis*, Vol. 2. Leipzig.

BIBLIOGRAPHY

Wissowa, G. 1880. *De Macrobii Saturnaliorum fontibus capita tria*. Breslau.

———. 1913. "Athenaeus und Macrobius." *Nachrichten von der Gesellschaft der Wissenschaften zu Göttingen, Philologisch-historiche Klasse*. Göttingen. 325–37.

Wolfsdorf, D. "The Dramatic Date of Plato's *Protagoras*." *RhM* 140: 223–30.

SATURNALIA

MACROBII AMBROSII THEODOSII VIRI CLARISSIMI ET ILLVSTRIS

CONVIVIORVM PRIMI DIEI SATVRNALIORVM[1]

1. Multas variasque res in hac vita nobis, Eustathi fili, natura conciliavit; sed nulla nos magis quam eorum qui e nobis essent procreati caritate devinxit eamque nostram in his educandis atque erudiendis curam esse voluit, ut parentes neque—si id quod cuperent ex sententia cederet—tantum ulla alia ex re voluptatis neque—si contra eveniret—tantum maeroris capere possint. 2. hinc est quod mihi quoque institutione tua nihil antiquius aestimatur, ad cuius perfectionem compendia longis anfractibus anteponenda ducens moraeque omnis impatiens non opperior ut per haec sola promoveas quibus ediscendis naviter ipse invigilas, sed ago ut ego quoque tibi legerim, et quicquid mihi—vel te iam in lucem edito vel antequam nascereris—in diversis seu Graecae seu Romanae linguae voluminibus elaboratum est, id totum sit tibi scientiae supellex et quasi de quo-

---

[1] CONVIVIORVM . . . SATVRNALIORVM *om.* GₛVC, *post* SATVRNALIORVM *add.* incipit NFA, incipit feliciter BR, liber incipit DX, liber ·i· incipit P

THE RIGHT HONORABLE AND ILLUSTRIOUS MACROBIUS AMBROSIUS THEODOSIUS

THE FESTIVITIES OF THE FIRST DAY OF THE SATURNALIA

1. Nature has formed many different attachments for us in this life, Eustathius my child, but she has forged no bond of affection stronger than the one that binds us to our offspring: so intent has she wished us to be on their upbringing and instruction that parents can neither find a greater source of pleasure, if all goes according to plan, nor experience greater grief, should things turn out otherwise. 2. For this reason I judge nothing dearer than your education,[1] and in making it complete I prefer shortcuts to long roundabouts: being impatient of delay, I am not waiting for you to make progress only in the subjects you are learning through your own wakeful efforts, but I have made a point of reading on your behalf, so that all that I have toiled through—in various books of Greek or Latin, both before and since you were born—might be available to you as a

---

1 §2 is based on Gell. Praef. 2.

dam litterarum peno, siquando usus venerit aut historiae
quae in librorum strue latens clam vulgo est aut dicti fac-
tive memorabilis reminiscendi, facile id tibi inventu atque
depromptu sit.

3. Nec indigeste tamquam in acervum congessimus
digna memoratu, sed variarum rerum disparilitas, auctoribus diversa, confusa temporibus, ita in quoddam digesta
corpus est, ut quae indistincte atque promiscue ad subsi-
dium memoriae adnotaveramus, in ordinem instar membrorum cohaerentia convenirent. 4. nec mihi vitio vertas,
si res quas ex lectione varia mutuabor ipsis saepe verbis
quibus ab ipsis auctoribus enarratae sunt explicabo, quia
praesens opus non eloquentiae ostentationem sed noscen-
dorum congeriem pollicetur; et boni consulas oportet, si
notitiam vetustatis modo nostris non obscure, modo ipsis
antiquorum fideliter verbis recognoscas, prout quaeque se
vel enarranda vel transferenda suggesserint.

5. Apes enim quodammodo debemus imitari, quae va-
gantur et flores carpunt, deinde quicquid attulere disponunt ac per favos dividunt et sucum varium in unum sapo-
rem mixtura quadam et proprietate spiritus sui mutant.
6. nos quoque quicquid diversa lectione quaesivimus com-
mittemus stilo, ut in ordinem eodem digerente coalescat.
nam et in animo melius distincta servantur, et ipsa distinc-
tio non sine quodam fermento, quo conditur universitas, in
unius saporis usum varia libamenta confundit, ut etiam si

---

2 §§5–10 are based on Sen. *Moral Epistles* 84.2–10.

fund of knowledge. If ever the need arises for a piece of history, say, that lurks hidden from the common run of men in a mass of books, or to call to mind some memorable deed or saying, you will be able to find and produce it easily as though from your own private store of culture.

3. Nor have I haphazardly deployed these items that are worth remembering, as though in a heap: I have organized the diverse subjects, drawn from a range of authors and a mix of periods, as though in a body, so that the things I initially noted down all a jumble, as an *aide mémoire*, might come together in a coherent, organic whole. 4. Please do not fault me if I often set forth the accounts I draw from my varied reading in the very words that the authors themselves used; the work before you promises not a display of eloquence but an accumulation of things worth knowing. You should, furthermore, count it as a bonus if you sometimes gain acquaintance with antiquity plainly in my own words, at other times through the faithful record of the ancients' own words, as each item lends itself to being cited or transcribed.

5. We ought to imitate bees, if I can put it that way:[2] wandering about, sampling the flowers, they arrange whatever they've gathered, distributing it among the honeycomb's cells, and by blending in the peculiar quality of their own spirit they transform the diverse kinds of nectar into a single taste. 6. I too will commit to writing all that I have sought out in my varied reading, so that by being arranged consistently it will come together in an orderly whole. Things made distinct are more readily remembered, and the very process of distinction involves a kind of fermentation that gives zest to the whole, blending the varied samples so that we experience a single flavor:

quid apparuerit unde sumptum sit, aliud tamen esse quam unde sumptum noscetur appareat. 7. quod in corpore nostro videmus sine ulla opera nostra facere naturam: alimenta quae accipimus, quamdiu in sua qualitate perseverant et solida innatant, male stomacho oneri sunt; at cum ex eo quod erant mutata sunt, tum demum in vires et sanguinem transeunt. idem in his quibus aluntur ingenia praestemus, ut quaecumque hausimus non patiamur integra esse, ne aliena sint, sed in quandam digeriem concoquantur: alioquin in memoriam ire possunt, non in ingenium.

8. Ex omnibus colligamus unde unum fiat,[2] sicut unus numerus fit ex singulis. hoc faciat noster animus: omnia quibus est adiutus abscondat, ipsum tantum[3] ostendat quod effecit, ut qui odora pigmenta conficiunt ante omnia curant ut nullius sint odoris proprii[4] quae condientur, confusuri[5] videlicet omnium sucos in spiramentum unum. 9. vides quam multorum vocibus chorus constet, una tamen ex omnibus redditur. aliqua est illic acuta, aliqua gravis, aliqua media, accedunt viris feminae, interponitur fistula: ita singulorum illic latent voces, omnium apparent, et fit concentus ex dissonis. 10. tale hoc praesens opus volo: multae in illo artes, multa praecepta sint, multarum aetatium exempla, sed in unum conspirata. in quibus si neque ea quae iam tibi sunt cognita aspernaris nec quae ignota

---

[2] fiat B: fiat ex omnibus ω   [3] tantum *cod. Patav. Bibl. Anton. 27 "Disputationis Chori"*: tamen ω   [4] proprii O[2]A[vl]C: propria ω   [5] confusuri *ed. Ven. 1513*: -ura ω

---

[3] Cf. 7.8.2.

[4] Cf. [Arist.] *On the Universe* 5 396b7–19, Philo *On the Life of Moses* 2.256, *On the Contemplative Life* 88, Plut. *Mor.* 96E.

even if some item's source should be clear, it still seems different from that evident source. 7. We see nature do just that in our bodies, with no effort of our own:[3] as long as the foods we take in remain just as they are, floating as solids in the stomach, they are an unpleasant burden, but when they have been changed from what they were, then and only then do they become sources of strength and blood. We should make the same provision in the case of things that nourish our wits: we should not allow what we have taken in to remain intact and alien but should digest and distribute it; otherwise it can pass into memory, but not become part of our thought.

8. We should draw upon all our sources with the aim of making a unity, just as one number results from a sum of individual numbers. Let this be the mind's goal: to conceal its sources of support and to display only what it has made of them, just as those who make perfumes take particular care that the specific odor of any ingredient not be perceptible, since they aim to blend all the aromatic essences into a single fragrant exhalation. 9. You know how a chorus consists of many people's voices, and yet they all produce a single sound. One voice is high-pitched, another low, another in the middle, men are joined by women, a pipe is added to the mix: individual voices disappear while the voices of all are revealed, and the disparate tones produce a harmony.[4] 10. That is my goal for the present work: it comprises many different disciplines, many lessons, examples drawn from many periods, but brought together into a harmonious whole. If you neither disdain the things already familiar to you nor shun those you do not know, you will find many

sunt vites, invenies plurima quae sit aut voluptati legere aut cultui legisse aut usui meminisse. 11. nihil enim huic operi insertum puto aut cognitu inutile aut difficile perceptu, sed omnia quibus sit ingenium tuum vegetius, memoria adminiculatior, oratio sollertior, sermo incorruptior —ni sicubi nos, sub alio ortos caelo, Latinae linguae vena non adiuvet. 12. quod ab his, si tamen quibusdam forte non numquam tempus voluntasque erit ista cognoscere, petitum impetratumque volumus ut aequi bonique consulant, si in nostro sermone nativa Romani oris elegantia desideretur.

13. Sed ne ego incautus sum, qui venustatem reprehensionis incurri a M. quondam Catone profectae in A. Albinum qui cum L. Lucullo consul fuit. 14. is Albinus res Romanas oratione Graeca scriptitavit. in eius historiae primo[6] scriptum est ad hanc sententiam: neminem succensere sibi convenire, si quid in illis libris parum composite aut minus eleganter scriptum foret. "nam sum," inquit, "homo Romanus natus in Latio, et eloquium Graecum a nobis alienissimum est." ideoque veniam gratiamque malae existimationis, si quid esset erratum, postulavit. 15. ea cum legisset M. Cato, "ne tu," inquit, "Aule, nimium nugator es, cum maluisti culpam deprecari quam culpa vacare. nam petere veniam solemus aut cum imprudentes erravimus aut cum noxam imperio compellentis admisimus. te," in-

6 principio *Gell*.

---

5 §11 is modeled on Gell. Praef. 16   6 The conventional surmise is Africa: see Introd. §1.   7 For brief biographical notes on all persons mentioned in the text, see the "Index of Proper Names"; for sketches of the participants, see Introd. §2.

8

things that are either a pleasure to read or a mark of culti-
vation to have read or useful to remember. 11. I judge that
I have included nothing that is either useless to know or
difficult to learn:[5] everything here will make your mind
more active, your memory better stocked, your speech
more skillful, your language more refined—save here and
there where the natural flow of the Latin language might
fail me, who was born under an alien sky.[6] 12. And if others
chance at some point to have the time and desire to make
this work's acquaintance, I hope that they will, as I request,
be fair and righteous judges, should my discourse lack the
native elegance of the Roman tongue.

13. But here I have gone and carelessly exposed myself
to the witty criticism Marcus Cato[7] once made of Aulus
Albinus, who was Lucius Lucullus' colleague as consul
[151 BCE]. 14. In the first book of his Roman history, which
he wrote in Greek, Albinus included a remark to the effect
that people could not reasonably be irritated if they found
anything in the work insufficiently well arranged or smartly
written,[8] "For I am," he said (no. 812 fr. 1b *FGrH* = fr. 1b
Ch.), "a Roman born in Latium, and have very little famil-
iarity with Greek eloquence." He accordingly asked his
readers to indulge him and spare him their bad opinion if
he made mistakes. 15. On reading that, Cato said, "My
word, Aulus, you really are too big a fool, preferring to beg
indulgence for a fault instead of avoiding it. We usually ask
forgiveness when we've incautiously made a *faux pas* or
been guilty of wrongdoing under the constraint of force;

---

[8] §§14–15 are based on Gell. 11.8.2; cf. also Polyb. 29.1.4–8,
Plut. *Cato the Elder* 12.5.

quit, "oro quis perpulit ut id committeres quod priusquam faceres, peteres ut ignosceretur?" 16. nunc argumentum quod huic operi dedimus velut sub quodam prologi habitu dicemus.

1   Saturnalibus apud Vettium Praetextatum Romanae nobilitatis proceres doctique alii congregantur et tempus sollemniter feriatum deputant colloquio liberali, convivia quoque sibi mutua comitate praebentes nec discedentes a se nisi ad nocturnam quietem. 2. nam per omne spatium feriarum meliorem diei partem seriis disputationibus occupantes cenae tempore sermones conviviales agitant, ita ut nullum diei tempus docte aliquid vel lepide proferendi vacuum relinquatur, sed erit in mensa sermo iucundior, ut habeat voluptatis amplius, severitatis minus. 3. nam cum apud alios quibus sunt descripta convivia, tum in illo Platonis symposio non austeriore aliqua de re convivarum sermo, sed Cupidinis varia et lepida descriptio est, in quo quidem Socrates non artioribus, ut solet, nodis urget atque implicat adversarium sed eludendi magis quam decertandi modo adprehensis dat elabendi prope atque effugiendi locum. 4. oportet enim versari in convivio sermones ut castitate integros, ita adpetibiles venustate. matutina vero erit robustior disputatio, quae viros et doctos et praeclarissimos deceat. neque enim Cottae, Laelii, Scipiones amplis-

---

9 On the plan of the work see Introd. §4.

10 Lit. "conversation worthy of a free man" (*colloquium liberale*), the adjective alluding to the *artes liberales*—'the skills worthy of a free man'—that included grammar, dialectic, rhetoric, geometry, arithmetic, astronomy, and music, treated in that order by M.'s contemporary Martianus Capella in *The Wedding of Philology and Mercury and the Seven Liberal Arts*.

but you," he said, "pray tell me, who forced you to do a thing you ask to be forgiven for doing before you've done it?" 16. Now, as a sort of prologue, I will tell you the story line that I have given this work.

It is the Saturnalia:[9] the leading members of the Roman 1 nobility and other learned men are gathered at the home of Vettius Praetextatus, where they are devoting the time of the customary religious observance to cultured conversation,[10] sharing meals with good fellowship all around, nor leaving each other's company save to take their night's rest. 2. During the length of the holiday they spend the better part of the day discussing serious topics and hold festive conversations at dinner-time, so that no time of day is left empty of learned or beguiling contributions. But the conversation at table is of a lighter sort, more pleasurable and less austere. 3. For not only in the works of others who have described banquets,[11] but especially in the great *Symposium* of Plato, the banqueters did not converse about some more serious subject but described Love in various witty ways: in that setting Socrates does not, in his usual way, press his opponent and tie him up in tight argumentative knots but—in a way more playful than combative—almost offers those in his grasp the chance to give him the slip and get away. 4. At a banquet the conversations should be as pleasurably beguiling as they are morally unimpeachable; the morning's discussion, on the other hand, will be more vigorous, as befits men both learned and very highly distinguished. In truth, if men like Cotta and Laelius and Scipio are to hold forth on the most sub-

[11] On the *Saturnalia*'s debts to the genre of sympotic dialogues, see Introd. §3.

simis de rebus, quoad Romanae litterae erunt, in veterum libris disputabunt, Praetextatos vero, Flavianos, Albinos, Symmachos et Eustathios, quorum splendor similis et non inferior virtus est, eodem modo loqui aliquid licitum non erit.

5. Nec mihi fraudi sit si uni aut alteri ex his quos coetus coegit matura aetas posterior saeculo Praetextati fuit, quod licito fieri Platonis dialogi testimonio sunt. quippe Socrate ita Parmenides antiquior ut huius pueritia vix illius adprehenderit senectutem, et tamen inter illos de rebus arduis disputatur; inclitum dialogum Socrates habita cum Timaeo disputatione consumit, quos constat eodem saeculo non fuisse. 6. Paralus vero et Xanthippus, quibus Pericles pater fuit, cum Protagora apud Platonem disserunt secundo adventu Athenis morante, quos multo ante infamis illa pestilentia Atheniensis absumpserat.[7] annos ergo coeuntium mitti in digitos, exemplo Platonis nobis suffragante, non convenit. 7. quo autem facilius quae ab omnibus dicta sunt apparere ac secerni possent, Decium de Postumiano quinam ille sermo aut inter quos fuisset sciscitantem fecimus. et ne diutius lectori desideria moremur,

---

[7] absumpserat P²G²XVAC: ads- *vel* ass- ω

---

[12] Lucius Aurelius Cotta is a participant in Cicero's *On the Nature of the Gods*, Gaius Laelius and Publis Cornelius Scipio Aemilianus in *On the Commonwealth* and *On Old Age*; Laelius is represented as speaking of his relationship with Scipio in *On Friendship*.   [13] On the anachronistic inclusion of Servius and Avienus, see Introd. §2.   [14] M. knew Athenaeus' discussions of Plato's anachronisms at 216F-218E; cf. also next n.

[15] Sim. Athen. 505F; the dramatic date of the *Parmenides* is ca. 450 BCE, when Socrates was 19 and Parmenides of Elea is said

stantial topics in the books of the ancients as long as Roman literature exists,[12] there is nothing to prevent men like Praetextatus, Flavianus, the Albini, Symmachus, and Eustathius—whose brilliance is comparable and their excellence not inferior—to say their piece in the same way.

5. And let no one fault me if one or two of those whom this gathering has brought together did not reach their maturity until after the age of Praetextatus.[13] This is permitted, as Plato's dialogues testify:[14] Parmenides was so much older than Socrates that the latter's boyhood scarcely overlapped the other's old age—and yet they discussed difficult issues;[15] Socrates spends a glorious dialogue in discussion with Timaeus, though it is common knowledge that they did not live at the same time.[16] 6. Indeed, Plato has Paralus and Xanthippus, Pericles' sons, converse with Protagoras on his second visit to Athens, though the ill-famed Great Plague at Athens [430–29 BCE] had carried them off long before.[17] So with Plato's example as my support, I did not think it appropriate to tote up the guests' ages on my fingers. 7. But so that each speaker's words could more easily be made plain and distinct from the others', I have represented Decius as asking Postumianus what the conversation was and who participated. Not to stand in the eager

to have visited Athens at the age of ca. 65 (*Parm.* 127B, cf. *Soph.* 217C).   [16] A curious statement, since the Pythagorean Timaeus of Locri is known only from the dialogue that bears his name.   [17] It is impossible to define a single dramatic date for the *Protagoras* (Wolfsdorf 1997); M. is following Athen. 218B-C, where Protagoras' 2nd visit to Athens is placed late in the 420s and the dialogue is more generally convicted of multiple anachronisms.

13

iam Decii et Postumiani sermo palam faciet quae huius colloquii vel origo fuerit vel ordo processerit.

2 "Temptanti mihi, Postumiane, aditus tuos et mollissima consultandi tempora commodo adsunt feriae quas indulget magna pars mensis Iano dicati. ceteris enim ferme diebus qui perorandis causis opportuni sunt hora omnino reperiri nulla potest, quin tuorum clientum negotia vel defendas in foro vel domi discas. nunc autem—scio te enim non ludo sed serio feriari—si est commodum respondere id quod rogatum venio, tibi ipsi, quantum arbitror, non iniucundum, mihi vero gratissimum feceris. 2. requiro autem abs te id primum, interfuerisne convivio per complusculos dies continua comitate renovato eique sermoni quem praedicare in primis quemque apud omnes maximis ornare laudibus diceris? quem quidem ego ex patre audissem, nisi post illa convivia Roma[8] profectus Neapoli moraretur: aliis vero nuper interfui admirantibus memoriae tuae vires, universa quae tunc dicta sunt per ordinem saepe referentis."

3. "Hoc unum, Deci, nobis—ut et ipse, quantum tua sinit adulescentia, videre et ex patre Albino audire potuisti—in omni vitae cursu optimum visum est, ut quantum cessare a causarum defensione licuisset, tantum ad erudi-

---

[8] Roma D[vl]: Romana ω

---

[18] On M.'s debt to Plato in creating this frame for the dialogue, see Introd. §3; cf. also Lucian *Symp.* 1.   [19] Cf. *A.* 4.293–94.

[20] Decius means the Agonalia (9 January: cf. 1.4.7n.) and Carmentalia (11 and 15 January: cf. 1.16.6nn.), appropriately for the time of the dialogue, but not for long thereafter: in August 389 Rufius Albinus, a participant in the dialogue (and possibly Decius'

reader's way any longer, Decius and Postumianus will now make plain the discussion's origin and the order it followed.[18]

"Just in time, Postumianus—as I 'try to approach and test the times when you are susceptible'[19] to inquiry— those holidays are at hand that much of the month devoted to Janus grants to us.[20] For on practically all other days that are available for arguing cases, not an hour can be found when you are not either in the forum defending your clients' interests or at home working their cases up. But now, since I know that you are well and truly on holiday, if this is a good time for you to answer the question I've come to ask, it will be, so far as I can judge, not burdensome to you and a very great favor to me. 2. But first I want to ask: were you present at that banquet that continued for several days with uninterrupted good cheer, and at the conversation you are said especially to commend and praise to the skies to everyone you meet? I would have learned of it from my father,[21] had he not left Rome for a stay in Naples after the banquet. But I have recently been in the company of others who marvel at your powers of memory and say that you often repeat, in order, everything that was said then."

3. "In all of life's course, Decius—as you yourself (to the degree your youth allows) have been able to see and hear in the case of your father, Albinus—this one practice has seemed best: to devote as much free time as my labors at

uncle: Introd. §2) who was then urban prefect, received from the emperor a rescript ordering that "all days are to be juridical" (*CTh.* 2.8.19), with a very few exceptions that included New Year's Day and the two weeks surrounding Easter.   [21] I.e., Caecina Albinus, one of the participants in the dialogue (cf. Introd. §2).

torum hominum tuique similium congressum aliquem ser-
monemque conferrem. 4. neque enim recte institutus animus requiescere aut utilius aut honestius usquam potest
quam in aliqua opportunitate docte ac liberaliter collo-
quendi interrogandique et respondendi comitate. 5. sed
quodnam istud convivium? an vero dubitandum non est
quin id dicas quod doctissimis procerum ceterisque nuper
apud Vettium Praetextatum fuit et discurrens post inter
reliquos grata vicissitudo variavit?"

"De hoc ipso quaesitum venio et explices velim quale
illud convivium fuerit, a quo te afuisse propter singularem
omnium in te amicitiam non opinor."

6. "Voluissem equidem neque id illis, ut aestimo, ingra-
tum fuisset; sed cum essent amicorum complures mihi
causae illis diebus pernoscendae, ad cenam tum rogatus
meditandi non edendi illud mihi tempus esse respondi
hortatusque sum ut alium potius nullo involutum negotio
atque a cura liberum quaererent. 7. itaque factum est. nam
facundum et eruditum virum Eusebium, rhetorem inter
Graecos praestantem omnibus idem nostra aetate professis, doctrinae Latiaris haud inscium, Praetextatus meum in
locum invitari imperavit."

8. "Unde igitur illa tibi nota sunt quae tum iucunde et
comiter ad instituendam vitam exemplis, ut audio, rerum
copiosissimis et variae doctrinae ubertate prolata diges-
taque sunt?"

9. "Cum solstitiali die, qui Saturnaliorum festa quibus
illa convivia celebrata sunt consecutus est, forensi cura va-

---

[22] Cf. 1.5.13 and 1.6.2.   [23] 25 December: the feast of
Sol Invictus (Invincible Sun) and, for Christians, Christmas; M.
leaves unstated which he means.

the bar have allowed to meeting and speaking with scholars and people like yourself. 4. A well-bred spirit can find no more useful or more honorable form of relaxation than in the sort of learned conversation worthy of free men, and in the gracious exchange of questions and answers. 5. But what banquet do you have in mind? Surely you mean the one recently held at Vettius Praetextatus' home for the most learned of the nobility and his other guests, which thereafter gained a pleasing variety as invitations were exchanged and the group reassembled at the homes of other hosts?"

"The very one I'm here to ask about! Do please describe the sort of banquet it was—I'm sure that you were on hand, given the special friendship that all men feel for you."

6. "For my part, I wish I had been, nor do I think they would have found it displeasing. But I had such a large number of my friends' cases to work up over those days that when I was invited to dinner I replied that it was time for me to prepare, not dine,[22] and I urged them to look for someone else who was carefree and not wrapped up in business. 7. And so they did: Praetextatus bade the eloquent and learned gentleman Eusebius be invited in my place, foremost among the Greek rhetoricians of the day, and by no means ignorant of Latin lore."

8. "How then did you come to know of the proceedings that were mounted and presented delightfully and generously on that occasion, with (I'm told) plenty of applications for the conduct of life and with an abundance of diverse learning?"

9. "On the day of the winter solstice,[23] following the celebration of the Saturnalia when those festivities were held,

17

cuus laetiore animo essem domi, eo Eusebius cum paucis e
sectatoribus suis venit 10. statimque vultu renidens, 'per-
magna me,' inquit, 'abs te, Postumiane, cum ex aliis tum
hoc maxime gratia fateor obstrictum, quod a Praetextato
veniam postulando mihi in cena vacuefecisti locum. itaque
intellego non studium tantum tuum sed ipsam quoque, ut
aliquid abs te mihi fiat commodi, consentire atque adspi-
rare fortunam.' 11. 'visne,' inquam, 'restituere id nobis
quod debitum tam benigne ac tam libenter fateris nos-
trumque hoc otium, quo perfrui raro admodum licet, eo
ducere ut his quibus tunc tu interfueris nunc nos interesse
videamur?' 12. 'faciam,' inquit, 'ut vis. narrabo autem tibi
non cibum aut potum, tam etsi ea quoque ubertim cas-
teque adfuerunt. sed et quae vel in conviviis vel maxime
extra mensam ab isdem per tot dies dicta sunt, in quantum
potero, animo repetam.' 13. quae quidem ego cum audi-
rem, ad eorum mihi vitam qui beati a sapientibus diceren-
tur accedere videbar: nam et quae pridie quam adesset[9] inter eos dicta sunt Avieno mihi insinuante comperta sunt, et
omnia scripto mandavi, ne quid subtraheret oblivio. quae
si ex me audire gestis, cave aestimes diem unum referendis
quae per tot dies sunt dicta sufficere."

14. "Quemnam igitur et inter quos aut unde ortum sermonem, Postumiane, fuisse dicebat? ita praesto sum inde-
fessus auditor." 15. tum ille, "declinante," inquit, "in ves-
perum die quem Saturnale festum erat insecuturum, cum

[9] adesset *scripsi*: adessem ω

---

[24] Cf. 1.6.4, for Eusebius' arrival.

[25] Cf. Hor. *Satires* 2.4.1–3. If the written record is Postumianus', it explains occasions when, as narrator, he refers to "the

I was at home, free from the courtroom's cares and feeling rather cheerful, when Eusebius arrived with some of his followers. 10. Immediately he said, with a broad smile, 'I am much in your debt, Postumianus, for any number of reasons, but above all because you opened a place for me at that dinner by making your excuses to Praetextatus: I know that not just your goodwill but lady luck herself conspired to see that some good would come my way from you.' 11. 'Would you like to repay that debt,' I said, 'which you so kindly and gladly acknowledge, and spend this day's leisure, which I so rarely can enjoy, in allowing me to feel now that I am among those whose company you then enjoyed?' 12. 'I'll do as you wish,' he said, 'though I'll not tell you about the food and drink, generously and yet temperately provided though they were. Instead I will summon up from my memory, to the extent I can, all that was said throughout those days, whether in the course of their dining or, especially, away from the table.' 13. As I listened, I thought to myself that I was entering on the kind of life enjoyed by those whom sages call 'blessed.' And thanks to Avienus, I've found out what was said on the day before he arrived:[24] so as not to forget anything, I've committed it all to writing.[25] If you're eager to hear all this from me, don't suppose that one day will be enough to relate what it took so many days to say."

14. "How did he describe the conversation, Postumianus? Who took part and how did it start? I'm all ears, and indefatigable." 15. Then Postumianus said, "It was getting on toward evening, on the day before the Saturnalia was to

reader" (e.g., 1.16.30, 5.7.4, 7, 5.13.27) and to himself as writing (e.g., 3.13.6, 5.21.19).

Vettius Praetextatus domi convenire se gestientibus copiam faceret, eo venerunt Aurelius Symmachus et Caecina Albinus, cum aetate tum etiam moribus ac studiis inter se coniunctissimi. hos Servius inter grammaticos doctorem recens professus, iuxta doctrina mirabilis et amabilis verecundia, terram intuens et velut latenti similis sequebatur. 16. quos cum aspexisset obviamque processisset ac perblande salutavisset, conversus ad Rufium Albinum, qui tum forte cum Avieno aderat: 'visne,' ait, 'mi Albine, cum his quos advenisse peropportune vides quosque iure civitatis nostrae lumina dixerimus eam rem de qua inter nos nasci coeperat sermo communicemus?' 17. 'quidni maxime velim?' Albinus inquit, 'nec enim ulla alia de re quam de doctis quaestionibus colloqui aut nobis aut his potest esse iucundius.' 18. cumque consedissent, tum Caecina, 'quidnam id sit, mi Praetextate, tam etsi adhuc nescio, dubitare tamen non debeo esse scitu optimum, cum et vobis ad colloquendum causam adtulerit et nos eius esse expertes non sinatis.' 19. 'atqui scias oportet eum inter nos sermonem fuisse, [ut][10] quoniam dies crastinus festis Saturno dicatis initium dabit, quando Saturnalia incipere dicamus, id est quando crastinum diem initium sumere existimemus. 20. et inter nos quidem parva quaedam de hac disputatione libavimus; verum quia te quidquid in libris latet investigare notius est quam ut per verecundiam negare possis, pergas volo in medium proferre quicquid de hoc quod quaerimus edoctum tibi comprehensumque est.'

3   Tum Caecina: 'cum vobis qui me in hunc sermonem ad-

---

[10] ut *delevi*

---

[26] 16 December, the Saturnalia starting on 17 December.

begin,[26] when Vettius Praetextatus opened his house to those who were eager to visit him. Aurelius Symmachus and Caecina Albinus arrived, very close both in age and in their characters and pursuits, followed by Servius, who had recently established himself as a teacher among the grammarians, both marvelously learned and likably modest, with his eyes upon the ground and looking as though he were trying to hide. 16. When Vettius, catching sight of them, had come forward to meet them and greet them warmly, he turned to Rufius Albinus, who happened to be on hand with Avienus, and said, 'That subject we had just begun to discuss, my dear Albinus, would you like to share it with these new and very timely arrivals, whom we rightly declared the luminaries of our community?' 17. 'I'd like nothing better,' Albinus said. 'Neither we nor these gentlemen can take more pleasure in any discussion than one involving matters of scholarship.' 18. When they had taken a seat, Caecina said, 'Though I do not yet know what the matter might be, I ought not doubt that it is well worth knowing, since it gave you two something to talk about and you want us to share in it.' 19. 'Then you should know that this was the topic of conversation: since tomorrow will mark the start of the feast-days dedicated to Saturn, when should we say the Saturnalia begin—that is, when should we judge that tomorrow begins? 20. Between the two of us we've skimmed the surface of the discussion; but since it's well known that you track down any lore that lurks in books—too well known for you to deny it out of modesty— please do go ahead and put before us whatever you've learned and come to understand on this question.'

Then Caecina said: 'Those of you drawing me into this   3

ducitis nihil ex omnibus quae veteribus elaborata sunt aut ignoratio neget aut oblivio subtrahat, superfluum video inter scientes nota proferre. sed ne quis me aestimet dignationem consultationis gravari, quidquid de hoc mihi tenuis memoria suggesserit paucis revolvam.' post haec, cum omnes paratos ad audiendum erectosque vidisset, ita exorsus est:

2. 'M. Varro in libro Rerum humanarum quem de diebus scripsit, "homines," inquit, "qui ex media nocte ad proximam mediam noctem his horis viginti quattuor nati sunt uno die nati dicuntur." 3. quibus verbis ita videtur dierum observationem divisisse ut qui post solem occasum ante mediam noctem natus sit, illo quem nox secuta est, contra vero qui in sex noctis horis posterioribus nascitur, eo die videatur natus qui post eam noctem diluxerit. 4. Athenienses autem aliter observare idem Varro in eodem libro scripsit eosque a solis occasu[11] ad solem iterum occidentem omne id medium tempus unum diem esse dicere, Babylonios porro aliter—a sole enim exorto ad exortum eiusdem incipientem id spatium unius diei nomine vocare—Umbros vero unum et eundem diem esse dicere a meridie ad insequentem meridiem. 5. "quod quidem," inquit Varro, "nimis absurdum est. nam qui Kalendis hora sexta apud Umbros natus est, dies eius natalis videri debebit et Kalendarum dimidiatus et qui post Kalendas erit usque ad horam eius diei sextam."

6. 'Populum autem Romanum ita uti Varro dixit dies

[11] a sole occaso *Gell.*

conversation have learned, and well remember, all that the ancients developed to perfection, so I see no point in telling the knowledgeable what they already know. But lest anyone suppose that I find disagreeable the honor of being asked, I'll briefly review whatever my slender recollection might suggest on this topic.' Having said that, and seeing that all the others were ready and eager to listen, he began as follows:[27]

2. 'In the book of his *Human Antiquities* that he wrote on the subject of days, Marcus Varro says (lib. 16 fr. 2), "People born in the twenty-four hours that run from one midnight to the next are said to be born on a single day." 3. That formula seems to distinguish the day's reckoning so that a person born between sunset and midnight has his birthday on the day that the night followed, whereas a person born in the six hours after midnight has his birthday on the day that dawned after that night. 4. In the same book Varro also wrote that the Athenians reckon differently—holding that all the time extending from one sunset to the next is a single day—and the Babylonians differently again—calling a single day the stretch of time from one sunrise to the next—while the Umbrians says that a single day runs from one noon to the next. 5. "And that," says Varro (*Ant. hum.* lib. 16 fr. 3), "is too absurd: if an Umbrian is born at noon on the Kalends, his birthday will have to be considered half of the first day of the month plus the second day of the month, until noon."

6. 'But there are many proofs to show that the Roman

27 §§2–10 are based on Gell. 3.2 (cited by Serv. on *A.* 5.738), sim. Pliny *Natural History* 2.188, Plut. *Mor.* 284C-F, Cens. 23.3–5, John Lydus *On the Months* 2.2.

singulos adnumerare a media nocte ad mediam proximam multis argumentis ostenditur. sacra sunt enim Romana partim diurna, alia nocturna, et ea quae diurna sunt[12]
. . . ab hora sexta noctis sequentis nocturnis sacris tempus
impenditur. 7. ad hoc ritus quoque et mos auspicandi eandem esse observationem docet. nam magistratus, quando
uno die eis et auspicandum est et id agendum super quo
praecessit auspicium, post mediam noctem auspicantur et
post exortum solem agunt auspicatique et eodem egisse
die dicuntur. 8. praeterea tribuni plebis, quos nullum diem
integrum abesse Roma licet, cum post mediam noctem
proficiscuntur et post primam facem ante mediam noctem
sequentem revertuntur, non videntur afuisse diem, quoniam ante horam noctis sextam regressi partem aliquam
illius in urbe consumunt.

9. 'Quintum quoque Mucium iureconsultum dicere solitum legi[13] non esse usurpatam mulierem quae cum Kalendis Ianuariis apud virum matrimonii causa esse coepisset, a. d. IIII Kalendas Ianuarias sequentes usurpatum

---

[12] *post* sunt *lacunam asterisco notat* P2, ab initio diei ad medium noctis protenduntur *suppl. Tricassinus 514 (teste La Penna;
cf. Guittard MEFRA 88 [1976], 819–20)*

[13] legi *ed. Colon. 1521 ex Gell.*: lege ω, legi lege *ed. Lugd. Bat.
1597, Willis*

---

[28] The diurnal rites were devoted to the "gods above" (*di
superi*), the nocturnal rites to the gods of the Underworld (*di
inferi*/"gods below").

[29] There is a lacuna in the manuscripts but the general sense is
provided by a conjectural supplement found in a late 12th-cent.
MS, Troyes 514, reported by A. La Penna: "extend from dawn un-

people counted from one midnight to the next, just as Varro said: the Romans' sacred rites are partly diurnal, partly nocturnal,[28] and those that are diurnal . . . ,[29] while the time from midnight on is devoted to the nocturnal rites of the following day. 7. The customary ritual for taking auspices also shows that the reckoning is the same: since magistrates must both take the auspices and perform the action to which the auspices were a prelude all on a single day,[30] they take the auspices after midnight and perform the action after sunrise, and are thereby said to have taken the auspices and to have acted on the same day. 8. Furthermore, though tribunes of the plebs are not permitted to be absent from Rome for a full day,[31] when they leave the city after midnight and return after sunset, but before the next midnight, they are not regarded as having been absent for a day: by returning before midnight, they spend some part of the day in the city.

9. 'I've also read that the legal expert Quintus Mucius used say (fr. 2 *IAH* 1:81 = fr. 7 *IAR*[6]) that a woman did not interrupt her husband's authority over her if she began to live with him for the purpose of marriage on January 1 and then left, for the purpose of interrupting his authority, on

---

til midnight" (*ab initio diei ad medium noctis protenduntur*).

[30] By taking auspices a magistrate asked the gods, not whether a given action was good or bad *per se*, but whether there was an obstacle to performing it at a specific place and time.

[31] Cf. Gell. 13.12.9: "tribunes of the plebs seem to have been created . . . so that they might serve as intercessors—something that requires their presence—in order to ward off a wrong that was being done before their eyes; and for that reason they lost the right to spend the night away [from Rome]. . . ."

isset: non enim posse impleri trinoctium quo abesse a viro usurpandi causa ex duodecim tabulis deberet, quoniam tertiae noctis posteriores sex horae alterius anni essent, qui inciperet ex Kalendis.

10. Vergilius quoque id ipsum ostendit, ut hominem decuit poeticas res agentem, recondita atque operta veteris ritus significatione. "torquet," inquit,

> medios nox umida cursus
> et me saevus equis oriens adflavit anhelis.

his enim verbis diem quem Romani civilem appellaverunt a sexta noctis hora oriri admonet. 11. idem poeta quando nox quoque incipiat expressit in sexto. cum enim dixisset,

> hac vice sermonum roseis Aurora quadrigis
> iam medium aetherio cursu traiecerat axem,

mox suggessit vates,

> nox ruit, Aenea: nos flendo ducimus horas.

ita observantissimus civilium definitionum diei et noctis initia descripsit.

---

[32] Lit. "four days before 1 January" = 27 December according to the pre-Julian calendar of Mucius Scaevola's time, when December had only 29 days, reckoning inclusively in the Roman manner (four days before 1 January = December 27, 28, 29 + January 1 itself). The principle at issue concerns the wife's relation to the legal authority (*manus*) of her husband: cf. Gaius *Institutes* 1.111 (noting that it was obsolete), Treggiari 1991, 18–21.

[33] I.e., the equivalent of the hours between midnight and sunrise on what we call "New Year's Eve."

[34] Serv. on *A.* 6.255 acknowledges the interpretation found

the December 27 following:[32] according to the Twelve Tables (6.5 *RS*) she would have to spend three nights in the year away from her husband to achieve that purpose, but she would not spend three whole nights because the last six hours of the third night[33] would belong to the following year, which would begin on January 1.

10. 'Virgil too makes this very point with a subtle and veiled allusion to the ancient custom, as befits a person dealing with poetic material. "The damp night," he says (*A. 5.738–39**),

> wheels round the midpoint of her course
> and I have felt the panting breath of the fierce East's horses.

With these words he gives notice that the 'civil day' (as the Romans called it) begins at the sixth hour of the night. 11. The same poet also made plain in Book 6 when the night begins:[34] after he has said (*A. 6.535–36*),

> while they conversed, Dawn had already crossed the
>   sky's midpoint
> in her four-horse team's heavenly course, glowing
>   rose-red,

the Sibyl soon adds (*A. 6.539*),

> night comes rushing on, Aeneas: we pass the hours in
>   weeping.

Thus he marked out the starting-points of day and night, paying strict attention to the terms laid down by civil law.

here but prefers to take "night is rushing" (*nox ruit*) as = the end of night.

12. 'Qui dies ita dividitur: primum tempus diei dicitur mediae noctis inclinatio, deinde gallicinium, inde conticuum—cum et galli conticescunt et homines etiam tum quiescent—deinde diluculum—id est cum incipit dinosci dies—inde mane, cum dies clarus est. 13. mane autem dictum aut quod ab inferioribus locis, id est a Manibus, exordium lucis emergat aut—quod verius mihi videtur—ab omine boni nominis. nam et Lanuvini mane pro bono dicunt, sicut apud nos quoque contrarium est immane, ut immanis belua vel immane facinus et hoc genus cetera, pro non bono.[14] 14. deinde a mane ad meridiem, hoc est ad medium diei, inde iam supra vocatur tempus occiduum et mox suprema tempestas, hoc est diei novissimum tempus, sicut expressum est in duodecim tabulis: "solis occasus suprema tempestas esto." 15. deinde vespera, quod a Graecis tractum est: illi enim ἑσπέραν a stella Hespero dicunt, unde et Hesperia Italia quod occasui subiecta sit nominatur. ab hoc tempore prima fax dicitur, deinde concubia, et inde intempesta, quae non habet idoneum tempus rebus gerendis. haec est diei civilis a Romanis observata divisio. 16. ergo noctu futura, cum media esse coeperit, auspicium Saturnaliorum erit, quibus die crastini mos inchoandi est.'

---

[14] pro non bono P²Aᵐ: non pro bono ω

---

[35] §§12–15: cf. Varro *Latin Language* 6.4–7, 7.77–79, Fronto *Letters to Marcus Caesar* 2.8.3, Cens. 24, Serv. on *A.* 2.268 (citing Varro), (D)Serv. on *A.* 3.587.　　　[36] "Morning": cf. *LALE* 363–64. The etymologically correct connection between *mane* = "morning"/"good time" and *Manes* (cf. 1.10.15n.) is made also at Paul. Fest. p. 112.24–25, DServ. on *A.* 3.63.

[37] The rule concerned legal proceedings, which were to go forward only during daylight hours: cf. *RS* 2:594–96.

12. 'The day is divided as follows:[35] first there's "midnight's turning," then "cock crow," then "deep silence"—when both cocks are silent and human beings too are at rest—then "day-glow"—that is, when you begin to make out daylight—then "morning," when the daylight is bright. 13. "Morning" [*mane*] got its name either because first light rises from the nether regions —that is, from the Good Ones [*Manes*]—or (as seems more correct to me) from the favorable omen attaching to a good name:[36] for the people of Lanuvium say *mane* when they mean "good," just as among us Romans *immane* ["monstrous"] denotes the opposite, as in "*immanis* beast" or "*immane* deed" and other phrases of this kind, where we mean "not good." 14. Then there's the period from morning to noon [*meridiem*], that is, to mid-day [*medium diei*], then the period beyond that is called the "setting time," and soon after that the "final period," that is, the last moments of daylight, as it is put in the Twelve Tables (1.9 *RS*): "Let the sun's setting be the final period."[37] 15. Then there's "Vespers," a term derived from the Greeks:[38] for they speak of *hespera*, from the evening star [*Hesperus*], and that is why Italy is called "Hesperia," because it lies beneath the setting sun.[39] After this is the period called "first torchlight," then "bed time," and then "dead of night" [lit. "night without time"], which has no time suitable for conducting business. These are the divisions of the civil day observed by the Romans. 16. By night to come, therefore, the stroke of midnight will inaugurate the Saturnalia, which we customarily start to observe on the day of tomorrow.'

[38] Cf. *LALE* 640.   [39] "Hesperia" is "the western land" from the point of view of mainland Greece, but Spain from the point of view of Italy (Serv. on *A.* 1.530), cf. *LALE* 275.

4   Hic cum omnes quasi vetustatis promptuarium Albini memoriam laudavissent, Praetextatus Avienum videns Rufio insusurrantem, 'quidnam hoc est, mi Aviene,' inquit, 'quod uni Albino indicatum, clam ceteris esse velis?' 2. tum ille: 'moveor quidem auctoritate Caecinae, nec ignoro errorem in tantam non cadere doctrinam. aures tamen meas ista verborum novitas perculit, cum "noctu futura" et "die crastini" magis quam "futura nocte" et "die crastino" dicere, ut regulis placet, maluit. 3. nam "noctu" non appellatio sed adverbium est. porro "futura," quod nomen est, non potest cum adverbio convenire, nec dubium est hoc inter se esse "noctu" et "nocte" quod "diu" et "die." et rursus "die" et "crastini" non de eodem casu sunt, et nisi casus idem nomina in huius modi elocutione non iungit. "Saturnaliorum" deinde cur malimus quam "Saturnalium" dicere opto dinoscere.' 4. ad haec cum Caecina renidens taceret et Servius a Symmacho rogatus esset quidnam de his existimaret, 'licet,' inquit, 'in hoc coetu non minus doctrina quam nobilitate reverendo magis mihi discendum sit quam docendum, famulabor tamen arbitrio iubentis et insinuabo primum de Saturnalibus, post de ceteris, unde sit sic eloquendi non novitas.

5. 'Qui "Saturnalium" dicit regula innititur: nomina enim quae dativum pluralem in "bus" mittunt numquam genetivum eiusdem numeri syllaba crevisse patiuntur, sed aut totidem habet, ut "monilibus monilium" "sedilibus se-

---

[40] The translation exaggerates the oddity of the first two phrases, which differ grammatically from standard Latin in ways that cannot be replicated in English.

When all present had praised Albinus' memory as a   4
storehouse of antique lore, Praetextatus noticed Avienus
whispering to Rufius Albinus and said, 'Why in the world,
my dear Avienus, do you want to keep secret from the rest
of us what you've disclosed to Albinus alone?' 2. Then
Avienus: 'I am of course much moved by Caecina's authority, and I know full well that such great learning is not subject to error: still, my ears were struck by his novel usage,
when he chose to say "by night to come" [*noctu futura*]
and "on the day of tomorrow" [*die crastini*] rather than
"on the coming night" [*futura nocte*] and "tomorrow" [*die
crastino*], according to the rules of grammar.[40] 3. For *noctu*
is an adverb, not a noun; furthermore, *futura*, which is
an adjective, cannot be used with an adverb. And it's certainly the case that *noctu* and *nocte* differ from each other
in same way as *diu* [an adverb] and *die* [a noun]. As for
die and *crastini*, they're not in the same grammatical case,
and only the same case can link words in this kind of
phrase. Then there's *Saturnaliorum*: I'd like to know why
we would choose to use that form rather than *Saturnalium*.' 4. As Caecina smiled silently in response, Symmachus asked Servius what he thought of these matters:
'Though in this gathering,' he said, 'which demands respect no less for its learning than for its nobility, it is more
fitting for me to learn than to teach, I will do Symmachus'
bidding and speak first about the word *Saturnalia*, then
about the rest, to show that no novel usage is involved in
speaking thus.'

5. 'Someone who says *Saturnalium* relies upon the rule
that nouns with a dative plural ending in *–bus* never allow
the genitive plural to be a syllable longer than the dative: it
either has the same number of syllables, like *monilibus*

dilium," aut una syllaba minus est, ut "carminibus carminum" "liminibus liminum": sic ergo "Saturnalibus" rectius "Saturnalium" quam "Saturnaliorum." 6. sed qui "Saturnaliorum" dicunt auctoritate magnorum muniuntur virorum. nam et Sallustius in tertia "Bacchanaliorum" ait, et Masurius Fastorum secundo, "Vinaliorum dies," inquit, "Iovi sacer est, non, ut quidam putant, Veneri." 7. et ut ipsos quoque grammaticos in testimonium citem, Verrius Flaccus in eo libello qui Saturnus inscribitur, "Saturnaliorum," inquit, "dies apud Graecos quoque festi habentur," et in eodem libro, "dilucide me," inquit, "de constitutione Saturnaliorum scripsisse arbitror." item Iulius Modestus de feriis, "Saturnaliorum," inquit, "feriae"; et in eodem libro, "Antias," inquit, "Agonaliorum repertorem Numam Pompilium refert."

8. 'Haec tamen, inquies, auctoritas quaero an possit aliqua ratione defendi. plane quatenus alienum non est committi grammaticum cum sua analogia, temptabo suspicionibus eruere quid sit quod eos a solita enuntiatione detorserit, ut mallent "Saturnaliorum" quam "Saturnalium" dicere. 9. ac primum aestimo quod haec nomina quae sunt festorum dierum neutralia carentque numero singulari di-

---

[41] Cf. Non. p. 786

[42] So also Varro *Latin Language* 6.16, Masurius' probable source. As the name suggests, the Vinalia (23 April and 19 August) was a festival of wine, and it does seem to have been originally associated with Jupiter (cf. 3.5.10n.), though Venus came to be associated with it (see esp. Ov. *F.* 4.863ff.); cf. *FCRR* 106–7.

[43] The Agonalia or *dies agonales* (the name is of uncertain derivation: cf. Varro *Latin Language* 6.12, Ov. *F.* 1.317ff.) were observed 4 times each year (9 Jan., 17 March, 21 May, 11 Dec.),

monilium, sedilibus sedilium, or is one syllable shorter, like *carminibus carminum, liminibus liminum*. So, then, *Saturnalibus Saturnalium* is more correct than *Saturnalibus Saturnaliorum*. 6. But those who say *Saturnaliorum* are supported by the authority of great figures: Sallust in the third book of his *Histories* says *Bacchanaliorum* (*Hist.* 3.31),[41] and Masurius in the second book of his *Calendar* says (fr. 1 *IAH* 2.1:363 = fr. 8 *IAR*6), "the day of the Vinalia [*Vinaliorum*] is sacred to Jupiter, not Venus, as some think."[42] 7. And to cite the testimony of the grammarians themselves: Verrius Flaccus, in his book titled *Saturn*, says (test. 10 *GRF* 1:510), "The days of the Saturnalia [*Saturnaliorum*] are considered holidays among the Greeks too," and in the same book he says, "I judge that I have clarified the founding of the Saturnalia [*Saturnaliorum*]." So too Julius Modestus, writing on religious festivals, uses the phrase "festival of the Saturnalia [*Saturnaliorum*]" (cf. *GRF* 2:9) and in the same book says, "Antias relates that Numa Pompilius was the originator of the Agonalia [*Agonaliorum*]" (fr. 6).[43]

8. "'Nonetheless, I wonder,'" you'll say, "if this authoritative usage can be backed up by some rational principle." Of course it can; and insofar as it's proper for a grammarian to have recourse to his favorite principle—that of grammatical analogy—I'll rely on the clues available to discover what turned those men aside from the customary form of expression and caused them to prefer to say *Saturnaliorum* rather than *Saturnalium*. 9. In the first place, I judge that they wished to treat these nouns, which are holiday names

when the priest in charge of sacrifices (1.15.9n.) offered up a ram in the Regia (1.12.6n.): cf. *FCRR* 60–61.

versae condicionis esse voluerunt ab his nominibus quae
utroque numero figurantur. "Compitalia" enim et "Bacchanalia" et "Agonalia" "Vinaliaque" et reliqua his similia
festorum dierum nomina sunt nec singulariter nominan-
tur; aut si singulari numero dixeris, non idem significabis
nisi adieceris "festum," ut "Bacchanale festum," "Agonale
festum" et reliqua, ut iam non positivum sit, sed adiecti-
vum, quod Graeci ἐπίθετον vocant. 10. animati sunt ergo
ad faciendam discretionem in genetivo casu ut ex hac de-
clinatione exprimerent nomen sollemnis diei, scientes in
non nullis saepe nominibus dativo in "bus" exeunte nihilo
minus genetivum in "rum" finiri, ut "domibus domorum"
"duobus duorum" "ambobus amborum."

11. 'Ita et "viridia" cum ἀντὶ ἐπιθέτου accipiuntur, genetivum in "um" faciunt, ut "viridia prata, viridium pratorum": cum vero ipsam loci viriditatem significare volumus,
"viridiorum" dicimus, ut cum dicitur "formosa facies viridiorum": tunc enim viridia quasi positivum ponitur, non
accidens. 12. tanta autem apud veteres fuit licentia huius
genetivi, ut Asinius Pollio "vectigaliorum" frequenter
usurpet, cum[15] "vectigal" non minus dicatur quam "vectigalia." sed et cum legamus,

laevaque ancile gerebat,

[15] cum J²: quod ω

---

[44] On the Compitalia, 1.4.27n.; on the Agonalia, 1.4.7n.; on
the Vinalia, 1.4.6n. The Bacchanalia was not a holiday on the Roman sacral calendar; the term is most often applied to the Bacchic
cult that the Roman authorities suppressed in 186 BCE (Livy 39.8–
18).   [45] As did Cicero (*Letters* fr. XV 1.1), Varro (fr. 53 *GRF*
1:208), and Suetonius (*Aug.* 101.4, *Cal.* 16.3).

that occur in the plural only, differently from nouns that have both singular and plural forms: *Compitalia* and *Bacchanalia* and *Agonalia* and *Vinalia*[44] and all the others like them are the names of holidays and are not used in the singular—or if you were to use the singular form, it would not mean the same thing unless you added "holiday," as in "the Bacchanal holiday," "the Agonal holiday," and so on, using the word not as a substantive but as an adjective, what the Greeks call an "epithet." 10. They intended, then, to mark the difference in the genitive case, so that by declining the noun thus they would give a distinct form to the name of the holy day, fully aware that in some nouns that have the dative ending in *–bus* the genitive still often ends in *–rum*, as in *domibus domorum, duobus duorum, ambobus amborum*.

11. 'So too the word *viridia*: when it's understood to have served as an epithet, it produces its genitive in *–um*, as in the phrase "green meadows," *viridia prata, viridium pratorum*; but when we want to indicate a place's actual "greenery," we use the form *viridiorum*, as in the expression "the beautiful appearance of the greenery," *formosa facies viridiorum*, the word being used in that instance as a substantive, not an attribute. 12. The ancients, however, took such liberties in using this genitive that Asinius Pollio frequently goes so far as to say *vectigaliorum* (fr. 45 *ORF*²),[45] although the singular form *vectigal* is no less common than the plural *vectigalia*. But even though we read (*A.* 7.188*),[46]

and in his left hand he carried a small shield [*ancile*],

[46] Cf. also Servius' commentary on Donatus, *GL* 4:435.3.

tamen et "anciliorum" relatum est. 13. videndum ergo ne magis varietas veteres delectaverit quam ut adamussim verum sit festorum dierum nomina sic vocata. ecce enim et praeter sollemnium dierum vocabula alia quoque sic declinata reperimus, ut praecedens sermo patefecit, "viridiorum" et "vectigaliorum" et "anciliorum."

14. 'Sed et ipsa festorum nomina secundum regulam declinata apud veteres reperio, si quidem Varro "Feralium" diem ait a ferendis in sepulchra epulis dici. non dixit "Feraliorum,"[16] et alibi "Floralium," non "Floraliorum" ait, cum idem non ludos Florales illic sed ipsum festum Floralia significaret. 15. Masurius etiam secundo Fastorum, "Liberalium dies," inquit, "a pontificibus agonium Martiale appellatur," et in eodem libro, "eam noctem deincepsque insequentem diem, qui est Lucarium," non dixit "Lucariorum." itemque "Liberalium" multi dixerunt, non "Liberaliorum." 16. unde pronuntiandum est veteres indulsisse copiae per varietatem, ut dicebant "exanimos" et "exanimes" "inermes" et "inermos," tum "hilaros" atque

---

16 Feral- . . . Feral- J[2]: ferial- . . . ferial- ω

---

47 Cf. Hor. *Odes* 3.5.10.   48 The etymology generally agreed upon in antiquity: cf. *LALE* 228. 13–21 February comprised the Parentalia, the festival of the ancestors (*parentes*), marked by private observances at family tombs, with public ceremony on the final day, the Feralia (cf. *FCRR* 74–76).

49 I.e., Varro was using the word as a substantive, not an adjective, cf. §11 above. The Floralia was the festival of the vegetation goddess Flora at which the games in question were held (28 April–3 May: *FCRR* 110–11).

50 The Liberalia, a festival of Father Liber (= Bacchus = Dionysus), was 17 March, the Lucaria, of uncertain origin and sig-

the form *anciliorum* is nonetheless also found.[47] 13. We must consider the possibility, then, that variety just pleased the ancients, rather than its being strictly true that the names of holidays were used in that form. Note, in fact, that besides the terms used for days of religious observance we find other nouns declined in this way, as the preceding remarks have made plain in the case of *viridiorum* et *vectigaliorum* et *anciliorum*.

14. 'But I also find names of holidays declined according to the normal rule in the ancients' writings: so Varro says (fr. 407 *GRF* 1:353) that the day of the Feralia [*Feralium*] is derived from the custom of carrying [*ferre*] ritual meals to ancestors' tombs;[48] he did not use the form *Feraliorum*. Elsewhere he also uses the form *Floralium*, not *Floraliorum*, though he speaks there of the holiday of the Floralia itself and not the Games of Flora [*ludi Florales*].[49] 15. Masurius, too, in the second book of his *Calendar*, says (fr. 2–3 *IAH* 2.1:363 = fr. 9–10 *IAR*[6]), "The pontiffs call the day of the Liberalia [*Liberalium*] the agonium of Mars," and in the same book he spoke of "the night and then the following day, which is the day of the Lucaria [*Lucarium*]"; he did not say *Lucariorum*. Many people, too, similarly say *Liberalium*, not *Liberaliorum*.[50] 16. Accordingly, the verdict must be that the ancients used an abundance of forms for the sake of variety, saying both *exanimi* and *exanimes*, *inermes* and *inermi*, *hilari* and *hilares*,[51] and it is therefore

nificance (prob. connected with sacred groves, *luci*), on 19 and 21 July (*FCRR* 91f. and 166f., respectively).

[51] The examples comprise three adjectives ("lifeless," "unarmed," "cheerful") that had both second and third declension forms.

"hilares," et ideo certum est licito et "Saturnalium" et "Saturnaliorum" dici, cum alterum regula cum auctoritate, alterum etsi sola sed multorum defendat auctoritas.

17. 'Reliqua autem verba quae Avieno nostro nova visa sunt veterum nobis sunt testimoniis adserenda. Ennius enim—nisi cui videtur inter nostrae aetatis politiores munditias respuendus—"noctu concubia" dixit his versibus:

> qua Galli furtim noctu summa arcis adorti
> moenia concubia vigilesque repente cruentant.

18. quo in loco animadvertendum est non solum quod "noctu concubia" sed quod etiam "qua noctu" dixerit. et hoc posuit in Annalium septimo, in quorum tertio clarius idem dixit:

> hac noctu filo pendebit Etruria tota.

Claudius etiam Quadrigarius Annali tertio: "senatus autem de nocte convenire, noctu multa domum dimitti." 19. non esse ab re puto hoc in loco id quoque admonere, quod decemviri in duodecim tabulis inusitatissime "nox" pro "noctu" dixerunt. verba haec sunt: "si nox furtum faxit,[17] si im occisit, iure caesus esto." in quibus verbis id etiam notandum est, quod ab eo quod est "is" non "eum" casu accusativo sed "im" dixerunt.

---

[17] faxit *Cujas*: factum sit ω

---

[52] §§17–19 must be based on Gell. 8.1, of which only the summary heading survives.

[53] In 451 BCE all political authority at Rome was invested in a "Board of Ten" (*decemviri*), which drew up ten "tables" of law; a second "Board of Ten" added two more "tables" in 450. The resulting Twelve Tables marked the start of Roman jurisprudence.

certainly permissible to say both *Saturnalium* et *Saturnaliorum*: the one form is supported by the grammatical rule and authoritative usage, while the other is supported by authoritative usage alone—but it is the usage of many.

17. 'As for the other words that struck our friend Avienus as novel, we must champion them by relying on the ancients' testimony.[52] For Ennius—unless one thinks he fails the test of elegance in our refined age—used the phrase *noctu concubia* in these verses (*Ann.* 227 Sk.):

> And at that bedding down time of night [*noctu concubia*] the Gauls stole over
> the citadel's topmost walls and suddenly bloodied the watch.

18. Here we should note that he not only used the phrase *noctu concubia* but also the phrae *qua noctu*. This was in Book 7 of the *Annals*; in Book 3 he gives clearer testimony (*Ann.* 142 Sk.):

> On this night [*hac noctu*] all of Etruria will hang by a thread.

Claudius Quadrigarius, too, in Book 3 of his *Annals* (fr. 44): "The senate, however, was convening by night, and in deep night (*multa noctu*) was sent back home." 19. While we're on this topic it's not beside the point, I think, to remark that in the Twelve Tables the Board of Ten[53] used "night" [*nox*] in place of "by night" [*noctu*] in a most extraordinary way (1.17 *RS*): "If (someone) committed theft by night [*nox*], if (someone) committed murder [lit. 'killed him'], let him be rightly put to death"—where it should also be noted that for the pronoun 'he' they used *im*, not *eum*, in the accusative case.

20. 'Sed nec "diecrastini" a doctissimo viro sine veterum auctoritate prolatum est, quibus mos erat modo "diequinti," modo "diequinte" pro adverbio copulate dicere: cuius indicium est quod syllaba secunda corripitur, quae natura producitur cum solum dicitur "die." 21. quod autem diximus extremam istius vocis syllabam tum per "e" tum per "i" scribi, consuetum id veteribus fuit ut his litteris plerumque in fine indifferenter uterentur, sicuti "praefiscine" et "praefiscini," "proclive" et "proclivi." 22. venit ecce illius versus Pomponiani in mentem, qui est ex Atellania quae Maevia inscribitur:

> dies hic sextus, cum nihil egi:[18] diequarte moriar[19]
> fame.

23. "diepristine" eodem modo dicebatur, quod significabat die pristino, id est priore, quod nunc "pridie" dicitur, converso compositionis ordine, quasi "pristino die." 24. nec infitias eo lectum apud veteres "die quarto": sed invenitur hoc de transacto, non de futuro positum. nam Cn. Mattius, homo impense doctus, in Mimiambis pro eo dicit quod "nudius quartus" nos dicimus in his versibus:

> nuper—die quarto, ut recordor, et certe—
> aquarium urceum[20] unicum domi fregit.

[18] egi ω, *Gell.*: edi *ed. Lugd. Bat. 1597*
[19] moriar ω, *Gell.*: emoriar *Schoppe apud Gell.*
[20] urceum V2A, *Gell.* (urteum B2C): orci- *vel* orti- ω

---

[54] §§20–27 are based on Gell. 10.24.
[55] Named from Atella in Campania, the Atellan farce was a form of broad comic drama, performed in Latin, involving stock characters. [56] The speaker is probably a comic parasite complaining about his failure to secure an invitation to a free meal.

20. 'Nor did the very learned gentleman produce the form *die crastini* without the authority of the ancients, whose custom it was to use *diequinti* and *diequinte* by turns as compound adverbs (their character as compounds is clearly indicated by the shortened second syllable, as opposed to the naturally long quantity the syllable has when *die* is used by itself).[54] 21. As for the fact that the final syllable of that word is written, as I said, now with an *–e*, now with an *–i*, the ancients customarily used the two letters indifferently at the end of words, for example in *praefiscine* and *praefiscini* or *proclive* and *proclivi*. 22. Here now, this verse by Pomponius just came to mind, from the Atellan farce[55] titled *Maevia* (77 *SRPF*³ 2:284):

> This is now the sixth day that I've gotten nowhere;[56]
> on day four [*diequarte*] I'll just die of hunger.

23. 'In the same way they used to say *diepristine*,[57] meaning *die pristino*—that is, "on the prior day"—for what we mean now when we say *pridie* ["the day before"], with the order of the compound elements reversed, as though it were *pristino die*. 24. Nor will I deny that we read "on the fourth day" [*die quarto*] in the ancients' texts, but we find it used to refer to time past, not to the future. In his *Mimiambi* Cn. Mattius, an enormously learned man, does not say "four days ago" [*nudius quartus*], the expression that we use, but instead says (fr. 11 *FPL*³):

> Recently—on the fourth day, as I recall, not a
>   doubt—
> he broke the only water jug he had at home.

---

[57] This form is not attested.

hoc igitur intererit, ut "die quarto" quidem de praeterito dicamus, "diequarte" autem de futuro. 25. verum ne de "diecrastini" nihil rettulisse videamur, suppetit Coelianum illud ex libro Historiarum secundo: "si vis[21] mihi equitatum dare et ipse cum cetero exercitu me sequi, diequinti Romae in Capitolio curabo tibi cenam coctam." 26. hic Symmachus, 'Coelius tuus,' inquit, 'et historiam et verbum ex Originibus M. Catonis accepit, apud quem ita scriptum est: "igitur dictatorem Carthaginiensium magister equitum monuit: 'mitte mecum Romam equitatum: diequinti in Capitolio tibi cena cocta erit.'" 27. et Praetextatus: 'aestimo nonnihil ad demonstrandam consuetudinem veterum etiam praetoris verba conferre quibus more maiorum ferias concipere solet quae appellantur Compitalia. ea verba haec sunt: "dienoni populo Romano Quiritibus Compitalia erunt."'

5   Tum Avienus aspiciens Servium, 'Curius,' inquit, 'et Fabricius et Coruncanius, antiquissimi viri, vel etiam his antiquiores Horatii illi trigemini plane ac dilucide cum suis fabulati sunt neque Auruncorum aut Sicanorum aut Pelasgorum, qui primi coluisse in Italia[22] dicuntur, sed aetatis suae verbis loquebantur. tu autem, proinde quasi cum

---

[21] si vis S *corr. ex Gell.*: si quis ω (*cui* daret *aptant* PV, *mox* voles *post* sequi *add.* P[2]; *sim.* velit sequi C, *deinde* ei *pro* tibi)
[22] coluisse Italiam *Gell.*

---

[58] Though this form is attested at Plaut. *Most.* 881, the defense is purely analogical, relying on the forms *diequinti* and *dienoni*.
[59] One of the moveable feasts on the Roman calendar (cf. 1.16.4), the Compitalia was the festival of the crossroads and their

So we will draw this distinction, using *die quarto* about the past, *diequarte* about the future. 25. And lest I seem to have left *diecrastini* without comment,[58] consider the following, from the second book of Coelius' *Histories* (fr. 27): "If you're willing to provide the cavalry and to follow me yourself with the rest of the army, then five days hence [*diequinti*] I'll serve you a hot meal on the Capitoline in Rome.'" 26. Here Symmachus said, 'That Coelius of yours got both the story and the word from Marcus Cato's *Origines*, where we find he wrote (fr. 4.13): "So the cavalry commander told the Carthaginians' despot: 'Send the cavalry with me to Rome, and five days hence [*diequinti*] you'll have a hot meal on the Capitoline.'" 27. Praetextatus added: 'I think the ancients' usage is somewhat further clarified by the formula the praetor used, according to ancestral custom, to announce the religious festival called the Compitalia.[59] The words are these: "Nine days hence [*dienoni*] the Roman people, the Quirites, will observe the Compitalia.'"

At that point Avienus looked at Servius and said, 5 'Curius and Fabricius and Coruncanius, men of very great antiquity, or the three fabled Horatii, more ancient still, spoke clearly and plainly with their fellows, and they used the language of their own era, not that of the Aurunci or Sicani or Pelasgi, who are said to have first settled in Italy. But *you* want to call back into service words that disappeared from use many centuries ago—just as though you

presiding deities, the Lares; they could be held at any time between the Saturnalia (17 Dec.) and 5 Jan. (typically the first days of Jan.): cf. 1.7.34–35 and *FCRR* 58–60.

matre Euandri nunc loquare, vis nobis verba multis iam
saeculis oblitterata revocare, ad quorum congeriem praes-
tantes quoque viros, quorum memoriam continuus legen-
di usus instruit, incitasti. 2. sed antiquitatem vobis placere
iactatis quod honesta et sobria et modesta sit: vivamus ergo
moribus praeteritis, praesentibus verbis loquamur. ego
enim id quod a C. Caesare, excellentis ingenii ac pru-
dentiae viro, in primo analogiae libro scriptum est habeo
semper in memoria atque in pectore, ut "tamquam scopu-
lum, sic fugiam infrequens[23] atque insolens verbum."
3. mille denique verborum talium est quae cum in ore
priscae auctoritatis crebro fuerint, exauctorata tamen a sequenti aetate repudiataque sunt. horum copiam proferre
nunc possem, ni tempus noctis iam propinquantis neces-
sariae discessionis nos admoneret.'

4. 'Bona verba quaeso,' Praetextatus morali ut adsolet
gravitate subiecit, 'nec insolenter parentis artium antiqui-
tatis reverentiam verberemus, cuius amorem tu quoque
dum dissimulas magis prodis. cum enim dicis "mille verborum est," quid aliud sermo tuus nisi ipsam redolet vetusta-
tem! 5. nam licet M. Cicero in oratione quam pro Milone
concepit ita scriptum reliquerit, "ante fundum Clodii, quo
in fundo propter insanas illas substructiones[24] facile mille

[23] inauditum *Gell.*
[24] substruct- β_1R^2, *Gell.*: substitut- ω, subtract- B^2

[60] The mother of king Evander, who first settled the site of
Rome as an exile from Arcadia, was the prophetic nymph Car-
menta (or Carmentis: *A.* 8.335–40, Livy 1.7.8, Ov. *F.* 1.471–500,
Hyginus *Fab.* 277.2, DServ. on *A.* 8.51, cf. 1.16.6n.), who was also

were talking with Evander's mother[60]—and you've goaded even these excellent men, whose memory is well furnished by continuous reading, to heap them up. 2. As for your loud claim that antiquity appeals to you because it was honorable and austere and temperate: I say, let's follow the customs of the past in our lives, but let's use the language of today when we speak. For my part, I always have in my mind and heart what Gaius Caesar, a man of surpassing intelligence and practical wisdom, wrote in Book 1 of his work *On Analogy* (fr. 2 *GRF* 1:146): "I shall avoid the rare and unaccustomed word as though it were a reef."[61] 3. There's a thousand of such words that were frequently on the lips of authoritative men of old but have been cashiered and rejected by men of a later age. I could now produce a great abundance of these, did not the time of night remind us that the hour of parting is approaching.'

4. 'Please now, watch your tongue,' Praetextatus interjected, with his characteristic gravity, 'and let us not arrogantly and disrespectfully raise our hand against antiquity, the mother of all arts, for whom you, too, show your love even as you try to hide it. For when you say 'there's a thousand of words' [*mille verborum est*], your turn of phrase is redolent of nothing so much as antiquity itself! 5. True,[62] Marcus Cicero, in the speech that he undertook on Milo's behalf, wrote (53), "Before Clodius' estate, where easily a thousand of robust fellows [*mille hominum*] was milling

credited with the discovery of Latin writing (Serv. comm. on Donatus *GL* 4:421.2).
    [61] §§1–2 are based on Gell. 1.10.
    [62] §§5–9 are based on Gell. 1.16.

hominum[25] versabatur valentium"—non "versabantur,"
quod in libris minus accurate scriptis reperiri solet—et in
sexta in Antonium, "qui[26] umquam in illo iano inventus est
qui L. Antonio mille nummum ferret expensum?," licet
Varro quoque, eiusdem saeculi homo, in septimo decimo[27]
Humanarum dixerit "plus mille et centum annorum est,"
tamen fiduciam sic componendi non nisi ex anteceden-
tium auctoritate sumpserunt. 6. nam Quadrigarius in tertio Annalium ita scripsit: "ibi occiditur mille hominum"; et
Lucilius in tertio Saturarum:

> ad portam mille a porta est, sex inde[28] Salernum.

7. alibi vero etiam declinationem huius nominis exsecutus
est: nam in libro quinto decimo ita dicit,

> hunc milli[29] passum qui vicerit atque duobus
> Campanus sonipes subcursor[30] nullus sequetur
> maiore spatio ac diversus videbitur ire;

item in libro nono:

> tu milli nummum potes uno quaerere centum.

[25] mille hominum ω, *Gell.*: hominum mille *Cic.*
[26] qui ω, *cod.* V *Cic.*: quis *Gell.*, *Cic.*
[27] septimo decimo ω, XVII *codd.* VPR *Gell.*: XVIII *codd. recc.*
Gell.   [28] exinde *Gell.*
[29] milli PVOFA²C: mille αXBLδ
[30] succussor *Gell.*

---

[63] Cicero has just referred to "the middle arcade" (*medius
ianus*), an arched passageway near the forum customarily used
for financial transactions: cf. Cic. *On Appropriate Actions* 2.87,
LTUR 3: 93–94.

about because of his mad building projects . . . "—not "were milling about," as we regularly find in copies written with too little care—and in his sixth speech against Antony (*Phil*. 6.15), "Who was ever found in that arcade[63] who would advance a thousand of sesterces [*mille nummum*] to Lucius Antonius?" True, too, that Cicero's contemporary, Varro, said, in Book 17 of his *Human Antiquities* (lib. 18 fr. 2), "It is more than one thousand one hundred of years [*mille et centum annorum*]. . . ." Still, they could have drawn the confidence to phrase things that way only from the authority of their predecessors. 6. So Quadrigarius wrote in Book 3 of his *Annals* (fr. 43): "There a thousand of people [*mille hominum*] is slain"; and Lucilius in Book 3 of his *Satires* (fr. 125):

> From gate to gate there is a thousand [*mille . . . est*],
>   then six to Salernum.

7. Elsewhere he even declined this noun: so in Book 15 he says (fr. 511–13),

> Beat this horse though it might at a thousand of
>   paces, and two thousand,
> no jolting galloper from Campania will stay in the
>   race
> over a greater distance—in fact, it will seem to go
>   backwards.

similarly in Book 9 (fr. 331),

> With one thousand of sesterces you can make a
>   hundred thousand.

8. "milli passum" dixit pro "mille passibus" et "milli nummum" pro "mille nummis" aperteque ostendit "mille" et vocabulum esse et singulari numero dici et casum etiam capere ablativum eiusque plurativum esse "milia." 9. "mille" enim non ex eo ponitur quod Graece χίλια dicuntur sed quod χιλιὰς,[31] et sicut una χιλιὰς et duae χιλιάδες ita "unum mille" et "duo milia" veteres certa atque directa ratione dicebant. 10. et heus tu hisne tam doctis viris, quorum M. Cicero et Varro imitatores se gloriantur, adimere vis in verborum comitiis ius suffragandi et tamquam sexagenarios maiores de ponte deicies? 11. plura de hoc dissereremus, ni vos invitos ab invito discedere hora cogeret. sed vultisne diem sequentem, quem plerique omnes abaco et latrunculis conterunt, nos istis sobriis fabulis a primo lucis in cenae tempus, ipsam quoque cenam non obrutam poculis non lascivientem ferculis sed quaestionibus doctis pudicam et mutuis ex lecto relationibus exigamus? 12. sic enim ferias prae omni negotio fetas commodi senserimus, non animum, ut dicitur, remittentes—nam "remittere," inquit Musonius, "animum quasi amittere est"—sed demulcentes eum paulum atque laxantes iucundis honestisque sermonum inlectationibus. quod

---

[31] χίλια . . . χιλιὰς W[2]: chilia . . . chilias ω

---

[64] I.e., "a unit of one thousand" vs. "a thousand things."

[65] For the proverb see Otto 320–21. M. follows the interpretation that linked the proverb to a loss of suffrage by citizens over 60 years old, the "bridge" (*pons*) in question being the raised gangway along which Roman citizens walked to cast their ballot (cf. Varro *On the Way of Life of the Roman People* fr. 71).

8. He said "at a thousand of paces" [*milli passum*] instead of "at a thousand paces" [*mille passibus*] and "with a thousand of sesterces" [*milli nummum*] instead "with a thousand sesterces" [*mille nummis*], demonstrating plainly both that *mille* is a noun and that it is used in the singular and that it takes the ablative case, and that its plural is *milia*. 9. For *mille* is used to express what *khilias* does in Greek, not *khilia*,[64] and just as the Greeks say "one *khilias*" and "two *khiliades*," so the ancient Roman used to say "one *mille*" and "two *milia*," according to a fixed and straightforward principle. 10. But listen here now, these very learned men, whom Marcus Cicero and Varro are pleased to say they imitate—do you want to strip them of the right to vote at the polling-place of usage? Will you turn against our ancestors the custom of "hurling sexagenarians from the bridge"?[65] 11. I would expand on this subject, were not the hour compelling you to depart, unwilling though we are all around. But tomorrow is a day that most people waste on board games: do you want to spend it in the sorts of serious discussions you've been having, from first light to dinner-time—yes, and have a dinner that is itself not a riotous heap of cups and platters but modestly engaged with learned questions and mutual give-and-take based on our reading? 12. That's how we might experience a religious festival that brings profit beyond all our business engagements, not "relaxing the mind" (in the common phrase)—for as Musonius says (fr. 52), "relaxing the mind is the same as losing it"—but soothing it a bit and stretching it with the delightful and upright attractions of conversation.[66] If that

---

66 §12 is based on Gell. 18.2.1, itself an account of a symposium on the Saturnalia.

si ita decernitis, dis Penatibus meis huc conveniendo gratissimum feceritis.'

13. Tum Symmachus: 'nullus qui quidem se dignum hoc conventu meminerit sodalitatem hanc vel ipsum conventus regem repudiabit; sed ne quid ad perfectionem coetus desideretur, invitandos ad eundem congressum convictumque censeo Flavianum—qui quantum sit mirando viro Venusto patre praestantior, non minus ornatu morum gravitateque vitae quam copia profundae eruditionis adseruit—simulque Postumianum, qui forum defensionum dignatione nobilitat, et Eustathium, qui tantus in omni genere philosophiae est ut solus nobis repraesentet ingenia trium philosophorum de quibus nostra antiquitas gloriata est—14. illos dico quos Athenienses quondam ad senatum legaverant impetratum uti multam remitteret quam civitati eorum fecerat propter Oropi vastationem. ea multa fuerat talentum fere quingentum. 15. erant isti philosophi Carneades ex Academia, Diogenes Stoicus, Critolaus Peripateticus, quos ferunt seorsum quemque ostentandi gratia per celeberrima urbis loca magno conventu hominum dissertavisse. 16. fuit, ut relatum est, facundia Carneades violenta et rapida, scita et tereti Critolaus, modesta Diogenes et sobria; sed in senatum introducti interprete usi sunt Caelio[32] senatore. at hic noster cum sectas

---

[32] Caelio ω: C. Acilio *Lipsius apud Gell.* (Cacilio *vel* Cecilio *codd. Gell.*)

---

[67] §14–16 are based on Gell. 6.14.8–10, cf. Plut. *Cato the Elder* 22; the embassy occurred in 155 BCE.   [68] 500 talents (of silver) on the Attic standard = nearly 13000 kg.

[69] In fact this was prob. C. Acilius, senator and author of a his-

is your pleasure, you will do my household gods a very great favor by gathering here.'

13. At that Symmachus said, 'No one who fancies himself worthy of this assemblage will spurn such fellowship or the gathering's doyen himself. But to see that nothing is missing to make the gathering complete, I suggest that several men should be invited to join us: Flavianus, who has shown how far he surpasses his admirable father, Venustus, no less in his lustrous character and sober way of life than in his deep and abundant learning; also Postumianus, who ennobles the forum with his worthy work at the defense bar; and Eustathius, who is so distinguished in every form of philosophy that he can, by himself, make available to us the genius of the three philosophers of whom antiquity boasted—14. I mean the three whom Athens once sent as ambassadors,[67] to gain remission of the penalty (a fine of nearly 500 talents) that the senate had imposed on their community for the destruction of Oropus.[68] 15. They were Carneades of the Academy, the Stoic Diogenes, and the Peripatetic Critolaus, and each of them is said to have put on an individual display of their talents before a large crowd in the most heavily frequented parts of the city. 16. As report has it, Carneades' eloquence was forceful and swift, Critolaus' clever and well-turned, Diogenes' balanced and sober; but when they were brought into the senate they had a senator, Caelius,[69] serve as interpreter. But our friend Eustathius, having attended

tory in Greek, as Lipsius conjectured in correcting the readings of Gellius' manuscripts (*Cacilio* or *Cecilio*, cf. Plut. *Cato the Elder* 22.4); the reading *Caelius* is probably the one M. found in his own text of Gellius.

omnes adsecutus sed probabiliorem secutus sit omniaque haec inter Graecos genera dicendi solus impleat, inter nos tamen ita sui locuples interpres est ut nescias qua lingua facilius vel ornatius expleat operam disserendi.' 17. probavere omnes Q. Aurelii iudicium quo edecumatos elegit sodales atque his ita constitutis primum a Praetextato simul, deinde a se discedentes domum quisque suam regressi sunt.

6   Postero die ad aedes Vettii matutini omnes inter quos pridie convenerat adfuerunt. quibus Praetextatus in bibliothecam receptis, in qua eos opperiebatur, 2. 'praeclarum,' inquit, 'diem mihi fore video cum et vos adestis et adfuturos se illi quos ad conventus nostri societatem rogari placuit spoponderunt. soli Postumiano antiquior visa est instruendarum cura defensionum; in cuius abnuentis locum Eusebium Graia et doctrina et facundia clarum rhetorem subrogavi, insinuatumque omnibus ut ab exorto die se nobis indulgerent, quando quidem nullis hodie officiis publicis occupari fas esset: togatus certe vel trabeatus paludatusve seu praetextatus hac die videtur nullus.' 3. tum Avienus—ut ei interpellandi mos erat—'cum sacrum mihi,' ait, 'ac rei publicae nomen, Praetextate, tuum inter vocabula diversi habitus refers, admoneor non ludicrae, ut aestimo, quaestionis. cum enim vestitus togae vel trabeae seu paludamenti nullum de se proprii nominis usum fecerit, quaero abs te, cur hoc de solo praetextae habitu usur-

---

[70] Sc. 17 December.

[71] Or perhaps "augur's tunic," since the garment in question—knee-length and purple, with a scarlet border—was worn by both.

all the philosophical schools, has aligned himself with the one he most approved, and he fully employs, by himself, all the styles of speaking known to the Greeks; yet at Rome he is so much his own reliable interpreter that you would not know in which language he speaks more fluently or more resourcefully.' All present approved the judgment with which Quintus Aurelius selected these choice companions, and with matters arranged thus, together they took leave of Praetextatus, then each took leave of one another and returned home.

On the following morning[70] they all were on hand at   6 Vettius' home, as they had agreed the night before. When they had been received in the library, where Praetextatus was waiting for them, he said, 2. 'I see that I'm going to have a brilliant day, since you're all here and the others whom we decided to invite to join in the fellowship of our gathering have promised to be here. Only Postumianus thought that preparing his defense arguments took precedence: since he's declined, I've invited Eusebius to take his place, a rhetorician distinguished by his Greek learning and eloquence. I have suggested to them all that they give us the pleasure of their company from early morning, seeing that no occupation with public business is permitted on this day: no one today, surely, will be seen wearing a toga or knight's tunic [*trabea*][71] or officer's cloak [*paludamentum*] or toga praetexta [*praetextatus*]. 3. Then Avienus—interrupting, as was his habit—said, 'Praetextatus, hearing you mention your own name—one that I and the commonwealth hold sacred—among the names for different kinds of attire, I'm put in mind of a question that's not (I think) at all trifling. No one has ever been named "Togatus" or "Trabeatus" or "Paludatus": why did antiquity take this li-

SATURNALIA

paverit vetustas aut huic nomini quae origo contigerit?'
4. inter haec Avieni dicta Flavianus et Eustathius, par
insigne amicitiae, ac minimo post Eusebius ingressi ala-
criorem fecere coetum acceptaque ac reddita salutatione
consederunt, percontantes quidnam offenderint sermoci-
nationis. 5. tum Vettius, 'peropportune adfuistis,' inquit,
'adsertorem quaerenti. movet enim mihi Avienus noster
nominis quaestionem et ita originem eius efflagitat tamquam fides ab eo generis exigenda sit! nam cum nullus sit
qui appelletur suo nomine vel togatus vel trabeatus vel paludatus, cur praetextatus nomen habeatur postulat in medium proferri. 6. sed et cum posti inscriptum sit Delphici
templi, et unius e numero septem sapientum eadem sit ista
sententia γνῶθι σεαυτόν, quid in me scire aestimandus
sim, si nomen ignoro? cuius mihi nunc et origo et causa dicenda est.

7. 'Tullus Hostilius, rex Romanorum tertius, debellatis
Etruscis sellam curulem lictoresque et togam pictam
atque praetextam, quae insignia magistratuum Etrusco-
rum erant, primus ut Romae haberentur instituit. sed
praetextam illo saeculo puerilis non usurpabat aetas: erat
enim, ut cetera quae enumeravi, honoris habitus. 8. sed
postea Tarquinius, Demarati exulis Corinthii filius, Priscus

---

72 The saying (cf. *Comm.* 1.9.2), which Socrates is represented
as embracing (Pl. *Phileb.* 48C10, Xen. *Mem.* 4.2.24), is esp. associated with Chilon of Sparta among the Seven Sages (e.g., Diod. Sic.
9.10.1, Clem. *Strom.* 1.14.60, *Anth. Gr.* 9.366.3).
73 The "curule seat" was a folding chair made of ivory, used by
censors, consuls, praetors, and curule aediles. Lictors attended
magistrates with *imperium* (the authority to give a command that
could not be refused), carrying *fasces*, bundles of wooden rods

54

cense with the toga praetexta alone? How did this name happen to come about?' 4. In the midst of these remarks Flavianus and Eustathius entered—a distinguished pair of friends—followed quickly by Eusebius, adding to the gathering's good cheer. Having exchanged greetings all around, they took their seats and asked what topic of conversation they had come in upon. 5. Then Vettius said, 'You've come just when I need someone to take my side: our friend Avienus has stirred up a question about my name and so earnestly demands to know its origin you'd think the legitimacy of my family was at stake! Given that no one bears the personal name "Togatus" or "Trabeatus" or "Paludatus," why is "Praetextatus" considered a personal name? That's the question he demands be put before us. 6. But since "Know thyself" is inscribed on the doorpost of the temple at Delphi and is at the same time the wise saying of one of the Seven Sages,[72] what should I be thought to know about myself if I'm ignorant of my own name? I have no choice but tell how it came to be, and why.

7. 'After the Etruscans had been defeated in war, Tullus Hostilius, the Romans' third king, instituted the practice of using at Rome the curule seat, lictors, the toga picta, and the toga praetexta,[73] which were insignia of the Etruscans' magistrates. In that period, however, the toga praetexta was not the dress of childhood but was an honorific vestment,[74] like the other tokens I've enumerated. 8. But later on the son of the Corinthian exile Demaratus, Tarquinius

symbolizing the magistrate's power to compel obedience. The "toga picta" was a purple garment embroidered with gold thread, worn by a commander celebrating a triumph; the "toga praetexta" was distinguished by a purple border.   [74] Cf. Livy 1.8.3.

quem quidam Lucumonem vocitatum ferunt, rex tertius ab Hostilio, quintus a Romulo, de Sabinis egit triumphum. quo bello filium suum annos quattuordecim natum, quod hostem manu percusserat, et pro contione laudavit et bulla aurea praetextaque donavit, insigniens puerum ultra annos fortem praemiis virilitatis et honoris. 9. nam sicut praetexta magistratuum, ita bulla gestamen erat triumphantium, quam in triumpho prae se gerebant inclusis intra eam remediis quae crederent adversus invidiam valentissima. 10. hinc deductus mos ut praetexta et bulla in usum puerorum nobilium usurparentur ad omen ac vota conciliandae virtutis ei similis cui primis in annis munera ista cesserunt.

11. 'Alii putant eundem Priscum, cum is statum[33] civium sollertia providi principis ordinaret, cultum quoque ingenuorum puerorum inter praecipua duxisse instituisseque ut patricii bulla aurea cum toga cui purpura praetexitur uterentur, dumtaxat illi quorum patres curulem gesserant magistratum. 12. ceteris autem ut praetexta tantum uterentur indultum, sed usque ad eos quorum parentes equo stipendia iusta meruissent. libertinis vero nullo iure uti praetextis licebat ac multo minus peregrinis quibus nulla esset cum Romanis necessitudo. 13. sed postea libertinorum quoque filiis praetexta concessa est ex causa tali,

---

[33] is statum β_2: istatum *vel* ista tum ω, statum P[2]

---

[75] Cf. Livy 1.34.1–2.

[76] Cf. Pliny *Natural History* 33.10, Plut. *Mor.* 287F-288A; the amulet in question was the circular *bulla*, suspended from a chain or cord and worn around the neck.

[77] M. refers to the common belief that a hostile glance (*invidia*

Priscus (who some say was called Lucumo[75]), the third king after Hostilius and the fifth after Romulus, celebrated a triumph from his victory over the Sabines. He delivered an address before the assembled people praising his fourteen-year-old son because in that war he had killed one of the enemy with his own hand, and he gave the boy a golden amulet and the toga praetexta, using these rewards for manly honor to mark him out as gallant beyond his years.[76] 9. For just as the toga praetexta was worn by magistrates, so the amulet was worn by those celebrating a triumph: they carried it before them in the procession, containing spells believed to be most effective against the Evil Eye.[77] 10. That began the custom of having the amulet and toga praetexta used by the sons of the nobility, as an omen of, and prayer for, manly excellence like that of the one who first gained those gifts while still a child.

11. 'Others think that when Priscus was shrewdly organizing the citizen body, as befitted a prudent chief, he also attached particular importance to the dress of freeborn boys and established that patricians should use the golden amulet with purple-bordered toga, at least in the case of those whose fathers had held a curule magistracy.[78] 12. The rest, down to and including those whose fathers had completed the prescribed service in the cavalry, were granted use of the toga praetexta only; but freedmen had no legal right to wear the praetexta, still less foreigners who had no relationship with Roman citizens. 13. But freedmen's sons were later granted the praetexta; the rea-

> Engl. "envy") could have the effect of casting a spell (*fascinare* > Engl. "fascinate") and harming the person who was its object.

[78] See §7n., on the curule seat.

quam M. Laelius augur refert, qui bello Punico secundo
duumviros dicit ex senatus consulto propter multa prodi-
gia libros Sibyllinos adisse et inspectis his nuntiasse in
Capitolio supplicandum lectisterniumque ex collata stipe
faciendum, ita ut libertinae quoque, quae longa veste uterentur, in eam rem pecuniam subministrarent. 14. acta igitur obsecratio est pueris ingenuis itemque libertinis, sed et
virginibus patrimis matrimisque pronuntiantibus carmen:
ex quo concessum ut libertinorum quoque filii, qui ex iusta
dumtaxat matrefamilias nati fuissent, togam praetextam et
lorum in collo pro bullae decore gestarent.

15. 'Verrius Flaccus ait cum populus Romanus pestilentia laboraret essetque responsum id accidere quod di
despicerentur, anxiam urbem fuisse, quia non intellegere-
tur oraculum evenisseque ut Circensium die puer de cena-
culo pompam superne despiceret et patri referret quo ordine secreta sacrorum in arca pilenti composita vidisset:
qui cum rem gestam senatui nuntiasset, placuisse velari
loca ea qua pompa veheretur atque ita peste sedata puerum, qui ambiguitatem sortis absolverat, togae praetextae
usum munus impetravisse.

---

[79] The Sibylline Books comprised a set of Greek oracles that
by tradition dated to the reign of Tarquin the Proud and were typically consulted in times of crisis; they were preserved by a priestly
college, originally the Board of Two, which by the time of this
story had become a "Board of Ten" (*decemviri*; by the end of the
Republic, a "Board of Fifteen"). The "special banquet" was the
ritual of the *lectisternium* (lit. "spreading the bed [with blan-
kets]"), when images of the gods were placed on couches and
served a propitiatory meal.

son is reported by the augur Marcus Laelius (fr. 4 *IAR*⁶): in the Second Punic War, after numerous portents, the senate decreed that the Board of Two should consult the Sibylline books, and the books, when inspected, declared that supplication should be offered on the Capitoline and a special banquet should be offered to the gods, funded by contributions from the community;⁷⁹ freedwomen, who wore long garments, were also to contribute for that purpose. 14. So the ritual of supplication was performed, with a hymn sung by freeborn boys and freedmen's sons, and by girls of marriageable age with two living parents: as a consequence, freedmen's sons (at least those born to a legitimate marriage) gained the right to wear the praetexta and a leather thong around their necks in place of the amulet.

15. 'Verrius Flaccus reports that when the Roman people were in the grip of a plague and an oracle said it was happening because the gods "were being looked down upon," the city was seized by anxiety because the oracle was opaque; and it came to pass that on the days of the Circus Games⁸⁰ a boy was looking down on the procession from a garret, reporting to his father the arrangement of the secret sacred objects he saw in the cart's coffer. When his father told the senate what had happened, it decreed that the route of the procession should be covered with an awning; and when the plague had been put to rest, the boy who had clarified the ambiguous oracle gained the use of the praetexta as his reward.

⁸⁰ The chariot races held during the Roman Games (5–19 Sept.), when images of the gods were placed in carts and led in a procession: cf. 1.23.13.

16. 'Vetustatis peritissimi referunt in raptu Sabinarum unam mulierem nomine Hersiliam, dum adhaeret filiae, simul raptam: quam cum Romulus Hosto cuidam ex agro Latino, qui in asylum eius confugerat, virtute conspicuo uxorem dedisset, natum ex ea puerum antequam alia ulla Sabinarum partum ederet: eum, quod primus esset in hostico procreatus, Hostum Hostilium a matre vocitatum et eundem a Romulo bulla aurea ac praetextae insignibus honoratum. is enim cum raptas ad consolandum vocasset, spopondisse fertur se eius infanti quae prima sibi civem Romanum esset enixa inlustre munus daturum.

17. 'Non nulli credunt ingenuis pueris attributum ut cordis figuram in bulla ante pectus adnecterent, quam inspicientes ita demum se homines cogitarent si corde praestarent, togamque praetextam his additam ut ex purpurae rubore ingenuitatis pudore regerentur.

18. 'Diximus unde praetexta, adiecimus et causas quibus aestimatur concessa pueritiae: nunc idem habitus quo argumento transierit in usum nominis paucis explicandum est. 19. mos antea senatoribus fuit in curiam cum praetextatis filiis introire. cum in senatu res maior quaepiam consultabatur eaque in diem posterum prolata est,[34] placuit[35] ut hanc rem super qua tractavissent ne quis enuntiaret priusquam decreta esset. 20. mater Papirii pueri, qui cum parente suo in curia fuerat, percontatur filium quid-

---

[34] est β_1: esset ω [35] placuitque β_1, *Gell.*

---

[81] Hersilia is generally said to have been the wife of Romulus (Livy 1.11.2, Plut. *Rom.* 14.7–8, Serv. on *A.* 8.638), but with this version cf. Plut. *Rom.* 18.6–7, Dion. Hal. 3.1.2.

[82] §§19–25 are based on Gell. 1.23.4–14.

16. 'Scholars of antiquity report that in the theft of the Sabine women a woman named Hersilia was seized while clinging to her daughter:[81] after Romulus had given her as a wife to a certain Hostus (he had come from Latium and taken refuge in Romulus' asylum) as a reward for conspicuous valor, she bore a son, the first of the Sabine women to give birth. Because the boy was born in enemy territory [*in hostico*], she named him Hostus Hostilius, and Romulus honored him with the distinction of the golden bulla and the praetexta: for when he had called together the women who had been seized, so as to console them, he reportedly promised to give a gift of distinction to the baby of the woman who was the first to present him with a Roman citizen.

17. 'Some believe that freeborn boys were permitted to wear on their chests the bulla with a heart fastened to it, so that they would look upon it and reflect that if and only if they showed exceptional heart could they be truly human; and that they were also given the praetexta so that— consistent with the purple border's blush—they would be guided by the sense of shame proper to free birth.

18. 'I've spoken of the praetexta's origin and added, too, why it was judged permissible for children to wear it; now I must briefly unfold the story of how it came to be used as a name. 19. It was once the custom for senators to enter the senate-chamber with their sons dressed in their praetextae.[82] When some business of greater than usual importance was being discussed and it had to be put over until the following day, the senate resolved no one was to report the matter under discussion before a decree had been passed. 20. The mother of young Papirius, who had been in the chamber with his father, asked her son what business

nam in senatu egissent patres. puer respondit tacendum
esse neque id dici licere. mulier fit audiendi cupidior: secretum rei et silentium pueri animum eius ad inquiren-
dum everberat: quaerit igitur compressius violentiusque.
21. tum puer, urgente matre, lepidi atque festivi mendacii
consilium capit. actum in senatu dixit utrum videretur
utilius magisque e re publica esse unusne ut duas uxores
haberet an ut una apud duos nupta esset. 22. hoc illa ubi
audivit, animo compavescit, domo trepidans egreditur, ad
ceteras matronas adfert, postridieque ad senatum co-
piosae matrum familias catervae confluunt, lacrimantes
atque obsecrantes orant una potius ut duobus nupta fieret
quam ut uni duae. 23. senatores ingredientes curiam quae
illa mulierum intemperies et quid sibi postulatio istaec vellet mirabantur et ut non parvae rei prodigium illam vere-
cundi sexus impudicam insaniam pavescebant. 24. puer
Papirius publicum metum demit. nam in medium curiae
progressus quid ipsi mater audire institisset, quid matri
ipse simulasset sicuti fuerat enarrat. 25. senatus fidem
atque ingenium pueri exosculatur consultumque facit uti
posthac pueri cum patribus in curiam ne introeant praeter
illum unum Papirium, eique puero postea cognomentum
honoris gratia decreto inditum Praetextatus ob tacendi
loquendique in praetexta aetate prudentiam. 26. hoc cognomentum postea familiae nostrae in nomen haesit. non
aliter dicti Scipiones nisi quod Cornelius, qui cognominem
patrem luminibus carentem pro baculo regebat, Scipio

the senate fathers had transacted. The boy replied that he had to keep silent and wasn't allowed to speak of it. The woman became yet more eager to hear: the matter's concealment and the boy's silence goaded her to press her inquiry, and so she asked with greater urgency and force. 21. Pressed by his mother, the boy conceived a witty and playful lie: he said the senate was considering whether it would be judged more expedient and in the public interest for one man to have two wives or for one woman to be married to two men. 22. Hearing this, his mother became panic-stricken, left the house all atremble, and brought the report to all the other married women: next day saw large contingents of matrons streaming to the senate. In tearful supplication they begged that one woman be married to two men rather than vice versa. 23. Entering the chamber, the senators wondered what the women's furor and odd demand could mean, and they feared that such shameless frenzy on the part of the modest sex portended no small crisis. 24. Young Papirius calmed the general distress: advancing to the center of the chamber, he told how his mother had pressed him, and how he had made up the story to tell her, just as it had happened. 25. The senate hugely admired the boy's trustworthiness and wit and resolved that—except for Papirius—boys should henceforth not come into the chamber with their fathers. For Papirius it was decreed that he would henceforth be given the honorific surname Praetextatus, because of the wisdom he showed in both silence and speech while still of an age to wear the praetexta. 26. This surname thereafter attached itself to our family name, in much the same way that the Scipios got that name because a Cornelius used to guide his blind homonymous father, in place of a cane, and got

cognominatus nomen ex cognomine posteris dedit. sic Messala tuus, Aviene, dictus a cognomento Valerii Maximi qui postquam Messanam urbem Siciliae nobilissimam cepit Messala cognominatus est. 27. nec mirum si ex cognominibus nata sunt nomina, cum contra et cognomina ex propriis sint tracta nominibus, ut ab Aemilio Aemilianus, a Servilio[36] Servilianus.'

28. Hic subiecit Eusebius: 'Messala et Scipio, alter de pietate, de virtute alter, ut refers, cognomina reppererunt. sed Scrofa et Asina, quae viris non mediocribus cognomenta sunt, volo dicas unde contigerint, cum contumeliae quam honori propiora videantur.'

29. Tum ille: 'Nec honor nec iniuria sed casus fecit haec nomina. nam Asinae cognomentum Corneliis datum est quoniam princeps Corneliae gentis, empto fundo seu filia data marito, cum sponsores ab eo sollemniter poscerentur, asinam cum pecuniae onere produxit in forum quasi pro sponsoribus praesens pignus. 30. Tremellius vero Scrofa cognominatus est eventu tali. is Tremellius cum familia atque liberis in villa erat. servi eius cum de vicino scrofa erraret, subreptam conficiunt: vicinus advocatis custodibus omnia circumvenit nequa ecferri possit isque ad dominum appellat restitui sibi pecudem. Tremellius, qui ex vilico rem comperisset, scrofae cadaver sub centonibus collocat super quos uxor cubabat, quaestionem vicino permittit. cum ventum est ad cubiculum, verba iurationis concipit: nullam esse in villa sua scrofam, "nisi istam," inquit, "quae

---

---

83 On the family of Avienus see Introd. §2.
84 Cf. Sen. *On the brevity of life* 13.5.

the name Rod [*scipio*] and passed what began as a surname on to his descendants as part of the family name. So
too, Avienus, your own Messala[83] got his name from the
Valerius Maximus who received the surname Messala after
capturing Messana, the most renowned city in Sicily.[84]
27. Nor is it odd that family names should derive from
surnames, since surnames have been drawn, conversely,
from family names, like "Aemilianus" from "Aemilius"and
"Servilianus" from "Servilius."'

28. Here Eusebius interposed: 'Messala and Scipio
gained their surnames for valor or filial piety, as you say,
but could you please explain how Scrofa ["sow"] and Asina
["ass"] came to be the surnames of two exceptional men,
though they seem more like insults than honorifics?'

29. Praetextatus replied: 'These names are owed neither to honor nor to insult, but to chance. The Cornelii
gained the surname Asina because when a leader of the
Cornelian clan was asked to provide guarantors—either
for the purchase of an estate or the dowry of his daughter—he led into the forum an ass carrying a load of money,
a manifest surety (his point was) as good as any guarantors.
30. But Tremellius Scrofa got his surname as follows.
When Tremellius was in his villa with his household staff
and children, his slaves seized and killed a sow that had
wandered over from his neighbor's: calling his guards, the
neighbor surrounded the area so the sow couldn't be carried off and demanded of the master that his animal be returned. When Tremellius learned from his steward what
the matter was, he put the sow's carcass under some quilts
on which his wife was reclining and allowed his neighbor to
make a search. When they reached the bedroom, Tremellius swore an oath that there was no sow in the villa, "ex-

in centonibus iacet," lectulum monstrat. ea facetissima iu-
ratio Tremellio Scrofae cognomentum dedit.'

7   Dum ista narrantur, unus a famulitio, cui provincia
erat admittere volentes dominum convenire, Evangelum
adesse nuntiat cum Dysario, qui tunc Romae praestare videbatur ceteris medendi artem professis. 2. conrugato in-
dicavere vultu plerique de considentibus Evangeli inter-
ventum otio suo inamoenum minusque placido conventui
congruentem. erat enim amarulenta dicacitate et lingua
proterve mordaci procax ac securus offensarum, quas sine
dilectu cari vel non amici in se passim verbis odia serenti-
bus provocabat. sed Praetextatus, ut erat in omnes aeque
placidus ac mitis, ut admitterentur missis obviis imperavit.
3. quos Horus ingredientes commodum consecutus comi-
tabatur, vir corpore atque animo iuxta validus, qui post
innumeras inter pugiles palmas ad philosophiae studia
migravit sectamque Antisthenis et Cratetis atque ipsius
Diogenis secutus inter Cynicos non incelebris habebatur.
4. sed Evangelus, postquam tantum coetum adsurgentem
sibi ingressus offendit, 'casusne,' inquit, 'hos omnes ad te,
Praetextate, contraxit, an altius quiddam, cui remotis arbitris opus sit, cogitaturi ex disposito convenistis? quod si ita
est, ut aestimo, abibo potius quam me vestris miscebo
secretis, a quibus me amovebit voluntas, licet fortuna fecisset inruere.' 5. tunc Vettius, quamvis ad omnem patientiam constanter animi tranquillitate firmus, non nihil
tamen consultatione tam proterva motus, 6. 'si aut me,' in-

---

[85] A different origin, also tied to a remark by Tremellius
but involving a military exploit, is given at Varro *On Agriculture*
2.4.1–2.   [86] On the place of uninvited guests in the genre of
the symposium see Introd. §3.

cept that one over there, lying in the quilts," and pointed at the bed. That witty oath earned Tremellius the surname Scrofa.'[85]

While that story was unfolding, one of the household 7 responsible for admitting those who wished to see his master announced that Evangelus had come with Dysarius, who then was reputed to be the foremost physician in Rome.[86] 2. Most of the seated company frowned, making plain that they found Evangelus' interruption of their leisure disagreeable and ill-suited to the gathering's placid nature: given to sharply cutting remarks, with a bold tongue that left wounds, he was aggressive and careless of offense, which he gave to friend and foe alike with words that rankled. But Praetextatus, with the calm and gentle manner he displayed toward all, sent to meet them, with the order that they be shown in. 3. As they were entering Horus took the opportunity of accompanying them, a powerful fellow in mind and body alike, who after countless boxing victories had passed on to philosophical studies and—attaching himself to the school of Antisthenes, Crates, and Diogenes himself—gained something of a reputation among the Cynics. 4. But after entering and finding so large a gathering rising to greet him, Evangelus said, 'Has mere chance gathered all these men to you, Praetextatus, or is the meeting pre-arranged so you could conspire on some deeper matter better left unwitnessed? If that's the case (I judge it is), I'll leave rather than get involved in your hidden goings-on, from which I'll gladly distance myself, though I chanced to burst in upon them.' 5. Though Vettius' calm spirit allowed him to show firm and unswerving patience on all occasions, this impertinent question did not leave him unmoved: 6. 'Evangelus,' he

quit, 'Euangele, aut haec innocentiae lumina cogitasses, nullum inter nos tale secretum opinarere quod non vel tibi vel etiam vulgo fieri dilucidum posset, quia neque ego sum immemor nec horum quemquam inscium credo sancti illius praecepti philosophiae, sic loquendum esse cum hominibus tamquam di audiant, sic loquendum cum dis tamquam homines audiant: cuius secunda pars sancit ne quid a dis petamus, quod velle nos indecorum sit hominibus confiteri. 7. nos vero, ut et honorem sacris feriis haberemus et vitaremus tamen torporem feriandi atque otium in negotium utile verteremus, convenimus diem totum doctis fabulis velut ex symbola conferendis daturi. 8. nam si per sacra sollemnia rivos deducere religio nulla prohibebit, si salubri fluvio mersare oves fas et iura permittunt, cur non religionis honor putetur dicare sacris diebus sacrum studium litterarum? 9. sed quia vos quoque deorum aliquis nobis additos voluit, facite—si volentibus vobis erit—diem communibus et fabulis et epulis exigamus, quibus ut omnes hodie qui praesentes sunt adquiescant impetratum teneo.' 10. tunc ille: 'supervenire fabulis non evocatos haud equidem turpe existimatur, verum sponte inruere in convivium aliis praeparatum nec Homero sine nota vel in fratre memoratum est—et vide ne nimium arroganter tres tibi velis Menelaos contigisse, cum illi tanto regi unus evenerit.' 11. tum omnes Praetextatum iuvantes orare blandeque ad commune invitare consortium, Evangelum qui-

---

87 Sen. *Moral Epistles* 10.5 attributes a similar thought to the Stoic Athenodorus, pupil of Posidonius and friend of Cicero.

88 Cf. 1.15.21, 1.16.12, 3.3.10–12 (with the n. ad loc.).

89 Cf. *Il.* 2.408: the incident is invoked in a similar context at Plato *Symp.* 174B-C and Lucian *Symp.* 12.

said, 'if you had reflected on either my character or the integrity of these luminaries, you would not think us involved in any "hidden goings on" that could not be shown in the clear light of day to you or even one of the common mob: I am not unmindful, nor do I believe any of these men is ignorant, of that great and holy teaching of philosophy, that we should speak with our fellow men as if the gods might be listening, and speak with the gods as though our fellow men might hear. That second clause forbids us from asking anything of the gods that we could not confess to wanting without disgrace.[87] 7. But we aim both to honor this religious holy day and to avoid the typical holiday lethargy by turning our leisure to some useful employment: hence we've agreed to give the whole day over to sharing learned tales, like contributions to a common meal. 8. If no religious scruple forbids clearing stream-beds on a holiday, and if divine and human laws allow sheep to be given a curative dip,[88] why should religious scruple not be thought to receive due honor by dedicating to sacred days the sacred study of literature? 9. But since one of the gods wanted the three of you to join our number, let's spend the day in shared talk and meals, if you're willing: I know that all those here today agree with me in this suggestion.' 10. Evangelus said: 'For my part I think there's nothing disgraceful for the uninvited to overtake a conversation underway, but to willingly crash a party prepared for others—for that even a brother cannot escape censure, according to Homer. And seeing that on that occasion the great king Agamemnon had only one Menelaus come his way, watch out that you not claim too much for yourself in wanting three.'[89] 11. Then all, seconding Praetextatus, entreated and cajoled them to join the common undertaking,

dem saepius et maxime sed non nunquam et cum eo
pariter ingressos.

12. Inter haec Evangelus petitu omnium temperatus,
'M. Varronis,' inquit, 'librum vobis arbitror non ignotum ex
saturis Menippeis qui inscribitur "Nescis quid vesper vehat," in quo convivarum numerum hac lege definit, ut
neque minor quam Gratiarum sit neque quam Musarum
numerosior. hic video excepto rege convivii tot vos esse
quot Musae sunt: quid ergo perfecto numero quaeritis adi-
ciendos?' 13. et Vettius, 'hoc,' inquit, 'nobis praesentia ves-
tra praestabit, ut et Musas impleamus et Gratias, quas ad
festum deorum omnium principis aequum est convenire.'

Cum igitur consedissent, Horus Avienum intuens,
quem familiarius frequentare solitus erat, 14. 'in huius,' inquit, 'Saturni cultu, quem deorum principem dicitis, ritus
vester ab Aegyptiorum religiosissima gente dissentit. nam
illi neque Saturnum nec ipsum Sarapim receperant in arcana templorum usque ad Alexandri Macedonis occasum,
post quem tyrannide Ptolemaeorum pressi hos quoque
deos in cultum recipere Alexandrinorum more, apud quos
praecipue colebantur, coacti sunt. 15. ita tamen imperio
paruerunt ut non omnino religionis suae observata con-
funderent. nam quia numquam fas fuit Aegyptiis pecudi-
bus aut sanguine sed precibus et ture solo placare deos, his

---

90 §12 is based on Gell. 13.11.1–2.

91 *excepto rege* is usually understood as "except for the master
. . . ," in which case M. would have slipped, since there are only
eight invited guests; but *excipere* can also mean "receive/admit."

92 Sarapis = Osiris-Apis, the name given the sacred Apis bull at
Memphis after its death and embalming; his worship was much

Evangelus especially and repeatedly, but also the others who had entered with him.

12. Yielding as they all made their requests, Evangelus said, 'I imagine you are all familiar with that book of Varro's Menippean satires titled *You Know Not What the Evening Will Bring* (fr. 333 Cèbe), in which he defines the proper number of banquet guests according to the principle that they should be not fewer than the Graces nor more than the Muses.[90] Here I see that, counting[91] the Master of the Feast, there are as many of you as there are Muses: why do you want to add us to a number already complete?' 13. 'Your presence,' Vettius replied, 'will guarantee that we equal the number of both Muses and Graces, which is fitting and just for the celebration of the foremost of the gods.'

So when they had sat, Horus glanced at Avienus, with whom he was on more familiar terms: 14. 'In the cult you pay Saturn,' he said, 'whom you style the foremost of the gods, your practice differs from the Egyptians', a nation of most profound religious scruple. For they had received neither Saturn nor Sarapis himself into their temples' holy of holies all the way down to the death of Alexander of Macedon; after that, under the pressure of the Ptolemies' tyranny, they were forced to receive these gods too, following the custom of the Alexandrians, who paid them special cult.[92] 15. Still, they obeyed the command in such a way as to avoid overturning entirely their own religious observances. Because the Egyptians were never permitted to appease their gods using animals or blood, but only

promoted by the Ptolemies (cf. Diod. Sic. 1.84.8, Tac. *Hist*. 4.83–84, Plut. *Mor*. 361F-362A, 984A).

autem duobus advenis hostiae erant ex more mactandae, fana eorum extra pomerium locaverunt, ut et illi sacrificii sollemnis sibi cruore colerentur nec tamen urbana templa morte pecudum polluerentur: nullum itaque Aegypti oppidum intra muros suos aut Saturni aut Sarapis fanum recepit. 16. horum alterum vix aegreque a vobis admissum audio, Saturnum vero vel maximo inter ceteros honore celebratis. si ergo nihil est quod me hoc scire prohibeat, volo in medium proferatur.' 17. hic Avienus in Praetextatum expectationem consulentis remittens, 'licet omnes,' ait, 'qui adsunt pari doctrina polleant, sacrorum tamen omnium Vettius unice conscius potest tibi et originem cultus qui huic deo penditur et causam festi sollennis aperire.' quod cum Praetextatus in alios refundere temptasset, omnes ab eo impetraverunt ut ipse dissereret. tunc silentio facto ita exorsus est:

18. 'Saturnaliorum originem illam mihi in medium proferre fas est, non quae ad arcanam divinitatis naturam refertur, sed quae aut fabulosis admixta disseritur aut a physicis in vulgus aperitur. nam occultas et manantes ex mero veri fonte[37] rationes ne in ipsis quidem sacris enarrare permittitur, sed si quis illas adsequitur, continere intra conscientiam tectas iubetur. unde quae sciri fas est Horus noster licebit mecum recognoscat.

19. 'Regionem istam quae nunc vocatur Italia regno Ianus optinuit, qui—ut Hyginus Protarchum Trallianum

---

[37] ex mero veri fonte *scripsi*: ex meri veri fonte ω, ex veri fonte *Meurs*

with prayers and incense—whereas victims had to be sacrificed to these two newcomers in the customary way—their shrines were located beyond the sacred boundaries of their cities, so that the gods could receive their usual cult of blood-sacrifice, yet the city temples would not be polluted by the death of animals. Hence no town of Egypt received a shrine of either Saturn or Sarapis within its walls. 16. I gather that you have received the latter of these hardly at all, whereas you celebrate Saturn with the greatest honor, among all the others. If, then, there is nothing that I would be forbidden to learn, I would like you to make it known.' 17. Here Avienus redirected the expectant Horus to Praetextatus, saying, 'Though all present share the same potent learning, Vettius is nonetheless singularly well-informed about all religious rites and can reveal to you both the origin of the cult that is paid this god and the rationale behind the customary observance.' Though Praetextatus tried to put the task off onto others, they all prevailed upon him to give the account himself. When they were silent, then, he began as follows:

18. 'It is permissible for me to reveal the great origin of the Saturnalia—not the origin that touches on the secret nature of the divinity, but the one that is spoken of with an admixture of legendary elements or is revealed to all and sundry by the physical scientists. Telling the secret account that flows from the pure source of truth is forbidden even in the very midst of the rites, and if someone learns them, he is commanded to keep them hidden within his heart. Accordingly, our friend Horus will be allowed to review with me the things that may be known.

19. 'The region now called Italy was ruled by Janus, who—as Hyginus reports, following Protarchus of Tralles

secutus tradit—cum Camese aeque indigena terram hanc ita participata potentia possidebant, ut regio Camesene, oppidum Ianiculum vocitaretur. 20. post ad Ianum solum regnum redactum est, qui creditur geminam faciem praetulisse, ut quae ante quaeque post tergum essent intueretur: quod procul dubio ad prudentiam regis sollertiamque referendum est, qui et praeterita nosset et futura prospiceret, sicut Antevorta et Postvorta, divinitatis scilicet aptissimae comites, apud Romanos coluntur. 21. hic igitur Ianus, cum Saturnum classe pervectum excepisset hospitio et ab eo edoctus peritiam ruris ferum illum et rudem ante fruges cognitas victum in melius redegisset, regni eum societate muneravit. 22. cum primus quoque aera signaret, servavit et in hoc Saturni reverentiam, ut quoniam ille navi fuerat advectus, ex una quidem parte sui capitis effigies, ex altera vero navis exprimeretur, quo Saturni memoriam in posteros propagaret. aes ita fuisse signatum hodieque intellegitur in aleae lusu,[38] cum pueri denarios in sublime iactantes capita aut navia lusu teste vetustatis exclamant. 23. hos una concordesque regnasse vicinaque oppida communi opera condidisse—praeter Maronem, qui refert

[38] lusu GO²L: lusum ω

[93] DServ. on *A.* 8.330 records a tradition in which Camasena was the wife of Janus; Athen. 692E and John Lydus *On the Months* 4.2, his sister.   [94] Cf. Ov. *F.* 1.113–14, Athen. 692D, John Lydus ibid., *LIMC* 5,1:620–21, 5,2:421–22.

[95] I.e., "Turned Backward" and "Turned Forward." On Porrima and Postvorta, companions of Carmentis (cf. 1.5.1n.) who know the past and future, cf. Ov. *F.* 1.633–36 and DServ. on *A.* 8.336 (Postvorta was also a goddess of breech births, Varro *Divine Antiquities* fr. 103 = Gell. 16.16.4); Antevorta is otherwise unattested.

(fr. 6 *HRR* 2:73 = fr. 17 *GRF* 1:535)—held this land together with Cameses, another native, in a power-sharing
arrangement whereby the region was called Camesene,[93]
the settlement Janiculum. 20. This arrangement was later
reduced to the sole rule of Janus, who is held to have had
two faces, so that he could see what was in front of him and
what was behind[94]—something surely to be explained with
reference to the shrewdness and cleverness appropriate to
a king, who ought to know the past and foresee the future:
compare Antevorta and Postvorta, whom the Romans worship as very fitting companions of divination.[95] 21. When
Saturn arrived by ship, he was received hospitably by Janus
and taught him agriculture; and when Janus improved his
way of life, which had been wild and uncouth before the
fruits of the earth were discovered, he rewarded Saturn by
making him a partner in his rule. 22. When Janus became
the first to coin money, he maintained his respect for Saturn in this too: because Saturn had arrived by ship, he had
the likeness of his own head stamped on one side of the
coin, a ship on the other, to preserve the memory of Saturn
for posterity.[96] We know that the bronze was stamped that
way from the gambling game in which boys throw denarii
high in the air and shout "heads" or "ships," bearing
witness to antiquity thereby. 23. We know that Janus and
Saturn ruled together in harmony and collaborated in
founding neighboring settlements from Maro, who reports
(*A.* 8.358),

[96] Cf. Ov. *F.* 1.229–40, Pliny *Natural History* 33.45, Plut. *Mor.*
274E, Lact. *Divine Institutes* 1.13.7; sim. Athen. 692E, DServ. on
A. 8.357, Paul. Nol. *Carmina* 32.73–77 (attributing the nautical
arrival to Janus).

Ianiculum huic, illi fuerat Saturnia nomen—

etiam ⟨ob⟩[39] illud in promptu est, quod posteri quoque
duos eis continuos menses dicarunt, ut December sacrum
Saturni, Ianuarius alterius vocabulum possideret. 24. cum
inter haec subito Saturnus non comparuisset, excogitavit
Ianus honorum eius augmenta ac primum terram omnem
dicioni suae parentem Saturniam nominavit, aram deinde
cum sacris tamquam deo condidit, quae Saturnalia nominavit. tot saeculis Saturnalia praecedunt Romanae urbis
aetatem. observari igitur eum iussit maiestate religionis
quasi vitae melioris auctorem: simulacrum eius indicio est,
cui falcem, insigne messis, adiecit. 25. huic deo insertiones
surculorum pomorumque educationes et omnium cuius-
cemodi fertilium tribuunt disciplinas. Cyrenenses etiam,
cum rem divinam ei faciunt, ficis recentibus coronantur
placentasque mutuo missitant, mellis et fructuum repertorem Saturnum aestimantes. hunc Romani etiam Stercu-
lium vocant, quod primus stercore fecunditatem agris
comparaverit. 26. regni eius tempora felicissima feruntur,
cum propter rerum copiam tum et quod nondum quisquam servitio vel libertate discriminabatur, quae res intellegi potest quod Saturnalibus tota servis licentia permittitur.

[39] ob *supplevi*

[97] The Janiculum, on the Tiber's right bank, retained its name;
Saturnia (in some sources, Saturnius) came to be called the Capitoline, cf. §27 below, Varro *Latin Language* 5.42, 45, Fest. p.
430.31–32, Dion. Hal. 1.34.1, 5.   [98] Cf. Enn. *Ann.* 21 Sk.,
Verg. *G.* 1.273, *A.* 1.569, 8.329, Ov. *F.* 1.235–37, 5.625, Colum.
1.pr.20, *LALE* 546.   [99] Cf. Fest. p. 432.11–13, and 1.8.9 below.   [100] Such names were catnip to Christian polemicists,

This [settlement's] name was Janiculum, that one's Saturnia,[97]

and it's also obvious from the fact that later generations dedicated two neighboring months to them, so that December has the festival of Saturn while January has the other's name. 24. When Saturn suddenly disappeared in the middle of their reign, Janus devised a way to increase his honors. First he named his entire kingdom "Saturnia,"[98] then he established an altar, as though for a god, and sacred rites that he called the "Saturnalia": by so many centuries do these rites antedate the city of Rome. He accordingly commanded that Saturn be revered with the solemn grandeur of religious scruple, as the source of a better way of life, a status indicated by his image, to which Janus added a sickle, the symbol of the harvest.[99] 25. To Saturn people attribute the practice of grafting shoots, cultivating fruit trees, and methodically raising all produce of every conceivable kind. The people of Cyrene, when they sacrifice to him, even wear garlands of fresh figs and send each other honey-cakes, believing that he discovered honey and fruit. The Romans also call him Sterculius, because he first fertilized fields with manure [*stercus*].[100] 26. The time of his reign is said to have been the happiest, both because of its material abundance and also because the distinction between slavery and freedom did not yet exist,[101] as is made plain by the fact that slaves are allowed complete license during the Saturnalia.

cf. Tert. *To the Heathens* 2.9.20, 2.17.3, *Apol.* 25.3, Lact. *Divine Institutes* 1.20.36, Aug. *City of God* 18.15, *Ep.* 17, Prudent. *Peristeph.* 2.449–51. Acc. to Serv. on *A.* 9.4 (cf. *G.* 1.21, citing Varro), the title Sterculinius was given to Pitumnus for the same reason.

101 Cf. Justin 43.1.3–4.

27. 'Alia Saturnaliorum causa sic traditur. qui erant ab Hercule in Italia relicti—ut quidam ferunt, irato quod incustoditum fuisset armentum, ut non nulli aestimant, consulto eos relinquente ut aram suam atque aedem ab incursionibus tuerentur—hi ergo cum a latronibus infestarentur, occupato edito colle Saturnios se nominaverunt, quo ante nomine etiam idem collis vocabatur, et quia se huius dei senserunt nomine ac religione tutos, instituisse Saturnalia feruntur ut agrestes vicinorum animos ad maiorem sacri reverentiam ipsa indicti festi observatio vocaret.

28. 'Nec illam causam quae Saturnalibus adsignatur ignoro, quod Pelasgi, sicut Varro memorat, cum sedibus suis pulsi diversas terras petissent, confluxerunt plerique Dodonam et incerti quibus haererent locis eius modi accepere responsum:

> στείχετε μαιόμενοι Σικελῶν Σατούρνιον αἶαν
> ἠδ' Ἀβοριγινέων,[40] Κοτύλην, οὗ νᾶσος ὀχεῖται,
> οἷς ἀναμειχθέντες δεκάτην ἐκπέμπετε Φοίβῳ
> καὶ κεφαλὰς Ἅιδῃ καὶ τῷ πατρὶ πέμπετε φῶτα.

acceptaque sorte cum Latium post errores plurimos appulissent, in lacu Cutiliensi enatam insulam deprehenderunt.

---

[40] Ἀβοριγινέων Marinone: ΑΒΟΡΕΙΓΕΝ- ω

---

[102] On the theft of Hercules' cattle, §31 below.
[103] Cf. also *Ant. div.* fr. 244   [104] Dodona, in NW Epirus, was the site of an oracle of Zeus (1.18.23n.); this oracle, presumably quoted by Varro, is also recorded at Dion. Hal. 1.19.3.
[105] In the territory of Reate, identified with the lake near mod. Paterno, ca. 83 km NE of Rome: for the island, cf. Varro *Latin*

27. 'Another origin of the Saturnalia is handed down, as follows. Hercules left behind some of his people in Italy, out of anger (some say) because they had left his herd unguarded[102] or with the plan (others judge) of having them protect his altar and temple from attacks: when these people were beset by brigands, they seized a high hill and adopted the name "Saturnians"—which was also the name of the hill—and because they felt protected by the god's awesome name, they are said to have established the Saturnalia, so that the very act of observing this festival might summon their neighbors' uncivilized souls to greater reverence for what is holy.

28. 'Nor am I unaware that the following origin is attributed to the Saturnalia: when the Pelasgi were driven from their homes, as Varro records (*Ant. hum.* lib. 2 fr. 2),[103] and set out for different land, most of them converged on Dodona and, uncertain where to settle, received a response along these lines (*Anth. Gr.* App. c. 6 no. 177, 3:500 Cougny):[104]

Go in pursuit of the Sicels' Saturnian land
and the Aborigines' Cotulê, where an island floats:
when you have joined with them, offer a tithe to
    Phoebus
and heads to Hades, and send a man [*phôta*] to the
    father.

They accepted the response and, having landed in Latium after much wandering, they came unexpectedly upon an island that had risen up in Lake Cutilia.[105]

Language 5.71, Fest. p. 44.22–23, Sen. *Natural Questions* 3.25.8, Pliny *Natural History* 3.109.

29. amplissimus enim caespes, sive ille continens limus
seu paludis fuit coacta compage virgultis et arboribus in
silvae licentiam comptus, iactantibus perenne[41] fluctibus
vagabatur, ut fides ex hoc etiam Delo facta sit, quae celsa
montibus, vasta campis, tamen per maria migrabat. 30. hoc
igitur miraculo deprehenso, has sibi sedes praedictas esse
didicerunt vastatisque Siciliensibus incolis occupavere regionem, decima praedae secundum responsum Apollini
consecrata erectisque Diti sacello et Saturno ara, cuius
festum Saturnalia nominarunt. 31. cumque diu humanis
capitibus Ditem et virorum victimis Saturnum placare se
crederent propter oraculum in quo erat,

$$καὶ\ κεφαλὰς\ Ἅιδῃ\ καὶ\ τῷ\ πατρὶ\ πέμπετε\ φῶτα,$$

Herculem ferunt postea cum Geryonis pecore per Italiam
revertentem suasisse illorum posteris ut faustis sacrificiis
infausta mutarent, inferentes Diti non hominum capita
sed oscilla ad humanam effigiem arte simulata et aras Sa-
turnias non mactando viro sed accensis luminibus excolen-
tes, quia non solum virum sed et lumina φῶτα[42] significat.
inde mos per Saturnalia missitandis cereis coepit.

[41] perenne *Willis*: per omnem ω (per omne B¹, mare *add.* B²,
per omnem lacum ϵ, per amnem P²B²)
[42] ΦΩΤΑ C²: fota ω

---

[106] For the story that the barren island of Delos floated over
the sea until Leto arrived and gave birth to Apollo see esp. Callim.
Hymn to Delos.
[107] Dis (also Dis Pater, "Father Dis") was the chief god of the
underworld; cf. esp. 3.9.10.

29. With very thick turf—the ground being either silt or compacted marshland—and an adornment of brush and trees, like a forest growing wild, it wandered about in the ever-tossing waves, making credible the story of Delos, which has lofty mountains and wide open fields but nonetheless used to travel through the seas.[106] 30. Having come upon this marvel, then, they understood that this was their foretold settlement: they wiped out the Sicels who were dwelling there, seized the land, followed the oracle by dedicating a tenth of the booty to Apollo, and set up a shrine to Dis[107] and an altar to Saturn, whose holiday they called the Saturnalia. 31. And though they long believed that they were appeasing Dis with human heads and Saturn with men as victims, because of the oracle's words,

> . . . and heads to Hades, and send a man [*phôta*] to the father,

they say that Hercules, returning through Italy with Geryon's cattle,[108] persuaded their descendants to replace those ill-omened sacrifices with favorable ones, offering to Dis not human heads but masks with skillfully fashioned human faces and honoring Saturn's altar not by slaughtering a man but by kindling lights—for *phôta* means not only 'man' but also 'lights':[109] hence the custom of exchanging candles during the Saturnalia.[110]

108 Cf. Livy 1.7.4–15, Verg. *A.* 8.185–287, Dion. Hal. 1.34.

109 *phôta* is both the accusative (objective case) singular of *phôs* = "man" and the nominative/accusative plural of *phôs* = "light" (a contracted form of *phaos* used in the Attic dialect).

110 The ref. is to the custom of exchanging small gifts on the Sigillaria (23 Dec.), cf. 1.11.47–49.

32. 'Alii cereos non ob aliud mitti putant quam quod hoc principe ab incomi et tenebrosa vita quasi ad lucem et bonarum artium scientiam editi sumus. 33. illud quoque in litteris invenio, quod cum multi occasione Saturnaliorum per avaritiam a clientibus ambitiose munera exigerent idque onus tenuiores gravaret, Publicius tribunus plebi tulit non nisi cerei ditioribus missitarentur.'

34. Hic Albinus Caecina subiecit, 'qualem nunc permutationem sacrificii, Praetextate, memorasti invenio postea Compitalibus celebratam, cum ludi per urbem in compitis agitabantur, restituti scilicet a Tarquinio Superbo Laribus ac Maniae ex responso Apollinis, quo praeceptum est ut pro capitibus capitibus supplicaretur. 35. idque aliquamdiu observatum, ut pro familiarum sospitate pueri mactarentur Maniae deae, matri Larum. quod sacrificii genus Iunius Brutus consul pulso Tarquinio aliter constituit celebrandum. nam capitibus alii et papaveris supplicari iussit, ut responso Apollinis satis fieret de nomine capitum remoto scilicet scelere infaustae sacrificationis, factumque est ut effigies Maniae suspensae pro singulorum foribus periculum, si quod immineret familiis, expiarent, ludosque ipsos ex viis compitorum in quibus agitabantur Compitalia appellitaverunt. sed perge cetera.'

36. Et Praetextatus: 'bene et opportune similis emen-

---

[111] On candles sent to "superiors" as gifts, Varro *Latin Language* 5.64, Fest. p. 47.27–28.

[112] Cf. 1.4.27n.

[113] Cf. Paul. Fest. 273.7–9, Ov. *F.* 2.613–16.

[114] Cf. Varro *Latin Language* 9.61.

32. 'Others think that candles are exchanged precisely because it was under Saturn's guidance that we passed out from a dark and uncultured way of life to the light cast by the knowledge of beneficial skills. 33. I also find it recorded that when many men used the occasion of the Saturnalia to extort gifts from clients out greedy self-interest, so that the less well off were burdened, Publicius, a tribune of the plebs, carried a measure forbidding anything but candles to be sent to the wealthy.'[111]

34. Here Caecina Albinus interposed: 'The sort of change in sacrifice that you mentioned just now, Praetextatus, I find to have been observed later in the case of the Compitalia, when the games used to be celebrated at the crossroads throughout the city,[112] after Tarquin the Proud reestablished them in honor of the Lares[113] and Mania, in accordance with an oracle of Apollo directing that the gods' favor be sought "with heads on behalf of heads." 35. For some time it was the practice of sacrificing children to Mania, mother of the Lares,[114] to assure the well-being of household members. After the expulsion of Tarquin, the consul Junius Brutus decided that the sacrifice should be celebrated differently, ordering that the gods' favor be sought with heads of garlic and poppy: that way the terms of Apollo's oracle stipulating "heads" could be satisfied, while the crime attaching to the ill-omened sacrifice would be avoided. So it came to be that likenesses of Mania hung before each household's door to avert any danger that might threaten the household's members, and the games themselves came to be called the Compitalia, from the crossroads [compita] in which they were celebrated. But please do complete your account.'

36. Praetextatus said: 'Your account of that similar cor-

datio sacrificiorum relata est; sed ex his causis, quae de origine huius festi relatae sunt, apparet Saturnalia vetustiora esse urbe Roma, adeo ut ante Romam in Graecia hoc sollemne coepisse L. Accius in Annalibus suis referat his versibus:

37. maxima pars Graium Saturno et maxime Athenae
conficiunt sacra, quae Cronia esse iterantur ab illis
eumque diem celebrant: per agros urbesque fere
    omnes
excercent epulas[43] laeti famulosque procurant
quisque suos. nostrisque itidem est[44] mos traditus
    illinc
iste, ut cum dominis famuli epulentur ibidem.

8   'Nunc de ipso dei templo pauca referenda sunt. Tullum Hostilium, cum bis de Albanis, de Sabinis tertio triumphasset, invenio fanum Saturno ex voto consecravisse et Saturnalia tunc primum Romae instituta, quamvis Varro libro sexto, qui est de sacris aedibus, scribat aedem Saturni ad forum faciendam locasse L. Tarquinium regem, Titum vero Larcium dictatorem Saturnalibus eam dedicasse. nec

---

[43] epulas *Baehrens*: -is ω   [44] nostrisque itidem est *ed. Lugd. Bat. 1670*: nostrique itidem et ω

---

[115] Cf. also Athen. 639B. The fragment presumes the equivalence of Kronos and Saturn, cf. §6–12 below.

[116] Cf. Dion. Hal. 3.32.4. 672–41 BCE are the traditional dates of Hostilius' reign as Rome's third king.

[117] I.e., Lucius Tarquinius Superbus (Dion. Hal. 6.1.4), Rome's last king (534–510 BCE are the traditional dates of his reign). Titus Larcius was dictator in 498 (Dion. Hal. 5.72.3) or 501 (Livy 2.18.5, cf. *MRR* 1:10 n.3.); but both Livy 2.21.2 and Dion.

rection of ritual practice was well timed; but from the explanations of the festival's origin that I've reported it's clear that the Saturnalia is older than the city of Rome—so much so that the custom began in Greece before Rome, as Lucius Accius recounts in these verses from his *Annals* (fr. 3 *FPL*[3]):

37. Most of the Greeks, and especially Athens, conduct rites
in honor of Saturn, which they call the Cronia, and they
celebrate the day: throughout the countryside and almost
all the towns they carry on feasting and care for their slaves,
each one his own: just so did our countrymen receive
the custom of slaves dining together with their masters.[115]

'Now I should give a brief account of the god's temple. I 8 find that after Tullus Hostilius celebrated two triumphs from victories over the Albans and a third from the Sabines, he consecrated a shrine that he had vowed to Saturn and established the Saturnalia for the first time in Rome.[116] But in Book 6, concerning sacred buildings (*Ant. div.* fr. 73 C.), Varro writes that king Lucius Tarquinius contracted for construction of the temple of Saturn by the forum, whereas the dictator Titus Larcius dedicated it at the time of the Saturnalia.[117] Nor am I unaware that ac-

Hal. 6.1.4 ascribe the temple's dedication to the consulship of A. Sempronius and M. Minucius in 497. On the temple, in the forum at the foot of the Capitoline, cf. *LTUR* 4: 234–36.

me fugit Gellium scribere senatum decresse ut aedes Saturni fieret eique rei L. Furium tribunum militum praefuisse. 2. habet aram et ante Senaculum: illic Graeco ritu capite aperto res divina fit, quia primum a Pelasgis, post ab Hercule ita eam a principio factitatam putant.

3. 'Aedem vero Saturni aerarium Romani esse voluerunt, quod tempore quo incoluit Italiam fertur nullum in eius finibus furtum esse commissum aut quia sub illo nihil erat cuiusque privatum:

> nec signare solum[45] aut partiri limite campum
> fas erat: in medium quaerebant . . .

Ideo apud eum locaretur populi pecunia communis, sub quo fuissent cunctis universa communia. 4. illud non omiserim, Tritonas cum bucinis fastigio Saturni aedis superpositos, quoniam ab eius commemoratione ad nostram aetatem historia clara et quasi vocalis est, ante vero muta et obscura et incognita, quod testantur caudae Tritonum

---

[45] ne signare quidem *Verg.*

---

[118] From 444 to 367 BCE the consuls' functions were performed by a board of military tribunes (staff officers) with consular power. Three different Lucii Furii Medullini held that rank, on 12 different occasions, from 432 to 370 BCE (summary at *MRR* 2:569), but that period is too late for the building of the temple, which all other traditions ascribe to the first years of the Republic: one of these Furii might have been charged with repairing the temple, perhaps after the Gallic sack of 390.

[119] When a meeting of the senate was called, senators gathered to await the presiding magistrate's decision on a venue: the gathering-place was called a senaculum. Since the senate customarily met in several different venues, there were several different

cording to Gellius (fr. 25) the senate decreed that the temple of Saturn be built, with the military tribune Lucius Furius in charge.[118] 2. The god also has an altar before the Senaculum, where sacrifice is offered in the Greek manner, with uncovered head, because they think that it was offered that way from the beginning, first by the Pelasgi and later by Hercules.[119]

3. 'Now, the Romans wanted the temple of Saturn to be the treasury, because it is said that when he dwelt in Italy no theft was committed in his territory, or else because in his reign no one held private property (Verg. G. 1.126–27):

marking out the ground and dividing the field with a
    border line
was a sin: all gain was sought for the common
    good. . . .

Hence the money belonging in common to the people was placed in his temple, because under his rule all men had all things in common. 4. I should not omit to mention the Tritons[120] with their trumpets that were placed atop the temple's roof: that's because from the time of the god's commemoration down to our own day history shines bright and all but speaks, whereas it was previously mute, shrouded in darkness, unknown—as is indicated by the

senacula. We know of 3: one centrally located, on the rise of the Capitoline near the senate house (*curia Hostilia*); one just outside the porta Capena in the city's SE quadrant; and one in the Campus Martius near the temple of Bellona (cf. *LTUR* 4: 348). On sacrifice in the "Greek manner" cf. 1.17.28n.   [120] Beings that were half-human, half-fish, often represented in art, as here, blowing horns or conch shells: cf. *LIMC* 8,2:45, 49, 51, 53, 58.

humi mersae et absconditae. 5. cur autem Saturnus ipse in compedibus visatur Verrius Flaccus causam se ignorare dicit, verum mihi Apollodori lectio sic suggerit: Saturnum Apollodorus alligari ait per annum laneo vinculo et solvi ad diem sibi festum id est mense hoc Decembri, atque inde proverbium ductum, deos laneos pedes habere; significari vero decimo mense semen in utero animatum in vitam grandescere, quod donec erumpat in lucem, mollibus naturae vinculis detinetur.

6. ʽEst porro idem Κρόνος καὶ Χρόνος. Saturnum enim in quantum mythici fictionibus distrahunt, in tantum physici ad quandam veri similitudinem revocant. hunc aiunt abscidisse Caeli patris pudenda, quibus in mare deiectis Venerem procreatam, quae a spuma unde coaluit Ἀφροδίτη nomen accepit. 7. ex quo intellegi volunt, cum chaos esset, tempora non fuisse, si quidem tempus est certa dimensio quae ex caeli conversione colligitur. [tempus coepit][46] inde ab ipso natus putatur Κρόνος qui, ut diximus, Χρόνος est. 8. cumque semina rerum omnium post caelum gignendarum de caelo fluerent et elementa universa quae mundo plenitudinem facerent ex illis semini-

---

[46] *secl. Willis*

---

[121] §§5–12 are perhaps based on Cornelius Labeo (Wissowa 1880, 42–43, Mastandrea 1977, 214–15).

[122] Cf. 1.4.7 above.

[123] M.'s explanation departs from other applications of the proverb, which concern instead the tendency of the gods to come late to punish (Otto 110–11).

[124] The equivalence is first attested for Pherecydes of Syros (mid-6th cent. BCE), fr. 9.5–6 D.-K., cf. [Arist.] *On the Universe* 7

Tritons' tails, which are buried beneath the surface and hidden away. 5. As for why Saturn himself is seen to be in bondage:[121] Verrius Flaccus[122] says he does not know, but my reading of Apollodorus suggests the following (no. 244 fr. 118 *FGrH*). Apollodorus says that Saturn is bound throughout the year with a woolen bond and is released on the day of his festival, that is, in this month of December, and that this is the source of the proverb, "The gods have woolen feet";[123] further, this signifies that in the tenth month the seed in the womb, which is held by the delicate bonds of nature until it emerges into the light, quickens and grows.

6. 'Furthermore, Kronos [= Saturn] is the same as Khronos [= Time]:[124] for as much as the mythographers offer different versions of Saturn in their tales , the physical scientists restore him to a certain likeness to the truth. They say that he cut off the genitals of his father, Heaven, and that when these were cast into the sea Venus was engendered, taking the name Aphrodite from the foam[125] from which she was formed.[126] 7. They interpret this to mean that when chaos existed, time did not, since time is a fixed measurement computed from the rotation of the heavens. Hence Kronos, who as I said is Khronos, is thought to have been born from heaven itself. 8. Because the seeds for engendering all things after heaven flowed down from heaven, and because all the elements that fill the world took their start from those seeds, when the world

401a15, Cic. *On the Nature of the Gods* 2.64 (citing Chrysippus), Cornut. p.4.1–2, Plut. *Mor.* 266F, 363D.

[125] In Greek, *aphros*: cf. 1.12.8.
[126] Cf. 1.12.8, Hes. *Theog.* 188–98.

bus fundarentur, ubi mundus omnibus suis partibus membrisque perfectus est, certo iam tempore finis factus est producendi[47] de caelo semina ad elementorum conceptionem, quippe quae iam plena fuerant procreata. animalium vero aeternam propagationem ad Venerem generandi facultas ex umore translata est, ut per coitum maris feminaeque cuncta deinceps gignerentur. 9. propter abscisorum pudendorum fabulam etiam nostri eum Saturnum vocitaverunt παρὰ τὴν σάθην, quae membrum virile declarat, veluti Sathurnum: inde etiam satyros veluti sathyros,[48] quod sint in libidinem proni, appellatos opinantur. falcem ei quidam aestimant attributam quod tempus omnia metat exsecet et incidat. 10. hunc aiunt filios suos solitum devorare eosdemque rursus evomere, per quod similiter significatur eum tempus esse, a quo vicibus cuncta gignantur absumanturque et ex eo denuo renascantur. 11. eundem a filio pulsum quid aliud est quam tempora senescentia ab his quae post sunt nata depelli? vinctum autem, quod certa lege naturae conexa sint tempora vel quod omnes fruges quibusdam vinculis nodisque alternentur. 12. nam et falcem volunt fabulae in Siciliam decidisse, quod sit terra ista vel maxime fertilis.

[47] producendi *scripsi*: procedendi ω
[48] Sathurnum . . . sathyros *Jan*: Sathunnum . . . sathunos ω

---

[127] Cf. Σ Theoc. 4.62–63e, Orion *Etym.* Σ p. 147.14–15, *Etym. mag.* p. 709.6, [Zon.] *Lexicon* Σ p. 1627.   [128] Cf. Hes. *Theog.* 453–67.   [129] The assumed equivalence of Cronos and Saturn is matched by the equivalence of Zeus and Jupiter.

[130] The Latin here is especially obscure: the rendering suits the context, but I am not confident that it is correct.

was complete in all its parts and members, the process of bringing forth seeds from heaven for the creation of the elements came to an end at a fixed moment in time, since a full complement of elements had by then been created. The capacity for engendering living things in an unbroken sequence of reproduction was transferred from water to Venus, so that all things would thenceforth come into being through the intercourse of male and female. 9. Because of the story of castration, too, our countrymen called him "Saturn" after the Greek work *sathê*, which denotes the penis—"Sathurn," as it were—just as they also think satyrs are called, as it were, "sathyrs,"[127] because they are given to lust. Some judge that the sickle was attributed to him because time crops, cuts off, and severs all things. 10. They say that he was accustomed to swallowing his sons and then vomiting them back up:[128] this also signifies that he is time, which by turns creates and destroys all things and then gives birth to them again. 11. As for the story that he was driven out by his son,[129] what does that mean but that as times grow old they are pushed aside by those come next? He is bound, however, because one moment is tied to the next by the fixed law of nature, or because all the fruits of the earth are produced in a rotation organized, as it were, by firmly knotted bonds.[130] 12. Legend has it, too, that the sickle fell into Sicily,[131] because that land is supremely fertile.

[131] Acc. to a tradition going back to Hecataeus of Miletus (no. 1 fr. 72 *FGrH*), Zancle (later Messana, mod. Messina) got its name from the sickle (*zanklon* in Sicilian) that fell there, creating the sickle-shaped mole that protects the city's harbor.

9   'Et quia Ianum cum Saturno regnasse memoravimus,
de Saturno autem quid mythici, quid physici aestiment
iam relatum est: de Iano quoque quid ab utrisque iactetur
in medium proferemus. 2. mythici referunt regnante Iano
omnium domos religione ac sanctitate fuisse munitas id-
circoque ei divinos honores esse decretos et ob merita introitus et exitus aedium eidem consecratos. 3. Xenon
quoque primo Italicon tradit Ianum in Italia primum dis
templa fecisse et ritus instituisse sacrorum, ideo eum in
sacrificiis praefationem meruisse perpetuam. 4. quidam
ideo eum dici bifrontem putant quod et praeterita scive-
rit et futura providerit. 5. sed physici eum magnis conse-
crant argumentis divinitatis. nam sunt qui Ianum eundem
esse atque Apollinem et Dianam dicant et in hoc uno
utrumque exprimi numen adfirment. 6. etenim, sicut Nigidius quoque refert, apud Graecos Apollo colitur qui Θυ-
ραῖος vocatur, eiusque aras ante fores suas celebrant,
ipsum exitus et introitus demonstrantes potentem. idem
Apollo apud illos et Ἀγυιεὺς nuncupatur, quasi viis praepositus urbanis; illi enim vias quae intra pomeria sunt
ἀγυιὰς appellant, Dianae vero ut Triviae viarum omnium
tribuunt potestatem. 7. sed apud nos Ianum omnibus

132 Much of the balance of this chapter is derived from Cornelius Labeo's *Fasti*: Mastandrea 1977, 21–32, 35–43.

133 Xenon, otherwise unknown, has probably replaced Conon
(cf. DServ. on *A.* 7.738 = no. 26 fr. 3 *FGrH*) through an error of M.,
his source, or a scribe.

134 Cf. Cic. *On the Nature of the Gods* 2.67, Anon. *Origin of
the Roman Nation* 3.7, John Lydus *On the Months* 4.2.

135 Cf. 1.7.20, with Paul. Nol. *Carmina* 32.69–72, *Anth. Lat.*
1,1.352.3–4 (Luxorius).

'I've recalled now that Janus ruled with Saturn and 9
what the mythographers and physical scientists have to say
about the latter: now I'll present what both groups claim
about Janus.[132] 2. The mythographers report that under Janus' rule everyone's homes were well fortified by an aura of
holiness and religious scruple: for that reason it was decreed that he be worshipped as a god, and because of his
benefactions the entrances and exits of buildings were
consecrated to him. 3. Xenon[133] too, in the first book of his
Italica, relates (no. 824 fr. 1 *FGrH*) that Janus was the first
to build temples to the gods in Italy and to establish sacred
rites, and for that reason he earned the right always to be
named first when rituals are performed.[134] 4. Some think
that he is said to have had two faces because he both knew
past events and foresaw the future.[135] 5. But the physical
scientists marshal substantial proofs of his divinity: for
some say that Janus is the same as Apollo and Diana and assert that he represents the divine essence of both all by
himself. 6. Indeed, as Nigidius also relates (fr. 73), the
Greeks worship Apollo under the name Thyraios [= 'of
the doorway'] and tend his altars in front of their doors,
thereby showing that entrances and exits are under his
power. The Greeks also call Apollo Agyieus, as if he over-
saw the city's streets; for they call the roads inside their
cities' sacred boundaries *agyiai*, whereas they assign the
power over all roadways to Diana as Trivia.[136] 7. But the

---

[136] Trivia = "she of the place where three roads meet." The
cult name Agyieus is a well-attested for Apollo (e.g., Pausan.
2.19.8, 8.32.4, Cornut. p. 69.9–10, 73.7, Steph. Byz. 1.50, Σ Ar.
Thes. 489, *LIMC* 2,1:327–32, 2,2:279–83), Thyraios only at Tert.
On Idolatry 15 (~ *On the Soldier's Crown* 13.9).

praeesse ianuis nomen ostendit, quod est simile Θυραίῳ.
nam et cum clavi ac virga figuratur, quasi omnium et porta-
rum custos et rector viarum. 8. pronuntiavit Nigidius
Apollinem Ianum esse Dianamque Ianam, adposita d littera, quae saepe i litterae causa decoris adponitur: "reditur"
"redhibetur" "redintegratur" et similia.

9. 'Ianum quidam solem demonstrari volunt et ideo geminum—quasi utriusque ianuae caelestis potentem—qui
exoriens aperiat diem, occidens claudat invocarique primum, cum alicui deo res divina celebratur, ut per eum pa-
teat ad illum cui immolatur accessus, quasi preces suppli-
cum per portas suas ad deos ipse transmittat. 10. inde et
simulacrum eius plerumque fingitur manu dextera trecentorum et sinistra sexaginta et quinque numerum tenens ad
demonstrandam anni dimensionem, quae praecipua est
solis potestas. 11. alii mundum id est caelum esse voluerunt Ianumque ab eundo dictum, quod mundus semper
eat dum in orbem volvitur et ex se initium faciens in se refertur: unde et Cornificius Etymorum libro tertio, "Cicero," inquit, "non Ianum sed Eanum nominat, ab eundo."
12. hinc et Phoenices in sacris imaginem eius exprimentes
draconem finxerunt in orbem redactum caudamque suam

---

137 The dominant ancient etymology (*LALE* 290) correctly
connected the name of the god *Ianus* with the word for "door,"
ianua.

138 Cf. Ov. *F.* 1.99, Arnob. 6.25, John Lydus *On the Months* 4.1.

139 The "d" is phonetically motivated in the compounds of *re-*
cited here, but that has no bearing on the initial "d" in Diana's
name.

140 Cf. DServ. on *A.* 7.610, John Lydus *On the Months* 4.2.

141 Cf. Arnob. 3.29, DServ. ibid.   142 That is, keeping its
fingers bent in the positions to convey "300" and "65," acc. to the

name we give Janus' shows that he has power over all doorways, and in that it is similar to *Thyraios*.[137] He is also
shown holding a key and a rod,[138] to signify that he is
guardian of all gates and the regent of all roads. 8. Nigidius
declared that Apollo is Janus and Diana is Iana, with a "d,"
as usual, put before the "i" for the sake of euphony, as in
reditur, redhibetur, redintegratur and the like.[139]

9. 'Some claim that Janus is shown to be the sun and has
his two-fold nature because both heavenly doorways are in
his power, as he opens the day by rising and closes it by setting;[140] and further that when some god's rite is being celebrated, he is called upon first so that he might open the way
to the god to whom the sacrifice is being made, as though
sending suppliants' prayers on to the gods through his own
gateways.[141] 10. Hence, too, his likeness is commonly represented keeping the number 300 in its right hand and 65
in its left,[142] to indicate the measure of the year, which
is the sun's chief function. 11. Others have claimed that
he is the universe—that is, the heavens—and that he is
called Janus from the verb "to go" [*ire*], because the universe is always in motion as it revolves, starting from itself and returning to the same point: hence Cornificius,
in the third book of his *Origins*, says (fr. 2 *GRF* 1:475),
"Cicero calls him not Janus but Eanus, from *eundo* ["going"]."[143] 12. Hence, too, when the Phoenicians fashioned
his likeness for their rites they represented him as a serpent shaped like a circle, swallowing its own tail, to make

system of signifying numbers referred to at 7.13.9–10 (n.); cf.
Pliny *Natural History* 34.33 (*digitis figuratis*), John Lydus *On the
Months* 4.1. The representation must postdate Julius Caesar's re-
form of the calendar.   [143] Cf. Cic. *On the Nature of the
Gods* 2.67, DServ. ibid. (an allusion at Ov. *F.* 1.126).

devorantem, ut appareat mundum et ex se ipso ali et in
se revolvi. 13. ideo et apud nos in quattuor partes spectat,
ut demonstrat simulacrum eius Faleris advectum. Gavius
Bassus in eo libro quem de dis composuit Ianum bifrontem fingi ait quasi superum atque inferum ianitorem, eundem quadriformem quasi universa climata maiestate com-
plexum. 14. Saliorum quoque antiquissimis carminibus
"deorum deus" canitur. M. etiam Messala, Cn. Domitii in
consulatu collega idemque per annos quinquaginta et
quinque augur, de Iano ita incipit:

> qui cuncta fingit eademque regit aquae terraeque
> vim ac naturam gravem atque pronam in profun-
> dum dilabentem, ignis atque animae levem in im-
> mensum sublime fugientem copulavit circumdato
> caelo: quae vis caeli maxima duas vis dispares colli-
> gavit.

15. 'In sacris quoque invocamus "Janum Geminum,"
"Ianum Patrem," "Ianum Iunonium," "Ianum Consi-
vium," "Ianum Quirinum," "Ianum Patulcium" et "Clusivium." 16. cur Geminum invocemus supra iam diximus,

---

144 For the image, cf. Mart. Cap. 1.70; Lipìnski 1995 provides
no evidence of a "Phoenician Janus."

145 When the Etruscan city of Falerii (mod. Cività Castellana)
was destroyed in 241 BCE, its quadriform statue of Janus was
brought to Rome, where it was displayed well into the imperial period (Serv. on A. 7.607 refers to its location in the *forum
transitorium* = Forum of Nerva); it was also represented on a coin
of Hadrian. Cf. Martial 10.28, Serv. ibid. (sim. 12.198), *LIMC*
5,1:620–21, 5,2:422 no.21; quadriform representations of Janus
are still found on the Tiber island's Fabrician bridge.

146 Cf. John Lydus *On the Months* 4.2

plain that the universe is fed by itself alone and moves in a self-contained circle.[144] 13. Among us, too, he looks to the four regions of the world, as is shown by the image of him that was brought from Falerii.[145] In his book *On the Gods*, Gavius Bassus says (fr. 9 *GRF* 1:491) that Janus is represented with two faces as the doorkeeper of both heaven and the underworld, and as a compound of four figures because his majesty embraces the cardinal points of the world.[146] 14. The Salii, too, sing of him as the "god of gods" in their very ancient hymn.[147] Marcus Messala, Gnaius Domitius' colleague as consul [53 BCE] and fifty-five years an augur, begins his account of Janus as follows:

> He who fashions all and rules all has joined together, beneath the surrounding heavens, the nature and essence of water and earth, heavily falling headlong into the depths, and of fire and spirit, lightly escaping into the immeasurable spaces above: the vast power of heaven has bound together these two opposing forces.

15. 'In our rituals, too, we call upon "Two-fold Janus," "Father Janus,"[148] "Junonian Janus," "Janus Consivius," "Janus Quirinus," "Janus Patulcius," and "Janus Clusivius."[149] 16. I've already said above why we call him "Two-

---

[147] The Salii were a priestly brotherhood known at Rome and other towns in central Italy, usually associated with the god of war; their name derives from the distinctive dance (*salire*) that they performed during their processions. Janus is associated with their hymn also at John Lydus ibid.   [148] Cf. Gell. 5.12.5.

[149] Cf. Ov. *F*.1.129–30, DServ. on *A*. 7. 610, John Lydus *On the Months* 4.1 (citing Cornelius Labeo).

"Patrem" quasi deorum deum, "Iunonium" quasi non solum mensis Ianuarii sed mensium omnium ingressus te-
nentem; in dicione autem Iunonis sunt omnes Kalendae,
unde et Varro libro quinto rerum divinarum scribit Iano
duodecim aras pro totidem mensibus dedicatas; "Consi-
vium" a conserendo, id est a propagine generis humani,
quae Iano auctore conseritur; "Quirinum"[49] quasi bellorum potentem, ab hasta quam Sabini "curin" vocant; "Patulcium" et "Clusivium" quia bello caulae eius patent, pace
clauduntur. huius autem rei haec causa narratur.

17. 'Cum bello Sabino, quod virginum raptarum gratia
commissum est, Romani portam quae sub radicibus collis
Viminalis erat (quae postea ex eventu Ianualis vocata est)
claudere festinarent, quia in ipsam hostes ruebant, postquam est clausa, mox sponte patefacta est; cumque iterum
ac tertio idem contigisset, armati plurimi pro limine, quia
claudere nequibant, custodes steterunt, cumque ex alia
parte acerrimo proelio certaretur, subito fama pertulit fu-
sos a Tatio nostros. 18. quam ob causam Romani, qui adi-
tum tuebantur, territi profugerunt cumque Sabini per portam patentem inrupturi essent, fertur ex aede[50] Iani per
hanc portam magnam vim torrentium undis scatentibus

---

[49] Quirinum Vβ_2: -inium $\alpha\beta_1$AC[2] [50] aede β_2: sede ω

---

[150] Cf. §9 above and 1.7.20.
[151] Cf. John Lydus On the Months 4.2.
[152] Cf. Varro Divine Antiquities fr. 91, with 3.9.4n. on Ops
Consivia.   [153] Cf. Ov. F. 2.477–78, Paul. Fest. p. 43.1–4,
Plut. Rom. 29.1, Mor. 285C, Serv. on A. 1.292.
[154] Cf. Verg. A. 7.607–15, Hor. Epistles 2.1.255, Ov. F. 1.281–
82, Livy 1.19.2–3, who adds that the temple was closed only once,

Fold."[150] We call him "Father" as the god of gods, "Junonian" because he controls the entry-way not just of January but of all the months, and all the Kalends are under Juno's authority; that is why Varro, in Book 5 of his *Divine Antiquities*, writes (fr. 67) that twelve altars are dedicated to Janus, to equal the number of months.[151] We call him "Consivius" from the verb meaning to "sow" [*conserere*][152]—that is to say, from the sowing of human-kind's progeny under Janus' authority—and "Quirinus" as a god of war, from *curis*, the Sabine word for "spear."[153] We call him "Patulcius" and "Clusivius" because his temple's doors are open [*patere*] during war and closed [*cludere*] in peace:[154] the reason for this is told in the following story.

17. 'In the war with the Sabines over their kidnapped maidens, the enemy were attacking the city-gate at the base of the Viminal—later called "Ianus' Gate," from the outcome of this story—and the Romans were hurrying to close it.[155] No sooner was it closed than it opened again of its own accord. After this happened two more times and they were unable to close the gate, a mass of armed men stood guard at its threshold, and while fierce fighting was going on in another part of the city, a rumor suddenly circulated that our men had been routed by Tatius. 18. At that, the Romans who were guarding the entry fled in terror, and it is said that just as the Sabines were about to burst through the open gate, a great torrent of boiling water erupted from Janus' temple and poured through the

at the end of the first Punic War, before Augustus' victory at Actium.

155 §17–18: cf. Ov. *F.* 1.263–77, *Met.* 14.785–804, Serv. on *A.* 1.291.

erupisse multasque perduellium catervas aut exustas fer-
venti aut devoratas rapida voragine deperisse. ea re placi-
tum ut belli tempore, velut ad urbis auxilium profecto deo,
fores reserarentur. haec de Iano.

10   'Sed ut ad Saturnalia revertamur, bellum Saturnalibus
sumere nefas habitum, poenas a nocente isdem diebus exi-
gere piaculare est. 2. apud maiores nostros Saturnalia die
uno finiebantur, qui erat a. d. quartum decimum Kalendas
Ianuarias, sed postquam C. Caesar huic mensi duos addixit
dies, sexto decimo coepta celebrari. ea re factum est ut
cum vulgus ignoraret certum Saturnaliorum diem, non
nullique a C. Caesare inserto die et alii vetere more cele-
brarent, plures dies Saturnalia numerarentur—licet et
apud veteres opinio fuerit septem diebus peragi Saturnalia, si opinio vocanda est quae idoneis firmatur auctoribus.
3. Novius enim Atellanarum probatissimus scriptor ait,

    olim expectata veniunt septem Saturnalia.

Mummius quoque, qui post Novium et Pomponium diu
iacentem artem Atellaniam suscitavit, "nostri," inquit,
"maiores, velut bene multa instituere, hoc optime: a frigore
fecere summo dies septem Saturnalia."

---

[156] Cf. Varro *Latin Language* 5.165.
[157] Cf. 1.16.16–17.
[158] Cf. 1.14.9; both dates correspond to 17 December.
[159] Cf. 1.4.21n.

gate, killing many companies of combatants who were either scalded by the burning water or swallowed up by the swift whirlpool. It was therefore decided that since the god had sallied forth to help the city, the doors of his temple would be left unbarred in time of war.[156] So much for Janus.

'But to return to the Saturnalia: it is considered to be   10 against divine law to wage war on the Saturnalia, and punishing a guilty man on the same days is an act requiring expiation.[157] 2. Among our ancestors the Saturnalia was confined to one day, the fourteenth before the Kalends of January, but after Gaius Caesar gave the month two more days, it began to be celebrated on the sixteenth day before the Kalends.[158] As a result, since the common people did not know the exact date of the Saturnalia—with some celebrating it on the day inserted by Caesar, others according to the old custom—more days were counted as the Saturnalia; though note that even among the ancients there was the opinion that the Saturnalia spanned seven days—if indeed a view that is supported by suitable authorities should be called mere "opinion." 3. For Novius, a highly respected writer of Atellan farce,[159] says (fr. 104 *SRPF*[3] 2:328),

Long awaited, the seven Saturnalia are now at hand.

Mummius too, who revived the Atellan art when it was long neglected after Novius and Pomponius, says (fr. 3–5 *SRPF*[3] 2:332), "Our ancestors instituted many fine customs, and this the best: from the deepest chill they produced the seven-day Saturnalia."

4. sed Mallius ait eos qui se, ut supra diximus, Saturni nomine et religione defenderant per triduum festos instituisse dies et Saturnalia vocavisse, "unde et Augustus
huius," inquit, "rei opinionem secutus in legibus iudiciariis
triduo servari ferias iussit."

5. 'Masurius et alii uno die, id est quarto decimo Kalendas Ianuarias, fuisse Saturnalia crediderunt, quorum sententiam Fenestella confirmat, dicens Aemiliam virginem
XV Kalendarum Ianuariarum esse damnatam, quo die
si Saturnalia gererentur, nec causam omnino dixisset.
6. deinde adicit, "sequebantur eum diem Saturnalia." mox
ait "postero autem die, qui fuit XIII Kalendarum Ianuariarum, Liciniam[51] virginem ut causam diceret iussam," ex
quo ostendit XIII Kalendarum profestum[52] esse. 7. duodecimo vero feriae sunt divae Angeroniae, cui pontifices in
sacello Volupiae sacrum faciunt. quam Verrius Flaccus
Angeroniam dici ait quod angores ac sollicitudines animorum propitiata depellat. 8. Masurius adicit simulacrum
huius deae ore obligato atque signato in ara Volupiae propterea collocatum quod qui suos dolores anxietatesque dis-

---

[51] Liciniam *ed. Ven. 1472*: luciniam ω
[52] profestum RF: profectum ω

---

[160] This is perhaps the early 1st-cent. BCE scholar variously
cited as "Manilius," "Manlius," and "Mallius" (the confusions are
common) by Varro and Festus (= Verrius Flaccus), cf. *GRF* 1:84–
85, *IAH* 1:107.   [161] 1.7.27.   [162] Cf. §23.

[163] Cf. Cic. *Brut.* 160, Livy *Per.* 63, Ascon. p. 45.27ff., Plut.
Mor. 284B. The trials of Aemilia and Licinia took place in 114 BCE;
Licinia, first found innocent, was condemned with a third Vestal,
Marcia, early the next year.

4. But Mallius[160] says that those who fortified themselves with Saturn's awesome name, as I said above,[161] established a three-day holiday and called it the Saturnalia, "whence Augustus too," he says, "followed this opinion and in his judicial laws ordered the holiday to be observed for three days."[162]

5. 'Masurius (fr. 4 *IAH* 1:363 = fr. 11 *IAR*[6]) and others held that the Saturnalia fell on one day, the fourteenth before the Kalends of January, and their view is corroborated by Fenestella (fr. 11 *HRR* 2:82), who says that the Vestal Virgin Aemilia was condemned on the fifteenth day before the Kalends: if the Saturnalia were being celebrated on that day, her case would not even have been heard. 6. Then he adds, "The Saturnalia falls on the following day," and soon says, "On the day after that, however, the thirteenth before the Kalends, the Vestal Virgin Licinia was ordered to plead her case,"[163] which shows that the thirteenth before the Kalends was not a holiday. 7. But on the twelfth day before the Kalends there is the holy day of the goddess Angeronia, to whom the pontiffs sacrifice in the shrine of Volupia;[164] Angeronia is so called, Verrius Flaccus says (fr. 28 *GRF* 1:521), because when she has been propitiated she dispels the mind's anxieties and worries. 8. Masurius adds (fr. 5 *IAH* 1:363 = fr. 12 *IAR*[6] = fr. 5 *GRF* 2:361–62) that this goddess' image on the altar of Volupia has a bound and sealed mouth[165] because those who keep quiet about their

---

[164] This goddess of pleasure is otherwise known from Varro (*Latin Language* 5.165), on whom Augustine drew (*On the City of God* 4.8.1, cf. Tert. *To the Heathens* 2.11). The festival of Angeronia was called the Divalia (*FCRR* 209–10).

[165] Cf. Solin. 1.6.

simulant perveniant patientiae beneficio ad maximam voluptatem. 9. Iulius Modestus ideo sacrificari huic deae dicit quod populus Romanus morbo qui angina[53] dicitur praemisso voto sit liberatus. 10. undecimo autem Kalendas feriae sunt Laribus dedicatae, quibus aedem bello Antiochi Aemilius[54] Regillus praetor in campo Martio curandam vovit.

11. 'Decimo Kalendas feriae sunt Iovis quae appellantur Larentinalia, de quibus—quia fabulari libet—hae fere opiniones sunt. 12. ferunt enim regnante Anco aedituum Herculis per ferias otiantem deum tesseris provocasse, ipso utriusque manum tuente, adiecta condicione ut victus cena scortoque multaretur. 13. victore itaque Hercule illum Accam Larentiam, nobilissimum id temporis scortum, intra aedem inclusisse cum cena eamque postero die distulisse rumorem quod post concubitum dei accepisset munus, ne commodum primae occasionis cum se domum reciperet offerendae aspernaretur. 14. evenisse itaque ut egressa templo mox a Carutio capto eius pulchritudine compellaretur. cuius voluntatem secuta adsumptaque nuptiis post obitum viri omnium bonorum eius facta compos, cum decederet, populum Romanum nuncupavit heredem. 15. et ideo ab Anco in Velabro,[55] loco celeberrimo

53 angina US, anguina L: -ginia ω
54 Antiochi Aemilius *ed. Paris. 1585*: Antiochiae mil(l)ius ω
55 Velabro P²J²W²: bel(l)abro ω

---

166 Cf. Paul. Fest. p.16.12–14
167 Cf. Livy 40.52.4; the vow was made to the *Lares Permarini*, who preside over seafaring, during a naval battle, 190 BCE.
168 "Larentalia" is the more usual form of the name (cf. Varro *On the Latin Language* 6.23, Ov. *F.* 3.57), but the form M. uses is found also at Lact. *Divine Institutes* 1.20.4.

grief and anguish achieve the greatest satisfaction through the good effects of patience. 9. Julius Modestus says (fr. 2 *GRF* 2:9) that sacrifice is made to this goddess because the Roman people were freed of the disease called angina after making a vow to her.[166] 10. The eleventh day before the Kalends is the holy day dedicated to the Lares, to whom the praetor Aemilius Regillus, in the war against Antiochus, vowed that he would raise a temple in the Campus Martius.[167]

11. 'The tenth day before the Kalends is the holy day of Jupiter called the Larentinalia,[168] about which—since it's fun telling tales—I can offer this range of views. 12. They say that in the reign of Ancus the temple warden of Hercules was enjoying his holiday leisure and challenged the god to a game of dice (he would handle the dice for both of them), adding the stipulation that the loser would be penalized the cost of a meal and a prostitute.[169] 13. So when Hercules won, the warden locked up Acca Larentia, the most notorious prostitute of the day, in the temple with a meal; the next day she put about the rumor that after sleeping with her the god told her, as a kind of tip, that she should not fail to benefit from the first opportunity that presented itself when she returned home. 14. And so it happened that soon after leaving the temple she was propositioned by Carutius, who had been taken by her beauty. She did as he desired and married him, then after his death came into all his possessions: when she died, she named the Roman people her heir.[170] 15. For that reason Ancus buried her in the Velabrum, the most frequented

[169] §§12–14: cf. Varro *Divine Antiquities* fr. 220a-b, Plut. *Rom.* 5.1–4, *Mor.* 272E-273B. [170] Cf. Gell. 7.7.6.

SATURNALIA

urbis, sepulta est ac sollenne sacrificium eidem constitutum, quo dis Manibus eius per flaminem sacrificaretur,
Iovique feriae consecratae, quod aestimaverunt antiqui
animas a Iove dari et rursus post mortem eidem reddi.
16. Cato ait Larentiam meretricio quaestu locupletatam
post excessum suum populo Romano agros Turacem,
Semurium, Lintirium et Solonium[56] reliquisse et ideo se-
pulcri magnificentia et annuae parentationis honore
dignatam. 17. Macer Historiarum libro primo Faustuli
coniugem Accam Larentiam Romuli et Remi nutricem
fuisse confirmat, hanc regnante Romulo Carutio cuidam
Tusco diviti denuptam auctamque hereditate viri, quam
post Romulo, quem educasset, reliquit et ab eo parentalia
diemque festum causa pietatis statutum.

18. 'Ex his ergo omnibus colligi potest et uno die Saturnalia fuisse et non nisi quarto decimo Kalendarum Ianuariarum celebrata. quo solo die apud aedem Saturni convivio dissoluto Saturnalia clamitabantur, qui dies nunc
Opalibus inter Saturnalia deputatur, cum primum Saturno

---

[56] Solonium (*cf. Cic. Div. 1.79, Fest. p. 296.16*)] solinium ω

---

[171] Members of the college of pontiffs, the *flamines* were each
assigned to the cult of a specific god; there were 3 major *flamines*—the *flamen Dialis* (Jupiter: cf. 1.15.16, 1.16.30, 2.2.13),
flamen Martialis (Mars: cf. 3.13.11), *flamen Quirinalis* (Quirinus)—and 12 minor (cf. 1.12.18); Acca Larentia is not among the
deities known to have been assigned a *flamen*. The "Good Gods"
were the spirits of the dead (*Di Manes*, also simply *Manes*, cf.
1.3.13, 3.9.10: the name is an apotropaic euphemism); originally
applied to the dead collectively, the phrase is used from the late
Republic on, as here, to refer to an individual's spirit.

106

spot in the city, and established a solemn sacrifice to her in which a flamen makes an offering to her Good Gods,[171] and the holiday is consecrated to Jupiter, because the ancients believed that he bestows souls and receives them back after death. 16. Cato says (fr. 1.23) that Larentia became wealthy from her prostitution and after she passed away left the Roman people the *ager Turax, ager Semurius, ager Lintirius*, and *ager Solonius* and was for that reason deemed worthy of a splendid tomb and the honor of annual offerings at the Parentalia.[172] 17. In Book 1 of his *Histories*, Macer establishes that Acca Larentia, the wife of Faustulus, was the nurse of Romulus and Remus (fr. 2):[173] during Romulus' reign she was married off to a rich Etruscan named Carutius, came into his estate, and later left it to Romulus, whom she had raised and who out of filial devotion established her holiday and the offerings at the Parentalia.

18. 'From all this, then, we can conclude both that the Saturnalia comprised a single day and that it was the fourteenth day before the Kalends of January: on that day alone the Saturnalia used to be proclaimed in the temple of Saturn in the course of a relaxed banquet. That day is

[172] The first two parcels are otherwise unattested (cf. *LTUR Sub.* 5:210), the *ager Semurius* mentioned once elsewhere (Cic. *Phil.* 6.14); the *ager Solonius* was on the coast SE of Ostia. On the Parentalia, the festival for appeasing the *Manes* of one's ancestors, cf. 1.4.14n.

[173] Faustulus and Acca Larentia: cf. Livy 1.4.7, 1.5.5, Dion. Hal. 1.84.4, Plut. *Rom.* 4.4 (= Fabius Pictor no. 809 fr. 4 *FGrH* = fr. 7a.10–17 Ch.), Strabo 5.3.2, Appian *Basil.* fr. 1a.7, Anon. *Origin of the Roman Nation* 20.3 (= Enn. *Annals* 1.xliv), Zon. *Epitome* 2:88–89. For the following story cf. also Gell. 7.7.5–8.

pariter et Opi fuerit adscriptus. 19. hanc autem deam
Opem Saturni coniugem crediderunt et ideo hoc mense
Saturnalia itemque Opalia celebrari, quod Saturnus eiusque uxor tam frugum quam fructuum repertores esse cre-
dantur, itaque omni iam fetu agrorum coacto ab hominibus
hos deos coli quasi vitae cultioris auctores. 20. quos etiam
nonnullis caelum ac terram esse persuasum est Satur-
numque a satu dictum cuius causa de caelo est et terram
Opem cuius ope humanae vitae alimenta quaeruntur, vel
ab opere, per quod fructus frugesque nascuntur. 21. huic
deae sedentes vota concipiunt terramque de industria tan-
gunt, demonstrantes ipsam matrem terram esse mortalibus adpetendam.

22. 'Philochorus Saturno et Opi primum in Attica statuisse aram Cecropem dicit eosque deos pro Iove terraque
coluisse instituisseque ut patres familiarum et frugibus et
fructibus iam coactis passim cum servis vescerentur, cum
quibus patientiam laboris in colendo rure toleraverant. de-
lectari enim deum honore servorum, contemplatu laboris.
hinc est quod ex instituto peregrino huic deo sacrum aperto capite facimus.

23. 'Abunde iam probasse nos aestimo Saturnalia uno
tantum die, id est quarto decimo Kalendas, solita celebra-

---

174 The Opalia, in honor of Saturn's consort, was celebrated on
19 Dec. (Varro *Latin Language* 6.22, *FCRR* 207); see also 3.9.4n.,
on Ops Consivia.

175 This is the Varronian etymology (*Latin Language* 5.64 with
LALE 546), as opposed to the derivation from *saturare*/"make
full" (Cic. *On the Nature of the Gods* 2.64 with *LALE* 546–47).

176 Cf. Strabo 1.18.7 with Jacoby's commentary on Philochorus, *FGrH* IIIB (Supplement) 1:402–3.   177 Cf. 1.8.2.

now assigned to the Opalia, in the course of the Saturnalia, though it was originally assigned both to Ops and to Saturn.[174] 19. The goddess Ops was believed to be Saturn's spouse, and the Saturnalia and Opalia were both celebrated in this month because Saturn and his wife were thought to have discovered both grains and fruits: when all the produce of the fields has been gathered people pay cult to these gods as the sources of a more civilized way of life. 20. Some have believed that they are the heaven and the earth: on this view, Saturn's name derives from 'sowing' [*satus*], which originates in the heavens,[175] and Ops is the earth, from whose bounty [*ops*] the sustenance of human life is sought, or else her name derives from toil [*opus*], which causes fruits and grains to grow. 21. People make vows to her while seated and deliberately touch the earth, signifying that mortals cannot help but seek their very mother, the earth.

22. 'Philochorus says (no. 328 fr. 97 *FGrH*) that Cecrops set up the first altar to Saturn and Ops in Attica, paid them cult as Jupiter and Earth,[176] and established the custom whereby heads of households, after the fruits and grains have been harvested, dine with the slaves with whom they bore labor's suffering in working the fields. The god (he says) is pleased by the honor given the slaves and by the reflection given to labor. The foreign origin of the cult explains why we sacrifice to the god with uncovered heads.[177]

23. 'I judge that I've now abundantly demonstrated that the Saturnalia used to be celebrated on one day only, the fourteenth before the Kalends, but that it was later ex-

ri, sed post in triduum propagata, primum ex adiectis a
Caesare huic mensi diebus, deinde ex edicto Augusti quo
trium dierum ferias Saturnalibus addixit. a sexto decimo
igitur coepta in quartum decimum desinunt, quo solo fieri
ante consueverant. 24. sed Sigillariorum adiecta celebritas
in septem dies discursum publicum et laetitiam religionis
extendit.'

11   Tunc Evangelus, 'hoc quidem,' inquit, 'iam ferre non
possum, quod Praetextatus noster in ingenii sui pompam
et ostentationem loquendi vel paulo ante honori alicuius
dei adsignari voluit quod servi cum dominis vescerentur,
quasi vero curent divina de servis aut sapiens quisquam
domi suae contumeliam tam foedae societatis admittat, vel
nunc Sigillaria, quae lusum reptanti adhuc infantiae oscil-
lis fictilibus praebent, temptat officio religionis adscribere
et quia princeps religiosorum putatur non nulla iam et
superstitionis admiscet; quasi vero nobis fas non sit Praetextato aliquando non credere.'

    2. Hic cum omnes exhorruissent, Praetextatus reni-
dens: 'superstitiosum me, Evangele, nec dignum cui cre-
datur existimes volo, nisi utriusque tibi rei fidem ratio
adserta monstraverit. et ut primum de servis loquamur, io-
cone an serio putas esse hominum genus quod di immorta-
les nec cura sua nec providentia dignentur? an forte servos
in hominum numero esse non pateris? audi igitur quanta
indignatio de servi supplicio caelum penetraverit.

    3. 'Anno enim post Romam conditam quadringente-

---

178 The celebration thus ended on the 10th day before the
Kalends = 23 Dec. The Sigillaria, on which small gifts were exchanged (1.11.47–49 with 1.7.30–33), was not part of the Roman
sacral calendar.

tended to three, first as a result of the days that Caesar added to the month, and then by the edict of Augustus (fr. 21 Malc.) in which he assigned to the Saturnalia a three-day holiday. As a result, they begin on the sixteenth day before the Kalends and end on the fourteenth, when the one-day observance was formerly held. 24. But the addition of the Sigillaria extends the public bustle and religious celebration to seven days.'[178]

Then Evangelus said, 'I really cannot stand this: in the showy pageant of his wit and eloquence our friend Praetextatus a little while ago tried to chalk up to some god's honor the custom of slaves dining with their masters—as if divinities care about slaves, or any wise man would indulge in such outrageously disgusting fellowship in his own home! Or take the Sigillaria he just mentioned: the holiday and its clay figurines are meant to amuse infants who haven't yet learned to walk, but he tries to make it a matter of religious duty, and because he's held to be the Prince of the Pious, he even adds in some matters of sheer humbug—as if it were against divine law for us to disbelieve Pratextatus now and then.' 11

2. When the whole company had shuddered at this, Praetextatus smiled: 'Evangelus, I actually want you to judge me a humbug unworthy of belief if the explanation I provide fails to persuade you on both topics. To start with slaves: are you joking, or do you seriously believe that there is a category of human being for which the immortal gods deign neither to care nor to provide? Or is it perhaps that you can't stand the thought that slaves are to be reckoned human? Listen, then, and learn how outraged heaven was by a slave's punishment.

3. 'In the four hundred seventy-fourth year after

simo septuagesimo quarto Autronius quidam Maximus
servum suum verberatum patibuloque constrictum ante
spectaculi commissionem per circum egit: ob quam causam indignatus Iuppiter Annio cuidam per quietem imperavit ut senatui nuntiaret non sibi placuisse plenum crudelitatis admissum. 4. quo dissimulante filium ipsius mors
repentina consumpsit, ac post secundam denuntiationem
ob eandem neglegentiam ipse quoque in subitam corporis
debilitatem solutus est. sic demum ex consilio amicorum
lectica delatus senatui rettulit et vix consummato sermone,
sine mora recuperata bona valitudine, curia pedibus egres-
sus est. 5. ex senatus itaque consulto et Maenia lege ad propitiandum Iovem additus est illis Circensibus dies, isque
instauraticius dictus est non a patibulo, ut quidam putant,
Graeco nomine ἀπὸ τοῦ σταυροῦ, sed a redintegratione,
ut Varroni placet, qui instaurare ait esse instar novare.

6. 'Vides quanta de servo ad deorum summum cura
pervenerit. tibi autem unde in servos tantum et tam inane
fastidium, quasi non ex isdem tibi et constent et alantur
elementis eundemque spiritum ab eodem principio car-
pant? 7. vis tu cogitare eos, quos ius tuos vocat,[57] isdem se-

---

[57] quos ius tuos vocat *Madvig Adv. crit. 3:250*: quos ius tuum
vocas ω (istum quem servum tuum vocas *Sen. EM 47.10*)

---

[179] *Comm.* 2.11.16 (destruction of Carthage, 146 BCE = 607th
year after the founding, reckoned inclusively) implies that M.
himself used the chronology of the *fasti Capitolini* (founding =
752 BCE, cf. also 1.13.20n.), not the Varronian dating (753 BCE),
but we cannot know which system his source followed: the date
given therefore = either 280 or 279 BCE, both of which are contra-
dicted by the date provided by Livy 2.36, 490 BCE. Since the latter
= the 264th year from the founding, on the Varronian chronology,

Rome's founding a certain Autronius Maximus beat his slave, tied him to a gibbet, then drove him through the Circus before the start of the show.[179] Outraged at this, Jupiter ordered a certain Annius,[180] in a dream, to tell the senate that he was displeased by such a cruel offense. 4. When Annius kept the vision to himself, his own son suddenly died, and after disregarding a second message, he himself suddenly became enfeebled. At long last, heeding the advice of friends, he had himself carried in a litter to the senate, where he told the whole story: he had scarcely finished when his health was immediately restored and he was able to leave the curia on his own two feet. 5. So by decree of the senate and the law of Maenius a day was added to the Circus Games, to propitiate Jupiter: it is called the *dies instauricius*, not (as some think) from the gibbet— that is, *stauros* in Greek—but from the act of making whole again, as Varro holds (fr. 430 *GRF* 1:362), noting that *instaurare* means "to replace the equivalent amount" [*instar novare*].[181]

6. 'You can see how concerned the highest god was about a slave. But tell me, how do you come by this hugely foolish disgust for slaves, as though they neither derive their existence and sustenance from the same elements as you nor draw the same breath of life from the same source? 7. Why not reflect that those whom the law calls "yours"

the error presumably arose when M., his source, or a scribe misread "CCLXIV" as "CDLXXIV." For versions of the story cf. Cic. *On Divination* 1.55, Dion. Hal. 7.68.3–69.2, 73.5, Val. Max. 1.7.4, Lact. *Divine Institutes* 2.7.20–21, Aug. *City of God* 4.26.

180 Called "T. Latinius" by Livy and Dionysius, "Ti. Atinius" by Lactantius.   181 Cf. Paul. Fest. 98.29–30, Serv. on *A.* 2.15, DServ. on *A.* 2.669.

minibus ortos eodem frui caelo, aeque vivere, aeque mori?
servi sunt: immo homines. servi sunt: immo conservi, si
cogitaveris tantundem in utrosque licere fortunae. tam tu
illum videre liberum potes quam ille te servum. nescis qua
aetate Hecuba servire coeperit, qua Croesus, qua Darei
mater, qua Diogenes, qua Platon ipse? 8. postremo quid ita
nomen servitutis horremus? servus est quidem, sed neces-
sitate, sed fortasse libero[58] animo. servus est: hoc illi noce-
bit, si ostenderis quis non sit. alius libidini servit, alius ava-
ritiae, alius ambitioni, omnes spei, omnes timori: et certe
nulla servitus turpior quam voluntaria. 9. at nos iugo a Fortuna imposito subiacentem tamquam miserum vilemque
calcamus, quod vero nos nostris cervicibus inserimus non
patimur reprehendi.

10. 'Invenies inter servos aliquem pecunia fortiorem,
invenies dominum spe lucri oscula alienorum servorum
manibus infigentem. non ergo fortuna homines aestimabo
sed moribus: sibi quisque dat mores, condicionem casus
adsignat. quemadmodum stultus est qui empturus equum
non ipsum inspicit sed stratum eius ac frenos, sic stultissi-
mus est qui hominem aut ex veste aut ex condicione quae
nobis vestis modo circumdata est aestimandum putat.

---

[58] *an* liber, *ut Sen.*?

---

[182] §§7–15 are based on Sen. *Moral Epistles* 47, which M.
takes apart, abridges, and rearranges, in his usual fashion.

[183] Seneca refers to Hecuba's capture at the fall of Troy and
Cyrus' conquest of Croesus (who in the dominant traditions is not
enslaved). The capture of Sisigambis, mother of Darius III, after
Alexander defeated her son at the Issus in 333 BCE, is described by
Curt. Ruf. 3.11.24–25; on Diogenes of Sinope cf. §42n. below;
Plato was sold into slavery after angering the tyrant Dionysius of
Syracuse but was soon ransomed (Diog. Laert. 3.19–20).

spring from the same beginning, enjoy the same heaven, live the same as you, die the same?[182] "They're slaves": no, human beings. "They're slaves": no, fellow slaves, if you reflect that chance has the same power over us both. You can look on him as a free man as easily as he can see you as a slave. Are you unaware how late in life Hecuba was enslaved, or Croesus, or Darius' mother, or Diogenes, or Plato himself?[183] 8. Finally, why does the name "slave" make us shudder? "He's in fact a slave": but from force of circumstances—yet perhaps his mind is free. "He's a slave": this will count against him if you show who is not. One man is a slave to lust, another to greed, another to ambition—and we're all slaves to hope and to fear. And surely no slavery is worse than the one we chose for ourselves. 9. Yes, we trample on the man who lies fallen beneath the yoke that bad luck has put upon him, as though he were wretched and of no account—but we don't stand criticism for the yoke that we've placed on our own necks.

10. 'You will find among slaves someone who can't be bribed, and you'll find a master who from hope of gain plants kisses on the hands of another man's slaves: I will therefore judge a man's value not according to his luck but according to his character, for each of us is responsible for his character, while chance determines our circumstances. If someone intent on buying a horse inspects its blanket and bridle, but not the horse itself, he's a fool;[184] more foolish still is the man who thinks a person's worth can be judged either from his garments or from the circumstances that merely enfold us like a garment.

[184] Cf. Sen. *Moral Epistles* 80.9, Apul. *On the God of Socrates* 23.

11. 'Non est, mi Evangele, quod amicum tantum in foro et in curia quaeras: si diligenter attenderis, invenies et domi. tu modo vive cum servo clementer, comiter quoque, et in sermonem illum et non numquam in necessarium admitte consilium. nam et maiores nostri omnem dominis invidiam, omnem servis contumeliam detrahentes, dominum patrem familias, servos familiares appellaverunt. 12. colant ergo te potius servi tui, mihi crede, quam timeant. dicet aliquis nunc me dominos de fastigio suo deicere et quodam modo ad pilleum servos vocare, quos debere dixi magis colere quam timere. hoc qui senserit, obliviscetur id dominis parum non esse quod dis satis est. deinde qui colitur etiam amatur: non potest amor cum timore misceri. 13. unde putas adrogantissimum illud manasse proverbium quo iactatur totidem hostes nobis esse quot servos? non habemus illos hostes sed facimus, cum in illos superbissimi contumeliosissimi crudelissimi sumus, et ad rabiem nos cogunt pervenire deliciae, ut quicquid non ex voluntate respondit iram furoremque evocet. 14. domi enim nobis animos induimus tyrannorum, et non quantum decet sed quantum licet exercere volumus in servos. nam ut cetera crudelitatis genera praeteream, sunt qui, dum se mensae copiis et aviditate distendunt, circumstantibus servis movere labra nec in hoc quidem ut loquantur licere permittunt: virga murmur omne compescitur, et ne fortuita quidem verberibus excepta sunt; tussis, sternutamentum, singultus magno malo luitur. 15. sic fit ut

11. 'There's no reason, my dear Evangelus, to seek a friend only in the forum and the senate chamber: if you pay careful attention, you'll fine one at home too. Just treat your slave mercifully, even courteously, engage him in conversation, and occasionally in your serious planning. Our ancestors, too, made the master's position less invidious, the slave's less insulting, by calling the master "the household's father" and slaves "household members." 12. Believe me, it's better that your slaves respect you than fear you. Now someone will say that I'm knocking masters down off their high horses and, so to speak, inviting slaves to claim their freedom, by saying they should respect rather than fear. Someone who feels this way is forgetting that what is sufficient for the gods is not insufficient for masters. Furthermore, the person who is respected is also loved: love cannot be mingled with fear. 13. What do you suppose is the source of that utterly arrogant proverb that claims, "We have as many enemies as we have slaves"? We don't "have" them as enemies, we make them that way when we behave toward them with supreme arrogance, contempt, and cruelty—and when sheer caprice drives us to this madness, so that anything that doesn't respond to us as we'd like provokes an insane rage. 14. In our homes we adopt the attitude of tyrants, and we want to exert power over our slaves, taking as our limit not what's appropriate, but what's allowed. For to set aside all other forms of cruelty, there are those who—while gorging themselves greedily at a full table—do not allow the slaves around them to move their lips even to speak. Every murmur is suppressed with the rod and not even chance noises escape a beating: a cough, a sneeze, a hiccup carries a large price-tag in pain. 15. So it happens that slaves who aren't permit-

isti de domino loquantur, quibus coram domino loqui non licet. at illi quibus non tantum praesentibus dominis sed cum ipsis erat sermo, quorum os non consuebatur, parati erant pro domino porrigere cervicem et periculum imminens in caput suum vertere: in conviviis loquebantur sed in tormentis tacebant.

16. 'Vis exercitas in servili pectore virtutes recenseamus? primus tibi Vrbinus occurrat: qui cum iussus occidi in Reatino lateret, latebris proditis unus ex servis anulo eius et veste insignitus in cubiculo ad quod inruebant qui persequebantur pro domino iacuit militibusque ingredientibus cervicem praebuit et ictum tamquam Vrbinus excepit. Vrbinus postea restitutus monumentum ei fecit titulo scriptionis qui tantum meritum loqueretur adiecto.

17. 'Aesopus libertus Demosthenis, conscius adulterii quod cum Iulia patronus admiserat, tortus diutissime perseveravit non prodere patronum, donec aliis coarguentibus consciis Demosthenes ipse fateretur. 18. Et ne aestimes ab uno facile celari posse secretum, Labienum ope libertorum latentem ut indicarent liberti nullo tormentorum genere compulsi sunt.

'Ac ne quis libertos dicat hanc fidem beneficio potius libertatis acceptae quam ingenio debuisse, accipe servi in dominum benignitatem cum ipse a domino puniretur. 19. Antium enim Restionem proscriptum solumque nocte

---

185 Cf. Val. Max. 6.8.6 (where the man's name is "Urbinius"), sim. Sen. *On Benefits*. 3.25, Cass. Dio 47.10.2–3.

186 Not the Athenian orator but an otherwise unknown contemporary of Augustus.

187 Cf. Cassius Dio 48.40.5–6, on Labienus' escape at the end of his unsuccessful venture among the Parthians in 39 BCE.

ted to speak in the master's presence talk about him behind his back—but those who were allowed to speak not just in front of their masters but with them, whose lips weren't sewn shut, were ready to offer their necks in their master's place and to shift a danger hanging over his head onto their own. They talked at the banquet but were silent under torture.

16. 'Shall we review the virtues that have found employment in the heart of a slave? Think first of Urbinus. When he was in hiding from a death warrant on his estate at Reate and his hiding place was revealed, one of his slaves took on his identity, with his signet-ring and clothing, and lay in his master's place in the bedroom where the searchers were rushing: when the soldiers entered, he offered his neck and received the blow as though he were Urbinus. When Urbinus was later restored, he raised a monument to the slave, with an inscription describing his great service.[185]

17. 'Demosthenes'[186] freedman Aesopus was aware of the affair his former owner had conducted with Julia but held out for a very long time under torture and did not betray him: in the end, Demosthenes himself confessed when others who were in on the affair provided evidence. 18. You might suppose that this was just a case of one man easily keeping a secret. Don't: when Labienus was hiding with his freedmen's help,[187] no sort of torture could force them to betray him.

'And lest anyone say that freedmen owed this sort of loyalty in return for gift of freedom they'd received, rather than out of their own nature, here's a story about a slave who showed kindness to a master who had actually punished him. 19. Antius Restio had been proscribed and was fleeing alone in the night: while his other slaves were plun-

fugientem, diripientibus bona eius aliis, servus compeditus inscripta fronte, cum post damnationem domini aliena esset misericordia solutus, fugientem persecutus est hortatusque ne se timeret scientem contumeliam suam fortunae imputandam esse, non domino, abditumque ministerio suo aluit. 20. cum deinde persequentes adesse sensisset, senem quem casus obtulit iugulavit et in constructam pyram coniecit. qua accensa occurrit eis qui Restionem quaerebant, dicens damnatum sibi poenas luisse, multo acrius a se vexatum quam ipse vexarat, et fide habita Restio liberatus est.

21. 'Caepionem quoque qui in Augusti necem fuerat animatus, postquam detecto scelere damnatus est, servus ad Tiberim in cista detulit pervectumque Ostiam inde in agrum Laurentem ad patris villam nocturno itinere perduxit. comes deinde[59] navigationis naufragio una expulsum dominum Neapoli dissimulanter occuluit exceptusque a centurione nec pretio nec minis ut dominum proderet potuit adduci. 22. Asinio etiam Pollione acerbe cogente Patavinos ut pecuniam et arma conferrent dominisque ob hoc latentibus, praemio servis cum libertate proposito qui dominos suos proderent, constat servorum nullum victum praemio dominum prodidisse.

---

[59] comes deinde *Madvig adv. crit. 3:250–51*: cum isdem de α, cum (h)is deinde β

---

188 §18–20: cf. Val. Max. 6.8.7. The man is conceivably the same Antius Restio who was tribune of the plebs in 68 BCE (3.17.13n.), twenty-five years before the proscriptions; another Antius Restio, perhaps the latter's son, is attested ca. 46 BCE as a

dering his goods, one slave—a tattoo on his forehead and shackles on his feet, until someone took pity and released him after his master was condemned—followed after him as he fled, urging him not to be afraid: he knew (he said) that his outrageous treatment should be chalked up to fortune, not his master. Then he hid Restio and ministered to his needs. 20. When he realized that their pursuers were upon them, he killed an old man whom chance brought their way, built a pyre, and put the corpse upon it. After lighting the pyre he ran up to the men looking for Restio, saying that he had exacted the penalty himself and had got the better of it when it came to handing out abuse. He was believed, and Restio was rescued.[188]

21. 'When Caepio intended to kill Augustus and was condemned after the crime was exposed, a slave brought him to the Tiber in a chest, conveyed him to Ostia, and from there escorted him to his father's villa in the territory of Laurentum, traveling at night. Next, he accompanied his master by boat, was cast ashore with him in a shipwreck, and then concealed him in Naples. Though he was caught by a centurion, neither a reward nor threats could bring him to betray his master.[189] 22. When Asinius Pollio, too, was harshly pressuring the people of Padua to contribute money and weapons, the masters took to hiding, and a reward, including freedom, was promised to slaves who betrayed their masters: it is an established fact none of the slaves yielded to the reward and betrayed his master.[190]

moneyer (*MRR* 2:431), a position typically held by a man at the start of his public career.

[189] 22 BCE, cf. Vell. 2.91.2, Cass. Dio 54.3.

[190] 40 BCE, cf. Vell. 2.76.2.

23. 'Audi in servis non fidem tantum sed et fecundum[60] bonae inventionis ingenium. cum premeret obsidio Grumentum, servi relicta domina ad hostes transfugerunt. capto deinde oppido impetum in domum habita conspiratione fecerunt et extraxerunt dominam vultu poenam minante ac voce obviis adserente, quod tandem sibi data esset copia crudelem dominam puniendi raptamque quasi ad supplicium obsequiis plenis pietate tutati sunt.

24. 'Vide in hac fortuna etiam magnanimitatem exitum mortis ludibrio praeferentem. C. Vettium Pelignum Italicensem, comprehensum a cohortibus suis ut Pompeio traderetur, servus eius occidit ac se, ne domino superstes fieret, interemit. 25. C. Gracchum ex Aventino fugientem Euporus servus vel, ut quidam tradunt, Philocrates, dum aliqua spes salutis erat, indivulsus comes qua potuit ratione tutatus est, super occisum deinde animam scissis proprio vulnere visceribus effudit. 26. Ipsum P. Scipionem Africani patrem, postquam cum Hannibale conflixerat, saucium in equum servus imposuit et ceteris deserentibus solus in castra perduxit.

27. 'Parum fuerit dominis praestitisse viventibus: quid

[60] foecundum *ed. Colon. 1521*: facundum ω

---

[191] §§23–24: cf. Sen. *On Benefits* 3.23 (M. includes details not found in Seneca). Both anecdotes are set in the Social War, 91–88 BCE: in §24, Italica was the name given to Corfinium, on Italy's east coast, when the Italian confederates made it their capital.

[192] The man is called Publius Vettius (Scato) at Cic. *Phil.* 12.27.

[193] 121 BCE: cf. Vell. 2.6.6, Val. Max. 6.8.3, Plut. *Ti. and C. Gracch.* 38.2–3.

23. 'Now listen to a story about slaves who were not just loyal but also richly ingenious and inventive.[191] When Grumentum was under siege, slaves left their mistress and crossed over to the enemy: when the city was captured they attacked their mistress' house (this was part of their plot) and dragged her out with threatening looks, telling those they met that they had finally been given an opportunity to repay their cruel mistress. After carrying her off, as though to punish her, they protected her and attended her devotedly.

24. 'Consider too a largeness of spirit—in servile circumstances—that prefers death to dishonor. When Gaius Vettius,[192] a Paelignian of Italica, was seized by his own soldiers to be handed over to Pompey, his slave slew him and then killed himself, so that he might not survive his master. 25. When Gaius Gracchus was fleeing from the Aventine, his slave Euporus (or Philocrates, as some report) was his inseparable companion while there was any hope of safety, and protected him any way he could. When Gracchus was killed, Euporus stabbed himself in the guts and gave up the ghost over Gracchus' corpse.[193] 26. Publius Scipio himself, Africanus' father, after being wounded in a clash with Hannibal, was put on his horse by a slave, who escorted him into camp all alone, when everyone else deserted him.[194]

27. 'Serving masters while they still lived—that wouldn't amount to much: what do you make of the cour-

___

[194] 218 BCE: this version of the story is owed to the annalist Coelius Antipater (Livy 21.46.10 = Antipater fr. 18); in the more commonly told version, Scipio is saved by his son (Livy ibid., Polyb. 10.3, Val. Max. 5.4.2, Sen. *On Benefits* 3.33).

quod in his quoque exigendae vindictae reperitur animosi-
tas? nam Seleuci regis servus cum serviret amico eius a
quo dominus fuerat interemptus, cenantem in ultionem
domini confodit. 28. Quid quod duas virtutes, quae inter
nobiles quoque unice clarae sunt, in uno video fuisse man-
cipio, imperium regendi peritiam et imperium contem-
nendi magnanimitatem? 29. Anaxilaus enim Messenius,
qui Messanam in Sicilia condidit, fuit Rheginorum tyran-
nus. is cum parvos relinqueret liberos, Micytho servo suo
commendasse contentus est. is tutelam sancte gessit impe-
riumque tam clementer obtinuit ut Rhegini a servo regi
non dedignarentur. perductis deinde in aetatem pueris et
bona et imperium tradidit, ipse parvo viatico sumpto profectus est et Olympiae cum summa tranquillitate conse-
nuit.

30. 'Quid etiam in commune servilis fortuna profuerit
non paucis docetur. bello Punico cum deessent qui scribe-
rentur, servi pro dominis pugnaturos se polliciti in civitatem recepti sunt et volones, quia sponte hoc voluerunt, ap-
pellati. 31. Ad Cannas quoque victis Romanis octo milia
servorum empta militaverunt cumque minoris captivi
redimi possent, maluit se res publica servis in tanta tem-
pestate committere. sed et post calamitatem apud Trasi-

---

[195] 281 BCE: cf. Paus. 1.16.2, Justin 17.2.4–5; the friend was
Ptolemy Ceraunus.   [196] 476 BCE: cf. Hdt. 7.170 (~ Paus.
5.26.4), Diod. 11.48.2, 11.66.1–3, Justin. 4.2.5. The tyrant's name
is more usually given as "Anaxilas."   [197] Cf. Paul. Fest. p.
511.5–7; acc. to Livy (22.57.11, 23.35.6, 24.10.3, 24.14.3) these
levies occurred after the battle of Cannae (next anecdote).

[198] 217 BCE: cf. Livy 22.11.8. Acc. to Livy 22.61.1–2, the senate refused to ransom the Roman captives both for ideological

age these slaves showed in avenging their masters? When a slave of king Seleucus became the slave of Seleucus' friend—and murderer—the slave stabbed him to death at dinner, in revenge for his master.[195] 28. What about finding in one slave the two virtues that confer unique distinction even on nobles, skill in using supreme power and largeness of spirit in turning one's back on that same power? 29. Anaxilaus of Messene, who founded Messana in Sicily, was tyrant over the people of Rhegium: at his death he left two small children, whom he was content to entrust to his slave Micythus.[196] The slave then behaved irreproachably as the children's guardian and was so merciful in his exercise of power that the people of Rhegium thought it no disgrace to be ruled by a slave. When the children reached maturity, he handed over to them their estate and the power to rule, while he himself accepted a small travel-allowance and set off for Olympia, where he reached old age in utter tranquility.

30. 'There are not a few examples that also show how slaves contributed to the common good. When there was a shortage of recruits in the Punic War, slaves who promised to fight on their masters' behalf were given citizenship and called *volones*, since they had volunteered.[197] 31. When the Romans were defeated at Cannae, 8000 slaves were purchased for military duty, and though captive Romans could have been ransomed more cheaply, the commonwealth preferred to rely on slaves at that critical juncture.[198] But also after the disaster of the notorious blood-

reasons, as allegedly being contrary to precedent, and because they could not afford to, in part because of the money already spent in purchasing the slaves.

menum notae cladis acceptam libertini quoque in sacramentum vocati sunt. 32. Bello sociali cohortium duodecim ex libertinis conscriptarum opera memorabilis virtutis apparuit. C. Caesarem, cum milites in amissorum locum substitueret, servos quoque ab amicis accepisse et eorum forti opera usum esse comperimus. Caesar Augustus in Germania et Illyrico cohortes libertinorum complures legit, quas voluntarias appellavit.

33. 'Ac ne putes haec in nostra tantum contigisse re publica, Borysthenitae obpugnante Zopyrione servis liberatis dataque civitate peregrinis et factis tabulis novis hostem sustinere potuerunt. 34. Cleomenes Lacedaemonius, cum mille et quingenti soli Lacedaemonii qui arma ferre possent superfuissent, ex servis manu missis bellatorum novem milia conscripsit. Athenienses quoque consumptis publicis opibus servis libertatem dederunt.

35. 'Ac ne in solo virili sexu aestimes inter servos extitisse virtutes, accipe ancillarum factum non minus memorabile nec quo utilius reipublicae in ulla nobilitate reperias. 36. Nonis Iuliis diem festum esse ancillarum tam vulgo notum est ut nec origo et causa celebritatis ignota sit. Iunoni enim Caprotinae die illo liberae pariter ancillaeque sacrificant sub arbore caprifico in memoriam benignae

---

[199] 217 BCE: cf. Livy 22.7.1.   [200] Cf. Appian *Civil War* 1.49.212.   [201] On Augustus cf. Suet. *Aug.* 25. 2; the action of Julius Caesar is otherwise unattested.

[202] Borysthenes (also known as Olbia) lay on the river of the same name (mod. Dnieper).

[203] Cleomenes was king ca. 235–222 BCE; contrast Plut. *Cleom.* 11.2.

[204] Slaves fought at the battle of Marathon in 490 BCE (Paus.

bath experienced at Lake Trasimene, freedmen too were called to take the soldier's oath.[199] 32. In the Social War twelve cohorts of freedmen conscripts performed memorably and with courage.[200] We see that when Gaius Caesar was finding replacements for soldiers he had lost, he accepted slaves from his friends and employed their gallant service. In Germany and Illyricum Caesar Augustus enlisted quite a number of freedmen companies, which he called "voluntaries."[201]

33. 'Don't suppose, either, that this sort of thing has happened only in our commonwealth. When Zopyrio was besieging Borysthenes [325 BCE],[202] the people freed their slaves and gave citizenship to foreign residents: with the citizen-rolls thus redrawn, they were able to hold off the enemy. 34. When there remained only 1500 Lacedaemonians able to bear arms, Cleomenes enlisted 9000 warriors from slaves who had been freed.[203] When their public reserves were depleted, the Athenians too freed their slaves.[204]

35. 'And lest you judge that virtues emerged only among the males of the species, here is a deed of some slave girls no less memorable, and as much a contribution to the common good as any you'd find among the nobility.[205] 36. It's too well known that female slaves have a holiday on the Nones of July for there to be any mystery about when and why the celebration began. On that day women—free and slave alike—sacrifice to Juno Caprotina under the wild fig-tree in memory of the generosity and

1.32.3), and subsequently (Xen. *Hell.* 1.6.24, Demosth. 4.36 ["those living apart" = freedmen]).   [205] §§35–40: cf. Varro *Latin Language* 6.18, Plut. *Rom.* 29.3–6, *Cam.* 33.2–6.

virtutis, quae in ancillarum animis pro conservatione publicae dignitatis apparuit. 37. nam post urbem captam cum sedatus esset Gallicus motus, res publica vero esset ad tenue deducta, finitimi opportunitatem invadendi Romani nominis aucupati praefecerunt sibi Postumium Livium, Fidenatium dictatorem, qui mandatis ad senatum missis postulavit ut si vellent reliquias suae civitatis manere, matres familiae sibi et virgines dederentur. 38. cumque patres essent in ancipiti deliberatione suspensi, ancilla nomine Tutela seu Philotis pollicita est se cum ceteris ancillis sub nomine dominarum ad hostes ituram, habituque matrum familias et virginum sumpto hostibus cum prosequentium lacrimis ad fidem doloris ingestae sunt. 39. quae cum a Livio in castris distributae fuissent, viros plurimo vino provocaverunt, diem festum apud se esse simulantes. quibus soporatis ex arbore caprifico quae castris erat proxima signum Romanis dederunt. 40. qui cum repentina incursione superassent, memor beneficii senatus omnes ancillas manu iussit emitti dotemque iis ex publico fecit et ornatum quo tunc erant usae gestare concessit diemque ipsum Nonas Caprotinas nuncupavit ab illa caprifico ex qua signum victoriae ceperunt sacrificiumque statuit annua sollemnitate celebrandum, cui lac quod ex caprifico manat propter memoriam facti praecedentis adhibetur.

41. 'Sed nec ad philosophandum ineptum vel impar servile ingenium fuit. Phaedon ex cohorte Socratica Socratique et Platoni perfamiliaris, adeo ut Plato eius nomini

---

[206] Cf. Plut. *Rom.* 29.4 (Philotis or Tutola), *Cam.* 33.3 (Philotis or Tutula).

[207] §§41–44 are based on Gell. 2.18.

courage that shone forth from slave girls' hearts as they saved the state's honor. 37. After the Gallic threat was removed following the city's capture, when the commonwealth's resources were severely reduced, Rome's neighbors seized the opportunity to invade our realm and chose Postumius Livius of Fidenae as their leader. He sent orders to the senate demanding that the city's matrons and marriageable girls be surrendered to him, if they wanted any trace of their community to survive. 38. When the senate fathers could not make up their minds, a slave girl named Tutela (or Philotis)[206] promised to go to the enemy with all the other slave girls in the guise of their mistresses: so dressed in the matrons' and maidens' garments they were foisted off on the enemy, as their escorts' tears lent credibility to their grief. 39. When Livius had shared them out in his camp, they egged the men on to down a great amount of wine, pretending that it was a holiday of theirs, and when the men were fast asleep, they signaled the Romans from the wild fig nearest the camp. 40. When their sudden attack resulted in victory, the senate, mindful of the slave girls' contribution, ordered that they all be freed, gave them dowries from public funds, and granted them the garments that they had worn. The senate named the day the "Caprotine Nones," after the wild fig [*caprificus*] from which they received the victorious signal, and established that a sacrifice be celebrated in an annual ritual in which the milky sap that drips from the tree is used in memory of the bygone deed.

41. 'Furthermore, the wits of slaves have not been unsuited or unequal to philosophy.[207] Phaedo was a member of Socrates' entourage and so much an intimate of Socrates and Plato that Plato gave his name to that great and godlike

librum illum divinum de immortalitate animae dicaret, servus fuit forma atque ingenio liberali. hunc Cebes Socraticus hortante Socrate emisse dicitur habuisseque in philosophiae disciplinis, atque is postea philosophus inlustris emersit sermonesque eius de Socrate admodum elegantes leguntur.

42. 'Alii quoque non pauci servi fuerunt qui post philosophi clari extiterunt. ex quibus ille Menippus fuit, cuius libros M. Varro in saturis aemulatus est, quas alii Cynicas, ipse appellat Menippeas.

'Sed et Philostrati Peripatetici servus Pompylus et Zenonis Stoici servus qui Perseus vocatus est et Epicuri, cui Mys nomen fuit, philosophi non incelebres illa aetate vixerunt; Diogenes etiam Cynicus, licet ex libertate, in servitutem venum ierat. 43. quem cum emere vellet Xeniades Corinthius, ecquid artificii novisset percontatus est: "novi," inquit Diogenes, "hominibus liberis imperare." tunc Xeniades responsum eius demiratus e<mit et e>misit[61] manu filiosque suos ei tradens, "accipe," inquit, "liberos meos quibus imperes."

44. 'De Epicteto autem philosopho nobili, quod is quoque servus fuit, recentior est memoria quam ut possit

---

[61] emit et emisit *Jan* (*post* emit et misit *Meurs*): emisit ω

---

[208] Cf. Diog. Laert. 2.105.

[209] Rather, Theophrastus, Aristotle's successor (so Gell. 2.18.8, cf. Diog. Laert. 5.36); the confusion is more likely M.'s than a medieval scribe's.

[210] The man's Greek name was certainly *Persaios* = *Persaeus* in Latin (so Gell. ibid.): it is not clear whether the archetype's *Perseus* results from the common manuscript confusion of *ae* and

book on the immortality of the soul: he was a slave with the beauty and the mind worthy of a free man.[208] Socrates' follower Cebes is said to have purchased him at Socrates' urging and instructed him in philosophy, and he later turned out to be a brilliant philosopher whose very elegant dialogues about Socrates are in circulation.

42. 'There have been a large number of other slaves who also proved to be distinguished philosophers. One of these is the Menippus whose writings Marcus Varro rivaled in his satires, which others call "Cynic," but he called "Menippean."

'Furthermore, Pompylus, a slave of the Peripatetic philosopher Philostratus,[209] and the Stoic Zeno's slave called Perseus,[210] and Epicurus' slave named Mys were all noted philosophers who lived in that period; and Diogenes the Cynic, though of free birth, was sold into slavery.[211] 43. When Xeniades of Corinth wanted to buy him, he asked him what sort of skill he knew: "I know," Diogenes said, "how to command free men [*liberi*]." Admiring the reply, Xeniades bought and freed him, then handed over his sons to him, saying, "Here are my children [*liberi*] for you to command."

44. 'The memory of the noble philosopher Epictetus is too fresh for the fact that he was a slave to be forgotten and

e or from the fact that "Perseus" is simply the more famous name, belonging both to the slayer of Medusa and to a Macedonian king; it is similarly unclear whether the error is owed to M., his copy of Gellius, or a later scribe.

211 After being taken captive by pirates, Diog. Laert. 6.29 and 74; a version of the following anecdote appears in the latter passage, cf. also ibid. 29–31.

inter oblitterata nesciri. 45. cuius etiam de se scripti duo versus feruntur, ex quibus illud[62] latenter intellegas, non omni modo dis exosos esse qui in hac vita cum aerumnarum varietate luctantur, sed esse arcanas causas ad quas paucorum potuit pervenire curiositas:

δοῦλος Ἐπίκτητος γενόμην καὶ σῶμ' ἀνάπηρος,
καὶ πενίην Ἶρος καὶ φίλος ἀθανάτοις.

46. habes, ut opinor, adsertum non esse fastidio despiciendum servile nomen, cum et Iovem tetigerit cura de servo et multos ex his fideles providos fortes, philosophos etiam extitisse constiterit. nunc de Sigillaribus, ne ridenda me potius aestimes quam sancta dixisse, paucis recensendum est.

47. Epicadus refert Herculem occiso Geryone cum victor per Italiam armenta duxisset, ponte qui nunc Sublicius dicitur ad tempus instructo, hominum simulacra pro numero sociorum quos casu[63] peregrinationis amiserat in fluvium demisisse, ut aqua secunda in mare advecta pro corporibus defunctorum veluti patriis sedibus redderentur et inde usum talia simulacra fingendi inter sacra mansisse. 48. sed mihi huius rei illa origo verior aestimatur

---

62 illud C: aliud ω (*om.* XL)
63 casu Vβ₂: casus ω

---

212 Said from the perspective of Gellius, M.'s source, who was a young man when Epictetus died in the mid-2nd cent. CE.
213 A name derisively given the beggar Arnaios by the suitors in the *Odyssey*, because he served as a go-between like Iris, the messenger of the gods.   214 Cf. 1.7.31 and 1.11.1.
215 Acc. to the dominant tradition, the Sublician bridge, which

unknown.[212] 45. A couplet that he wrote about himself is in circulation: its point, made obliquely, is that the gods do not utterly hate those who struggle in this life with various miseries, but there are hidden causes, which a few men, by careful inquiry, are able to grasp (*Anth. Gr.* 7.676):

> I, Epictetus, was born a slave, maimed in my body,
> an Irus[213] in my poverty, and dear to the gods.

46. 'I think I've made the case that the name "slave" should not be viewed with disgust and contempt, both because Jupiter felt concern for a slave and because many slaves have proved to be loyal, shrewd, gallant, and even philosophers. Now I should briefly review the case of the Sigillaria, so you will not judge that my remarks[214] had more to do with humor than with religion.

47. 'Epicadus reports (test. 6 *GRF* 1:103) that when Hercules had slain Geryon and led his cattle victoriously through Italy, he built the Sublician bridge (as it's now called)[215] so that he could cast into the river human effigies equal in number to the companions he had lost to mischance on his journey: that way, they could be carried along by the current to the sea and be restored, in a sense, to their ancestral homes in place of the bodies of the dead. That (according to Epicadus) is why the practice of fashioning such effigies has remained part of the rites.[216] 48. But I think the explanation I reported a bit earlier is more accurate:[217] namely, that when a more auspicious reading of

spanned the river downstream from the Tiber island, near the Forum Boarium, was built by Ancus Marcius (Livy 1.33.6).

216 Cf. Ov. *F.* 5.629–60 (Paul. Fest. p. 14.22–23), Lact. *Divine Institutes* 1.21.6–8 (citing Varro and Ovid).

217 Cf. 1.7.28–31.

quam paulo ante memini rettulisse: Pelasgos, postquam
felicior interpretatio capita non viventium sed fictilia et
φωτὸς aestimationem non solum hominem sed etiam lumen significare docuisset, coepisse Saturno cereos potius
accendere et in sacellum Ditis arae Saturni cohaerens
oscilla quaedam pro suis capitibus ferre. 49. ex illo tradi-
tum ut cerei Saturnalibus missitarentur et sigilla arte fictili
fingerentur ac venalia pararentur quae homines pro se
atque suis piaculum pro Dite Saturno facerent. 50. ideo
Saturnalibus talium commerciorum coepta celebritas septem occupat dies, quos tantum[64] feriatos facit esse, non
festos omnes. nam medio id est tertio decimo Kalendas
fastum probavimus et aliis hoc adsertionibus ab his proba-
tum est qui rationem anni mensium dierumque et ordinationem a C. Caesare digestam plenius retulerunt.'

12   Cumque hic facere vellet finem loquendi, subiecit Aurelius Symmachus: 'pergin Praetextate eloquio tam dulci
de anno quoque edissertare, antequam experiaris moles-
tiam consulentis, si quis forte de praesentibus ignorat quo
ordine vel apud priscos fuerit vel certioribus postea regulis
innovatus sit? ad quod discendum ipse mihi videris au-
dientum animos incitasse de diebus mensi additis disse-
rendo.' tum ille eodem ductu orandi reliqua contexuit:

[64] tantum *ed. Ven. 1472 (iam cod. Patav. Bibl. Anton. 27 'Disputationis Chori'):* tamen ω

---

[218] Cf. 1.7.30n.   [219] There was significant overlap between "festive days" (*dies festi*) and "days of religious observance"
(*dies feriati*), but they were not synonymous: days of mourning
would qualify as the latter but not as the former, days of public
Games (*ludi*) as the former but not as the latter (the examples are
from Michels 1967, 82; cf., for the 4th cent., Salzman 1990, 119).

the oracle showed that "heads" meant "figurine heads," not "human heads," and that *phôs* could mean both "person" and "lights," the Pelasgi began to light candles to Saturn and to bring a kind of mask, in place of their own heads, to the shrine of Dis[218] contiguous with Saturn's altar. 49. From there was handed down the custom of exchanging candles on the Saturnalia and purchasing figurines fashioned from clay for people to offer to Saturn, in place of Dis, in expiation of themselves and their kin. 50. That's why those common exchanges, begun on the Saturnalia, extend for seven days, which makes them only festive days [*festi*], not all days of religious observance [*feriati*],[219] since (as I've shown) the middle day—that is, the thirteenth before the Kalends—is a day of ordinary legal business,[220] and this has otherwise been shown by those who have treated in more detail the organization of the year, months, and days and Gaius Caesar's ordering of the calendar.'

And though he wished to stop there, Aurelius Symmachus interposed: 'Won't you go on, Praetextatus, and extend your pleasant discourse to the year also, before you're burdened with questions, in case anyone present does not know how the earliest people organized the year and how it was later reorganized along more reliable lines? You yourself, I think, have whetted your listeners' appetite for this lesson by talking about the days that were added to the month.' Then the other picked up the thread of his remarks and wove together all that follows:[221]

12

220 20 Dec.: cf. 1.10.6.
221 For much of 1.12–16 Cornelius Labeo's *Fasti* is the source, used also by (esp.) John Lydus: Mastandrea 1977, 47–65.

2. 'Anni certus modus apud solos semper Aegyptios fuit, aliarum gentium dispari numero, pari errore nutabat; et ut contentus sim referendo paucarum morem regionum, Arcades annum suum tribus mensibus explicabant, Acarnanes sex, Graeci reliqui trecentis quinquaginta quattuor diebus annum proprium computabant. 3. non igitur mirum in hac varietate Romanos quoque olim auctore Romulo annum suum decem habuisse mensibus ordinatum, qui annus incipiebat a Martio et conficiebatur diebus trecentis quattuor, ut sex quidem menses, id est Aprilis Iunius Sextilis September November December, tricenum essent dierum, quattuor vero, Martius Maius Quintilis October, tricenis et singulis expedirentur, qui hodieque septimanas habent Nonas, ceteri quintanas. 4. septimanas autem habentibus ab Idibus revertebantur Kalendae ad diem septimum decimum, verum habentibus quintanas ad octavum decimum remeabat initium Kalendarum.

5. 'Haec fuit Romuli ordinatio, qui primum anni mensem genitori suo Marti dicavit. quem mensem anni primum fuisse vel ex hoc maxime probatur, quod ab ipso Quintilis quintus est et deinceps pro numero nominabantur. 6. huius etiam prima die ignem novum Vestae aris accendebant, ut incipiente anno cura denuo servandi novati ignis inciperet. eodem quoque ingrediente mense tam in regia curiisque atque flaminum domibus laureae veteres

---

222 Cf. 1.14.3.

223 Cf. Pliny *Natural History* 7.155, Plut. *Numa* 18.4, Cens. 19.4, 7, Solin. 1.34, Aug. *City of God* 15.12.

224 Cf. Ov. *F.* 1.27–38, 3.99–100, 119–27, Cens. 20.2–3, Serv. on *G.* 1.43, John Lydus *On the Months* 1.16.

2. 'Only the Egyptians have always had a reliable calendar;[222] those of other nations got the calculations wrong in different ways, but all were in error. To limit myself to describing the habits of a few areas: the Arcadians used to unfold their year in three months, the Acarnanians in six,[223] while the rest of the Greeks reckoned a year of 354 days. 3. It's not strange, then, that amid this variety the Romans too once had their year organized in ten months, on the authority of Romulus: that year began with March and was completed in 304 days, with six months—April, June, Sextilis, September, November, December—having thirty days, four—March, May, Quintilis, October—being disposed of in thirty-one: the latter today have their Nones on the seventh, the rest on the fifth.[224] 4. For those with the Nones on the seventh, the Kalends recurs on the seventeenth day after the Ides, while for those with the Nones on the fifth, the Kalends recurs on the eighteenth day.

5. 'This was the organization of Romulus, who dedicated the first month of the year to Mars, who begot him. That it was the first month of the year is proved particularly clearly by the fact that the fifth [*quintus*] month after it was Quintilis, with the rest named according to their numerical order.[225] 6. On the first day of March, too, they kindled a new flame on the altars of Vesta, so that guardianship of the renewed flame could begin again at the beginning of the year. Also at the start of this month new laurel branches were substituted for the old in the Regia, the curias, and

[225] Cf. Plut. *Mor.* 268A-D, John Lydus *On the Months* 1.14, 4.102.

novis laureis mutabantur; eodem quoque mense et publice et privatim ad Annam Perennam sacrificatum itur, ut annare perennareque[65] commode liceat. 7. hoc mense mercedes exsolvebant magistris quas completus annus deberi fecit, comitia auspicabantur, vectigalia locabant, et servis cenas adponebant matronae, ut domini Saturnalibus: illae ut principio anni ad promptum obsequium honore servos invitarent, hi quasi[66] gratiam perfecti operis exsolverent.

8. 'Secundum mensem nominavit Aprilem, ut quidam putant cum adspiratione quasi Aphrilem, a spuma quam Graeci ἀφρὸν vocant, unde orta Venus creditur. et hanc Romuli asserunt fuisse rationem, ut primum quidem mensem a patre suo Marte, secundum ab Aeneae matre Venere nominaret, et hi potissimum anni principia servarent a quibus esset Romani nominis origo, cum hodieque in sacris Martem patrem, Venerem genetricem vocemus. 9. alii putant Romulum vel altiore prudentia vel certi numinis providentia ita primos ordinasse menses ut cum praecedens Marti esset dicatus, deo plerumque hominum necatori—ut Homerus naturae conscius ait,

[65] perennareque XBR[2]: perann- ω
[66] quasi *Salmasius ex Solin.*: quia ω

---

[226] The Regia was the house of King Numa just off the forum, used under the Republic for various religious purposes (*LTUR* 4: 189–92). Varro *Latin Language* 5.155 distinguishes two kinds of curia, one where priests look after (*curare*) the gods' affairs, one where the senate looks after human affairs (= the *curia Hostilia* under the Republic); both kinds were inaugurated *templa*. On the *flamines* cf. 1.10.15n.

[227] Cf. Ov. *F.* 3.145–46, 523–710.

the flamens' homes.[226] And in the same month both public and private sacrifice is offered to Anna Perenna,[227] so that we might prosperously pass the year [*annare*] and many years thereafter [*perennare*]. 7. In this month teachers used to be paid their fees, which came due at the end of the year, voting assemblies were inaugurated, taxes were farmed out, and matrons served meals to their slaves, as masters do on the Saturnalia, the former to encourage ready obedience in their slaves by this honor at the start of the year, the latter as though to give thanks for work completed.[228]

8. 'Romulus named the second month April, as though (some think) it were "Aphril," from the foam, called *aphros* in Greek, from which Venus is thought to have sprung. They claim that Romulus intended to name the first month for his father, Mars, the second for Aeneas' mother, Venus,[229] so that the year's first stages would chiefly be protected by those who are the source of Roman identity—for today too in offering sacrifices we call upon Mars as father and Venus as mother.[230] 9. Others think that Romulus ordered the first months that way out of a more profound wisdom or inspired by the foresight of a specific god, so that while the first month is dedicated to Mars, a god who for the most part destroys human beings—as Homer, with his knowledge of nature, says (*Il.* 5.31),

[228] On the matrons' meals cf. Solin. 1.35, John Lydus *On the Months* 3.22.
[229] Cf. Ov. *F.* 4.61, Cens. 22.9, John Lydus *On the Months* 4.64, cf. 1.8.6
[230] Cf. Ov. *F.* 4.25–28.

Ἆρες Ἆρες βροτολοιγέ, μιαιφόνε,
τειχεσιβλῆτα[67]—

secundus Veneri dicaretur, quae vim eius quasi benefica
leniret. 10. nam et in duodecim zodiaci signis, quorum certa certorum numinum domicilia creduntur, cum primum
signum Aries Marti adsignatus sit, sequens mox Venerem,
id est Taurus, accepit; 11. et rursus e regione Scorpius ita
divisus est ut deo esset utrique communis. nec aestimatur
rationc caelesti carere ipsa divisio, si quidem aculeo velut
potentissimo telo pars armata posterior domicilium Martis
est, priorem vero partem, cui Ζυγὸς apud Graecos nomen
est, nos Libram vocamus, Venus accepit, quae velut iugo
concordi iungit matrimonia amicitiasque componit.
12. sed Cingius in eo libro quem de fastis reliquit ait imperi-
rite quosdam opinari Aprilem mensem antiquos a Venere
dixisse, cum nullus dies festus nullumque sacrificium insigne Veneri per hunc mensem a maioribus institutum sit,
sed ne in carminibus quidem Saliorum Veneris ulla ut ceterorum caelestium laus celebretur. 13. Cingio etiam Varro consentit, adfirmans nomen Veneris ne sub regibus quidem apud Romanos vel Latinum vel Graecum fuisse, et
ideo non potuisse mensem a Venere nominari. 14. sed cum

[67] -πλῆτα *Aristarch., codd. plerique Hom.*

---

[231] Cf. John Lydus ibid.   [232] Vettius Valens *Anthol.* 2.37,
41, Porph. *CCAG* 5,4:197, Serv. on *G.* 1.33, John Lydus *On the
Months* ibid.   [233] Cf. Hygin. *Astron.* 4.5, Serv. ibid., Mart.
Cap. 8.839, John Lydus *On the Months* 4.34.   [234] The name
of Lucius Cincius is consistently represented thus in M.'s manuscripts and is presumably the form of the name M. knew.

Ares, Ares, bane to man, murderous, destroyer of city
    walls—

the second is dedicated to Venus, who mitigates his violence as our benefactor.[231] 10. In the twelve signs of the zodiac, too, among which specific signs are believed to house
specific divinities, the first sign, Aries, has been assigned
to Mars, the next sign, Taurus, has welcomed Venus.[232]
11. Right across from those two signs Scorpio is divided in
such a way that both gods share it,[233] and that very division
is thought the work of a heavenly plan, since Scorpio's tail,
armed with the spear-like telson, is the house of Mars,
while its front end—the Greeks call it *Zygos* ["Yoke"], we
call it Libra ["Scale"]—belongs to Venus, who joins people
in marriage and brings friends together as though with a
yoke of harmony. 12. But Cingius,[234] in the book he left on
the calendar (fr. 1 *IAH* 1:252 = fr. 1 *IAR*[6]), says the view of
some, that the ancients named April after Venus,[235] is un-
informed, since our ancestors established not a single holy
day nor any significant sacrifice to Venus in the course of
this month—moreover, there's not even celebratory praise
of Venus, as there is of all the other gods, in the hymns of
the Salii.[236] 13. Varro, too, agrees with Cingius, maintaining that under the kings Venus' name did not even exist
among the Romans in either Latin or Greek, and so a
month could not have been named after her (*Ant. hum.* lib.
17 fr. 2 = fr. 409 *GRF* 1:355).[237] 14. But since the heavens

[235] I.e., Aphrodite, cf. Ov. *F.* 4.13–14, Plut. *Numa* 19.2, Cens.
22.9, John Lydus ibid.
[236] On the Salii, cf. 1.9.14 n.
[237] Cf. Varro *Latin Language* 6.33.

fere ante aequinoctium vernum triste sit caelum et nubibus obductum, sed et mare navigantibus clausum, terrae
etiam ipsae aut aqua aut pruina aut nivibus[68] contegantur
eaque omnia verno id est hoc mense aperiantur, arbores
quoque nec minus cetera quae continet terra aperire se in
germen incipiant: ab his omnibus mensem Aprilem dici
merito credendum est quasi Aperilem, sicut apud Athenienses Ἀνθεστηριὼν idem mensis vocatur ab eo quod
hoc tempore cuncta florescant. 15. non tamen negat Verrius Flaccus hoc die postea constitutum ut matronae Veneri sacrum facerent, cuius rei causam, quia huic loco non
convenit, praetereundum est.

16. 'Maium Romulus tertium posuit, de cuius nomine
inter auctores lata dissensio est. nam Fulvius Nobilior in
fastis quos in aede Herculis Musarum posuit Romulum dicit postquam populum in maiores iunioresque divisit, ut
altera pars consilio altera armis rem publicam tueretur, in
honorem utriusque partis hunc Maium, sequentem Iunium mensem vocasse. 17. sunt qui hunc mensem ad nos-

68 nivibus R²FC: nubibus ω

---

238 Cf. Varro ibid., Ov. *F.* 4.89, Plut. ibid., Cens. 22.11, Serv. on
G. 1.43, 1.217, John Lydus ibid.

239 This account connects the name Anthesterion with Gk.
anthos, "flower," probably correctly, though the month corre-
sponds to late February and early March, not April.

240 M. presumably refers to the Veneralia, the feast of Venus
observed on 1 April, when the cult statue of the goddess was
bathed and women also performed a ritual cleansing, which perhaps explains M.'s reticence: cf. Ov. *F.* 4.133–62, Plut. *Numa* 19.2,
John Lydus *On the Months* 4.65.

are usually overcast and cloud-covered before the vernal equinox, the sea closed to navigation, and the very land, too, covered with water or frost or snow, since all these open up [*aperire*] in the month of spring—the month under discussion—and since trees, too, and all else that the earth contains begin to open themselves up to sprout: for all these reasons we should rightly believe that the month is called "April" as though it were "Aperil,"[238] just as the Athenians call the same month *Anthesterion*, because then everything is in bloom.[239] 15. Still, Verrius Flaccus does not deny that a sacrifice offered by matrons to Venus was later established on this day (I need not go into the reason, which is irrelevant to our topic).[240]

16. 'Romulus placed May third.[241] About its name there is wide disagreement among our authorities.[242] In the calendar he set up in the temple of Hercules of the Muses,[243] Fulvius Nobilior says that after Romulus divided the people into "elders" [*maiores*] and "juniors" [*iuniores*], so that one set could protect the commonwealth with its wise planning, the other with arms, he named this month May, the next month June, in honor of the two divisions, respectively.[244] 17. Some report that this month entered our cal-

---

[241] Cf. Varro *On the Latin Language* 6.33, Ov. *F.* 1.41.

[242] Cf. *LALE* 360.

[243] Prob. dedicated sometime after Nobilior's triumph in 187, in the SW Campus Martius (*LTUR* 3: 17–19): the name M. gives (so also Suet. *Aug.* 29.5) is explained only in a late source (Eumen. *Latin Panegyrics* 9.7–8, alleging a Greek tradition in which Hercules was a leader of the Muses) and differs from the name given by Serv. on *A.* 1.8 ("Hercules and the Muses").

[244] Cf. Varro ibid., Ov. *F.* 5.73, 427, Plut. *Numa* 19.3, Cens. 22.9, Serv. on *G.* 1.43, John Lydus *On the Months* 4.76, 88.

tros fastos a Tusculanis transisse commemorent, apud quos nunc quoque vocatur deus Maius, qui est Iuppiter, a magnitudine scilicet ac maiestate dictus. 18. Cingius mensem nominatum putat a Maia quam Vulcani dicit uxorem argumentoque utitur quod flamen Vulcanalis Kalendis Maiis huic deae rem divinam facit. sed Piso uxorem Vulcani Maiestam, non Maiam dicit vocari. 19. contendunt alii Maiam Mercurii matrem mensi nomen dedisse, hinc maxime probantes quod hoc mense mercatores omnes Maiae pariter Mercurioque sacrificant. 20. adfirmant quidam, quibus Cornelius Labeo consentit, hanc Maiam cui mense Maio res divina celebratur terram esse, hoc adeptam nomen a magnitudine, sicut et Mater Magna in sacris vocatur, adsertionemque aestimationis suae etiam hinc colligunt quod sus praegnans ei mactatur, quae hostia propria est terrae. et Mercurium ideo illi in sacris adiungi dicunt quia vox nascenti homini terrae contactu datur, scimus autem Mercurium vocis et sermonis potentem. 21. auctor est Cornelius Labeo huic Maiae, id est terrae, aedem Kalendis Maiis dedicatam sub nomine Bonae Deae

---

245 Cf. Fest. p. 120.6–8 ("many Latin communities"), Ov. *F.* 5.427–28. Here and in §20 (on Maia) the proposed etymology looks to *maior/maius* ("greater")—the comparative degree of the adj. *magnus*—or to the cognate noun *maiestas* ("greatness").

246 Cf. Gell. 13.23.2, Cens. 22.12.

247 One of the minor *flamines*, cf. 1.10.15n.

248 Cf. Ov. *F.* 5.85–88, John Lydus 4.76. This account implies the identification of Mercury with the Greek god Hermes, whose birth from the union of Atlas' daughter Maia and Zeus is the subject of the *Homeric Hymn to Hermes*.

249 For this festival, held on 15 May, see Ov. *F.* 5.663–92 (with Livy 2.27.5), *FCRR* 122, cf. John Lydus *On the Months* 4.80.

endar via the people of Tusculum,[245] who even now have a god called Maius, who is identified with Jupiter and whose name is of course derived from "magnitude" and "majesty." 18. Cingius thinks (fr. 3 *IAH* 1:252 = fr. 3 *IAR*[6]) the month was named after Maia, who he says is the wife of Vulcan,[246] and he bases his argument on the fact that the flamen of Vulcan[247] sacrifices to this goddess on the Kalends of May; but Piso says (fr. 44) that Vulcan's wife is named Maiesta, not Maia. 19. Others contend that Mercury's mother, Maia, gave her name to the month,[248] stressing particularly that in this month all merchants sacrifice to Maia and Mercury alike.[249] 20. Some assert—and Cornelius Labeo agrees (fr. 5)—that the Maia who receives cult in May is the earth, and that she got this name from her magnitude, just as she is also called "Great Mother" [*Mater Magna*] in her rites. They also derive support for this view from the fact that Maia receives the sacrifice of a pregnant sow, which is the victim appropriate to the earth.[250] They also say that Mercury is associated with her in her cult because at their births human beings get the power of speech from contact with the earth,[251] and we know that Mercury has speech and utterance in his power. 21. Cornelius Labeo supports the view (ibid.) that on the Kalends of May a temple was dedicated to this Maia (that

[250] I.e., the festival of 1 May noted in §18; cf. Paul. Fest. p. 243.2–3. For sacrifice of a sow to Earth cf. also Cic. *On Divination* 1.101, Fest. p. 274.6, Ov. *F.* 1.671–72, Arnob. 7.22.2–4, Serv. on *A.* 8.84; the same offering to Dêmêtêr/Ceres is more common still (cf. §23).

[251] Cf. John Lydus *On the Months* 4.80, the only other ancient source to document this notion.

et eandem esse Bonam Deam et terram ex ipso ritu occul-
tiore sacrorum doceri posse confirmat: hanc eandem Bonam Faunamque, Opem et Fatuam pontificum libris indi-
gitari, 22. Bonam quod omnium nobis ad victum bonorum
causa est, Faunam quod omni usui animantium favet,
Opem quod ipsius auxilio vita constat, Fatuam a fando
quod, ut supra diximus, infantes partu editi non prius vocem edunt quam attigerint terram. 23. sunt qui dicant
hanc deam potentiam habere Iunonis ideoque regale
sceptrum in sinistra manu ei additum. eandem alii Proserpinam credunt porcaque ei rem divinam fieri quia segetem
quam Ceres mortalibus tribuit porca depasta est. alii
Χθονίαν Ἑκάτην, Boeoti Semelam credunt.

24. 'Nec non eandem Fauni filiam dicunt obstitisseque
voluntati patris in amorem suum lapsi, ut et virga myrtea
ab eo verberaretur cum desiderio patris nec vino ab eodem

---

252 Cf. *FCRR* 116–17, *LTUR* 1: 197–98. The goddess was also
celebrated each Dec. in nocturnal rites "for the well-being of the
Roman people" (Cic. *On the Soothsayers' Responses* 12) held at
the house of a consul or praetor and supervised by the magistrate's
wife (men were rigorously excluded); cf. *FCRR* 199–200.

253 Cf. DServ. on *G.* 1.10; the dominant ancient etymology
derived the names "Faunus" and "Fauna" from *fari*, "to speak"
(*LALE* 226)

254 On Ops, the wife of Saturn, cf. 1.10.18–20.

255 Cf. Varro *Latin Language* 6.55, *LALE* 225.

256 Extant images of the Bona Dea typically represent her with
a libation-bowl (*patera*) and/or serpent (cf. §§24–25) in her right
hand and a cornucopia in her left; the scepter M. mentions is not
found (*LIMC* 3,1:121–22 with 3,2:96–97).

is, the earth) under the name of the Good Goddess,[252] and he maintains that her identity with the Good Goddess and the earth can be learned from an exceptionally secret ritual of her cult: the pontiffs' books invoke the same goddess as the Good Goddess, Fauna, Ops, and Fatua, 22. Good, because she causes all things that are good for us in living our lives; Fauna, because she nurtures [*favere*] all that is useful to living creatures;[253] Ops, because life depends on her assistance;[254] and Fatua from speaking [*fari*],[255] because (as I said above) newborn babies do not make a sound before they have touched the earth. 23. Some say that this goddess has Juno's power and for that she was given a scepter to hold in her left hand.[256] Others believe the same goddess is Proserpina and receives a pig in sacrifice because a pig ate the crop that Ceres gave to mortals.[257] Still others believe her to be Chthonian Hecate,[258] the Boeotians, Semele.[259]

24. 'They say that the same goddess is Faunus' daughter, who resisted her father when he fell in love with her: as a result, he beat her with a myrtle branch because she had not yielded to his desire, even when he had plied her with

[257] Abducted by Hades, Proserpina (Gk. Persephonê) subsequently spent 6 months upon the earth, 6 below, causing Ceres to mourn, and the world of men to be barren, for half the year: the story is the centerpiece of the *Homeric Hymn to Dêmêtêr*. The pig earned its place as victim by destroying the first crops: cf. Ov. *Met.* 15.111–13, Hygin. *Fab.* 277, Serv. on *A.* 8.43.

[258] Goddess of the underworld, associated with magic, the moon, and crossroads, and identified with various other goddesses, esp. Artemis.

[259] Cf. John Lydus *On the Months* 4.51. Semelê was the mother, by Zeus, of Dionysus.

pressa cessisset. transfigurasse se tamen in serpentem pater creditur et coisse cum filia. 25. horum omnium haec proferuntur indicia: quod virgam myrteam in templo haberi nefas sit; quod super caput eius extendatur vitis qua maxime eam pater decipere temptavit; quod vinum in templum eius non suo nomine soleat inferri sed vas in quo vinum inditum est mellarium nominetur et vinum lac nuncupetur; serpentesque in templo eius nec terrentes nec timentes indifferenter appareant. 26. quidam Medeam putant, quod in aede[69] eius omne genus herbarum sit ex quibus antistites dant plerumque medicinas, et quod templum eius virum introire non liceat propter iniuriam quam ab ingrato viro Iasone perpessa est. 27. haec apud Graecos θεὸς γυναικεία dicitur, quam Varro Fauni filiam tradit adeo pudicam ut extra γυναικωνῖτιν numquam sit egressa, nec nomen eius in publico fuerit auditum, nec virum umquam viderit vel a viro visa sit, propter quod nec vir templum eius ingreditur. 28. unde et mulieres in Italia sacro Herculis non licet interesse, quod Herculi, cum boves Geryonis per agros Italiae duceret, sitienti respondit mulier aquam se non posse praestare, quod feminarum deae celebraretur dies, nec ex eo apparatu viris gustare fas esset. propter quod Hercules facturus sacrum detestatus est praesentiam feminarum et Potitio ac Pinario sacrorum

---

[69] aede *ed. Colon. 1521*: aedem ω

---

[260] A version of this story, in which the goddess is Faunus' wife, is told at Plut. *Mor.* 268D-E, Lact. *Divine Institutes* 1.22.11 (citing Sextus Clodius), Arnob. 5.18.
[261] Cf. Plut. ibid.
[262] Most extant representations of Bona Dea are statuettes,

wine.[260] Her father is believed, nonetheless, to have taken the form of a snake and to have lain with her. 25. For all this the following evidence is offered: it is against divine law for a myrtle branch to be kept in her temple;[261] above her head there stretches a grapevine, the special instrument of her father's trickery;[262] when wine is brought into her temple it is not referred to as such, but the vessel in which it's stored is called the "honeypot" and the wine is called "milk"; and snakes appear in her temple without either causing or experiencing fear. 26. Some think she's Medea, because her shrine contains all kinds of herbs from which her priests often make medicines, and because it is forbidden for a man to enter her temple in view of the wrong done to her by her ungrateful husband, Jason. 27. The Greeks call her the women's goddess, who Varro reports was Faunus' daughter (*Ant. div.* fr. 218 = *ant. hum.* lib. 17 fr. 3), so modest that she never set foot outside the women's quarter of the house: her name was never heard in public, she never saw a man, and vice versa.[263] That's the reason no man enters her temple. 28. For a similar reason women, too, are forbidden to attend the rites of Hercules in Italy: when he was thirsty from driving Geryon's cattle through the fields of Italy, a woman told him she could not give him water because the holy day of the women's goddess was being celebrated and it was against divine law for men to drink from a vessel used in the rites. As a result, Hercules placed women under a curse if they were present when he was going to offer a sacrifice, and he ordered Potitius and

where this feature would not appear; it is absent in the few reliefs that survive (*LIMC* ibid.)

263 Cf. Lact. *Divine Institutes* 1.22.10 (also citing Varro).

custodibus iussit ne mulierem interesse permitterent.
29. ecce occasio nominis, quo Maiam eandem esse et terram et Bonam Deam diximus, coegit nos de Bona Dea
quaecumque comperimus protulisse!

30. 'Iunius Maium sequitur aut ex parte populi, ut supra diximus, nominatus aut ut Cingius arbitratur quod Iu-
nonius apud Latinos ante vocitatus diuque apud Aricinos
Praenestinosque hac appellatione in fastos relatus sit, adeo
ut (sicut Nisus in commentariis fastorum dicit) apud maiores quoque nostros haec appellatio mensis diu manserit,
sed post detritis quibusdam litteris ex Iunonio Iunius dictus sit. nam et aedes Iunoni Monetae Kalendis Iuniis dedi-
cata est. 31. non nulli putaverunt Iunium mensem a Iunio
Bruto qui primus Romae consul factus est nominatum,
quod hoc mense, id est Kalendis Iuniis, pulso Tarquinio
sacrum Carnae deae in Caelio monte voti reus fecerit.
32. hanc deam vitalibus humanis praeesse credunt. ab ea
denique petitur ut iecinora et corda quaeque sunt intrinse-
cus viscera salva conservet, et quia cordis beneficio, cuius
dissimulatione brutus habebatur, idoneus emendationi
publici status extitit, hanc deam quae vitalibus praeest

---

264 Cf. Prop. 4.9, Plut. *Mor.* 278E, Gell. 11.6.2, Anon. *Origin
of the Roman Nation* 6.7.

265 Cf. Ov. *F.* 6.25–26, 59–60, Paul. Fest. p. 92.6–7, Plut. *Numa*
19.3, *Mor.* 285A, Serv. on *G.* 1.43.

266 Cf. Livy 7.28.4, Ov. *F.* 6.183–84, John Lydus *On the Months*
4.89.

267 Though Ovid makes Carna, who had her festival on 1 June
(*FCRR* 128), the goddess of the door-hinge (*cardo: F.* 6.101–30,
cf. Tert. *On the Soldier's Crown* 13.9, Aug. *On the City of God*

Pinarius, the wardens of his rites, to prevent women from participating.[264] 29. And look at that: just happening upon the name—saying that Maia is identified with the earth and the Good Goddess—compelled me to produce everything I know about the Good Goddess!

30. 'June follows May. It takes its name either from a segment of the people, as I said above [§16], or from the fact that—as Cingius holds (fr. 4 *IAH* 1:253 = fr. 4 *IAR*[6])—it was called Junonius by the Latin people and was long recorded in that form in the calendars of Aricia and Praeneste; and as Nisus says in his commentary on the calendar (fr. 8 *GRF* 2:340), even among our own ancestors too the month kept this name for a long time, though after some letters were removed it was called June [*Iunius*] instead of Junonius.[265] Note too that the temple to Juno Moneta was dedicated on the Kalends of June.[266] 31. Some have thought that June was named after Junius Brutus, Rome's first consul, because in this month—specifically, on the Kalends of June—he discharged a vow by sacrificing to the goddess Carna on the Caelian Hill after the expulsion of Tarquin. 32. This goddess is thought to hold human vital organs in her power and is accordingly called upon to keep our livers, hearts, and all our innards healthy.[267] Brutus turned out to be the right man to improve our constitution by virtue of his wits [lit. "heart"]—which he concealed, and so was thought doltish [*brutus*][268]—and for that reason he dedicated a temple to the

4.8), he also tells an etiological story (ibid. 169–82) to show how Carna—as M. says—cares for our internal organs.

[268] Cf. Livy 1.56.8.

templo sacravit. 33. cui pulte fabaria[70] et larido sacrifica-
tur, quod his maxime rebus vires corporis roborentur. nam
et Kalendae Iuniae fabariae vulgo vocantur, quia hoc
mense adultae fabae divinis rebus adhibentur.

34. 'Sequitur Iulius qui, cum secundum Romuli ordinationem Martio anni tenente principium Quintilis a numero vocaretur, nihilo minus tamen etiam post praepositos a
Numa Ianuarium ac Februarium retinuit nomen, cum non
videretur iam quintus esse sed septimus. sed postea in honorem Iulii Caesaris dictatoris legem ferente M. Antonio
M. filio consule Iulius appellatus est, quod hoc mense a. d.
quartum Idus Quintiles Iulius procreatus sit. 35. Augustus
deinde est, qui Sextilis antea vocabatur donec honori Augusti daretur ex senatus consulto cuius verba subieci:

> cum Imperator Caesar Augustus mense Sextili et
> primum consulatum inierit et triumphos tres in ur-
> bem intulerit et ex Ianiculo legiones deductae secu-
> taeque sint eius auspicia ac fidem, sed et Aegyptus
> hoc mense in potestatem populi Romani redacta
> sit finisque hoc mense bellis civilibus impositus sit
> atque ob has causas hic mensis huic imperio felicis-
> simus sit ac fuerit, placere senatui ut hic mensis Au-
> gustus appelletur.

[70] fabaria G²: fabacia ω

---

[269] Cf. Ov. *F.* 1.169–82, with Varro *On the Way of Life of the
Roman People* fr. 21, Pliny *Natural History* 18.118.

[270] Cf. §5 above.

[271] Cf. John Lydus *On the Months* 4.102, *MRR* 2:315.

[272] In August of 43 three legions guarding the treasury on the
Janiculum transferred their allegiance from the senate to Octa-

goddess in charge of vital organs. 33. The goddess receives an offering of bean porridge and bacon,[269] which are especially conducive to bodily strength. The Kalends of June is also called the "bean Kalends," because in this month ripe beans are used in sacrifice.

34. 'Then follows July: in Romulus' system, where March came first, this month was called Quintilis from its numerical position,[270] and it still kept that name even after Numa put January and February at the start of the year, though it then appeared seventh, not fifth. Later on, under a law carried by Mark Antony, the son of Marcus, as consul, it was named July in honor of Julius Caesar, because he was born on the fourth day of Quintilis.[271] 35. Next, August is the month that was previously called Sextilis, before it was granted as an honor to Augustus, by a decree of the senate that I've quoted here (SC 42 *FIRA*[2] 1:280–81):

> Whereas in the month of Sextilis Commander Caesar Augustus both entered his first consulship [43 BCE] and brought three triumphal processions into the city [29 BCE], and legions led down from the Janiculum followed his auspices and tutelage [43 BCE];[272] and whereas in this month Egypt was brought under the power of the Roman people [30 BCE]; and whereas in this month the civil wars were ended;[273] and whereas for these reasons this month is and has been the most fortunate for this realm; it is the senate's will that this month be called "August."

vian; he was elected consul for the first time shortly thereafter (Appian *Civil War* 3.91.373ff.).

[273] Cf. John Lydus *On the Months* 4.111.

item plebiscitum factum ob eandem rem Sexto Pacuvio tribuno plebem rogante.

36. 'Mensis September principalem sui retinet appellationem: quem Germanici appellatione, Octobrem vero suo nomine Domitianus invaserat. 37. sed ubi infaustum vocabulum ex omni aere vel saxo placuit eradi, menses quoque usurpatione tyrannicae appellationis exuti sunt: cautio postea principum ceterorum diri ominis infausta vitantium mensibus a Septembri usque ad Decembrem prisca nomina reservavit.

38. 'Haec fuit a Romulo annua ordinata dimensio, qui, sicut supra iam diximus, annum decem mensium, dierum vero quattuor et trecentorum habendum esse constituit mensesque ita disposuit ut quattuor ex his tricenos singulos, sex vero tricenos haberent dies. 39. sed cum is numerus neque solis cursui neque lunae rationibus conveniret, non numquam usu veniebat ut frigus anni aestivis mensibus et contra calor hiemalibus proveniret, quod ubi contigisset, tantum dierum sine ullo mensis nomine patiebantur absumi quantum ad id anni tempus adduceret quo caeli habitus instanti mensi aptus inveniretur.

13   'Sed secutus Numa, quantum saeculo rudi et[71] adhuc impolito solo ingenio magistro comprehendere potuit, vel quia Graecorum observatione forsan instructus est, quin-

---

[71] saeculo rudi et *Meurs*: sub caelo rudi et saeculo ω

---

[274] 8 BCE: cf. Suet. *Aug.* 31.2, Cassius Dio 55.6.6–7, Cens. 22.16

[275] Cf. Suet. *Dom.* 13.3, Plut. *Numa* 19.4.

[276] On the practice of effacing the memory of disgraced leaders (*damnatio memoriae*) see Hedrick 2000 and Flower 2006.

A plebiscite was adopted to the same end on the motion of Sextus Pacuvius, tribune of the plebs.[274]

36. 'The month of September has retained its original name, though Domitian assaulted it with the name "Germanicus," as he did October with his own name.[275] 37. But when it was decided that his ill-omened name be erased from every inscription in bronze or stone,[276] the months, too, were freed from the presumptuous grip of the tyrant's name: all emperors since then have exercised caution, wanting to avoid the foul omen's grim outcome, and retained the original names for the months from September to December.

38. 'This was the measure of the year set in order by Romulus, who, as I said above [§3], established that the year should be reckoned at ten months or 304 days, and arranged the months so that four of them had thirty-one days, while six had thirty. 39. But since that number matched neither the revolution of the sun nor the phases of the moon, it sometimes happened that the cold season fell out in the summer months and, conversely, the hot season in the winter months: when that happened, they let pass as many days—assigned to no particular month—as were needed to bring them to the time of year when the condition of the heavens matched the month they were in.[277]

'But Numa followed Romulus. With all the under- 13 standing he could muster, following his wits alone in an age still uncouth and unrefined—or perhaps because he learned from the Greeks[278]—he added fifty days,[279] ex-

---

[277] Cf. Plut. *Caes*. 59.1.

[278] Cf. Plut. *Numa* 1.2, on Numa's alleged friendship with Pythagoras.   [279] Cf. Cens. 20.4–5, Solin. 1.38.

quaginta dies addidit, ut in trecentos quinquaginta et quattuor dies quibus duodecim lunae cursus confici credidit annus extenderetur. 2. atque his quinquaginta diebus a se additis adiecit alios sex retractos illis sex mensibus qui triginta habebant dies, id est de singulis singulos, factosque quinquaginta et sex dies in duos novos menses pari ratione divisit. 3. ac de duobus priorem Ianuarium nuncupavit primumque anni esse voluit, tamquam bicipitis dei mensem, respicientem ac prospicientem transacti anni finem futurique principia; secundum dicavit Februo deo, qui lustrationum potens creditur. lustrari autem eo mense civitatem necesse erat, quo statuit ut iusta dis Manibus solverentur.

4. 'Numae ordinationem finitimi mox secuti totidem diebus totidemque mensibus ut Pompilio placuit annum suum computare coeperunt; sed hoc solo discrepabant, quod menses undetricenum tricenumque numero alternaverunt. 5. paulo post Numa in honorem imparis numeri, secretum hoc et ante Pythagoram parturiente natura, unum adiecit diem quem Ianuario dedit, ut tam in anno quam in mensibus singulis praeter unum Februarium impar numerus servaretur. nam quia duodecim menses, si singuli aut pari aut impari numero putarentur, consummationem parem facerent, unus pari numero institutus universam putationem imparem fecit. 6. Ianuarius igitur

---

280 Cf. Varro *Latin Language* 6.13 (~ *Ant. div.* lib. 16 fr. 231), identifying the Lupercalia (15 Feb.) as a rite of purification (*februatio*), sim. ibid. 6.34, Paul. Fest. p. 75.23–24, Plut. *Numa* 19.5, Cens. 22.13–14, John Lydus *On the Months* 4.25, cf. *FCRR* 76–78; according to Serv. on *G.* 1.43, Februus = the chthonian god Dis (cf. §7 below). On the various derivations of the name, see *LALE* 227.

tending the year to the 354 days he thought comprised twelve lunar cycles. 2. To these additional fifty days he added another six taken from the months that had thirty days—that is, one day from each—and divided the resulting fifty-six days into two months of equal length. 3. The first of these he named January and decided it should be the first month of the year, the month of the two-headed god, looking back to the end of the year past and ahead to the start of the year to come. The second he dedicated to the god Februus, who is believed to control rites of purification:[280] the community had to be purified in that month, when he determined that the Good Gods be paid the offerings due them.[281]

4. 'Rome's neighbors soon followed Numa's system and began to reckon their year as comprising the same number of months and days as Pompilius decided on, with one difference: they alternated the months of twenty-nine and thirty days.[282] 5. Numa soon added one day to January, paying honor to the mystery of the odd number that nature revealed even before Pythagoras:[283] as a result, both the year as a whole and the individual months (save February) had an odd number of days.[284] (If all twelve months had either an odd or even number of days, their total would be an even number; but arranging for one month to have an even number produced an odd-numbered total.) 6. So January,

---

[281] Cf. Varro *Latin Language* 6.34, Ov. *F.* 1.43–44; on the "Good Gods" (*Di Manes*), cf. 1.10.15n.   [282] Cf. John Lydus *On the Months* 3.10.   [283] Cf. Solin. 1.39, DServ. on *E.* 8.75 (citing Varro). Acc. to Arist. *Metaphysics* 1.5.5 986a and Plut. *Mor.* 288C, Pythagoreans regarded even as finite and female, odd as infinite and male.   [284] Cf. Cens. 20.4.

Aprilis Iunius Sextilis September November December undetricenis censebantur diebus et quintanas Nonas habebant, ac post Idus in omnibus a. d. septimum decimum Kalendas computabatur. 7. Martius vero Maius Quintilis et October dies tricenos singulos possidebant. Nonae in his septimanae erant similiterque post Idus decem septem dies in singulis usque ad sequentes Kalendas putabantur, sed solus Februarius viginti et octo retinuit dies quasi inferis et deminutio et par numerus conveniret. 8. cum ergo Romani ex hac distributione Pompilii ad lunae cursum sicut Graeci annum proprium computarent, necessario et intercalarem mensem instituerunt more Graecorum.

9. 'nam et Graeci cum animadverterent temere se trecentis quinquaginta quattuor diebus ordinasse annum—quoniam appareret de solis cursu, qui trecentis sexaginta quinque diebus et quadrante zodiacum conficit, deesse anno suo undecim dies et quadrantem—intercalares stata ratione commenti sunt, ita ut octavo quoque anno nonaginta dies, ex quibus tres menses tricenum dierum composuerunt, intercalarent. 10. id Graeci fecerunt, quoniam operosum erat atque difficile omnibus annis undecim dies et quadrantem intercalare. itaque maluerunt hunc numerum octies multiplicare et nonaginta dies, qui nascuntur si quadrans cum diebus undecim octies componatur, inserere in tres menses, ut diximus, distribuendos. hos dies

---

285 Cf. 1.14.7, Solin. 1.40, Serv. on *E.* 5.66 (= Porph. fr. 477 Smith, remarking the chthonian gods' preference for the even number), John Lydus *On the Months* 3.10, 4.64. On the month's association with the dead see 1.4.14n.

286 Cf. Plut. *Caes.* 59.2, Cens. 18.2, Solin. 1.42.

April, June, Sextilis, September, November, and December were counted as having twenty-nine days, with the Nones on the fifth and seventeen days between the Ides and the following Kalends. 7. But March, May, Quintilis, and October had thirty-one days each: in these the Nones were on the seventh and, again, there were seventeen days after the Ides to the following Kalends. Only February kept twenty-eight days, as though both the lesser number and its evenness were appropriate to the spirits of the dead.[285] 8. As a result of Pompilius' apportionment, then, the Romans reckoned their year according to a lunar calendar, like the Greeks, and so like the Greeks they had to begin to observe intercalary months.[286]

9. 'When the Greeks, too, noticed that they had rashly arranged the year in 354 days—for it was clear that their year was eleven and one quarter days shorter than the sun's course, which completes the cycle of the zodiac in 365¼ days—they came up with the intercalary months according to a regular system: every eight years they inserted ninety days, from which they made three months of thirty days each.[287] 10. The Greeks chose this system because it was burdensome and difficult to intercalate eleven and one quarter days every year: they preferred to multiply that number by eight and to insert ninety days (the product of adding eleven and one quarter days eight times), distributed, as I said, into three months. They called these

[287] Cf. Cens. 18.4, Solin. ibid. The days were not inserted all at once in the eighth year, as M. seems to imply, but in stages, by turns in the second, fifth, and eighth year and the third, sixth, and eighth year.

ὑπερβαίνοντας,[72] menses vero ἐμβολίμους appellita-
bant. 11. hunc ergo ordinem Romanis quoque imitari placuit, sed frustra, quippe fugit eos diem unum, sicut supra
admonuimus, additum a se ad Graecum numerum in honorem imparis numeri. ea re per octennium convenire numerus atque ordo non poterat. 12. sed nondum hoc errore
comperto per octo annos nonaginta quasi superfunden-
dos Graecorum exemplo computabant dies alternisque
annis binos et vicenos, alternis ternos vicenosque interca-
lantes expensabant intercalationibus quattuor. sed octavo
quoque anno intercalares octo affluebant dies ex singulis quibus vertentis anni numerum apud Romanos super
Graecum abundasse iam diximus.

13. 'Hoc quoque errore iam cognito haec species
emendationis inducta est. tertio quoque octennio ita inter-
calandos dispensabant dies ut non nonaginta sed sexaginta
sex intercalarent, compensatis viginti et quattuor diebus
pro illis qui per totidem annos supra Graecorum numerum creverant. 14. omni autem intercalationi mensis Februarius deputatus est quoniam is ultimus anni erat, quod
etiam ipsum de Graecorum imitatione faciebant. nam et
illi ultimo anni sui mensi superfluos interserebant dies,
ut refert Glaucippus, qui de sacris Atheniensium scripsit.
15. verum una re a Graecis differebant. nam illi confecto
ultimo mense, Romani non confecto Februario sed post
vicesimum et tertium diem eius intercalabant, Terminali-

---

[72] hyperballontas *Solin.*

---

[288] Cf. Solin. ibid., using the term *hyperballontas* = "excessive"; no Greek source attests either term in this connection.

days "transgressive" [*hyperbainontes*],[288] the months, "inserted" [*embolimoi*].[289] 11. The Romans also decided to imitate this arrangement—to no avail, since they overlooked the fact that they had added one day to the number chosen by the Greeks, in honor of the odd number, as I mentioned above [§5]. For that reason the number and arrangement of the days could not square with an eight-year cycle. 12. This error was not detected immediately, however: in eight year cycles they followed the Greek example of adding ninety "overflow" days, parceling out the total in four intercalations of, alternately, twenty-two and twenty-three days; but every eighth year there were eight intercalary days too many, because of the one day by which, as I've noted [§5], the Romans' yearly cycle exceeded the Greeks'.

13. 'When this error too was finally recognized, they corrected it in the following way. In every third eight-year period they parceled out not ninety but sixty-six intercalary days, to compensate for the twenty-four days by which they had exceeded the Greek model every twenty-four years. 14. February was set aside for the intercalation because it was the last month of the year, and in this too they imitated the Greeks, who also inserted the added days in the last month of the year, according to Glaucippus (no. 363 fr. 1 *FGrH*), who wrote on the rites of the Athenians.[290] 15. They departed from the Greeks in one respect, however: whereas the latter intercalated when the final month was over, the Romans intercalated after the twenty-third

---

[289] Cf. Hecataeus of Abdera (no. 264 *FGrH*) fr. 25.501, Solin. ibid., Hesych. E.2306.   [290] Cf. Varro *Latin Language* 6.13, Plut. *Numa* 18.2, Cens. 20.6.

bus scilicet iam peractis. deinde reliquos Februarii mensis dies, qui erant quinque, post intercalationem subiungebant, credo vetere religionis suae more, ut Februarium omni modo Martius consequeretur.

16. 'Sed cum saepe eveniret ut nundinae modo in anni principem diem, modo in Nonas caderent—utrumque autem perniciosum rei publicae putabatur—remedium quo hoc averteretur excogitatum est, quod aperiemus si prius ostenderimus cur nundinae vel primis Kalendis vel Nonis omnibus cavebantur. 17. nam quotiens incipiente anno dies coepit qui addictus est nundinis, omnis ille annus infaustis casibus luctuosus fuit, maximeque Lepidiano tumultu opinio ista firmata est. 18. Nonis autem conventus universae multitudinis vitandus existimabatur quoniam populus Romanus exactis etiam regibus diem hunc Nonarum maxime celebrabat quem natalem Servii Tullii existimabat: quia cum incertum esset quo mense Servius Tullius natus fuisset, Nonis tamen natum esse constaret, omnes Nonas celebri notitia frequentabant, veritos ergo qui diebus praeerant ne quid nundinis collecta universitas ob desiderium regis novaret, cavisse ut nonae a nundinis segregarentur. 19. unde dies ille quo abundare annum diximus eorum est permissus arbitrio qui fastis praeerant, uti cum vellent intercalaretur, dum modo eum in medio Terminaliorum vel mensis intercalaris ita locarent, ut a suspecto

---

291 The Terminalia honored Terminus, god of boundaries and boundary markers (*FCRR* 79–80). The account of intercalation is incorrect: a 27-day month called Interkalaris was added, sometimes after 23 February, sometimes after the 24th, and the remaining days of February were suppressed.

day of February, at the conclusion of the Terminalia. They then added on the last five days of February after the intercalary period, acting on the religious scruple of ancient custom, I think, so that March would follow on February no matter what.[291]

16. 'But when it often happened that a market day fell out, now on the first day of the year, now on a Nones—either occurrence being thought perilous for the commonwealth—a way was devised to avoid this: I'll reveal this remedy[292] after I've first made plain why a market day was avoided on the first Kalends of the year and on every Nones.[293] 17. Whenever a year began with a market day, dreadful calamities made the year one long period of mourning, a view that was especially corroborated during the sedition of Lepidus [78 BCE]. 18. As for the Nones, it was thought that the multitudes should avoid mass meetings then because after the kings were expelled, the Roman people particularly celebrated what they took to be Servius Tullius' birthday: because crowds notoriously thronged all the Nones—it being well-known that Servius was born on the Nones, though the exact month was uncertain—those in charge of the calendar were afraid that if the whole population gathered on a market day it might start to revolt out of yearning for the king, and so they took the precaution of keeping the Nones and market days distinct. 19. Accordingly, the day on which I've said the year "overflows" was entrusted to the judgment of those in charge of the calendar: they can insert it when they wish, provided they put it in the middle of the Terminalia or of the interca-

[291] See 1.16.28ff.
[293] Cf. Cass. Dio 48.33.4, John Lydus *On the Months* 4.10.

die celebritatem averteret nundinarum. atque hoc est quod quidam veterum rettulerunt non solum mensem apud Romanos verum etiam diem intercalarem fuisse.

20. 'Quando autem primum intercalatum sit varie refertur. et Macer quidem Licinius eius rei originem Romulo adsignat; Antias libro secundo Numam Pompilium sacrorum causa id invenisse contendit; Iunius Servium Tullium regem primum intercalasse commemorat, a quo et nundinas institutas Varroni placet. 21. Tuditanus[73] refert libro tertio magistratuum decem viros qui decem tabulis duas addiderunt de intercalando populum rogasse. Cassius eosdem scribit auctores, Fulvius autem id egisse M'. Acilium[74] consulem dicit ab urbe condita anno quingentesimo sexagesimo secundo, inito mox bello Aetolico. sed hoc arguit Varro scribendo antiquissimam legem fuisse incisam in columna aerea a L. Pinario et ⟨P.⟩[75] Furio consulibus, cui mensis[76] intercalaris adscribitur. haec de intercalandi principio satis relata sint.

14   'Verum fuit tempus cum propter superstitionem inter-

[73] Tuditanus W²S: tutidianus α, tutidanus β
[74] M'. Acilium *Jan*: marcium ω
[75] P. *addidi, om.* ω
[76] mensis *ed. Lips. 1774*: mentio ω

---

[294] The "overflow" day was the 355th day of the pre-Julian year, the one day by which the Roman calendar exceeded the Greek (§5). However, we hear nothing about any such adjustments for 1 January until after the Julian reform (52 BCE certainly started on the *nundinae*), and avoiding coincidence with the Nones would have been virtually impossible under either the pre-Julian or the reformed calendar.

lary month in a way that deflected the market day's crowds from the day that is a cause of concern.[294] This is why some of the ancients have said that the Romans had not just an intercalary month but also an intercalary day.

20. 'There are different accounts of when intercalation began. Licinius Macer actually attributes the beginning of the practice to Romulus (fr. 6); Antias contends (fr. 7) in his second book that Numa Pompilius devised it for the sake of religious rituals; Junius records that king Servius Tullius first performed intercalation (fr. 4 *IAH* 1:38 = fr. 9 *IAR*[6]), and Varro adds that he also instituted market days (*Ant. hum.* lib. 16 fr. 5). 21. In the third book of his *Magistracies* Tuditanus reports (fr. 7 *HRR* 1:146 = fr. 1 *IAR*[6]) that the Board of Ten, who added Two Tables to the original Ten,[295] put a motion concerning intercalation before the people. Cassius also writes (fr. 21) that the Board of Ten were responsible, but Fulvius[296] says that Manius Acilius did it in the 562nd year after the founding of the city,[297] at the start of the Aetolian War. But Varro refutes this idea, writing (ibid.) that a very ancient law to which an intercalary month is attributed was inscribed on a bronze column under the consuls Lucius Pinarius and ⟨Publius⟩ Furius [472 BCE]. Let this suffice as an account of the start of intercalation.

'There was, however, a time when intercalation was entirely neglected out of superstition, while sometimes the   14

---

[295] Cf. 1.4.19n.

[296] Cf. 1.12.16.

[297] Since Manius Acilius Glabrio was consul in 191 BCE, the Capitoline date (cf. 1.11.3n.) for the city's founding (752 BCE) is implied here.

calatio omnis omissa est, non numquam vero per gratiam sacerdotum, qui publicanis proferri vel imminui consulto anni dies volebant, modo auctio, modo retractio dierum proveniebat et sub specie observationis emergebat maior confusionis occasio. 2. sed postea C. Caesar omnem hanc inconstantiam temporum vagam adhuc et incertam in ordinem statae definitionis coegit, adnitente sibi M. Flavio scriba, qui scriptos dies singulos ita ad dictatorem retulit ut et ordo eorum inveniri facillime posset et invento certus status perseveraret. 3. ergo C. Caesar exordium novae ordinationis initurus dies omnes qui adhuc confusionem poterant facere consumpsit, eaque re factum est ut annus confusionis ultimus in quadringentos quadraginta tres dies protenderetur. post hoc imitatus Aegyptios, solos divinarum rerum omnium conscios, ad numerum solis, qui diebus trecentis sexaginta quinque et quadrante cursum conficit, annum dirigere contendit. 4. nam sicut lunaris annus mensis est, quia luna paulo minus quam mensem in zodiaci circumitione consumit, ita solis annus hoc dierum numero colligendus est quem peragit dum ad id signum se denuo vertit ex quo digressus est, unde annus vertens vo-

---

298 Cf. Cens. 20.7, Solin. 1.43. Lengthening the year would benefit the tax farmers, since their profit lay in collecting more taxes than the amount for which they had contracted (cf. Cassius Dio 54.21.5, on a provincial procurator who allegedly persuaded the Gauls that there were 14 months in the year for a similar purpose); the advantage of having it shortened presumably lay with the opportunity to begin collecting taxes again more quickly.

299 Cf. Cic. *On the Laws* 2.29.

300 Cf. Solin. 1.45.

301 Caesar is known to have relied on the help of mathematicians (Pliny *Natural History* 18.211), but this Flavius is otherwise unknown, and M.'s description of his contribution is unclear.

influence of the priests, who wanted the year to be longer or shorter to suit the tax farmers,[298] saw to it that the number of days in the year was now increased, now decreased, and under the cover of a scrupulous precision the opportunity for confusion increased.[299] 2. But Gaius Caesar took all this chronological inconsistency, which he found still ill-sorted and fluid, and reduced it to a regular and well-defined order;[300] in this he was assisted by the scribe Marcus Flavius, who presented a table of the individual days to Caesar in a form that allowed both their order to be determined and, once that was determined, their relative position to remain fixed.[301] 3. When he was on the point of starting this new arrangement, then, Gaius Caesar let pass all the days still capable of creating confusion: when that was done, the final year of confusion was extended to 443 days.[302] Then imitating the Egyptians, who alone know all things concerned with the divine, he undertook to reckon the year according to the sun, which completes its course in 365¼ days.[303] 4. For just as one month is a "year" for the moon—since the moon completes its circuit of the zodiac in a little under a month—so the solar year must be calculated according to the number of days the sun takes to return to the sign from which it began: that's why it's called the "turning year" and is considered

[302] 46 BCE, which had 445 days: the 27 days of the intercalary month were added, the last 4 days of February were suppressed (i.e., 355 + 27 − 4 = 378 days), and two more intercalary months totaling 67 days were added.   [303] Cf. Diod. Sic. 1.50.1–2, John Lydus *On the Months* 3.5. That the Egyptian calendar was neither solar nor composed of 365¼ days was known already to Herodotus (2.4.1); a leap day, bringing the year to 365¼, was first introduced by the Canopus Decree of 239 BCE (*OGIS* 56).

catur et habetur magnus, cum lunae annus brevis putetur.
5. horum Vergilius utrumque complexus est:

Interea magnum sol circumvolvitur annum.

hinc et Ateius Capito annum a circuitu temporis putat dictum, quia veteres "an" pro "circum" ponere solebant, ut
Cato in Originibus: "arator[77] an terminum," id est circum
terminum, et ambire dicitur pro circumire. 6. Iulius igitur
Caesar decem dies observationi veteri super adiecit, ut annum trecenti sexaginta quinque dies quibus sol zodiacum
lustrat efficerent, et ne quadrans deesset, statuit ut quarto
quoque anno sacerdotes qui curabant mensibus ac diebus unum intercalarent diem, eo scilicet mense ac loco
quo etiam apud veteres mensis intercalabatur id est ante
quinque ultimos Februarii mensis dies, idque bissextum
censuit nominandum. 7. dies autem decem quos ab eo additos diximus hac ordinatione distribuit. in Ianuarium et
Sextilem et Decembrem binos dies inseruit, in Aprilem
autem Iunium Septembrem Novembrem singulos; sed
neque mensi Februario addidit diem, ne deum inferum

---

[77] arator *Jan*: oratorum ω

---

[304] The conception of the sun's year as "great" relative to the
moon's "short year" is unique to this passage; in other conceptions
the "great year" is realized by the completion of a cycle comprising a certain number of solar years (there is no agreement on the
number): cf. Cic. *On the Commonwealth* 6.24, *On the Nature of
the Gods* 2.51–52, Tac. *Dialogue* 16.4–7, Aelian *Historical Miscellany* 10.7 (citing Oenopides), Cens. 18–19, Serv. on *A.* 1.269, M. at
Comm. 2.11.10–12.

"great,"[304] although the lunar "year" is thought to be short. 5. Virgil embraced both of these facts (*A. 3.284**):

> Meanwhile the sun rolls back around through the great year.

That's also why Ateius Capito thinks (fr. 17 *IAH* 2.1:277 = fr. 13 *IAR*[6]) the year [*annus*] is named after a temporal "cycle," because the ancients used to use *an* instead of *circum* ["around"], as Cato does in his *Origins* (fr. inc. 5)— "plow *an terminum*, that is, *circum terminum* ["around the boundary-marker"]—and as *ambire* is used instead of *circumire* ["to go around"]. 6. Julius Caesar, then, added ten days to the old practice, so that the 365 days in which the sun circles the zodiac would make a year; and to account for the one-quarter day, he ordained that the priests who attended to the months and days[305] would insert one day every fourth year, in the same month and place where the ancients used to intercalate a month, that is, before the last five days of February, and he decreed that it be called "the twice sixth."[306] 7. He distributed the ten days that I said he added in the following way: he added two days each to January, Sextilis, and December, and one day each to April, June, September and November; but he added no days to February, so that the religious observances offered

305 That is, the college of pontiffs, who had charge of the calendar among their other responsibilities: it was as chief pontiff (*pontifex maximus*) that Caesar undertook his reform.

306 I.e., it was added before 24 February (= the sixth day before 1 March, acc. to the Romans' inclusive reckoning) and so became the first of two days to count as the sixth day before the Kalends of March; cf. Cens. 20.10, John Lydus *On the Months* 3.7.

religio immutaretur, et Martio Maio Quintili Octobri servavit pristinum statum, quod satis pleno erant numero, id
est dierum singulorum tricenorumque. 8. ideo et septimanas habent Nonas, sicut Numa constituit, quia nihil in his
Iulius mutavit: sed Ianuarius Sextilis December, quibus
Caesar binos dies addidit, licet tricenos singulos habere
post Caesarem coeperint, quintanas tamen habent Nonas,
et ab Idibus illis sequentes Kalendae in[78] undevicesimum
revertuntur, quia Caesar quos addidit dies neque ante
Nonas neque ante Idus inserere voluit, ne Nonarum aut
Iduum religionem, quae stato erat die, novella comperen-
dinatione corrumperet. 9. sed nec post Idus mox voluit inserere, ne feriarum quarumque violaretur indictio, sed peractis cuiusque mensis feriis locum diebus advenis fecit. et
Ianuario quidem dies quos dicimus quartum et tertium
Kalendas Februarias dedit, Aprili sextum Kalendas Maias,
Iunio tertium Kalendas Iulias, Augusto quartum et ter-
tium Kalendas Septembres, Septembri tertium Kalendas
Octobres, Novembri tertium Kalendas Decembres, Decembri vero quartum et tertium Kalendas Ianuarias.

10. 'Ita factum est ut cum omnes hi menses, quibus dies

---

[78] in H², *om.* ω

---

[307] Cf. 1.13.3, John Lydus *On the Months* 3.10, 4.64.

[308] Cf. Cens. 20.9.

[309] Or rather Romulus before him: 1.12.3.

[310] Since the festivals concerned were *stativae*, not *conceptivae* or *imperativae* (cf. 1.16.6), it must have been the custom to
announce them as occurring a specific number of days after the
Ides.

[311] This was after the Parilia (21 April) and Robigalia (25

to the gods of the dead would not be changed[307] and did not change the original status of March, May, Quintilis, and October, because the thirty-one days each had was a sufficiently full complement.[308] 8. They also have their Nones on the seventh, as Numa ordained,[309] because Julius changed nothing about them. As for January, Sextilis, and December, they still have their Nones on the fifth, though they began to have thirty-one days after Caesar added two days to each, and it is nineteen days from their Ides to the following Kalends, because in adding the two days Caesar did not want to insert them before either the Nones or the Ides, lest an unprecedented postponement mar religious observance associated with the Nones or Ides themselves, which have a fixed date. 9. But neither did he want to insert the days soon after the Ides and thereby interfere with the declaration of any religious festival;[310] instead, he made room for the new days after the completion of each month's festivals. Thus he gave to January the days we call the fourth and third before the Kalends of February [= January 29–30]; to April, the sixth before the Kalends of May [= April 26];[311] to June, the third day before the Kalends of July [= June 29]; to August, the third and fourth days before the Kalends of September [= August 29–30]; to September, the third day before the Kalends of October [= September 29]; to November, the third day before the Kalends of December [= November 29]; and to December, the third and fourth days before the Kalends of January [= December 29–30].

10. 'Thus it happened that whereas all the months that

April) but, necessarily, before the Floralia, which before Caesar's reform began on 28 April and continued into May.

addidit, ante hanc ordinationem habuissent mensis sequentis Kalendas ad septimum decimum revertentes, postea ex augmento additorum dierum hi qui duos acceperunt ad nonum decimum, qui vero unum, ad octavum decimum haberent reditum Kalendarum. 11. feriarum tamen cuiusque mensis ordo servatus est. nam si cui fere tertius ab Idibus dies festus aut feriatus fuit et tunc a. d. sextum decimum dicebatur, etiam post augmentum dierum eadem religio servata est, ut tertio ab Idibus die celebraretur, licet ab incremento non iam a. d. sextum decimum Kalendas sed a. d. septimum decimum, si unus, aut a. d. octavum decimum,[79] si duo sunt additi, diceretur. 12. nam ideo novos dies circa finem cuiusque mensis inseruit, ubi finem omnium quae in mense erant repperit feriarum, adiectosque omnes a se dies fastos notavit, ut maiorem daret actionibus libertatem, et non solum nullum nefastum sed nec comitialem quemquam de adiectis diebus instituit, ne ambitionem magistratuum augeret adiectio. 13. sic annum civilem Caesar habitis ad limam dimensionibus constitutum edicto palam posito publicavit, et [error][80] hucusque stare potuisset, ni sacerdotes sibi errorem novum ex ipsa emendatione fecissent. nam cum opor-

---

[79] decimum P, *om.* ω   [80] error *secl. Eyss.*

---

[312] Cf. John Lydus *On the Months* 3.10.

[313] For the distinction between "festive days" and "days of religious observance," see 1.11.50n.   [314] A voting assembly (*comitia*) could be held only on a day specifically designated for it (*dies comitialis*); comitial days and "days of ordinary legal business" (*dies fasti*) were mutually exclusive. The ref. to magistrates' "ambition" presumably concerns their use of *comitia* to further

gained days had had seventeen days between their Ides and the following Kalends before the change, those that gained two days subsequently had nineteen days between their Ides and next Kalends and those that gained one day had eighteen days between Ides and Kalends.[312] 11. Yet each month kept its system of religious festivals intact: for if any month had (say) the third day after the Ides as a festive day or day of religious observance[313]—that is, the sixteenth day before the Kalends, as it was called then—the religious scruple attaching to the day was preserved even after the number of days was increased: it was still celebrated on the third day after the Ides, even though it was no longer said to be the sixteenth day before the Kalends, because of the increase, but either the seventeenth day (if one day was added) or the eighteenth day (if two were added). 12. That's why he inserted the new days toward the end of every month, where he found the end of all of the month's religious observances, and he designated all the days he inserted as days of ordinary legal business, to increase the opportunity to conduct legal proceedings; and not only was none of the new days a day of religious observance, none was even eligible for a voting assembly, because he did not want the added days to increase magistrates' ambition.[314] 13. When the precise calculations that had been made placed the civil year on a firm footing, Caesar published it with a decree that was publicly posted, and it would have continued in that form down to the present day, if the priests had not introduced a new error in the course of their corrections. For though they were sup-

legislative agenda; electoral *comitia* were already confined to a limited period in the middle of the year.

teret diem qui ex quadrantibus confit quarto quoque anno
confecto antequam quintus inciperet intercalare, illi quarto non peracto sed incipiente intercalabant. 14. hic error
sex et triginta annis permansit, quibus annis intercalati
sunt dies duodecim cum debuerint intercalari novem. sed
hunc quoque errorem sero deprehensum correxit Augustus, qui annos duodecim sine intercalari die transigi iussit,
ut illi tres dies qui per annos triginta et sex vitio sacerdota-
lis festinationis excreverant sequentibus annis duodecim
nullo die intercalato devorarentur. 15. post hoc unum
diem secundum ordinationem Caesaris quinto quoque incipiente anno intercalari iussit et omnem hunc ordinem
aereae tabulae ad aeternam custodiam incisione manda-
vit.'

15   Tunc Horus, 'dies quidem hic,' inquit, 'intercalaris antequam quintus annus incipiat inserendus cum Aegypti
matris artium ratione consentit. sed nihil in illorum mensibus explicandis videtur operosum, quos tricenum dierum
omnes habent, eoque explicitis duodecim mensibus id est
trecentis sexaginta diebus exactis tunc inter Augustum
atque Septembrem reliquos quinque dies anno suo red-
dunt, adnectentes quarto quoque anno exacto intercalarem, qui ex quadrantibus confit. 2. at hic non a primo in ultimum mensis diem ad incrementum continuum numerus
accedit, sed post Kalendas dirigitur in Nonas: inde ad
quasdam Idus deflecti audio, post rursus ni fallor, immo ut
nunc quoque rettulisti, in sequentes Kalendas. 3. quae omnia quid sibi velint scire equidem vellem. nam illud nec

315 Cf. Solin. 1.46; on the problem, Brind'Amour 1983, 11–15.
316 I.e., because the extra day was in effect being intercalated
every third year, not every fourth.   317 Cf. Solin. 1.47.

posed to insert the day that made good the four quarters at the completion of every fourth year, before the fifth began, they were intercalating not at the end of the fourth year but at the beginning.[315] 14. This error continued for thirty-six years, in the course of which twelve days were intercalated instead of the nine that were needed.[316] But though it was caught only late, the error was corrected by Augustus, who ordered that twelve years pass without an intercalated day, so that the three excess days the priests' hasty error had produced over those thirty-six years would be swallowed up when no days were intercalated during the next twelve.[317] 15. After that, he ordered that one day be intercalated at the start of every fifth year, as Caesar ordained, and he ordered that the whole system be inscribed on a bronze tablet and so be preserved forever.'

Then Horus said, 'Inserting the intercalary day before the fifth year begins is in line with the system of Egypt, the mother of all crafts. But the Egyptians have no difficulty sorting out the months: all their months are thirty days long, and so when the sequence of months is finished—360 days having passed—they make the year complete by adding five days between August and September; then after four years have passed they add the intercalary day that comprises the four quarters. 2. But in Rome the days of the month are not counted from first to last in a steadily rising sequence; instead, after the Kalends they're reckoned relative to the Nones, then I gather the reckoning is shifted to something called the "Ides," and after that, if I'm not mistaken—or rather, as you just now said—to the following Kalends. 3. For my part, I'd like to know what that's all about; then too, I haven't a hope of understanding the la-

consequi posse me spero, ut vocabula comprehendam quae singulis apud vos diebus adduntur, dum alios fastos variisque alios nominibus nuncupatis. nundinas quoque vestras nescire me fateor, de quibus observatio tam diligens, tam cauta narratur. haec nec mihi erubescendum est ignorare peregrino, a te vero, Praetextate, discere nec civem puderet.'

4. Tunc Praetextatus 'non solum tibi,' inquit, 'Hore, cum sis Aegypto oriundus, sed ne nobis quidem quibus origo Romana est erubescendum puto quaerere quod quaesitu dignum omnes veteres putaverunt. nam de Kalendis Nonis et Idibus deque feriarum variis observationibus innumeros auctores cura quaestionis exercuit, et ideo nos quae de his ab omnibus dicta sunt in unum breviter collegimus.[81] 5. Romulus cum ingenio acri quidem sed agresti statum proprii ordinaret imperii, initium cuiusque mensis ex illo sumebat die quo novam lunam contigisset videri. 6. quia non continuo evenit ut eodem die semper appareat, sed modo tardius, modo celerius ex certis causis videri solet, contigit ut cum tardius apparuit, praecedenti mensi plures dies aut cum celerius, pauciores darentur, et singulis quibusque mensibus perpetuam numeri legem primus casus addixit. sic factum est ut alii triginta et unum, alii undetriginta sortirentur dies. 7. omnibus tamen mensibus ex die Nonarum Idus nono die repraesentari placuit, et inter Idus ac sequentes Kalendas constitutum est sedecim dies esse numerandos. ideo mensis uberior duos illos quibus augebatur dies inter Kalendas suas et Nonas habe-

---

[81] collegimus *Disp. Chori*: collig-ω

---

[318] Cf. John Lydus *On the Months* 3.10.

bels that you give to individual days, calling some "days for legal business" [*fasti*] and giving other names to others. I also confess that I don't understand your "market days" [*nundinae*], which as you tell it are observed with such wary precision. Ignorance of these matters need not cause me to blush, foreigner that I am, nor would it shame a citizen, Praetextatus, to learn of them from you.'

4. Then Praetextatus said, 'Not just you, Horus, who come from Egypt, but those of us, too, whose roots are Roman need not blush to ask about a topic that the ancients always thought worthy of inquiry. In fact, careful inquiry about the Kalends, Nones, and Ides and about the varied observances of religious holidays has kept countless authorities busy: I've therefore pulled together what they've all said into one brief account. 5. When Romulus was organizing his realm—with wits that were sharp, to be sure, but unrefined—he had every month begin with the day that coincided with the new moon. 6. Since that does not inevitably fall out on the same day but appears now later, now sooner, for specific reasons,[318] it happened that he gave more days to the preceding month when the new moon appeared later, or fewer when it appeared sooner, and that first occurrence permanently fixed the lawful number of days for each month: that's how it happened that some were allotted thirty-one days, others twenty-nine. 7. But he decided to mark the Ides on the ninth day[319] from the Nones every month, and to establish an interval of sixteen days between the Ides and the following Kalends. A longer month therefore had its two extra days between the Kalends and the Nones: that's why the fifth

[319] Ninth day reckoned inclusively, in the Roman manner (cf. 1.3.10n.): we would say "eighth day."

bat. hinc aliis quintus a Kalendis dies, aliis septimus Nonas
facit. 8. Caesar tamen, ut supra diximus, stata sacra custo-
diens nec in illis mensibus quibus binos adiecit dies ordinem voluit mutare Nonarum, quia peractis totius mensis
feriis dies suos rei divinae cautus inseruit. 9. priscis ergo
temporibus, antequam fasti a Cn. Flavio scriba invitis patribus in omnium notitiam proderentur, pontifici minori
haec provincia delegabatur, ut novae lunae primum ob-
servaret aspectum visamque regi sacrificulo nuntiaret.
10. itaque sacrificio a rege et minore pontifice celebrato
idem pontifex calata, id est vocata, in Capitolium plebe
iuxta curiam Calabram, quae casae Romuli proxima est,
quot numero dies a Kalendis ad Nonas superessent pro-
nuntiabat, et quintanas quidem dicto quinquies verbo
calo, septimanas repetito septies praedicabat. 11. verbum
autem calo[82] Graecum est, id est voco, et hunc diem, qui ex
his diebus qui calarentur primus esset, placuit Kalendas
vocari. hinc et ipsi curiae ad quam vocabantur Calabrae
nomen datum est, et classi, quod omnis in eam populus vo-

[82] calo . . . calo *Timpanaro*: καλῶ . . . καλῶ ω

---

[320] Cf. 1.14.8–9   [321] But with the support of Appius Claudius Caecus (304 BCE): on Cn. Flavius cf. Piso fr. 30, Licin. Macer
fr. 19, Cic. *Speech on Behalf of Murena* 25, *Att.* 6.1.8, Livy 9.46,
Val. Max. 2.5.2, Pliny *Natural History* 33.17, with *MRR* 1:168 n. 1,
3:92.   [322] Lit. "king who performs the sacrifice" (*rex sacri-
ficulus*, also called *rex sacrorum*), the title given to the priest who
performed the sacrifices that had been the kings' responsibility
before the monarchy was overthrown.   [323] The original hut
of Romulus was scrupulously preserved on the Palatine until late
antiquity; the house here mentioned was a duplicate built in the
precinct of Jupiter Optimus Maximus on the Capitoline: cf. *LTUR*

178

day from the Kalends marks the Nones in some months, the seventh day in others. 8. However, as I said previously,[320] Caesar was careful to preserve the existing system of religious observances and did not want to change the regular location of the Nones in the months to which he added two days: taking careful account of sacred practice he inserted those days after all the holy days of the month had been observed. 9. In earliest times, then, before the scribe Gnaius Flavius made knowledge of the calendar available to all, against the senate's wishes,[321] it was a lesser pontiff's duty to watch for the first appearance of the new moon and to report the sighting to the priest in charge of sacrifices.[322] 10. And so the latter, after performing the sacrifice with the lesser pontiff, called [*calata*]—which is to say, summoned—the common people to the Capitoline near the *curia Calabra*, close to the house of Romulus,[323] and announced how many days remained from the Kalends to the Nones, repeating the verb *calo* five times if the Nones fell on the fifth, seven times if it fell on the seventh.[324] 11. The verb *calo* is Greek, meaning "I call" [=καλῶ], and it was decided that the first of the days "called" should be named the Kalends.[325] For this reason, too, the assembly hall [*curia*] to which the people were called was itself named the *Calabra*, as was the assembly [*classis*], because the entire citizen body was called to it.

1: 241 and, on the meeting place called the *curia Calabra*, ibid. 330.   [324] Cf. Varro *Latin Language* 6.27 (with different detail), (D)Serv. on *A.* 8.654.

[325] Cf. Varro and (D)Serv. ibid., Varro *On the Way of Life of the Roman People* fr. 18, Paul. Fest. p. 251.25–26, Plut. *Mor.* 269C, John Lydus 3.10, *LALE* 321.

caretur. 12. ideo autem minor pontifex numerum dierum qui ad Nonas superesset calando prodebat, quod post novam lunam oportebat Nonarum die populares qui in agris essent confluere in urbem accepturos causas feriarum a rege sacrorum sciturosque quid esset eo mense faciendum. 13. unde quidam hinc Nonas aestimant dictas quasi novae initium observationis, vel quod ab eo die semper ad Idus novem dies putentur, sicut apud Tuscos Nonae plures habebantur, quod hi nono quoque die regem suum salutabant et de propriis negotiis consulebant.

14. ʾIduum porro nomen a Tuscis, apud quos is dies Itis vocatur, sumptum est. Item autem illi interpretantur Iovis fiduciam. nam cum Iovem accipiamus lucis auctorem (unde et Lucetium Salii in carminibus canunt) et Cretenses Δία τὴν ἡμέραν vocant, ipsi quoque Romani Diespitrem appellant ut diei patrem, 15. iure hic dies Iovis fiducia vocatur, cuius lux non finitur cum solis occasu sed splendorem diei et nocte continuat inlustrante luna, quod semper in plenilunio id est medio mense fieri solet. diem igitur, qui vel nocturnis caret tenebris, Iovis fiduciam Tusco nomine vocaverunt, unde et omnes Idus Iovis ferias observandas sanxit antiquitas. 16. alii putant Idus, quod ea die plena luna videatur, a videndo "vidus" appellatas, mox

---

326 Cf. John Lydus ibid.

327 The second etymology is correct: the Nones was the ninth (*nonus*) day before the Ides, the interval between them being a *nundinae* (§7 above); cf. *LALE* 414.

328 Cf. Varro *Latin Language* 6.28, Plut. *Mor.* 269D. The etymology of *Idus* is in fact obscure; the explanations canvassed in §§16–17 are all fanciful. Cf. *LALE* 292.

12. The lesser pontiff revealed the number of days remaining to the Nones by "calling" because after the new moon[326] citizens in the countryside were obliged to gather in the city on the Nones, to receive an account of the month's holy days from the priest in charge of sacrifices and to find out what they had to do in the course of the month. 13. Hence some think that the Nones got its name as the start of a new [*nova*] process of ritual observance, or because nine [*novem*] days are always reckoned from it to the Ides,[327] just as the Etruscans used to observe several Nones, because they greeted their king every ninth [*nonus*] day and sought his advice on their personal affairs.

14. The name of the Ides was taken from the Etruscans, who call that day Itis,[328] which they take to mean "Jupiter's surety." For we regard Jupiter as the source of light [*lux*]—hence the Salii sing of him as "Lucetius" in their hymns[329]—and the Cretans call the day "Zeus," while the Romans themselves call him Diespiter, as father [*pater*] of the day [*dies*]:[330] 15. this day is rightly called "Jupiter's surety," then, because its light does not end with sunset but extends the day's brilliance into the night thanks to the moonlight, since the day usually coincides with the full moon, that is, with the middle of the month. So to the day that lacks even the darkness of night they gave the Etruscan name "Jupiter's surety," and from that arose the ancient provision that every Ides should be observed as Jupiter's holy day. 16. Others think that because the moon then appears full, the Ides [*Idus*] was named "Vidus" from "vi-

---

[329] Cf. fr. 2 *FPL*[3] (*Leucesie*), Paul. Fest. p. 102.4–5, Gell. 5.12.6; on the Salii, 1.9.14n.   [330] Cf. Varro *Latin Language* 5.66, Gell. 5.12.5, Serv. on *A.* 9.567, *LALE* 187–88.

litteram v detractam, sicut contra, quod Graeci ἰδεῖν dicunt, nos v littera addita "videre" dicimus. non nullis placet Idus dictas vocabulo Graeco, οἷον ἀπὸ τοῦ εἴδους, quod eo die plenam speciem luna demonstret. sunt qui aestiment Idus ab ove iduli dictas, quam hoc nomine vocant Tusci et omnibus Idibus Iovi immolatur a flamine. 17. nobis illa ratio nominis vero propior aestimatur, ut Idus vocemus diem qui dividit mensem. "iduare" enim Etrusca lingua "dividere" est, unde "vidua" quasi "valde idua" id est "valde divisa," aut "vidua" id est "a viro divisa." 18. ut autem Idus omnes Iovi, ita omnes Kalendas Iunoni tributas et Varronis et pontificalis adfirmat auctoritas. quod etiam Laurentes patriis religionibus servant, qui et cognomen deae ex caerimoniis addiderunt, Kalendarem Iunonem vocantes, sed et omnibus Kalendis a mense Martio ad Decembrem huic deae [Kalendarum die][83] supplicant. 19. Romae quoque Kalendis omnibus, praeter quod pontifex minor in curia Calabra rem divinam Iunoni facit, etiam regina sacrorum, id est regis uxor, porcam vel agnam in regia Iunoni immolat. a qua etiam Ianum Iunonium cognominatum diximus, quod illi deo omnis ingressus, huic deae cuncti Kalendarum dies videntur adscripti. 20. cum enim initia mensium maiores nostri ab exortu lunae servaverint, iure Iunoni ad-

---

[83] Kalendarum die *seclusi*

---

[331] Cf. Plut. ibid., John Lydus *On the Months* 3.10.

[332] Cf. Paul. Fest. p. 93.3; the flamen of Jupiter (*flamen Dialis*) was one of the major *flamines*, cf. 1.10.15n.

[333] Cf. Ov. *F.* 1.55–56, John Lydus *On the Months* ibid.

[334] Cf. §9 n. above.   [335] Cf. 1.9.16

[336] Since M. has said that the Ides usually coincides with the full moon (§15), he should mean to say that the Kalends coincides,

sion" [*videre*], the letter v being subsequently lost, just as, conversely, the Greeks say *idein* ["to see"] whereas we say *videre*, with the letter "v" added. Some judge that Ides is Greek by origin, as though from *eidos* ["form"], because on that day the moon displays its form completely.[331] There are those who judge that the Ides is named after the Ides-sheep [*ovis Idulis*], so called by the Etruscans, which is sacrificed to Jupiter by his flamen every Ides.[332] 17. I judge the following explanation to be closer to the truth: we call the day that separates the month into two parts the Ides because *iduare* in Etruscan means "to separate," whence our "widow" [*vidua*], as though from *valde idua*, that is, "very separated," or else "widow" as though "separated from a husband" [*a viro divisa*]. 18. That every Ides is dedicated to Jupiter, just as every Kalends is dedicated to Juno,[333] is corroborated by the authority of both Varro (*Ant. hum.* lib. 16 fr. 8) and the pontiffs. The people of Laurentum also have that among their ancestral religious customs and give the goddess a surname based on the practice, calling her "Juno of the Kalends"; they also offer supplication to this goddess on every Kalends from March to December. 19. At Rome, too, on every Kalends not only does the lesser pontiff sacrifice to Juno in the *curia Calabra*, but the "queen of sacrifices"—that is, the wife of the priest in charge of sacrifices[334]—offers a sow or a ewe to Juno in the Regia. As I've already noted,[335] Janus received the surname "Junonian" from her, because he has authority over all entry-ways, she over all Kalends. 20. For since our ancestors marked the months' beginnings from the rising of the moon,[336] they rightly dedicated the Kalends

not with the moon's "rising" (*exortus*), but with the new moon (or, more strictly, conjunction).

dixerunt Kalendas, lunam ac Iunonem eandem putantes: vel quia luna per aerem meat, unde et Graeci lunam Ἄρτεμιν nuncuparunt id est ἀερότομιν, quod aera secat, Iuno autem aeris arbitra est, merito initia mensium, id est Kalendas, huic deae consecraverunt.

21. 'Nec hoc praetermiserim, quod nuptiis copulandis Kalendas Nonas et Idus religiosas, id est devitandas, censuerunt. hi enim dies praeter Nonas feriati sunt, feriis autem vim cuiquam fieri piaculare est: ideo tunc vitantur nuptiae, in quibus vis fieri virgini videtur. sed Verrium Flaccum iuris pontificii peritissimum dicere solitum refert Varro quia feriis tergere veteres fossas liceret, novas facere ius non esset, ideo magis viduis quam virginibus idoneas esse ferias ad nubendum. 22. subiciet aliquis: cur ergo Nonis, si feriatus dies non est, prohibetur celebritas nuptiarum? huius quoque rei in aperto causa est. nam quia primus nuptiarum dies verecundiae datur, postridie autem nuptam in domo viri dominium incipere oportet adipisci et

---

337 Cf. Varro *Latin Language* 5.69, Cic. *On the Nature of the Gods* 2.68, Ov. *F.* 1.55, John Lydus *On the Months* 3.10, 13.

338 Cf. Clem. Alex. *Stromata* 5.6.37, Porph. *On Statues* 8, *Homeric Questions* on *Il.* 20.67ff, John Lydus *On the Months* 2.2, Σ D on *Il.* 20.74, *Etym. Gud.* A p. 207, Eustath. *Comm. Il.* 4:371, *Etym. Mag.* p. 150.13.

339 Cf. *Comm.* 1.17.15, Cic. *On the Nature of the Gods* 2.66, Minuc. Fel. *Octavius* 19.10 (= Zeno fr. 169 *SVF* 1:43), Firm. Matern. *On the Error of Profane Religions* 4.1, Arnob. 3.30.2, Porph. ibid., Aug. *City of God* 4.10, Serv. on *G.* 2.325, *A.* 1.47, 71, 78, 4.122, 4.166, 7.311, 8.454, 12.139, DServ. on *A.* 2.296, 4.167. The equation of Hera/Juno with the air goes back to the Presocratics (Empedocles fr. 23 D.-K.).

340 Cf. Paul. Fest. p. 187.3–6, Plut. *Mor.* 289A-B.

to Juno, whom they identified with the moon;[337] or because the moon travels through the air (hence the Greeks called the moon Artemis, that is *aerotomis*, because she cuts through the air[338]), and Juno is the mistress of the air,[339] they rightly dedicated the months' beginnings, that is, the Kalends, to this goddess.

21. 'I would not want to omit the fact that the ancients judged the Kalends, Nones, and Ides taboo for forming the marriage bond, and to be avoided.[340] Except for the Nones, these are days of religious observance [*feriae*], and on all such days inflicting violence on anyone is a wrong demanding expiation: hence they are avoided as wedding days, when the maiden appears to suffer violence. But Varro reports that Verrius Flaccus, a most accomplished scholar of pontifical law, used to say that since it was permitted to clean out old drainage ditches on days of religious observance, but wrong to create new ones, such days were suited more to the weddings of widows than to the weddings of maidens.[341] 22. Someone will interject: why then are weddings banned on the Nones, if it's not a day of religious observance? The reason is plain. The first day of marriage is given over to matters of modesty,[342] whereas on the following day the bride must begin to exercise her authority in her husband's household and offer sacrifice.

[341] It is possible but very unlikely that Varro (d. 27 BCE) cited Verrius Flaccus (b. ca. 55 BCE) as an authority (cf. Kaster 1995, 342–43); more likely that the names were reversed by M. or his source, or that "Varro and Verrius Flaccus report . . . " became "Varro reports that Verrius Flaccus . . ." (a suggestion I owe to Alan Cameron).   [342] A euphemism that offers a sidelong glance at the sexual consummation of the marriage.

rem facere divinam, omnes autem postriduani dies seu post Kalendas sive post Nonas Idusve ex aequo atri sunt, ideo et Nonas inhabiles nuptiis esse dixerunt, ne nupta aut postero die libertatem auspicaretur uxoriam aut atro immolaret, quo nefas est sacra celebrari.

16 'Sed quia nos ad commemorationem dierum ordo deduxit, de hoc quoque quod Hori nostri consultatio continet pauca dicenda sunt. 2. Numa ut in menses annum, ita in dies mensem quemque distribuit, diesque omnes aut festos aut profestos aut intercisos vocavit. festi dis dicati sunt, profesti hominibus ob administrandam rem privatam publicamque concessi, intercisi deorum hominumque communes sunt. 3. festis insunt sacrificia epulae ludi feriae, profestis fasti comitiales comperendini stati proeliares. intercisi in se non in alia dividuntur: illorum enim dierum quibusdam horis fas est, quibusdam fas non est ius dicere. nam cum hostia caeditur fari nefas est, inter caesa et porrecta fari licet, rursus, cum adoletur non licet. ergo de divisione festorum et profestorum dierum latius disserendum est.

4. 'Sacra celebritas est vel cum sacrificia dis offeruntur vel cum dies divinis epulationibus celebratur vel cum ludi in honorem aguntur deorum vel cum feriae observantur.

---

343 Cf. 1.16. 21ff.   344 Cf. Varro *Latin Language* 6.31.

345 The "split days" (*dies intercisi = dies endotercisi*, marked "EN" on inscribed calendars) were 10 and 14 Jan., 16 and 26 Feb., 13 March, 22 Aug., 14 Oct., 12 Dec.

346 I.e., for the praetor to speak the three words, specified in §14 below, that are the essence of legal procedure.

347 "Between the slaying and the offering" was a proverbial expression = "at the last minute": cf. Cic. *Att*. 5.18.1, Otto 63–64.

But all days that follow the Kalends, Nones, or Ides are equally ill-omened,[343] and that's why they declared the Nones unsuitable for weddings: so that the bride would not either inaugurate her matronly privileges on the following day or offer sacrifice on an ill-omened day when it is against divine law for religious rites to be celebrated.

'But since the sequence I am following has brought me 16 to mention specific days, I should say a few words on the subject our friend Horus asked about. 2. As Numa apportioned the year into months, so he apportioned each month into days and designated all days as either religious [*festi*] or ordinary [*profesti*] or split [*intercisi*]. Religious days were dedicated to the gods, ordinary days were granted for people to take care of personal or public business, and split days were shared by the gods and human beings.[344] 3. On religious days there are sacrifices, religious feasts, games, and holidays; among ordinary days there are days for legal business, assembly days, days for resuming trials, appointed days, and days for battle; split days are not split for other activities but are internally divided, so that during some hours it is consistent with divine law to pronounce judgment, but during other hours it is not.[345] For when the victim is being slain, it is against divine law to speak,[346] but between the slaying and the offering[347] it is permitted, and then again it is forbidden when the offering is being burned. I should, then, explain at greater length the distinction between religious and ordinary days.

4. 'A sacred occasion is celebrated either when sacrifices are offered to the gods or when a day is marked by feasts for the gods or when games are staged in honor of the gods or when a holy festival is observed.

5. feriarum autem publicarum genera sunt quattuor. aut enim stativae sunt aut conceptivae aut imperativae aut nundinae. 6. et sunt stativae universi populi communes certis et constitutis diebus ac mensibus et in fastis statis observationibus adnotatae, in quibus praecipue servantur Agonalia Carmentalia Lupercalia. conceptivae sunt quae quotannis a magistratibus vel a sacerdotibus concipiuntur in dies vel certos vel etiam incertos ut sunt Latinae Sementivae Paganalia Compitalia. imperativae sunt quas consules vel praetores pro arbitrio potestatis indicunt. nundinae sunt paganorum itemque rusticorum, quibus conveniunt negotiis propriis vel mercibus provisuri. 7. sunt praeterea feriae propriae familiarum, ut familiae Claudiae vel Aemiliae seu Iuliae sive Corneliae et si quas ferias proprias quaeque familia ex usu domesticae celebritatis observat. 8. sunt singulorum, uti natalium fulgurumque susceptiones, item funerum atque expiationum. apud veteres quoque qui nominasset Salutem Semoniam Seiam Sege-

---

348 "Held every ninth day" = *nundinae*, otherwise translated here as "market day."

349 On the terminology of the fixed festivals cf. Varro *Latin Language* 6.12–24, Paul. Fest. p. 466.22–23. The Carmentalia, in honor of the prophetic nymph Carmenta or Carmentis (cf. 1.5.1n.), was observed on 11 and 15 Jan. On the Agonalia, cf. 1.4.7n.; on the Lupercalia, 1.13.3n.

350 On the terminology of the moveable festivals cf. Varro *Latin Language* 6.25–26. The Latin festival was celebrated, usually early in the year, by the consuls at the sanctuary of "Jupiter of the Latins" (*Iuppiter Latiaris*) in the Alban Hills 20 km SE of Rome (*FCRR* 111–15). Sementivae (< *semen*) and Paganalia (or Paganicae—Varro *Latin Language* 6.24, 26—from *pagus*, "rural district") may or may not have been two terms applied to the same

5. There are, moreover, four kinds of such public festivals: they are either fixed, or movable, or commanded, or held every ninth day.[348] 6. Fixed festivals are those celebrated by all the people together, with the month and day specifically established and the festival marked for fixed observance on the calendar: chief among these are the Agonalia, Carmentalia, and Lupercalia.[349] Movable feasts are those proclaimed from year to year by magistrates or priests for either specific or variable dates, like the Latin festival, the Sementivae, the Paganalia, and the Compitalia.[350] Commanded festivals are those that the consuls or praetors declare in accordance with their judgment and authority as magistrates.[351] The festivals held every ninth day provide the opportunities for the country folk and peasants[352] to gather for purposes of trade or to see to their personal affairs. 7. There are, besides, religious festivals that belong to specific clans, like Claudian or Aemilian or Julian or Cornelian festivals and any others that a given clan keeps as a consequence of its own domestic observances. 8. There are holidays proper to individuals, to mark birthdays or lightning strokes,[353] and similarly funerals and acts of expiation. Among the ancients, too, anyone who spoke the name of Salus, Semonia, Seia, Segetia, or

festival of sowing, also held early in the year (cf. Ov. *F.* 1.657ff. at 669–70 vs. Varro ibid.). On the Compitalia, cf. 1.4.27n.

[351] I.e., as celebratory or expiatory occasions.

[352] On the two terms M. uses here—*pagani* and *rustici*—see Introd. §1 ad fin.   [353] Unless it anticipates the *flaminica*'s response to thunder (noted end of next sentence), this perhaps refers to the private thanksgiving for an escape from danger exemplified by Hor. *Odes* 3.8.

tiam Tutilinam ferias observabat, item flaminica quotiens tonitrua audisset feriata erat donec placasset deos.

9. 'Adfirmabant autem sacerdotes pollui ferias si indictis conceptisque opus aliquod fieret. praeterea regem sacrorum flaminesque non licebat videre feriis opus fieri et ideo per praeconem denuntiabant ne quid tale ageretur, et praecepti neglegens multabatur. 10. praeter multam vero adfirmabatur eum qui talibus diebus imprudens aliquid egisset porco piaculum dare debere. prudentem expiare non posse Scaevola pontifex adseverabat, sed Vmbro negat eum pollui qui opus vel ad deos pertinens sacrorumve causa fecisset vel aliquid ad urgentem vitae utilitatem respiciens actitasset. 11. Scaevola denique consultus quid feriis agi liceret, respondit quod praetermissum noceret. quapropter si bos in specum decidisset eumque pater familias adhibitiis operis liberasset, non est visus ferias polluisse, nec ille qui trabem tecti fractam fulciendo ab imminenti vindicavit ruina. 12. unde et Maro omnium disciplinarum peritus, sciens lavari ovem aut lanae purgandae aut scabie

---

354 Seia, Segetia, and Tutilina, were deities of sown, grown, and harvested crops, respectively (cf. Pliny *Natural History* 18.8, Aug. *City of God* 4.8); Salus, of well-being (cf. 1.20.1n.). The meaning of "Semonia" is obscure: the term appears elsewhere only in a fragmentary passage of Festus (p. 404.18), and in a formula added at the end of a dedicatory inscription, again joined with Salus (*Salus Semonia——populi Victoria*, *CIL* 6.30975 [1 CE]: the two phrases, clearly added after the first cutting, frame the original inscription's final word), in a way that suggests the term might be an epithet derived from the name of the Sabine god (?) Semo.

355 Cf. 1.10.15n.

Tutilina used to keep a day of rest;[354] so too, whenever the wife of a flamen[355] heard thunder she observed a period of religious retirement until she had appeased the gods.

9. 'The priests, moreover, used to claim that religious festivals [*feriae*] became polluted if any work was undertaken once they had been proclaimed and formally scheduled. The priest in charge of sacrifices[356] and the flamens were also forbidden to observe any work being done during festivals: that's why their approach was announced by a herald, so that any such activity would cease, and anyone who ignored the announcement was fined.[357] 10. Indeed, besides the fine there was the rule that a person who out of ignorance performed some work on such occasions was obliged to offer expiation with a pig. Scaevola the pontiff used to claim (fr. 1b *IAH* 1:57 = fr. 11 *IAR*[6]) that one who intentionally acted thus could not offer expiation,[358] though Umbro denies that pollution is suffered by one who undertook a task that served the gods or their sacred rites or performed some action that met a vitally pressing need. 11. Scaevola, finally, when asked what one was permitted to do on a festival, replied (fr. 12 *IAH* 1:57 = fr. 12 *IAR*[6]), "What would cause harm if neglected." Accordingly, if an ox fell into a pit and the head of the household freed it with the aid of workmen, he was not seen as having polluted the festival, and similarly one who propped up a broken roof-beam and averted an imminent collapse. 12. Hence Maro too, familiar with every branch of learning and aware that a sheep is bathed either to cleanse the wool

[356] Cf. 1.15.9n.
[357] Cf. DServ. on *G.* 1.268.
[358] Cf. Varro *Latin Language* 6.30.

SATURNALIA

curandae gratia, pronuntiavit tunc ovem per ferias licere mersari, si hoc remedii causa fieret:

balantumque gregem fluvio mersare salubri.

adiciendo enim salubri ostendit avertendi morbi gratia tantum modo, non etiam ob lucrum purgandae lanae causa fieri concessum.

13. 'Haec de festis et qui inde nascuntur, qui etiam nefasti vocantur; nunc de profestis et qui ex his procedunt loquemur, id est fastis, comitialibus, comperendinis, statis, proeliaribus.

14. 'Fasti sunt quibus licet fari praetori tria verba sollemnia, "do dico addico." his contrarii sunt nefasti. comitiales sunt quibus cum populo agi licet, et fastis quidem lege agi potest, cum populo non potest, comitialibus utrumque potest; comperendini quibus vadimonium licet dicere; stati qui iudicii causa cum peregrino instituuntur, ut Plautus in Curculione,[84]

si status condictus cum hoste intercessit[85] dies.

"hostem" nunc more vetere significat "peregrinum."

---

[84] curculione V²: gurgulione ω (*fort. rectius* Gorgylione, *cf. Fontaine 2009, 61–68*)

[85] intercedit *Plaut.*

---

[359] Cf. (D)Serv. on *G.* 1.270.   [360] Cf. Varro *Latin Language* 6.30, Paul. Fest. p. 83.6–7, Ov. *F.* 1.47–48, *LALE* 224; M. leaves implied the (doubtful) connection between *fasti* and *fari* ("to speak") that other ancient etymologies make explicit. If the 3-word formula could not be uttered, a *legis actio*—the oldest form of Roman civil proceeding—could not go forward.

192

or to cure mange, affirmed that a sheep can be bathed if it is done for the sake of a cure (*G.* 1.272):

> plunge the bleating flock in the salubrious stream.

By adding "salubrious" he showed that cleaning the wool is permitted only to prevent illness, not for the sake of gain.[359]

13. 'So much for days of religious observance [*festi*] and their derivatives, which are also called "days unsuited to legal business" [*nefasti*]: now I will speak about ordinary days [*profesti*] and their derivatives, namely days of legal business, assembly days, days for resuming trials, appointed days, and days for battle.

14. 'Days of legal business [*fasti*] are those on which the praetor may pronounce the customary formula comprising the three verbs "I grant" [*do*], "I declare" [*dico*], "I assign" [*addico*]. The opposite of these are the days unsuited to legal business [*nefasti*].[360] Assembly days [*comitiales*] are those on which matters can be brought before the people for their action; on days of legal business matters can be brought before a judge but not before the people, whereas on assembly days both can be done. Days for resuming trials are those on which bond may be set for a future appearance in court; appointed days [*stati*] are those fixed for an appearance in court with a non-citizen,[361] as Plautus says in *Curculio* (5),

> if the appointed day agreed on with an outsider has intervened.

"Outsider" [*hostis*] here has the old sense of "non-citizen"

359 Cf. Paul. Fest. p. 415.5.

SATURNALIA

15. proeliares ab iustis non segregaverim, si quidem iusti
sunt continui triginta dies quibus exercitu imperato vexil-
lum russi coloris in arce positum est, proeliares autem omnes quibus fas est res repetere vel hostem lacessere.
16. nam cum Latiar, hoc est Latinarum sollemne, concipi-
tur, item diebus Saturnaliorum, sed et cum mundus patet,
nefas est proelium sumere, 17. quia nec Latinarum tempore, quo publice quondam indutiae inter populum Romanum Latinosque firmatae sunt, inchoari bellum dece-
bat, nec Saturni festo, qui sine ullo tumultu bellico
creditur imperasse, nec patente mundo, quod sacrum Diti
patri et Proserpinae dicatum est meliusque occlusa Pluto-
nis fauce eundum ad proelium putaverunt. 18. unde et
Varro ita scribit: "mundus cum patet, deorum tristium
atque inferum quasi ianua patet. propterea non modo
proelium committi, verum etiam dilectum rei militaris
causa habere ac militem proficisci, navem solvere, uxorem
liberum quaerendorum causa ducere religiosum est."
19. vitabant veteres ad viros vocandos etiam dies qui essent
notati rebus adversis, vitabant etiam ferias,[86] sicut Varro in
augurum libris scribit in haec verba: "viros vocare feriis

[86] ferias V²: feriis ω

---

[362] I.e., as distinct from "enemy," the common sense of *hostis*
in classical and post-classical Latin: cf. Varro *Latin Language* 5.3.

[363] Cf. Paul. Fest. p. 92.10–11, Serv. on A. 8.1.

[364] Seeking reparations (*res repetere*) was central to the con-
cept of a "just war" in the early Roman Republic and to the procedures that led to a declaration of war.   [365] Cf. §6n. above.

[366] Cf. Paul. Fest. p. 145.12–147.2 (~ Fest. p. 126.1–6), DServ.
on A. 3.134 ad fin. (differently Plut. *Rom.* 11.1–2): the *mundus* was

[*peregrinus*].³⁶² 15. I would not distinguish days for battle
[*proeliares*] from sanctioned days [*iusti*], seeing that sanctioned days comprise the thirty-day period when an army
has been mobilized and the red banner has been set up on
the citadel;³⁶³ but days for battle are all those on which divine law permits seeking reparations³⁶⁴ or challenging the
enemy. 16. For it is against divine law to engage battle
when the Latiar (that is, the Latin festival) is formally declared,³⁶⁵ similarly on the days of the Saturnalia, but also
when the *mundus* is open:³⁶⁶ 17. for it was appropriate to
start a war neither during the Latin festival, when the Roman people once reached an official armistice with the
Latins, nor during the feast of Saturn, who is believed to
have ruled without war's upheaval, nor when the *mundus* is
open, a time that is set aside as sacred to Dis and Proserpina,³⁶⁷ and it was reckoned better to go to battle when the
mouth of the Underworld is closed. 18. Hence Varro too
writes (*Ant. Div.* lib. 8, p. 55): "When the *mundus* is open,
it is as though the doorway of the baleful gods of the Underworld is open: for that reason it is taboo not just to join
battle but also to conduct a military levy, to set off on campaign, to set sail, and to take a wife for the purpose of pro-
creation."³⁶⁸ 19. The ancients avoided holding military levies also on days marked by disasters, and they avoided
holding levies on religious festivals, as Varro writes in his
book on augurs (*Ant. Div.* lib. 3, p. 41): "It is not right to
levy soldiers during religious festivals: if someone has done

a circular hole (location unknown: *LTUR* 3:288–89) that was
thought to give access to the Underworld; it was open on 24 July, 5
October, and 8 November.   ³⁶⁷ On Dis, 1.7.30n.; on Proserpina, 1.12.23n.   ³⁶⁸ Cf. Fest. p. 348.24–27.

non oportet: si vocavit, piaculum esto." 20. sciendum est tamen eligendi ad pugnandum diem Romanis tunc fuisse licentiam, si ipsi inferrent bellum. at cum exciperent, nullum obstitisse diem quo minus vel salutem suam vel publicam defenderent dignitatem. quis enim observationi locus, cum eligendi facultas non supersit?

21. 'Dies autem postriduanos ad omnia maiores nostri cavendos putarunt, quos etiam atros velut infausta appellatione damnarunt. eosdem tamen non nulli communes velut ad emendationem nominis vocitaverunt. horum causam Gellius Annalium libro quinto decimo et Cassius Hemina Historiarum libro secundo referunt. 22. anno ab urbe condita trecentesimo sexagesimo tertio a tribunis militum Vergilio Mallio Aemilio Postumio collegisque eorum in senatu tractatum, quid esset propter quod totiens intra paucos annos male esset afflicta res publica; 23. et ex praecepto patrum L. Aquinium, haruspicem in senatum venire iussum religionum requirendarum gratia dixisse Q. Sulpicium tribunum militum ad Alliam adversum Gallos pugnaturum rem divinam dimicandi gratia fecisse postridie Idus Quintiles, item apud Cremeram, multisque aliis temporibus et locis post sacrificium die postero celebratum male

---

369 Cf. 1.15.22. §§21–24, 26: cf. Gell. 5.17 (quoting Verrius Flaccus).   370 On the rank, cf. 1.8.1 n. In fact L. *Verginius* Tricostus, A. *Manlius*, L. Aemilius Mamercus and L. Postumius Albinus, with L. Valerius Poplicola and P. Cornelius, held office in 389 BCE, which was either the 365th year from Rome's founding (according to Varro) or the 364th (according to the *fasti Capitolini*, the system M. elsewhere follows, cf. 1.11.3n.): editors emend the incorrect forms of the two names found in M.'s manuscripts, though it is at least equally probable that M. himself was as misinformed about their names as he was about their date.

so, let it be an act demanding expiation." 20. Nonetheless, one should understand that the Romans had a certain freedom in choosing a day for battle when they themselves were the attackers. But when they were being attacked, no sort of day prevented them from saving their own lives and the good name of the Roman people: what room would there be for observing the rules when one was left no choice?

21. 'Our ancestors thought the day after the Kalends, Nones, and Ides should be avoided for all purposes,[369] and they even condemned them with the ill-omened name of "black days." Yet some have called them "shared days," as though to mitigate the label. Gellius, in Book 15 of his *Annals* (fr. 24), and Cassius Hemina, in Book 2 of his *Histories* (fr. 23), give the following account. 22. In the 363rd year after the city was founded the military tribunes Vergilius, Mallius, Aemilius, Postumius, and their colleagues brought before the senate the question why the commonwealth had suffered so many disasters in the space of a few years.[370] 23. When by the senate's directive the seer Lucius Aquinius was ordered to appear, so that the religious causes could be sought, he said that when the military tribune Quintus Sulpicius was preparing to fight the Gauls at the river Allia [390 BCE], he offered sacrifice to insure victory on the day after the Ides of Quintilis;[371] similarly at the river Cremera,[372] and at many other times and places, the battle had gone badly when sacrifice was of-

---

[371] I.e., 16 July.

[372] In the war against Veii in 477 BCE 306 members of the *gens Fabia* were said to have been killed on a single day (Livy 2.50.4–10, Gell. 17.21.13).

SATURNALIA

cessisse conflictum. 24. tunc patres iussisse ut ad colle-
gium pontificum de his religionibus referretur, ponti-
ficesque statuisse postridie omnes Kalendas Nonas Idus
atros dies habendos, ut hi dies neque proeliares neque puri
neque comitiales essent. 25. sed et Fabius Maximus Servilianus pontifex in libro duodecimo negat oportere atro die
parentare, quia tunc quoque Ianum Iovemque praefari
necesse est, quos nominari atro die non oportet. 26. ante
diem quoque quartum Kalendas vel Nonas vel Idus tamquam inominalem diem plerique vitant. eius observationis
an religio ulla sit tradita quaeri solet, sed nos nihil super ea
re scriptum invenimus nisi quod Q. Claudius Annalium
quinto cladem illam vastissimam pugnae Cannensis fac-
tam refert ante diem quartum Nonas Sextiles. 27. ad rem
sane militarem nihil attinere notat Varro utrum fastus vel
nefastus dies sit, sed ad solas hoc actiones respicere pri-
vatas.

28. 'Quod autem nundinas ferias dixi potest argui, quia
Titius[87] de feriis scribens nundinarum dies non inter ferias retulit sed tantum sollemnes vocavit, et quod Iulius
Modestus adfirmat Messala augure consulente pontifices,
an nundinarum Romanarum Nonarumque dies feriis te-
nerentur, respondisse eos nundinas sibi ferias non videri,

---

[87] Titius *ed. Lugd. Bat. 1670*: Titus ω

---

[373] The customary place for the two gods to be named, cf. Cato
Agr. 134, Livy 8.9.6.

[374] 2 August 216 BCE.

[375] In §5 above, cf. Fest. p. 176.24–27, DServ. on *G.* 1.275 (citing Varro).

[376] If "Titius" is correct ("Titus" can hardly be), he is probably

198

fered on a day after the Kalends, Nones, or Ides. 24. Then the senate ordered that the college of pontiffs be consulted on the religious issues involved, and the pontiffs established that all days that follow the Kalends, Nones, and Ides should be considered black days and so unsuitable for battle, for actions requiring religious purity, and for voting assemblies. 25. Furthermore, Fabius Maximus Servilianus the pontiff says, in Book 12 (fr. 4 *HRR* 1:118 = *IAH* 1:28), that it is wrong to make offerings to one's ancestors on a black day, since on that occasion too one must mention Janus and Jupiter at the start of one's prayer,[373] and it is not right that they be named on a black day. 26. Most people also avoid as ill-omened the fourth day before the Kalends, Nones, or Ides: it is often asked whether a tradition of religious sanction is tied to this practice, but I've been able to find nothing written on the matter save that in Book 5 of his *Annales* Quintus Claudius reports (fr. 52) that the utterly devastating disaster at the battle of Cannae occurred on the fourth day before the Nones of Sextilis.[374] 27. Of course, as Varro remarks (*Ant. hum.* lib. 16 fr. 4), the distinction between days fit [*fasti*] and unfit [*nefasti*] for legal business is relevant only to civil, not military, affairs.

28. 'As for my calling market day a religious festival [*feriae*],[375] that can be criticized: Titius, in writing on religious festivals, did not count market day among the festivals but called them only "customary occasions";[376] Julius Modestus is certain that when the augur Messala asked the pontiffs whether Roman market days and Nones are held to be religious festivals, they replied that they did not think

the Titius cited as a writer on priestly garments at Fest. 222.13–14 and 368.6–11 and by M. on ritual language at 3.2.11.

et quod Trebatius in libro primo religionum ait nundinis
magistratum posse manu mittere iudiciaque addicere.
29. sed contra Iulius Caesar sexto decimo auspiciorum libro negat nundinis contionem advocari posse, id est cum
populo agi, ideoque nundinis Romanorum haberi comitia
non posse. Cornelius etiam Labeo primo fastorum libro
nundinas[88] ferias esse pronuntiat. 30. causam vero huius
varietatis apud Granium Licinianum libro secundo diligens lector inveniet. ait enim nundinas Iovis ferias esse, si
quidem flaminica omnibus nundinis in regia Iovi arietem
soleat immolare, sed lege Hortensia effectum ut fastae essent, uti rustici, qui nundinandi causa in urbem veniebant,
lites componerent. nefasto enim die praetori fari non licebat. 31. ergo qui ferias dicunt a mendacio vindicantur patrocinio vetustatis, qui contra sentiunt aestimatu aetatis
quae legem secuta est vera depromunt.

32. 'Harum originem quidam Romulo adsignant, quem
communicato regno cum T. Tatio sacrificiis et sodalitati-
bus institutis nundinas quoque adiecisse commemorant,
sicut Tuditanus[89] adfirmat. 33. sed Cassius Servium Tullium fecisse nundinas dicit, ut in urbem ex agris convenirent urbanas rusticasque res ordinaturi. Geminus ait diem

[88] nundinas J²U²S: -nis ω
[89] Tuditanus *ed. Ven. 1472*: tutidanus β, tutidianus α

---

[377] The logical connection ("and so") exists because every voting assembly of the Roman people (*comitia*) had to be preceded
by a general (non-voting) assembly (*contio*).
[378] The fragments of the post-Hadrianic historian Granius
Licinianus are included as testimonia in Criniti's edition of the
London palimpsest (1981): this is testimonium 1A (p. xii).
[379] I.e., the *flamen Dialis*, cf. 1.10.15n.
[380] Cf. §14 above.

so; and Trebatius, in Book 1 of his *Religious Observances* (fr. 4 *IAH* 1:405 = fr. 2 *IAR*⁶), says that on a market day a magistrate can free a slave and award judgments. 29. Against this, however, Julius Caesar, in Book 16 of his *Auspices*, says (fr. 1 *IAR*⁶) that on a market day a non-voting assembly of the people (*contio*) cannot be called—that is, a matter cannot be brought before them—and so a voting assembly cannot be held on a market day.³⁷⁷ Cornelius Labeo, too, in Book 1 of his *Calendar* asserts (fr. 1 Mast.) that a market day is a religious festival [*feriae*]. 30. An attentive reader will find the reason for these divergent opinions in Granius Licinianus' second book:³⁷⁸ there he says that a market day is a festival of Jupiter, since it is the custom for the wife of the flamen³⁷⁹ to sacrifice a ram to Jupiter in the Regia on every market day, but that by the Hortensian law [287 BCE] they were made days of legal business [*fastus*], so that the peasants who came to market in the city could settle their lawsuits; for on a day not suited to legal business [*nefastus*], the praetor could not utter the formula of judgment.³⁸⁰ 31. So those who say that a market day is a religious day have ancient practice on their side to save them from a charge of falsehood, while those who take the opposite view render a true judgment in the view of the generations that came after that law.

32. 'Now, some credit Romulus with instituting the market days, claiming that when he shared his reign with Titus Tatius and established sacrifices and religious associations, he added the market day too: Tuditanus gives this sort of account (fr. 3). 33. But Cassius says (fr. 17) that Servius Tullius created market days so that people intending to set both their urban and their rural interests in order would gather in the city from the countryside. Geminus

nundinarum exactis iam regibus coepisse celebrari, quia
plerique de plebe repetita Servii Tullii memoria parenta-
rent ei nundinis. cui rei etiam Varro consentit. 34. Rutilius
scribit Romanos instituisse nundinas ut octo quidem diebus in agris rustici opus facerent, nono autem die inter-
misso rure ad mercatum legesque accipiendas Romam
venirent et ut scita atque consulta frequentiore populo re-
ferrentur, quae trinundino die proposita a singulis atque
universis facile noscebantur. 35. unde etiam mos tractus ut
leges trinundino die promulgarentur. ea re etiam candida-
tis usus fuit in comitium nundinis venire et in colle consistere unde coram possent ab universis videri. sed haec omnia neglegentius haberi coepta et post abolita, postquam
internundino etiam ob multitudinem plebis frequentes
adesse coeperunt. 36. est etiam Nundina Romanorum dea
a nono die nascentium nuncupata, qui lustricus dicitur. est
autem dies lustricus quo infantes lustrantur et nomen acci-
piunt; sed is maribus nonus, octavus est feminis.

37. 'Plene ut arbitror anni ac mensium constitutione digesta habet Horus quoque noster quod de dierum vocabulis et observatione consuluit. et scire equidem velim numquid sit quod argutus Niligena et gentis accola numerorum
potens ex hoc ordine Romanae dispensationis inrideat,

---

381 Cf. 1.13.18.

382 Cf. Varro *On Agriculture* 2 pr. 1, Dion. Hal. 7.58.3.

383 This interval of three market days, called the *trinundinum*,
meant that at least 17–24 days had to pass between the first public
notice of pending legislation and the vote (17 days if notice was
first given on a market day, 24 days if given on the day after a market day).   384 M. is the only author to mention this goddess.

385 Cf. Paul. Fest. p. 107.28–108.2, Plut. *Mor.* 288C-E.

says that the market day became a regular custom when the kings had already been driven out, because most of the plebs, recalling the memory of Servius Tullius, offered him the sacrifices due an ancestor on the market day;[381] and Varro agrees (*Ant. hum.* lib. 16 fr. 7). 34. Rutilius writes (fr. 1 *HRR* 1:187 = no. 815 fr. 6 *FGrH* = *IAH* 1:45 = *IAR*[6] 1:14f.) that the Romans established the market day so that the peasants would work in the field for eight days, then interrupt their work on the ninth day[382] and come to Rome to engage in trade and learn about laws, and also in order to have a larger segment of the community be made aware of popular resolutions and senatorial decrees: being posted on three successive market days, they would easily become known to one and all. 35. From this is derived the custom of promulgating proposed laws on each of three market days,[383] and for the same reason candidates for office used to come into the comitium on market days and stand on a hill where the entire populace could see them in person. But all these customs began to be treated carelessly and were later abolished, after there began to be large crowds on hand even between market days because the common people were so numerous. 36. The Romans also have a goddess Nundina, named from the ninth day [*nonus dies*] after a baby's birth:[384] that is the lustral day, when infants are purified and named (it's the ninth day for males, but the eighth for females[385]).

37. 'I think I've fully set forth the arrangement of the year and its months, so that our friend Horus has an answer to the question he asked about terminology and observances proper to the days. For my part, I'd like to know whether this clever son of the Nile, a native of the land that holds dominion over numbers, finds anything laughable in

an Tuscum quoque Thybrim aliquid ex disciplinis suis hau-
sisse consentiat.' 38. subiecit Eustathius, 'non solum Horus noster, gravis vir et ornatus, sed nec quisquam alius ut
aestimo tam futtilis posset esse iudicii qui Romani anni sic
ad unguem, ut aiunt, emendatum ordinem non probaret;
cui maiorem gratiam et tenax memoria et luculenta oratio referentis adiecit. nec mirum si haec digeries morsum
reprehensionis evasit, cui accersita est ab Aegypto pos-
tremae correctionis auctoritas. 39. nam Iulius Caesar ut si-
derum motus, de quibus non indoctos libros reliquit, ab
Aegyptiis disciplinis hausit, ita hoc quoque ex eadem institutione mutuatus est ut ad solis cursum finiendi anni tempus extenderet. 40. Latii vero veteres incolae, quia nihil
iam tum discere ab Aegypto licebat, ad quam nullus illis
commeatus patebat, morem Graeciae in numerandis mensium diebus secuti sunt, ut retroversum cedente numero
ab augmento in diminutionem computatio resoluta desi-
neret. 41. ita enim nos decimum diem, deinde nonum
et postea octavum dicimus, ut Athenienses δεκάτην καὶ
ἐνάτην φθίνοντος soliti sunt dicere. 42. Homerus quoque
cum ait,

τοῦ μὲν φθίνοντος μηνὸς, τοῦ δ' ἱσταμένοιο,

quid aliud nisi illum φθίνοντα dicit cuius paulatim defi-
cientis supputatio in nomen desinit secuturi et ἱστάμενον
illum qui praecedit numerum successurus priori in defec-

the Romans' system, or agrees that the Etruscan Tiber too has derived some good from his country's learning.' 38. Eustathius interposed: 'I doubt that anyone—not just our friend Horus, a serious and accomplished man, but anyone else—could be such a worthless judge that he would not agree that the organization of the Roman year has been refined, as they say, to perfection—a perfection made all the more pleasing by the speaker's unshakeable memory and brilliant way of speaking. And it's not surprising that this exposition has avoided criticism's sting, since it has the authority of utter correctness derived from Egypt. 39. For just as Julius Caesar owed to Egyptian learning his knowledge of the stars' movements, on which he left us some learned books (*On stars* test. 4 Klotz), so he borrowed from the same teachings in stretching the period by which the year is defined. 40. But because Latium's ancient inhabitants did not yet have the chance to learn from Egypt (travel there was closed to them), they followed the custom of Greece in reckoning the days of the months, so that the count moved backward, with the date dwindling by degrees from the greater number and ending with the lesser. 41. For just as we speak of the tenth day [sc. before the Kalends], then the ninth, and then the eighth, so the Athenians were accustomed to speak of the tenth and the ninth of the waning month. 42. And when Homer says (*Od.* 16.162):

With one month waning, another arising,

he must mean by "waning" the month in which the count gradually diminishes until it gives way to the name of the month to follow, and by "arising" the one that stands next in the series as it comes to succeed its shrinking predeces-

tum meanti? 43. quod et Homerus vester Mantuanus, intellegens illud stare dici ad quod acceditur, ait,

stat sua cuique dies,

extremum diem stare dicens, quasi ad quem per omnes eatur. 44. idem poeta doctrina ac verecundia iuxta nobilis, sciens Romanos veteres ad lunae cursum et sequentes ad solis anni tempora digessisse, utriusque saeculi opinioni reverentiam servans, "vos quoque,"[90] inquit,

. . . labentem caelo qui[91] ducitis annum,
Liber et alma Ceres,

tam lunam quam solem duces anni hac invocatione designans.'

17   Hic Avienus: 'hoc equidem mecum multum ac frequenter agitavi, quid sit quod solem modo Apollinem, modo Liberum, modo sub aliarum appellationum varietate veneremur. et quia sacrorum omnium praesulem esse te, Vetti Praetextate, divina voluerunt, perge, quaeso, rationem mihi tantae sub uno numine[92] in nominibus diversitatis aperire.'

2. Tum Vettius: 'cave aestimes, mi Aviene, poetarum gregem, cum de dis fabulantur, non ab adytis plerumque

---

[90] quoque *add. Macrob.*   [91] quae (*sc.* lumina) *Verg.*
[92] numine G¹: nomine ω

---

[386] M.'s comparison proceeds from the correct understanding that Lat. *stare* and Gk. *histêmi* are cognate; but because the Greek verb here (in the middle voice) has a sense, "arise," that the Latin verb never has, the point is obscured in translation.

sor. 43. Your Homer of Mantua, too, understood that a thing one approaches is said to "stand fixed" and so says (*A.* 10.467*):

> For each man his day [of death] stands fixed,

meaning that the final day toward which we move through all the rest stands fixed.[386] 44. This same poet—distinguished equally for his learning and his tact—knew that the ancient Romans organized the calendar according to the lunar cycle, their descendants according to the solar cycle, and showed his respect for the thinking of both ages by saying, "You too" (*G.* 1.5–7*),

> . . . who guide the year as it glides through the heavens,
> Liber [= Bacchus] and nurturing Ceres . . . ,

signifying by this invocation that both the moon and the sun are the year's "guides."'[387]

Here Avienus said: 'I've gone over this question in my mind, often and long: why is it that we worship the sun now as Apollo, now as Liber, now by various other names? Because the divine powers wished that you, Vettius Praetextatus, be master of all sacred lore, please, go on and reveal to me the reason that so many different names converge on a single godhead.'[388]

2. Then Vettius said: 'Careful, my good Avienus: do not suppose that when the flock of poets tell stories of the gods

[387] Identification in this verse of Bacchus with the sun, Ceres with the moon, is made explicit at 1.18.23.

[388] The solar "theology" developed in 1.17–23 has a large (but not exclusive) debt to Porphyry: see Introd. §4.

207

philosophiae semina mutuari. nam quod omnes paene
deos, dumtaxat qui sub caelo sunt, ad solem referunt, non
vana superstitio sed ratio divina commendat. 3. si enim sol,
ut veteribus placuit, dux et moderator est luminum reli-
quorum et solus stellis errantibus praestat, ipsarum vero
stellarum cursus ordinem rerum humanarum, ut quibusdam videtur, pro potestate disponunt, ut Plotino constat
placuisse, significant: necesse est ut solem, qui moderatur
nostra moderantes, omnium quae circa nos geruntur fa-
teamur auctorem. 4. et sicut Maro, cum de una Iunone diceret,

   quo numine laeso,

ostendit unius dei effectus varios pro variis censendos esse
numinibus, ita diversae virtutes solis nomina dis dederunt.
unde ἕν τὸ πᾶν sapientum principes prodiderunt. 5. virtutem igitur solis quae divinationi curationique praeest
Apollinem vocaverunt, quae sermonis auctor est Mercurii
nomen accepit. nam quia sermo interpretatur cogitationes
latentes, Ἑρμῆς ἀπὸ τοῦ ἑρμηνεύειν propria appellatione
vocitatus est. 6. virtus solis est quae fructibus . . . effectus

---

389 The gods "beneath heaven"—the realm contained within
the celestial sphere in which the fixed stars are set—were in principle comprehensible by human thought, as emanations of the
true God (the Good, the First Cause) who lay beyond both the celestial sphere and direct comprehension by the human mind (cf.
Comm. 1.2.14–15).

390 Cf. *Comm.* 1.20.1, Cic. *On the Commonwealth* 6.17.

391 Cf. *Enn.* 2.3.1ff., 3.1.5. The strong position, that the stars
determined earthly events, was the dominant view in ancient astrology.

they are not often borrowing germs of wisdom from the sacred shrine of philosophy. It's not empty superstition but divine reason that prompts them to relate almost all the gods—at least those beneath heaven[389]—to the sun. 3. If "the sun is guide and governor of all other stars in heaven,"[390] as the ancients judged, if it alone presides over the planets, and if the movements of the very stars have the power to determine (as some think) or foretell (as Plotinus is known to have held[391]) the sequence of human events, then we must acknowledge the sun—which governs those bodies that govern our affairs—as the source of all that goes on around us. 4. And just as Maro, in saying of Juno alone (*A.* 1.8*),

with what aspect of her divinity harmed,

shows that the different actions of a single god must be understood as different manifestations of her divinity, so the diverse special powers of the sun gave the gods their names: hence the foremost philosophers have revealed that "the all is one."[392] 5. So they called "Apollo" the special power of the son that presides over prophecy and healing, while the one that is the source of speech gained the name Mercury: since speech makes our hidden thoughts plain, Hermes got his name, appropriately, from "interpreting" [*hermêneuein*].[393] 6. It is the special power of the sun that

[392] The thought that "the all is one (ἕν τὸ πᾶν) and uncreated and spherical" can be traced back to Parmenides (A 7–8, 23, 25, fr. 8.3–6 D.-K., cf. Pl. *Soph.* 244B6, Arist. *Physics* 1.5 188a19–22).

[393] Cf. *Comm.* 1.12.14, Hyginus *Fab.* 143.2, Porph. *On Statues* 8, Hesych. A.7037, *Etym. Gud.* E p. 527, Eustath. *Comm. Il.* 1:279, *Etym. Mag.* p. 376.47.

eiusdem est qui frugibus praeest.[93] et hinc natae sunt appellationes deorum [sicut][94] ceterorum qui ad solem certa et arcana ratione referuntur et—ne tanto secreto nuda praestetur adsertio—auctoritates veterum de singulis consulamus.

7. 'Apollinis nomen multiplici interpretatione ad solem refertur, cuius rei ordinem pergam. Plato solem Ἀπόλλωνα cognominatum scribit ἀπὸ τοῦ ἀποπάλλειν τὰς ἀκτῖνας id est a iactu radiorum; Chrysippus [Apollinem],[95] ὡς οὐχὶ τῶν πολλῶν καὶ φαύλων οὐσιῶν τοῦ πυρὸς ὄντα, primam enim nominis litteram retinere significationem negandi, ἢ ὅτι μόνος ἐστὶ καὶ οὐχὶ πολλοί, nam et Latinitas eum, quia tantam claritudinem solus obtinuit, solem vocavit. 8. Speusippus, quod ex multis ignibus constet vis eius ὡς ἀπὸ πολλῶν οὐσιῶν πυρὸς αὐτοῦ συνεστῶτος, Cleanthes[96] ὡς ἀπ' ἄλλων καὶ ἄλλων τόπων τὰς ἀνατολὰς ποιουμένου, quod ab aliis atque aliis locorum declinationibus faciat ortus. 9. Cornificius arbitratur Apollinem nominatum ἀπὸ τοῦ ἀναπολεῖν, id est quia intra circuitum mundi quem Graeci πόλον appellant impetu latus ad ortus refertur. alii cognominatum Apollinem pu-

---

93 lacun. statuit Marinone[2] (virtus . . . praeest secl. Willis)
94 secl. Eyss.   95 Apollinem secl. Jan
96 ΚΛΕΑΝΘΗΣ Gr. litt. ω

---

394 §§7–65 ultimately depend on Apollodorus of Athens (no. 244 fr. 95 FGrH) through the medium of Cornutus (Jacoby FGrH IIB pp. 1046–63). Where M.'s Latin merely translates Greek phrases, I translate only the Greek.

395 Not in Plato's extant works (other etymologies are given at

. . . the fruits of the trees . . . and also his creative force that presides over the fruits of the fields. Hence too there came to be the names of the other gods, which relate to the sun in a fixed and secret system: let us ask the ancient authorities about them, one by one, lest so great a mystery be afforded no more than mere assertion.

7. 'Apollo's name is related to the sun by many different paths of understanding, which I shall pursue in order.[394] Plato writes[395] that the sun was named Apollo "as though from *apopallein tas aktînas*," that is, from casting his rays; Chrysippus (fr. 1095 *SVF* 2:319–20), "because he is *not* one of fire's many [*pollôn*] lowly substances"—for the first letter of his name keeps its negative force[396]—"or because the sun is one and *not* many [*polloi*]"—for Latin, too, called him "sun" [*sol*] because he alone [*solus*] is so bright;[397] 8. Speusippus (fr. 152 Parente), "because he is constituted from many [*apo pollôn*] of fire's substances"; Cleanthes (fr. 540 *SVF* 1:123), "because he rises now from one point, now from another [*ap' allôn*]" at different elevations. 9. Cornificius judges (fr. 3 *GRF* 1:475) that Apollo's name comes from "turning up again" [*anapolein*], that is, because he is carried forcefully around the vault of heaven, which the Greeks call the *polos*, and returns to the point of his rising. Others think that Apollo got his name from de-

Crat. 405C-406A), but cf. [Zon.] *Lexikon* A p. 235, *Etym. Gen.* A.1051, *Epimer. Hom. Il.* 1.21b.   [396] This (fanciful) explanation refers to the fact that the prefix *a-* in Greek has the same negative force as Lat. *in-* and Engl. "un-."

[397] Cf. *Comm.* 1.20.4, Varro *Latin Language* 5.68, Cic. *On the Nature of the Gods* 2.68, Mart. Cap. 2.188, John Lydus *On the Months* 2.4, *LALE* 572.

tant ὡς ἀπολλύντα τὰ ζῷα, exanimat enim et perimit animantes cum pestem intemperie caloris immittit, 10. ut Euripides in Phaethonte,

ὦ χρυσοφεγγὲς⁹⁷ ἥλι', ὡς μ' ἀπώλεσας,
ὅθεν σ' Ἀπόλλων ἐμφανῶς κλῄζει βροτός,⁹⁸

item Archilochus,

ἄναξ⁹⁹ Ἄπολλον, καὶ σὺ τοὺς μὲν αἰτίους
σήμαινε¹⁰⁰ καὶ σφᾶς ὄλλυ' ὥσπερ ὀλλύεις.

11. denique inustos morbo Ἀπολλωνοβλήτους καὶ ἡλιοβλήτους appellant, et quia similes sunt solis effectibus effectus lunae in iuvando nocendoque, ideo feminas certis adflictas morbis σεληνοβλήτους et Ἀρτεμιδοβλήτους vocant. 12. hinc est quod arcu et sagittis Apollinis simulacra decorantur, ut per sagittas intellegatur vis emissa radiorum, ⟨unde Homerus⟩,¹⁰¹

αὐτὰρ ἔπειτ' αὐτοῖσι βέλος ἐχεπευκὲς ἐφιεὶς
βάλλ'.

13. 'Idem auctor est et publicae sospitatis, quam creditur sol animantibus praestare temperie. sed quia perpe-

---

⁹⁷ καλλιφεγγὲς cod. Paris. Gr. 107B, Σ Eur. Or. 1388
⁹⁸ ὅθεν . . . βροτός] καὶ τόνδ'· Ἀπόλλων δ' ἐν βροτοῖς ὀρθῶς καλῇ cod. Paris., Σ Eur.
⁹⁹ ὦναξ Archil. (POxy. 2310 fr. 1 ii.5)
¹⁰⁰ πήμαινε ed. Basil. 1535, Archil. (POxy. 2310 fr. 1 ii.6)
¹⁰¹ unde Homerus suppl. ed. Ven. 1513

stroying [*apollunta*] living things,[398] as he does when he lets loose a plague with his immoderate heat, 10. as Euripides writes in the *Phaëthon* (fr. 781.11–2 *TrGF* 5,2:817):

> O sun of golden light, how you have destroyed
>   (*apôlesas*) me,
> whence mortal man frankly calls you "Apollo,"

similarly Archilochus (fr. 26.5 West[2]):

> You too, lord Apollo: mark out those who are
> guilty and destroy [*ollu'*] them as is your wont.

11. Finally, they call those withered by disease "Apollo-struck" and "sun-struck"; and because the actions of the moon are like those of the sun when it comes to helping and harming, they call women afflicted with certain diseases "moon-struck" and "Artemis-struck."[399] 12. That is why images of Apollo are adorned with a bow and arrows:[400] the arrows represent the force of his rays when they're shot forth, ⟨whence Homer⟩ (*Il.* 1.51–52):

> But then let loose your piercing shaft against them
> and strike.

13. 'Apollo is also the source of the general well-being he's thought to provide living creatures by tempering the climate. But because he continually provides health and

---

[398] Cf. Cornut. p. 65.20, 66.3–6, Plut. fr. 157.77, Euseb. *Preparation for the Gospel* 3.1.5, Serv. on *E.* 5.66 (= Porph. fr. 477 Smith).

[399] Neither "Apollo-struck" nor "Artemis-struck" is otherwise attested. For the effects of being "moon-struck," cf. 7.16.26.

[400] E.g., *LIMC* 2,2:188–89, 209–10, 212, 273–78, 311, 333.

tuam praestat salubritatem et pestilens ab ipso casus rarior est, ideo Apollinis simulacra manu dextera Gratias gestant, arcum cum sagittis sinistra, quod ad noxam sit pigrior, et salutem manus promptior largiatur. 14. hinc est quod eidem adtribuitur medendi potestas, quia temperatus solis calor morborum omnium fuga est. nam ὡς ἀπελαύνοντα τὰς νόσους Ἀπόλλωνα tamquam Ἀπέλλωνα cognominatum putant. 15. quae sententia Latinae quoque nominis enuntiationi congruens fecit, ne huius dei nomen verteremus, ut Apollinem apellentem mala intellegas, quem Athenienses Ἀλεξίκακον appellant. sed et Lindii colunt Apollinem Λοίμιον, hoc cognomine finita pestilentia nuncupatum. eadem opinio sospitalis et medici dei in nostris quoque sacris fovetur. namque virgines Vestales ita indigitant: Apollo Medice, Apollo Paean. 16. cum ergo sint huiusce sideris, id est solis, duo maximi effectus, alter quo calore temperato iuvat mortalium vitam, alter quo iactu radiorum non numquam pestiferum virus immittit, duo eademque cognomina circa singulos effectus propriis enuntiationibus signant, appellantes deum Ἰήιον atque Παιᾶνα. quae cognomina utrique effectui apta sunt, ut sit Ἰήιος ἀπὸ τοῦ ἰᾶσθαι, id est a sanando, et Παιὰν ἀπὸ τοῦ

---

401 Cf. Callim. *Aetia* fr. 114.1–15 Pf., Ister *FGrH* no. 334 fr. 52 (Graces in the left hand), Paus. 9.35.3, Σ Pind. *O.* 14.16, on the statue of Apollo at Delos, sim. Philo *Embassy to Gaius* 95; cf. *LIMC* 2,1:234–35, 2,2:214.

402 Cf. Cornut. p. 65.20, *Etym. Gud.* A p. 174.8, Σ Ar. *Wealth* 359, *Etym. Mag.* p. 130.19. Acc. to another common etymology of Apollo's name, not cited by M., he is so called because he releases (*apolyein*) human beings from woes: [Zon.] *Lexicon* A p. 235.6–8, *Etym. Gen.* A.1051, *Etym. Gud.* A p. 173.26–27, Eustath. *Comm. Il.* 1:53.5–6, *Etym. Mag.* ibid., *Epimer. Hom. Il.* 1.21b.

only rarely gives rise to sickness, images of Apollo hold the Graces in their right hand, a bow and arrows in the left, because he is slower to do harm while his readier hand is lavish with well-being.[401] 14. Hence the power of healing is attributed to him too: the sun's moderate warmth puts all diseases to flight and that is why they think Apollo was named from "driving away [*apelaunonta*] sicknesses," as though he were "Apello."[402] 15. That idea squared with the pronunciation of his name in Latin too, so there was no need to translate the god's name: as a consequence, you may take Apollo to be the one who drives woes away [*apellentem*],[403] whom the Athenians call "the one who wards off evil."[404] But the people of Lindus also worship Apollo "of the plague," so called because he ended a pestilence. The same conception of a saving and healing god is fostered in our rites too, for the Vestal Virgins invoke him with the formulas "Apollo Healer, Apollo Paean." 16. Since, then, there are two chief actions of this star, that is, the sun—one whereby he supports mortals' lives with well-regulated warmth, the other whereby he sometimes lets loose a pestilential miasma with the stroke of his rays—men mark each of these actions with the same two names, each with its own distinctive form, calling the god *Iêios* and *Paian*. Both of these names are appropriate to the sun's two actions: *Iêios* is from *iâsthai*, that is, "healing,"[405] and

---

[403] Cf. Paul. Fest. p. 20.27. The form M. uses, *apellentem*, represents the hypothetical present participle of a non-existent compound verb *a* ("from/away") + *pellere* ("to drive").

[404] Cf. Paus. 1.3.4, 6.24.6, 8.41.8.

[405] Cf. Herodian *GG* 3,2:185.11–13, 524.12–13, Hesych. I.363, Σ Soph. *OT* sch. Plan. 154, *Suda* I.223.

παύειν τὰς ἀνίας, et rursus Ἰήιος ἀπὸ τοῦ ἱέναι, ab im-
mittendo [βέλος ἐχεπευκὲς ἐφιείς],[102] et Παιὰν ἀπὸ τοῦ
παίειν, a feriendo. 17. obtinuit tamen ut cum sanitatem
dari sibi precantur, ἰὴ Παιάν per η litteram enuntient, id
est medere Paean;[103] cum autem ἱὲ Παιάν per ε litteram
dicunt cum adspiratione prioris litterae, significant hoc
dici in aliquem adversa precatione, βάλε Παιάν, id est im-
mitte feriendo. qua voce ferunt Latonam usam cum Apollinem hortaretur impetum Pythonis incessere sagittis,
cuius rei naturalem rationem suo loco reddam. 18. hanc
vocem, id est ἱὲ Παιάν, confirmasse fertur oraculum Delphicum Atheniensibus petentibus opem dei adversus
Amazonas Theseo regnante. namque inituros bellum iussit
his ipsis verbis semet ipsum auxiliatorem invocare horta-
rique. 19. Apollodorus in libro quarto decimo περὶ τῶν
θεῶν Ἰήιον solem scribit: ita appellari Apollinem ἀπὸ τοῦ
κατὰ τὸν κόσμον ἵεσθαι καὶ ἱέναι, quod sol per orbem
impetu fertur. 20. sed Timotheus ita:

σύ τε[104] ὦ τὸν ἀεὶ πόλον οὐράνιον
λαμπραῖς ἀκτῖσιν[105] ἥλιε βάλλων
πέμψον ἑκαβόλον ἐχθροῖς[106] βέλος
σᾶς ἀπὸ νευρᾶς ὦ ἱὲ Παιάν.

---

[102] secl. Willis   [103] ΠΑΙΑΝ Graece ω   [104] τε] τ' ed.
Basil. 1535   [105] ἀκτῖσ' Jan   [106] ἐχθροῖσι Jan

---

[406] Cf. Σ Ar. Wealth 636, Σ Soph. ibid., Etym. Gud. Π p.
446.50–51, Eustath. Comm. Il. 1:212.6–8, Etym. Mag. p. 657.11–
15, Lex. Seg. Π p. 295.33–34.   [407] Cf. Herodian. CG 3,
2:524.12–13, Hesych. I.363, Σ Soph. ibid., Orion Etym. I p.
75.24–27, Etym. Mag. p. 469.48–50, Suda I.221.
[408] Eustath. ibid.   [409] M.'s etymological theory connects

Paian is from "ending [*pauein*] woes";[406] and conversely, *Iêios* is from *ienai*, or "letting fly,"[407] and *Paian* is from *paiein*, or "striking."[408] 17. Still, the custom has prevailed of saying *iê Paian*—that is, "heal Paean"—with an eta, when praying for health, whereas when people say *hië Paian*, with an epsilon and a rough breathing on the first letter, they show that they intend a prayer to harm another, *balë Paian*, or "let fly and strike."[409] They say that that is the expression Latona used when she was urging Apollo to meet Python's attack with his arrows[410] (I'll give a scientific explanation of this episode in its proper place[411]). 18. It is said that the Delphic oracle ratified this expression—*hië Paian*—when the Athenians were seeking the god's aid against the Amazons during Theseus' reign: as they were about to start the war the god bade them to call upon him with those very words and urge him on as their ally. 19. In Book 14 of his *On the Gods*, Apollodorus writes (no. 244 fr. 95 *FGrH*) that *Iêios* is the sun and Apollo is so called from "moving speedily" [*hiësthai kai iënai*] through the universe. 20. But Timotheus writes as follows (fr. 24 *PMGr*):

> And you, o sun, who ever strike
> the vault of heaven with brilliant rays,
> send 'gainst the foe the shaft that hits its mark
> from your bowstring, o *hië Paian*.

iê with *iaömai* ("I heal"), *hië* with *hiêmi* ("I hurl/shoot"): the latter link can be traced to Aristotle's pupil Clearchus of Soli (Athen. 701B-E, cf. Callim. *Hymn to Apollo* 97–104, both referring to the slaying of Python), the former to Crates of Mallos (Σ Vet. *Il.* 15.365).   410 Beyond Clearchus and Callimachus, cf. Ephorus *FGrH* no. 70 fr. 31b.27–28, Duris *FGrH* no. 76 fr. 79, Ap. Rhod. 2.705–13 (~ Varro Atac. fr. 5 *FPL*³), Terent. 1586–91.
411 Cf. §§52–53 below.

21. eundem deum praestantem salubribus causis Οὔλιον appellant, id est sanitatis auctorem, ut ait Homerus:

οὐλέ τε καὶ μάλα[107] χαῖρε.

Maeandrius[108] scribit Milesios Ἀπόλλωνι Οὐλίῳ pro salute sua immolare. Pherecydes refert Thesea, cum in Cretam ad Minotaurum duceretur, vovisse pro salute atque reditu suo Ἀπόλλωνι Οὐλίῳ καὶ Ἀρτέμιδι Οὐλίᾳ. 22. nec mirum si gemini effectus variis nominibus celebrantur, cum alios quoque deos ex contrario in eadem re duplici censeri et potestate accipiamus et nomine, ut Neptunum quem alias Ἐνοσίχθονα id est terram moventem, alias Ἀσφαλίωνα id est stabilientem vocant. item Mercurius hominum mentes vel oculos et excitat et sopit, ut ait poeta,

εἴλετο δὲ ῥάβδον, τῇ τ᾽ ἀνδρῶν ὄμματα θέλγει,
⟨ὧν ἐθέλει, τοὺς δ᾽ αὖτε καὶ ὑπνώοντας
ἐγείρει⟩.[109]

23. 'Unde et Apollinem, id est solem, modo sospitatem modo pestem significantibus cognominibus adoramus; cum tamen pestis quae ab eo noxiis immittitur aperte hunc deum bonis propugnare significet. 24. hinc est quod apud Pachynum Siciliae promuntorium Apollo Libystinus exi-

---

107 μέγα codd. nonnull. Hom.
108 Maeandrius ed. Basil. 1535 in marg. (meandrius ω)
109 ὧν . . . ἐγείρει addidi

---

412 Cf. Strab. 14.1.6 (~ Eustath. Comm. Il. 1:53.6–8, cf. 1:535.1–3 and often), Suda O.905.

21. They call the same god who presides over the sources of health *Oulios*, or "author of well-being," as Homer says (*Od*. 24.402):

> Health to you, and much joy.

Maeandrius writes (no. 491 fr. 2 *FGrH*) that the people of Miletus sacrifice to Apollo *Oulios* for their health.[412] Pherecydes reports (no. 3 fr. 149 *FGrH* = fr. 149 *EGM*) that when Theseus was brought to Crete to face the Minotaur, he made a vow to Apollo *Oulios* and Artemis *Oulia* for his safe return. 22. Nor is it surprising if the god's two actions are celebrated under different names, since we learn that the other gods who have opposite effects in the same sphere are judged to have a twofold power and a double name, as in the case of Neptune, whom people call now *Enosichthôn*, or "earth-shaker," now *Asphaliôn*, or "he who steadies."[413] Similarly, Mercury both arouses and lulls to sleep men's minds or eyes, as the poet says (*Il*. 24.343–44):

> He took up his wand with which he beguiles men's
> sight,
> ‹those whom he wishes, and rouses them too when
> they sleep›.

23. 'So too we come to worship Apollo, that is, the sun, under names that signify survival and destruction by turns; yet the plague that the god lets loose upon the guilty still shows that he fights on behalf of the good. 24. Hence the reason why Apollo Libystinus ["of Libya"] is celebrated

---

[413] Cf. Strab. 1.3.16, Plut. *Theseus* 36.6, Paus. 3.11.9, Eustath. *Comm. Il.* 1:53.20–23, cf. 2:86.12–16 and often.

mia religione celebratur. nam cum Libyes invasuri Siciliam classem appulissent ad id promuntorium, Apollo, qui ibi colitur, invocatus ab incolis immissa hostibus peste et paene cunctis subita morte interceptis Libystinus cognominatus est. 25. nostris quoque continetur annalibus similis eiusdem dei praesentiae maiestas. nam cum ludi Romae Apollini celebrarentur ex vaticinio Marcii vatis carmineque Sibyllino, repentino hostis adventu plebs ad arma excitata occurrit hosti, eoque tempore nubes sagittarum in adversos visa ferri et hostem fugavit et victores Romanos ad spectacula dei sospitalis reduxit. hinc intellegitur proelii causa, non pestilentiae sicut quidam aestimant, ludos institutos.

26. 'Haec est autem huius aestimationis ratio quod tunc sol super ipsum nostrae habitationis verticem fulget. nam Cancer in aestivo tropico est, in quo meante sole radii temperatam nostram non eminus sed superne demissi rectis fulgoribus lustrant. unde aestimatum est a non nullis ad propitiandum tunc maxime deum caloris Apollinaribus litari. 27. sed invenio in litteris hos ludos victoriae, non valitudinis causa ut quidam annalium scriptores memorant, institutos. bello enim Punico hi ludi ex libris Sibyllinis pri-

---

[414] See Livy 25.12.3–15 (212 BCE), cf. Livy 26.23.3, Fest. p. 438.32–440.27 (211 BCE). First held in 212 BCE, in accordance with the story M. tells here, the Games of Apollo (*ludi Apollinares*) gained a permanent place on the Roman calendar (13 July) when a plague struck in 208 (Livy 27.23.4–5); they were gradually expanded to occupy 6–13 July. On the Sibylline Books and the Board of Ten (§27), see 1.6.13n.

[415] In astrological terms, the Sun enters Cancer at the summer solstice, the point at which the sun reaches the Tropic of Cancer

with extraordinary solemnity at Pachynus, the promontory
in Sicily: when the Libyans were going to invade Sicily and
put their fleet in at that promontory, the inhabitants called
upon Apollo, who has a cult-center there, and he let loose a
plague upon the enemy, nearly all of whom died immediately. From this he gained the name Libystinus. 25. Our
annals too tell a similar tale of the same god's greatness
made manifest:[414] when games were being celebrated at
Rome in Apollo's honor, in accordance with the divining of
the soothsayer Marcius and the Sibylline books, the enemy
suddenly appeared and the commons, summoned to arms,
ran to meet them; then a cloud of arrows was seen to bear
down on the enemy, putting them to flight and sending the
victorious Romans back to the spectacles in honor of the
savior god. From this we can conclude that the games were
established because of the battle, not a plague, as some
suppose.

26. 'The reason for that supposition is as follows. At the
time of these games the sun shines directly overhead in the
region where we dwell: Cancer is in the summer tropic,[415]
and as the sun passes through, its rays illuminate our temperate region not from afar but coming straight down from
above with unrefracted brilliance. That's why some think
that the games of Apollo are offered up to appease the god
of warmth precisely in that season. 27. But in the written
record I find that these games were established because of
the victory, not disease, as some historians say: during the
Punic War these games were instituted in accordance with

and turns ("tropic" < Gk. *tropai*, "turn") to move south toward the
equator; cf. §61, *Comm.* 2.7.11.

mum sunt instituti suadente Cornelio Rufo decemviro, qui
propterea Sibylla cognominatus est et postea corrupto nomine primus coepit Sylla vocitari. 28. fertur autem in carminibus Marcii vatis, cuius duo volumina inlata sunt in senatum, inventum esse ita scriptum:

> hostem, Romani, si ex agro expellere vultis, vomi-
> cam quae gentium venit longe, Apollini censeo vo-
> vendos ludos qui quotannis comiter Apollini fiant.
> his ludis faciendis praesit is praetor qui ius populo
> plebique dabit summum. decem viri Graeco ritu
> hostiis sacra faciant. hoc si recte facietis, gaudebitis
> semper fietque res publica melior: nam is divus ex-
> tinguet perduelles vestros qui vestros campos pas-
> cunt placide."

29. ex hoc carmine cum procurandi gratia dies unus rebus
divinis impensus esset, postea senatus consultum factum
uti decem viri, quo magis instruerentur de ludis Apollini
agundis reque divina recte facienda, libros Sibyllinos adi-
rent. in quibus cum eadem reperta nuntiatum esset, censuerunt patres Apollini ludos vovendos faciendosque,
inque eam rem duodecim milia aeris praetori et duas hos-
tias maiores dari, decemvirisque praeceptum ut Graeco
ritu hisce hostiis sacrum facerent, Apollini bove aurato et

---

416 Very likely an error, the earliest Sulla probably dating from
a generation earlier: *MRR* 1:214.   417 I.e., the urban praetor, the office held by Cornelius Rufus at the time of these proceedings.   418 Whereas Romans normally prayed and offered sacrifice with the head covered by a fold of the toga, one
sacrificing in the "Greek manner" had his head uncovered (cf.
3.6.17, 3.8.2) and wore a laurel wreath (cf. 3.12.1).

the Sibylline books, at the urging of Cornelius Rufus, one of the Board of Ten, who on that account got the surname Sibylla and, after the name suffered corruption, was the first man to be called Sulla.[416] 28. It is said, moreover, that among the prophecies of the soothsayer Marcius, whose two book-rolls were brought into the senate, the following was found (cf. *FPL*[3] pp. 14–15):

> If, Romans, you wish to expel the enemy from your land—the pus of nations come from afar—I hold that you must vow to Apollo a set of games that will graciously be mounted for the god each year. Let that praetor be in charge of these games who will have supreme judicial authority over the people and plebs.[417] Let the Board of Ten offer sacrifice with victims in the Greek manner.[418] If you do this correctly, you will always know joy and the commonwealth will become ever better: for that divinity will destroy your enemies, who graze placidly on your fields.

29. After one day had been set aside for religious observance, to administer the rites in line with this prophecy, the senate decreed that the Board of Ten should consult the Sibylline books, so that better arrangements could be made for mounting the games for Apollo and performing the rites correctly. When the Ten reported that they had found the same provisions in the books, the senate decreed that games should be vowed and produced for Apollo; that for that purpose 12,000 pounds of copper and two full-grown victims be provided; and that the Board of Ten be instructed to offer sacrifice in the Greek manner with these victims: for Apollo, an ox with gilded horns and two

223

capris duabus albis auratis, Latonae bove femina aurata. ludos in circo populus coronatus spectare iussus.

30. Haec praecipue traditur origo ludorum Apollinarium. Nunc ex aliis quoque huius dei nominibus eundem esse Apollinem et solem probemus. 31. Λοξίας cognominatur, ut ait Oenopides, ὅτι ἐκπορεύεται τὸν λοξὸν κύκλον ἀπὸ δυσμῶν ἐπ᾽ ἀνατολὰς κινούμενος, id est quod obliquum circulum ab occasu ad orientem pergit; aut, ut Cleanthes scribit, ἐπειδὴ καθ᾽ ἕλικας κινεῖται· λοξαὶ γάρ εἰσι καὶ αὗται, quod flexuosum iter pergit, ἢ ὅτι λοξὰς τὰς ἀκτῖνας ἵησιν ἐφ᾽ ἡμᾶς βορείους ὄντας νότειος ὤν, vel quod transversos in nos a meridie immittit radios, cum simus ad ipsum septentrionales. 32. Δήλιος[110] cognominatur ἀπὸ τοῦ δῆλα καὶ φανερὰ πάντα ποιεῖν τῷ φωτί, quod inluminando omnia clara demonstret.

33. Φοῖβος appellatur, ut ait Cornificius, ἀπὸ τοῦ φοιτᾶν βίᾳ, quod vi fertur, plerique autem a specie et nitore Φοῖβον id est καθαρὸν καὶ λαμπρόν dictum putant. 34. Item Φάνητα appellant ἀπὸ τοῦ φαίνειν, et Φανεόν,

---

110 Δήλιος] Delius ω

---

419 Presumably garlands of laurel, the plant of Apollo.

420 Cf. Cornut. p. 67.15–16 (treated as an interpolation by Lang), Suda Λ.673 (~ Etym. Mag. p. 569.48–50), sim. Diod. Sic. 1.98.3 (citing Oenopides), Chrysipp. fr. 650 SVF 2:195–96. The "oblique circuit" is the ecliptic, the apparent path along which the sun moves throughout the year: it can be imagined as a plane that intersects the plane of the equator at an oblique angle (cf. Comm. 2.7.10). Another common etymology derives the epithet from the "obliquity" of Apollo's oracles (e.g., Cornut. p. 67.14–15).

421 On the relative positions, north and south, cf. §48.

422 Cf. Cornut. p. 67.2–3, Plut. Mor. 385B, Eustath. Comm. Il.

white goats with gilded horns; for Latona, a cow with gilded horns. The people were ordered to watch the games in the Circus wearing garlands.[419]

30. 'This is the chief tradition concerning the origin of the games of Apollo. Now let me show that Apollo and the sun are one and the same on the basis of the god's other names too. 31. He has the surname *Loxias*, as Oenopides says (fr. 7 D.-K.), "because he follows an oblique [*loxos*] circuit from his setting to his rising";[420] or, as Cleanthes writes (fr. 542 *SVF* 1:123), "because he moves along a spiral path [*helikas*]—for oblique [*loxai*] and spiral paths are the same thing—or because, being to the south while we are to the north, he lets loose oblique [*loxai*] rays upon us."[421] 32. He has the surname *Delios* "from making all things clear [*dêla*] and bright with his light."[422]

33. 'He is named *Phoebos*, as Cornificius says (fr. 5 *GRF* 1:476), "from moving violently" [*phoitân bia*], though most people think he is called *Phoebos*—that is, pure [*katharos*] and bright [*lampros*]—from his shining appearance.[423] 34. Similarly, they call him *Phanês* from "shining" (*phainein*) and *Phaneos* "because he appears renewed

---

1:138.1–2. This is the first in a series of allegorizing etymologies given to epithets derived from place-names, in this case *Delios* = "of Delos": see also §45 *Napaios* (from Napê on Lesbos), §48 *Smintheus* and *Killaios* and §49 *Thymbraios* (all from towns in the Troad), §64 *Didymaios* (from Didymê on Miletus), §65 *Delphios* (from Delphi), and cf. §36n., on Apollo Lycius.

[423] Cf. Cornut. p. 66.18–19 (sim. p. 33.4–5, on *Phoebê* = Artemis), Heraclit. *Allegories* 7.7, Plut. *Mor.* 388F, 393C, Apollon. *Homeric Lexicon* p. 164.13–14, Orion *Etym.* Φ p. 157.1–2, Hesych. Α.2336, Phot. *Lexicon* Φ p. 652.1, [Zon.] *Lexicon* Φ p. 1816.13–15, *Etym. Gud.* Φ p. 555.21–22, 36, *Etym. Mag.* p. 796.54–56.

SATURNALIA

ἐπειδὴ φαίνεται νέος, quia sol cotidie renovat sese, unde Vergilius,

mane novum.

35. 'Camerienses, qui sacram Soli incolunt insulam, Ἀειγενέτῃ Apollini immolant, τῷ τὸν ἥλιον ἀεὶ γίνεσθαι καὶ ἀεὶ γεννᾶν, id est quod semper exoriens gignitur quodque ipse generat universa inseminando fovendo producendo alendo augendoque.

36. 'Apollinis Lycii plures accipimus cognominis causas. Antipater Stoicus Lycium Apollinem nuncupatum scribit ἀπὸ τοῦ λευκαίνεσθαι πάντα φωτίζοντος ἡλίου. Cleanthes Lycium Apollinem appellatum notat quod, veluti lupi pecora rapiunt, ita ipse quoque umorem eripit radiis. 37. prisci Graecorum primam lucem, quae praecedit solis exortus, λύκην appellaverunt ἀπὸ τοῦ λευκοῦ. id temporis hodieque λυκόφως cognominant. 38. de quo tempore poeta ita scribit:

ἦμος δ᾽ οὔτ᾽ ἄρ᾽ πω ἠώς, ἔτι δ᾽ ἀμφιλύκη νύξ,

---

424 *Phanês* is an Orphic name for the supreme deity, cf. 1.18.12; *Phaneos* is not otherwise attested.

425 Viz., Rhodes: the name of the town, Kameiros, was derived from a son of Heracles.

426 An epic epithet (in the form *aiei-*) for the gods in general ("immortal": *Il.* 3.296 *et al.*, Hes. fr. 283.3 M.-W.), not otherwise associated specifically with Apollo.

427 The name was commonly connected with wolves in antiquity (implied by Aesch. *Seven against Thebes* 145, cf. Menecrates *FGrH* no. 769 fr. 2 = fr. 2 *EGM*, Cornut. p. 69.5–9, Paus. 2.19.3–4, Porph. *On Vegetarianism* 3.17, Σ Vetera *Il.* 4.101b1, Eustath.

[*phainetai neos*]," since the sun renews itself every day:[424] hence Virgil's phrase "new morning" (*G.* 3.325).

35. 'The people of Camirus, who inhabit an island sacred to the sun,[425] sacrifice to Apollo *Aeigenetês*,[426] "the sun ever becoming [*aei gignesthai*] and ever begetting [*aei gennân*]," because the sun always comes into being as it rises and because it generates all things, by planting and fostering the seeds, bringing them forth, nurturing them, and making them grow.

36. 'I have learned many explanations for the surname of Apollo Lycius. The Stoic Antipater writes (fr. 36 *SVF* 3:249) that Apollo Lycius got his name "from the fact that all thing appear white [*leukainesthai*] when the sun shines." Cleanthes remarks (fr. 541 *SVF* 1:123) that Apollo is called "Lycius" because just as wolves [Gk. *lykoi*] snatch animals from the flocks so the sun itself takes away dampness with its rays.[427] 37. The earliest Greeks called the first light that precedes the dawn *lykê*, from "white" [*leukos*]; that's the time that nowadays they call "twilight" [*lykophôs*].[428] 38. About that time the poet writes (*Il.* 7.433):

. . . when it was not yet dawn, but still the half-lit [*amphilykê*] night,

Comm. Il. 1:708.2–10), probably correctly, although "Apollo of Lycia" remains a possibility (cf. §38n.).

[428] The term *lykê* said to have been used by the "earliest Greeks" is attested only in the compound adj. *amphilykê* (§38), which M. is about to connect to *lykophôs* (i.e., "white-light"), though etymologically the latter more likely means "wolf-light" (cf. Aelian *On the Nature of Animals* 10.26, [Zon.] *Lexicon* Λ p. 1323.6–11).

idem Homerus,

εὔχεο δ᾽ Ἀπόλλωνι Λυκηγενέι κλυτοτόξῳ,

quod significat τῷ γεννῶντι τὴν λύκην, id est qui generat exortu suo lucem. radiorum enim splendor propinquantem solem longe lateque praecedens atque caliginem paulatim extenuans tenebrarum parit lucem. 39. neque minus Romani, ut pleraque alia ex Graeco, ita et lucem videntur a λύκη figurasse. annum quoque vetustissimi Graecorum λυκάβαντα appellabant τὸν ὑπὸ τοῦ λύκου id est sole βαινόμενον καὶ μετρούμενον. 40. λύκον autem solem vocari etiam Lycopolitana Thebaidos civitas testimonio est, quae pari religione Apollinem itemque lupum, hoc est λύκον, colit, in utroque solem venerans, quod hoc animal rapit et consumit omnia in modum solis, ac plurimum oculorum acie cernens tenebras noctis evincit. 41. ipsos quoque λύκους a λύκη id est a prima luce appellatos quidam putant, quia hae ferae maxime id tempus aptum rapiendo pecori observant, quod antelucanum post nocturnam famem ad pastum stabulis expellitur.

42. ʼApollinem Πατρῷον cognominaverunt non pro-

---

429 The epithet is otherwise interpreted as "wolf-born" (Aelian ibid.) or, more commonly, "Lycian-born": Heraclit. *Allegories* 7.10, Arrian *FGrH* no. 156 fr. 9, Herodian *GG* 3,1:249.4–5, Menand: Rhet. *On Epideictic Speeches* p. 439.13–24, Hesych. Λ.1376, Σ Vetera *Il*.4.101, Eustath. *Comm. Il*. 1:554.4–7.

430 Lat. *lux* has a cognate (not source) in Gk. *leukos*, from which M. derives *lykê* in §37.

431 Otherwise most commonly explained as "shadowy passage" (*lygaiôs bainein*: e.g., Apollon. *Homeric Lexicon* p. 109.11–12 ~ *Etym. Gud.* Λ p. 374.48–50 ~ Hesych. Λ.1365 ~ Eustath.

and Homer again (*Il.* 4.101),

> pray to Apollo Lykêgenês, famed for his bow,

where the epithet means "he who begets light [*gennôn tên lykên*]" when he rises.[429] For in heralding the sun's approach far and wide and gradually diminishing the shadows' gloom, his rays' brilliance gives birth to light. 39. Just so, the Romans seem to have formed *lux* ["light"] from *lykê*, just as they derived most other words from Greek.[430] The most ancient Greeks also called the year "*lykabas*," from "that which the sun [*lykos*] passes over [*bainein*] and measures."[431] 40. That the sun is called *lykos* is attested by the community of Lycopolis in the Thebaid, which pays cult to both Apollo and the wolf—that is, *lykos*—in both cases worshipping the sun, because that animal snatches and consumes all things, like the sun, and overcomes night's shadows in seeing a great deal with its sharp eyes.[432] 41. Some think that *lykoi* ["wolves"] are named after *lykê*, or first light, because these animals look especially for that time to ravage the flock, which is driven from the fold just before dawn to pasture after the night's fast.

42. 'They named Apollo *Patrôios* ['Ancestral'], not be-

Comm. Il. 2:68.18) or "wolf passage" (*lykous bainein*: Eustath. ibid. 21–22 ~ Σ *Od.* 14.161, *Suda* Λ.793). [432] The Thebaid was a district in Upper Egypt extending from Abydos (mod. el-'Araba el Madfuna) to Aswan, named after its largest city, Thebes. At Lycopolis (mod. Asyut), on the Nile's left bank, Osiris/ Wepwawet, guide of the dead to the Underworld, was worshipped under the form of a wolf, and mummified wolves have been found in chambers near the site; cf. Diod. Sic. 1.88.6–7 = Hecataeus of Abdera no. 264 fr. 25 *FGrH*, Strabo 17.1.40, Plut. *Mor.* 380B.

pria gentis unius aut civitatis religione sed ut auctorem
progenerandarum omnium rerum, quod sol umoribus ex-
siccatis ad progenerandum omnibus praebuit causam, ut
ait Orpheus,

> πατρὸς ἔχοντα νόον καὶ ἐπίφρονα βουλήν.

unde nos quoque Ianum patrem vocamus, solem sub hac
appellatione venerantes. 43. Νόμιον Ἀπόλλωνα cognominaverunt non ex officio pastorali et fabula per quam
fingitur Admeti regis pecora pavisse, sed quia sol pascit
omnia quae terra progenerat. 44. unde non unius generis
sed omnium pecorum pastor canitur ut apud Homerum
Neptuno dicente

> Φοῖβε, σὺ δ' εἰλίποδας ἕλικας βοῦς
> βουκολέεσκες,

atque idem apud eundem poetam equarum pastor significatur, ut ait,

> τὰς ἐν Φηρίῃ[111] θρέψ' ἀργυρότοξος Ἀπόλλων,
> ἄμφω θηλείας, φόβον Ἄρηος φορεούσας.

45. praeterea aedes ut ovium pastoris sunt apud Camiren-
ses Ἐπιμηλίου, apud Naxios Ποιμνίου itemque deus

111 Φηρ- ω (-ιφι a, -ιηι β): Πηρείη *Hom.*

---

433 Applied to any god, the epithet meant (*pace* M.) that the
god in question was linked to a city as its ancestor and protector:
Athenians pointed to Apollo's (alleged) paternity of Ion to claim
him as *patrôios* (Pl. *Euthyd.* 302D., Harpocrat. *Lexicon* p. 48.13–
37).

cause of a belief specific to a single nation or community,[433] but as the source of generation for all things, because the sun dried up moisture and so began the general process of propagation, "having," as Orpheus says (*PEGr* fr. 544),

> a father's good sense and shrewd counsel.

For that reason we call Janus father, worshipping the sun under that form of address. 43. They gave Apollo the surname *Nomios*, not from his service as a shepherd[434]— according to the story in which he pastured king Admetus' flocks—but because the sun provides sustenance for all the things the earth generates.[435] 44. That's why he is celebrated as the shepherd, not of a single kind of flock, but of all flocks, as when Neptune says in Homer (*Il.* 21.448)

> Phoebus, you were herding the cattle with their
> twisted horns and shambling gait;

and the same poet represents him as pasturing mares, saying (*Il.* 2.766–67),

> . . . the ones that Apollo of the silver bow nurtured in
> Phêriê,
> both of them mares, bearing with them the terror of
> Ares.

45. Note too that he has temples as a shepherd at Camirus,[436] as Apollo *Epimêlios* ["guardian of flocks"]; on Naxos, as Apollo *Poimnios* ["of the sheep"] and similarly

---

[434] Alluding to Gk. *nomios*, "of or pertaining to shepherds"; for the story of Admetus and Apollo, see esp. Eur. *Alcestis* 1ff., Callim. *Hymn to Apollo* 51ff.

[435] Cf. Eustath. *Comm. Il.* 4:535.7–8.   [436] Cf. §35n.

Ἀρνοκόμης colitur, et apud Lesbios Ναπαῖος; et multa sunt cognomina per diversas civitates ad dei pastoris officium tendentia. quapropter universi pecoris antistes et vere pastor agnoscitur.

46. ʿApollo Ἐλελεὺς appellatur ἀπὸ τοῦ ἐλίττεσθαι περὶ τὴν γῆν, quod aeterno circa terram meatu veluti volvi videtur, ut ait Euripides,

Ἥλιε, θοαῖς ἵπποισιν εἰλίσσων φλόγα;

ἢ ὅτι συναλισθέντος πολλοῦ πυρὸς περιπολεῖ, ut ait Empedocles:

οὕνεκ᾽ ἀναλισθεὶς[112] μέγαν οὐρανὸν ἀμφιπολεύει.

Platon[113] ἀπὸ τοῦ συναλίζειν[114] καὶ συναθροίζειν τοὺς ἀνθρώπους, ὅταν ἀνατείλῃ, quod exoriens homines conducit in coetum.

47. ʿApollo Χρυσοκόμας cognominatur a fulgore radiorum, quos vocant comas aureas solis, unde et Ἀκερσικόμης, quod numquam radii possunt a fonte lucis avelli; item Ἀργυρότοξος, quod enascens per summum orbis

---

[112] οὕνεκ᾽ ἀναλισθεὶς ed. Basil. 1535 (οὕνεκ᾽ ἀναλλισθεὶς ω): ἀλλ᾽ ὁ μὲν ἁλισθεὶς Emped.   [113] Platon] ΠΛΑΤΩΝ ω
[114] συναλίζειν Jan: -ACKEIN ω, ut vid., ἁλίζειν Plato

---

[437] None of these is otherwise attested as an epithet of Apollo.
[438] M. surely means "Apollo of the dells" (napai), but the epithet is based on the town of Napê on Lesbos: Hellanicus FGrH no. 4 fr. 35a, Σ Ar. Clouds 144 (cf. §32n.).   [439] Otherwise attested only as a cult-name of Bacchus (Ov. Met. 4.15); Gk. eleleu is a cry of pain.   [440] A somewhat free quotation of Crat. 409A.
[441] All three are very ancient epithets of Apollo, the first used

as the god "with lamb's fleece" (*Arnokomês*);[437] and on Lesbos, as Apollo *Napaios*;[438] and there are many surnames, used in widely scattered communities, that point to his service as a god of pasturage. That is why he is recognized as the protector of every flock and herd, a pastoral god in the full sense.

46. 'He is called Apollo *Eleleus*[439] from "circling [*elittesthai*] around the world," because he seems to roll along, as it were, in an unending circuit of the earth, as Euripides says (*Phoen.* 3),

> Sun, whirling your flames around with your swift
> horses;

or because he makes his circuit after gathering [*synalizein*] together much fire to himself, as Empedocles says (fr. 41 D.-K.),

> why, having gathered himself together [*analistheis*],
> does he circle the great heavens?

Plato, "from gathering people together [*synaliskein*] and causing them to assemble whenever he rises."[440]

47. 'Apollo is surnamed *Khrysokomas* ["golden-haired"] from the brilliance of his rays, which people call the sun's golden locks, and for the same reason he is called *Akersikomês* ["of the unshorn hair"], because the rays can never be separated from the source of light; similarly *Argyrotoxos* ["of the silver bow"],[441] because when it rises

in the mid-7th cent. BCE by Tyrtaeus (*FGrH* no. 580 fr. 3b.4), the other two by Homer (respectively, *Il.* 20.39 and, e.g., *Il.* 2.766). With M.'s allegorizing interpretation cf. Cornut. p. 66.19–22, Mart. Cap. 1.13, 19, Eustath. *Comm. Il.* 1:53.21ff.

ambitum velut arcus quidam figuratur alba et argentea
specie, ex quo arcu radii in modum emicant sagittarum.
48. Σμινθεὺς cognominatur, ὅτι ζέων θεῖ, quia fervens
currit, Καρνεῖος, ἐπεὶ καιόμενος ὁρᾶται νέος, vel quod,
cum omnia ardentia consumantur, hic suo calore candens
semper novus constat. item Ἀπόλλων Κιλλαῖος, ὅτι τὰς
κινήσεις λαιὰς ποιεῖ, semper nobis ab austro currens.
49. Θυμβραῖος Ἀπόλλων ὁ τοὺς ὄμβρους θείς, quod est
deus imbricitor; Ἀπόλλων Φιλήσιος, quod lumen eius
exoriens amabile amicissima veneratione consalutamus.

50. Ἀπόλλων Πύθιος οὐκ ἀπὸ τῆς πεύσεως, id est non
a consultatione oraculorum dictus a physicis aestimatur,
sed ἀπὸ τοῦ πύθειν, id est σήπειν, quod numquam sine vi
caloris efficitur. 51. hinc ergo Πύθιον dictum aestimant,
licet hoc nomen ex nece draconis inditum deo Graeci fabu-
lentur, quae tamen fabula non abhorret ab intellectu naturalis arcani, quod apparebit si percurratur ordo qui de
Apolline nascente narratur, sicut paulo superius enarratu-
rum me esse promisi.

52. 'Latonae Apollinem Dianamque parituras Iuno
dicitur obstitisse, sed ubi quandoque partus effusus est,
draconem ferunt, qui Πύθων vocitabatur, invasisse cunas

On *Smintheus* and *Killaios* see §32n. The cult of Apollo
Karneios, centered in the Peloponnese, was reportedly founded
by one Karnos (Theopomp. *FGrH* no. 115 fr. 357, Paus. 3.13.4,
Hesych. K.842).

443 Cf. §31. When we face westward to follow the sun's path, it
is on our left = south, cf. 1.21.18 n.   444 Cf. §32n.

445 The epithet (cf. Arnob. 1.26.4, with Varro *Divine Antiquities* fr. 252 and Brown 2002, 235–36, on Conon fr. 1.xxxiii.19–20)
derives from the kiss (*philêma*) shared by Apollo and the beautiful

the outmost edge of its orb is shaped like a silvery-white bow, from which the rays flash like arrows. 48. He is surnamed *Smintheus* "because he boils as he runs [*zeôn thei*]"; *Karneios*, "because he appears new while he burns [*kaiomenos horatai neos*]," that is, though all things are consumed when they burn, he remains new while blazing with his own heat. Similarly, he is called Apollo *Killaios* "because he moves on the left [*kinêsieis laias*],"[442] always speeding from the south in relation to us.[443] 49. Apollo *Thymbraios* is "the one who sends showers," because he is the rain-god;[444] Apollo *Philêsios*, because when his dear [Gk. *philos*] light rises we greet it with most affectionate reverence.[445]

50. 'The physical scientists judge that Apollo *Pythios* is not named "from inquiring [*peusis*]"—that is, not from the consultation of his oracles—but "from causing to molder [*pythein*]"—that is, rot [*sêpein*]—which always requires the power of heat.[446] 51. That's the reason they think he's called *Pythios*, though the Greeks tell the tale that the god got this name from killing a serpent—a tale that is not inconsistent with an interpretation based on the mysteries of nature, as will be clear if I tell the story of baby Apollo from start to finish, as I promised I would do a little earlier [§17].

52. 'When Latona was going to give birth to Apollo and Diana, Juno is said to have stood in her way; but when at length she had delivered, they say that a serpent called *Py-*

boy Branchos, who (having been thus inspired) founded the oracle of Apollo at Didymê (cf. §64).

[446] For the first derivation, cf. Cornut. p. 67.9–11, Σ Ar. *Wealth* 39, Σ Pind. *P.* 1 inscr. b; for the second, cf. *Hom. Hymn to Apollo* 371, Σ Pind. ibid., Σ *Marciana* Dion. Thrax p. 346.31.

deorum Apollinemque in prima infantia sagittis beluam
confecisse. 53. quod ita intellegendum naturalis ratio demonstrat. namque post chaos ubi primum coepit confusa
deformitas in rerum formas et in elementa enitescere, terraque adhuc umida substantia molli atque instabili sede
nutaret, convalescente paulatim aetherio calore atque
inde seminibus in eam igneis defluentibus, haec sidera
edita esse creduntur et solem quidem maxima vi caloris in
superna raptum, lunam vero umidiore et velut femineo
sexu naturali quodam pressam tepore inferiora tenuisse,
tamquam ille magis substantia patris constet, haec matris.
54. si quidem Latonam physici volunt terram videri, cui
diu intervenit Iuno ne numina quae diximus ederentur:
hoc est aer, qui tunc umidus adhuc gravisque obstabat
aetheri ne fulgor luminum per umoris aerii densitatem
tamquam e cuiusdam partus progressione fulgeret. 55. sed
divinae providentiae vicit instantia, quae creditur iuvisse
partum. ideo in insula Delo ad confirmandam fidem fabulae aedes Providentiae, quam ναὸν Προνοίας Ἀθηνᾶς
appellant, apta religione celebratur. 56. propterea in insula
dicuntur enati, quod ex mari nobis oriri videntur. haec in-

---

447 Cf. [Apollod.] *Library* 1.22, Ov. *Met.* 1.438–50, Plut. *Mor.*
293C, and the refs. at §17n.

448 Cf. 7.6.17, 7.7.2–7.   449 I.e., Juno: cf. 1.15.20n.

450 Athena Pronoia was worshipped in Delphi (e.g., Demosth.
25.34, Paus. 10.8.7), not Delos. M. might confuse the two places
elsewhere (cf. 6.5.8n.), but the remarks that follow do not suggest
a mere slip here; perhaps he or a source was misled by Hyperides
fr. 67.9–11 (= Ael. Arist. *Panath.* 13), where Athena Pronoia is
imagined leading Leto to Delos.

451 I.e., as sun and moon.

thon attacked the gods' cradles and that the infant Apollo killed the beast with his arrows.[447] 53. Natural science shows that the story is to be understood in the following terms. After the time of chaos, when the formless confusion began to take on the visible shapes of things and their elements, and the earth, still moist, tottered on a shaky foundation of labile material, as the heaven's warmth gained strength and showered down fiery seeds upon the earth these two stars are believed to have been produced: the sun—carried up into the highest regions because its heat was greatest—and the moon—keeping to the lower regions, held in check by the moister kind of warmth that is natural to the female sex[448]—as though the one were composed of a father's elements, the other of a mother's. 54. Now the physical scientists want Latona to be seen as the earth, long hindered by Juno, who wished to prevent the divinities I've mentioned from being born: that is, the air,[449] which was then still moist and heavy, was blocking up the heavens and preventing the lights' brilliance from shining forth (as though in the natural sequence of birth) through the thick, moist air. 55. But the ineluctable force of divine providence, which is believed to have aided the birth, carried the day: hence on the island of Delos (to lend credibility to the tale) a temple of Providence, which they call the shrine of Athena *Pronoia* ["of foreknowledge"],[450] is tended with appropriate ceremony. 56. Apollo and Diana are said to have been born on an island because they seem to us to rise up out of the sea;[451] the island is called

sula ideo Delos vocatur, quia ortus et quasi partus luminum omnia facit δῆλα, id est aperta clarescere.

57. 'Haec est autem de nece draconis ratio naturalis, ut
scribit Antipater Stoicus. nam terrae adhuc umidae exhalatio, meando in supera volubili impetu atque inde sese,
postquam calefacta est, instar serpentis mortiferi in infera
revolvendo, corrumpebat omnia vi putredinis, quae non
nisi ex calore et umore generatur, ipsumque solem densitate caliginis obtegendo videbatur quodam modo lumen
eius eximere: sed divino fervore radiorum tandem velut
sagittis incidentibus extenuata exsiccata enecta, interempti draconis ab Apolline fabulam fecit. 58. est et alia ratio
draconis perempti. nam solis meatus licet ab ecliptica linea
numquam recedat, sursum tamen ac deorsum ventorum
vices certa deflexione variando iter suum velut flexum draconis involvit. 59. unde Euripides:

> πυριγενὴς δὲ δράκων ὁδὸν ἡγεῖται ταῖς
> τετραμόρφοις
> ὥραις[115] ζευγνὺς ἁρμονίᾳ πλούτου πολύκαρπον
> ὄχημα.

sub hac ergo appellatione caelestis itineris sol cum confecisset suum cursum, draconem confecisse dicebatur. inde
fabula exorta est de serpentis nece. 60. sagittarum autem

---

[115] ταῖς τετραμόρφοις ὥραις] ὥραισι Jan (anapaesticum
metrum censens), ταῖς et ὥραις eiec., -μόρφῳ coniec. Wilamowitz
(dactylicum metrum putans)

---

452 Cf. §32n.
453 Cf. 7.16.17–18.

Delos because the sun's and moon's rising—their birth, so
to speak—makes all things *dêla*, that is, plain and bright.[452]

57. The following is a natural-scientific explanation of
the serpent's death, according to the Stoic Antipater (fr. 46
SVF 3:250–51). The emanations of the still-damp earth
rose swiftly to the higher regions and, becoming warmed,
rolled back down to the lower regions like a deadly serpent, corrupting everything with the putrefying force to
which dampness and warmth give rise,[453] and it seemed
to blot out the very sun with its thick murk and, in a sense,
extinguish its light. But at last these emanations were
thinned out, dried out, and destroyed by the divine heat
of the sun's rays, falling like a shower of arrows—hence
the tale of the serpent slain by Apollo. 58. There is also another interpretation of the serpent's destruction: though
the sun's course never varies from the ecliptic, the shift-
ing winds vary their course with a regular up and down
movement,[454] rolling along like a slithering serpent.[455]
59. Hence Euripides says (fr. 1111a *TrGF* 5,2:1022),[456]

But the fire-born serpent leads the way for the four-
    fold
seasons, yoking with wealth's harmony a cart rich in
    fruit.

Under the name "Pythios" the sun was said to have put an
end to the serpent when it completed the proper course of
its heavenly journey. 60. The "arrows" must signify the

454 Cf. 1.19.10.
455 Cf. Pliny *Natural History* 2.67.
456 Editors regard the lines, which are not in Euripides' manner, as being of dubious authenticity: *TrGF* 5,2:1023.

SATURNALIA

nomine non nisi radiorum iactus ostenditur, qui tunc longissimi intelleguntur quo tempore altissimus sol diebus
longissimis solstitio aestivo conficit annuum cursum, inde
Ἑκηβόλος et Ἑκατηβόλος dictus ἔκαθεν τὰς ἀκτῖνας
βάλλων, e longissimo altissimoque radios in terram usque
demittens.

61. De Pythii cognomine sufficere ista potuissent ni
haec quoque se ratio eiusdem appellationis ingereret. cum
enim sol in signo Cancri aestivum solstitium facit, in quo
est longissimi dici terminus, et inde retrogressum agit ad
diminutionem dierum, Pythius eo tempore appellatur ὡς
πύματον θεῶν, ὅ ἐστιν τὸν τελευταῖον δρόμον τρέχων.
62. idem ei nomen convenit et cum Capricornum rursus
ingrediens ultimum brevissimi diei cursum intellegitur
peregisse, et ideo in alterutro signorum peracto annuo
spatio draconem Apollo, id est flexuosum iter suum, ibi
confecisse memoratur. hanc opinionem Cornificius in Ety-
mis retulit. 63. ideo autem iis duobus signis quae portae
solis vocantur, Cancro et Capricorno, haec nomina conti-
gerunt, quod cancer animal retro atque oblique cedit eademque ratione sol in eo signo obliquum ut solet incipit
agere retrogressum, caprae vero consuetudo haec in pastu
videtur ut semper altum pascendo petat, sed et sol in
Capricorno incipit ab imis in alta remeare.

Cf. *Etym. Gud.* E p. 443.21–22, Eustath. *Comm. Il.*
1:65.16–19.   Lit. "makes the summer *solstitium*," the
"solstice" being the time when "the sun stands still" (*sol + sistere*:
Varro *Latin Language* 6.8, cf. §26, *Comm.* 2.7.10).

I.e., the winter solstice.   Cf. *Comm.* 1.12.1, Numenius 5 fr. 32, Proclus *Comm. on Plato's Republic* 2:129.21–23.

Cf. 1.21.26, 1.22.6.

sun's rays, which are of course longest when the sun is completing its year-long course and stands at the highest point in the sky on the summer solstice, when the days are longest: hence the epithets "far-shooting" [*Hekêbolos*] and "who strikes from afar" [*Hekatêbolos*], since he casts [*ballôn*] his rays from far off [*hekathen*], sending them down to the earth from highest and farthest point.[457]

61. 'This account of the surname "Pythios" could have sufficed, were it not for another explanation of the name that thrusts itself forward. When the sun reaches its summer stopping point[458] in the sign of Cancer, delimiting the longest day, and then retreats, making the days shorter, it is called "Pythios" from "running last" (*pymaton theôn*), that is, running its final course. 62. The same name also suits him when he enters Capricorn[459] again and is taken to have "run the final course" of the shortest day: that is why Apollo is said to have put an end to the serpent—that is, to have ended his own sinuous journey—when he has completed his yearly course in one or the other of the two signs. Cornificius relates this account in his *Origins* (fr. 9 *GRF* 1:477). 63. The two signs that are called the "gates of the sun,"[460] Cancer ["Crab"] and Capricorn ["Goat's Horn"], got their names because the crab is an animal that moves backward and at an angle—just as the sun is accustomed to begin its backward and oblique course in that sign—while it seems to be the goat's habit at pasture always to seek the heights while grazing[461]—just as the sun in Capricorn begins to return to the heights from its nadir.

64. Ἀπόλλωνα Διδυμαῖον vocant, quod geminam speciem sui numinis praefert ipse inluminando formandoque lunam. etenim ex uno fonte lucis gemino sidere spatia diei et noctis inlustrat, unde et Romani solem sub nomine et specie Iani Didymaei Apollinis appellatione venerantur. 65. Ἀπόλλωνα Δέλφιον vocant, quod quae obscura sunt claritudine lucis ostendit ἐκ τοῦ δηλοῦν τὰ ἀφανῆ aut, ut Numenio placet, quasi unum et solum. ait enim prisca Graecorum lingua δέλφον unum vocari. unde et frater, inquit, ἀδελφός dicitur quasi iam non unus. 66. Hieropolitani praeterea, qui sunt gentis Assyriorum, omnes solis effectus atque virtutes ad unius simulacri barbati speciem redigunt eumque Apollinem appellant. 67. huius facies prolixa in acutum barba figurata est, eminente super caput calatho. simulacrum thorace munitum est, dextera erectam tenet hastam superstante Victoriae parvulo signo, sinistra floris porrigit speciem summisque ab umeris Gorgoneum velamentum redimitum anguibus tegit scapulas. aquilae propter ⟨caput⟩[116] exprimunt instar volatus, ante pedes imago feminea est, cuius dextera laevaque sunt signa feminarum, ea cingit flexuoso volumine draco. 68. radios in terram superne iaci barba demissa significat. calathus aureus surgens in altum monstrat aetheris summam, unde solis creditur esse substantia. hastae atque lo-

[116] caput *supplevi*

---

[462] Cf. §32n.   [463] Cf. 1.9.5.   [464] Cf. §32n.

[465] The form *delphos* is not attested.

[466] Hieropolis (more usually, Hierapolis) = Bambykê (mod. Manbij) in northern Syria ("Assyria" is a literary license); cf. Lightfoot 2003, 38–44. With §§66–70 compare Lucian *The Syrian*

64. 'They call Apollo *Didymaios* ["Twin"][462] because he presents the twofold aspect of his godhead in also giving the moon its light and form: from a single source of light he illuminates the reaches of day and night with twin stars, and that is why the Romans too worship the sun under the name and likeness of Janus,[463] with the epithet "Didymaean Apollo." 65. They call Apollo *Delphios*[464] because his bright light "reveals things unseen" [*dêloun ta aphanê*] or, as Numenius thinks (fr. 54), because he is the one and only: for he says that in the earliest form of Greek *delphos* meant "one"[465]—that, he claims, is why *adelphos* means "brother," that is, "one who is not [*a-*] any longer one [*delphos*]." 66. Furthermore, the people of Hieropolis,[466] who are Assyrian by origin, capture all of the sun's actions and powers in the form of a single bearded statue, which they call Apollo. 67. The statue has a full beard that ends in a point, with a basket high atop its head and a breastplate on its chest; its right hand holds an upright spear topped with a small image of Victory, while its left holds out the image of a flower; a cloak with a Gorgon's head and a border of snakes hangs down from the top of the shoulders and covers the back. Eagles next to ‹the head› represent flight; before its feet is a woman's likeness with images of women wreathed by serpent's coils to her left and right. 68. The beard extending downward signifies the sun's rays hurled down upon the earth from above; the golden basket rising high signifies the summit of heaven, whence the sun is believed to derive its essence. The

Goddess 35–37, on the "Apollo" of Hieropolis (i.e., Nebo = Babylonian Nabu, god of wisdom and writing), with Lightfoot 2003, 456–69, esp. 460–64, on the description of the statue that follows.

ricae argumento imago adiungitur Martis, quem eundem ac solem esse procedens sermo patefaciet. Victoria testatur cuncta submitti huius sideris potestati. floris species florem rerum protestatur, quas hic deus inseminat progenerat fovet nutrit maturatque. 69. species feminea terrae imago est, quam sol desuper inlustrat. signa duo aeque feminea quibus ambitur hylen naturamque significant confamulantes, et draconis effigies flexuosum iter sideris monstrat. aquilae propter altissimam velocitatem volatus altitudinem solis ostendunt. 70. addita est Gorgonea vestis, quod Minerva quam huius praesidem accipimus solis virtus sit, sicut et Porphyrius testatur Minervam esse virtutem solis quae humanis mentibus prudentiam subministrat. nam ideo haec dea Iovis capite prognata memoratur, id est de summa aetheris parte edita, unde origo solis est.

18   'Haec quae de Apolline diximus possunt etiam de Libero dicta existimari. nam Aristoteles, qui Theologumena scripsit, Apollinem et Liberum patrem unum eundemque deum esse cum multis aliis argumentis adserat, etiam apud Ligyreos ait in Thracia esse adytum Libero consecratum ex qua redduntur oracula. sed in hoc adyto vaticinaturi

---

467 Cf. 1.19.1–6.   468 Highest region: cf. 3.4.8n., with Arnob. 3.31.1 and Aug. *City of God* 7.16 (associating Minerva with the moon rather than the sun), Serv. on *A.* 4.201.

469 Much of 1.18 is derived from Cornelius Labeo, cf. Mastandrea 1977, 111–12, 159–61, 169–70; with §§1–4 cf. Arnob. 3.31–34.   470 The author in question was probably the mythographer Aristocles, author of a *Theogony* (no. 33 fr. 1 *FGrH*, cf. fr. 4), his name having been dislodged by Aristotle's more famous name already in Labeo, the common source of M. and Arnob. 3.31.1 ("Aristotle," also with citation of Granius [Flaccus], cf. §4 below); differently Mastandrea 1977, p. 111 n. 25.

spears and breastplate represent the likeness of Mars, who is identified with the sun, as my subsequent remarks will show.[467] The image of victory bears witness that all things are subject to this star's power, while the flower anticipates the blossoming of the things that the god fills with seed, brings to birth, fosters, nurtures, and makes ripe. 69. The woman's likeness represents the earth, on which the sun sheds its light from above, and the two female statues on either side signify the matter and the nature that serve her; the serpent's likeness points to the star's sinuous course, and the eagles, because they fly very high and fast, represent the sun's loftiness. 70. The garment with the Gorgon's image is added because Minerva, to whom we know the garment belongs, is the power of the sun: so Porphyry, too, bears witness (fr. 478 Smith) that Minerva is the power of the sun that makes human beings wise. That is why this goddess is said to have been born from Jupiter's head, which is to say, from the highest region of heaven,[468] which is also the origin of the sun.

'What I've said about Apollo can be taken to apply to Liber too.[469] For Aristotle, who wrote *Discourses on the Gods*,[470] advances many proofs to support his claim that Apollo and father Liber are one and the same,[471] including the fact that the Ligyreans in Thrace have a shrine consecrated to Liber from which oracles issue.[472] In this shrine the soothsayers drink a great deal of unmixed wine before

18

---

[471] Cf. Arnob. 3.33.2, Serv. on *A.* 6.78, *E.* 5.66 (= Porph. fr. 477 Smith), *G.* 1.5, Mart. Cap. 2.191.

[472] For prophetic drunkenness associated with Dionysus, cf. Athen. 38A. The Ligyreans of Thrace are not otherwise known.

plurimo mero sumpto, uti apud Clarium aqua pota, effantur oracula. 2. apud Lacedaemonios etiam in sacris quae Apollini celebrant, Hyacinthia vocantes, hedera coronantur Bacchico ritu. 3. item Boeotii, Parnassum montem Apollini sacratum esse memorantes, simul tamen in eodem et oraculum Delphicum et speluncas Bacchicas uni deo consecratas colunt; unde et Apollini et Libero patri in eodem monte res divina celebratur. 4. quod cum et Varro et Granius Flaccus adfirment, etiam Euripides his docet:

Διόνυσος[117] θύρσοισι καὶ νεβρῶν δοραῖς
καθαπτὸς ἐν πεύκαισι Παρνασσὸν κάτα
πηδᾷ χορεύων . . .

5. in hoc monte Parnasso Bacchanalia alternis annis aguntur, ubi et Satyrorum, ut adfirmant, frequens cernitur coetus et plerumque voces propriae exaudiuntur, itemque cymbalorum crepitus ad aures hominum saepe perveniunt. 6. et ne quis opinetur diversis dis Parnassum montem dicatum, idem Euripides in Licymnio, Apollinem Liberumque unum eundemque deum esse significans, scribit,

δέσποτα φιλόδαφνε Βάκχε, παιὰν Ἄπολλον
εὔλυρε.

[117] ὃς suppl. post Διόνυσος ed. Basil. 1535

---

[473] Cf. Pliny *Natural History* 2.232, Tac. *Ann.* 2.54, Iambl. *On the Mysteries* 3.11
[474] Cf. Paus. 10.32.7, Σ Ar. *Acharnians* 348b,d, *Suda* Π.679; acc. to Lucan 5.71–74, the semiannual rites mentioned in §5 are

pronouncing their prophecies, as those on Claros drink water.[473] 2. The Lacedaemonians also wear the ivy garlands of Bacchic cult in the rites they perform for Apollo, called the Hyacinthia. 3. Similarly, though the Boeotians say that Mount Parnassus is sacred to Apollo, they maintain the cult of the Delphic oracle and the caves of Bacchus in the same place at the same time, as consecrated to a single god, so that sacrifice is offered both to Apollo and Liber on the same mountain.[474] 4. Both Varro[475] and Granius Flaccus (fr. 2 *IAH* 1:262 = fr. 2 *IAR*[6] 1:54) support this view, and Euripides, too, teaches the same lesson in these lines (fr. 752 *TrGF* 5,2:743):

> Dionysus leaps and dances down Parnassus
> amid the pines, girt with the thyrsus and
> the skins of does . . .

5. Every other year on Mount Parnassus they celebrate the rites of Bacchus, where (they claim) a throng of satyrs is seen and their actual voices are usually heard, and the raucous sounds of cymbals often reach human ears. 6. And lest anyone suppose that Mount Parnassus is dedicated to two distinct gods, Euripides also writes as follows in his *Licymnian*, indicating that Apollo and Liber are one and the same god (fr. 477 *TrGF* 5,1:522):

> Lord Bacchus who loves the laurel, Paean Apollo
> skilled with the lyre,

offered to the "blended divinity" (*numine mixto*) of Apollo and Bacchus.

[475] Perhaps in *Divine Antiquities* Books 14–16, on the gods.

ad eandem sententiam Aeschylus,

ὁ κισσεὺς Ἀπόλλων ὁ Βακχεῖος ὁ μάντις.[118]

7. 'Sed licet illo prius adserto eundem esse Apollinem ac solem; edoctoque postea ipsum esse Liberum patrem qui Apollo est, nulla ex his dubitatio sit solem ac Liberum patrem eiusdem numinis habendum, absolute tamen hoc argumentis liquidioribus adstruetur. 8. in sacris enim haec religiosi arcani observatio tenetur, ut sol cum in supero id est in diurno hemisphaerio est, Apollo vocitetur: cum in infero id est nocturno, Dionysus qui est Liber pater habeatur. 9. item Liberi patris simulacra partim puerili aetate, partim iuvenis fingunt, praeterea barbata specie, senili quoque, uti Graeci eius quem Βασσαρέα, item quem Βρισέα appellant, et ut in Campania Neapolitani celebrant Ἥβωνα cognominantes. 10. hae autem aetatum diversitates ad solem referuntur, ut parvulus videatur hiemali solstitio, qualem Aegyptii proferunt ex adyto die certa,

---

[118] ὁ Βακχεῖος ὁ μάντις] ὁ βακχειόμαντις Ellis, alii alia

---

[476] Cf. Plut. *Mor.* 388F-389B, Serv. on *E.* 5.66 (= Porph. fr. 477 Smith).

[477] E.g., *LIMC* 3,1:479–82, 3,2:376–81.

[478] Cf. Cornut. p. 60.9–11.

[479] *Dionysos Bassareus* = "Dionysos of the maenads" (*bassarai/Bassarides*, so called from the fox-skins they wore): cf. Aesch. fr. 59 *TGrF* 3:180 (with ibid. 138–39), Hor. *Odes* 1.18.11, Prop. 3.17.30, Caesius Bassus fr. 2 *FPL*[3] = Anon. fr. 27 *FLP*[2]. *Dionysos Br(e)iseus* (*-saios*): a cult title derived in antiquity from Mt. Brêsa on Lesbos (Steph. Byz. 2.174 Billerbeck, *Etym. Gen.* B.263) or from the verb *brithein* ("prevail": *Etym. Gen.* ibid.), at-

and along the same lines Aeschylus writes (fr. 341 *TrGF* 3:412),

Apollo the ivy-crowned, the Bacchic seer.

7. 'But given the earlier proof that Apollo and the sun are the same, and the subsequent demonstration that father Liber is the very same as Apollo, there can be no doubt but that the sun and father Liber must be considered aspects of the same godhead—yet the point will be proved to perfection by the following, still more transparent arguments. 8. They observe the holy mystery in the rites by calling the sun Apollo when it is in the upper (that is, daytime) hemisphere; when it is in the lower (that is, night-time) hemisphere, it is considered Dionysus, who is Liber.[476] 9. Similarly, some images of father Liber are fashioned in the form of a boy,[477] others of a young man, sometimes also bearded, or even elderly,[478] like the image of the one the Greeks call *Bassareus*, and also the one they call *Briseus*, and like the one the people of Naples in Campania worship under the name *Hêbôn*.[479] 10. But the different ages are to be understood with reference to the sun. It is very small at the winter solstice, like the image the Egyptians bring out from its shrine on a fixed date, with the ap-

tested epigraphically at Smyrna (*ISmyrna* 600–1, 622, 639, 652); his beard is reported also at [Cornut.] *Schol. Pers.* 1.76(8). *Hêbôn* is not otherwise attested as a cult-title of Dionysus but appears in 2 inscriptions dedicated at Naples "to the most manifest god Hêbôn" (*IG* 14.716–17); if (as it seems) the name is a pres. participle of *hêbân* ("to be in one's prime"), it occupies an anomalous place in this catalogue. For the bearded Dionysus see, e.g., *LIMC* 3,1:430–33,437–38, 3,2:301, 303, 310.

quod tunc brevissimo die veluti parvus et infans videatur,
exinde autem procedentibus augmentis aequinoctio ver-
nali similiter atque adulescentis adipiscitur vires figuraque
iuvenis ornatur. postea statuitur eius aetas plenissima
effigie barbae solstitio aestivo, quo tempore summum sui
consequitur augmentum. exinde per deminutiones veluti
senescenti quarta forma deus figuratur. 11. item in Thracia
eundem haberi solem atque Liberum accipimus, quem illi
Sebazium[119] nuncupantes magnifica religione celebrant,
ut Alexander scribit, eique deo in colle Zilmisso aedes di-
cata est specie rotunda, cuius medium interpatet tectum.
rotunditas aedis monstrat huiusce sideris speciem, sum-
moque tecto lumen admittitur, ut appareat solem cuncta
vertice summo lustrare lucis inmissu, et quia oriente eo
universa patefiunt. 12. Orpheus quoque solem volens intellegi ait inter cetera:

> τήκων αἰθέρα δῖον ἀκίνητον πρὶν ἐόντα
> ἐξανέφηνε θεοῖσιν ὁρᾶν[120] κάλλιστον ἰδέσθαι,
> ὃν δὴ νῦν καλέουσι Φάνητά τε καὶ Διόνυσον
> Εὐβουλῆα τ᾽ ἄνακτα καὶ Ἀνταύγην ἀρίδηλον·

[119] Sebazium *scripsi* (*cf.*, *e.g.*, *IGBulg.* 2.678, 3,2.1588, 4.1985,
Sabazium *Meurs*): sebad- ω
[120] θεοῖς ⸉Ωρον *vel* ὥραν *Gesner* (*ed. 1764*)

---

480 For the image cf. Mart. Cap. 1.76.
481 Cf. Diod. Sic. 4.4.1, John Lydus *On the Months* 4.51, *Orphic Hymns* 48.1–2, Hesych. Σ.5, *Etym. Mag.* p. 707.15, Σ Ar.
Wasps 9, *Birds* 874. Probably of Phrygian origin, Sabazius was
commonly identified with Zeus/Jupiter, not Apollo and Dionysus.
The form of the name found in the archetype, *Sebadius*, is un-

pearance of a small infant, since it's the shortest day. Then, as the days become progressively longer, by the vernal equinox it resembles a vigorous young man and is given the form of a youth. Later, full maturity at the summer solstice is represented by a beard, by which point it has grown as much as it will grow. Thereafter, as the days become ever shorter, the god is rendered in the fourth shape, like a man growing old.[480] 11. Similarly, we learn that in Thrace the sun and Liber are considered the same: they call him Sebazius and worship him in a splendid ritual, as Alexander writes (no. 273 fr. 103 *FGrH*),[481] and on the hill Zilmissus[482] they dedicate to him a round temple, its center open to the sky. The temple's round shape points to the sun's shape, and light is let in through the roof to show that the sun purifies all things when it shines down from on high, and because the whole world opens up when the sun rises. 12. Orpheus too, intending a reference to the sun to be understood, says (among other things) (*PEGr* fr. 237),

Melting the bright ether that was before now
    unmoved,
he revealed to the gods the fairest sight to be seen,
the one they now call both Phanês and Dionysos,[483]
sovereign Euboulês and Antaugês[484] seen from afar:

attested elsewhere, though *Sebazius* is common on inscriptions from Thrace (a dozen examples in *IGBulg*).

[482] Not otherwise attested, although the cult title *Zylmyzdr(i)ênos* is found on inscriptions dedicated to Asclepius in Thrace.

[483] Cf. Diod. Sic. 1.11.3.

[484] This epithet, not glossed below, means "shining in response"; cf. *Orphic Hymns* 6.8–9, where it reappears with "Phanês."

ἄλλοι δ' ἄλλο καλοῦσιν ἐπιχθονίων ἀνθρώπων.
πρῶτος δ' ἐς φάος ἦλθε, Διώνυσος δ' ἐπεκλήθη,
οὕνεκα δινεῖται κατ' ἀπείρονα μακρὸν Ὄλυμπον·
ἀλλαχθεὶς δ' ὄνομ' ἔσχε, προσωνυμίας πρὸς
    ἑκάστων[121]
παντοδαπὰς[122] κατὰ καιρὸν ἀμειβομένοιο
    χρόνοιο.

13. Φάνητα dixit solem ἀπὸ τοῦ φωτὸς καὶ φανεροῦ, id est a lumine atque inluminatione, quia cunctis visitur cuncta conspiciens. Διόνυσος, ut ipse vates ait, ἀπὸ τοῦ δινεῖσθαι καὶ περιφέρεσθαι, id est quod circumferatur in ambitum. 14. unde Cleanthes ita cognominatum scribit ἀπὸ τοῦ διανύσαι, quia cotidiano impetu ab oriente ad occasum diem noctemque faciendo caeli conficit cursum. 15. physici Διόνυσον Διὸς νοῦν, quia solem mundi mentem esse dixerunt. mundus autem vocatur caelum, quod appellant Iovem. unde Aratus de caelo dicturus ait,

    ἐκ Διὸς ἀρχώμεσθα.

16. Liber a Romanis appellatur,[123] quod liber et vagus est, ut ait Laevius,[124]

---

[121] ἑκάστων *Vollgraff*: EKACTON ω
[122] προσωνυμίαις τ' ἐκέκαστο/παντοδαπαῖς *Lobeck (ed. 1829)*
[123] -tur *PFA*: -tus ω
[124] Laevius *Scaliger*: Naevius ω

---

485 Cf. Diod. ibid. Phanês is the creator- and ruler-god in Orphic theology.

among men who dwell on earth, some give him one
   name, others another.
First he came into the light, and was named
   Dionysos,
because he whirls along the limitless length of
   Olympos;
but then he changed his name and took on forms of
   address of every sort
from every source, as suits the alternating seasons.

13. He called the sun *Phanês* from "light [*phôs*] and illumi-
nation [*phaneros*],"[485] because in seeing all he is seen by
all, and *Dionysus*, as the inspired singer himself says, from
"whirling [*dineisthai*] about in a circle."[486] 14. Cleanthes
writes (fr. 546 *SVF* 1:124) that he is so named from "bringing to completion [*dianysai*]," because as he hastens every
day from east to west he completes the course of heaven
by creating day and night.[487] 15. The physical scientists
say Dionysus is "the mind of Zeus" [*Dios noun*],[488] claiming that the sun is the mind of the cosmic order, which is
called "the heavens," which in turn is addressed as Jupiter.
Thus Aratus, intending to speak about the heavens, says
(*Phaen.* 1):

Let us take our start from Zeus.

16. The Romans call the god Liber because he wanders
free [*liber*],[489] as Laevius says (fr. 31 *FPL*[3]),

---

[486] Cf. Porph. *On Statues* 8.
[487] Cf. Artemid. *Interpretation of Dreams* 2.37, Porph. ibid.
[488] Cf. Amm. Marc. 21.1.11, John Lydus *On the Months* 4.51.
[489] Cf. Catull. 64.390, John Lydus ibid., *LALE* 337.

Hac qua sol vagus igneas habenas
immittit propius iugatque terrae.

17. 'Idem versus Orphaici[125] Εὐβουλῆα vocantes boni
consilii hunc deum praestitem monstrant. nam si conceptu
mentis consilia nascuntur, mundi autem mentem solem
esse opinantur auctores, a quo in homines manat intelle-
gendi principium, merito boni consilii solem antistitem
crediderunt. 18. solem Liberum esse manifeste pronuntiat
Orpheus hoc versu:

Ἥλιος ὃν Διόνυσον ἐπίκλησιν καλέουσιν.

et is quidem versus absolutior, ille vero eiusdem vatis ope-
rosior:

εἷς Ζεὺς εἷς Ἀίδης εἷς Ἥλιος εἷς Διόνυσος.

19. huius versus auctoritas fundatur oraculo Apollinis Clarii, in quo aliud quoque nomen soli adicitur, qui in isdem
sacris versibus inter cetera vocatur ΙΑΩ. nam consultus
Apollo Clarius quis deorum habendus sit qui vocatur ΙΑΩ,
ita effatus est:

20. ὄργια μὲν δεδαῶτας ἐχρῆν νηπευθέα κεύθειν,
εἰ δ᾽ ἄρα τοι[126] παύρη σύνεσις καὶ νοῦς
ἀλαπαδνός.

---

[125] Orphaici *scripsi post Gronov. (coll. Comm. 1.12.12)*: Or-
pheici ω, Orphei S   [126] εἰ δ᾽ ἄρα τοι] ἐν δ᾽ ἀπάτῃ *Anth. Gr.*

---

[490] Cf. *Orphic Hymns* 30.6, 42.2, Plut. *Mor.* 714C.
[491] Cf. [Justin Martyr] *Exhortation of the Gentiles* 15.1, Julian
Or. 4.136A (replacing Dionysos with Sarapis).

Along the way where the wandering sun lets loose
his fiery reins and yokes his team closer to earth.

17. 'The same verses of Orpheus, by calling him *Euboulês*, show that he is the god of good counsel.[490] For if planning arises from ideas formed in the mind, and if the authorities think that the sun is the mind of the cosmic order, then they are right to believe that the sun is the guarantor of good counsel. 18. Orpheus explicitly declares that the sun is Liber in this verse (*PEGr* fr. 542–43):

The sun, whom they call with the surname Dionysus.

And while that verse is more unambiguous, this one by the same poet is more elaborate:

Zeus is one, Hades is one, the sun is one, Dionysus is
one.[491]

19. The authority of that verse is based on an oracle of Apollo of Claros, in which another name is also given to the sun, who in these same sacred verses is called (among other things) *Iaô*. For when Apollo of Claros was asked, concerning the god called *Iaô*,[492] which of the gods he should be considered, Apollo replied as follows (*Anth. Gr.* App. c. 6 no. 135, 3:490 Cougny):

20. Those who know the mysteries should conceal
    things not to be sought.
But if your understanding is slight, your mind feeble,

---

[492] Cf. Diod. 1.94.2, John Lydus *On the Months* 4.53 (citing Varro). Derived from *Yahu*, a form of the sacred name of the Jewish God, "Iaô" appears in syncretizing contexts, as here, in Gnostic texts, and as a name to conjure with in the magical papyri.

φράζεο τὸν πάντων ὕπατον θεὸν ἔμμεν ΙΑΩ,
χείματι μέν τ᾽ Ἀίδην, Δία δ᾽ εἴαρος ἀρχομένοιο,
Ἥλιον δὲ θέρευς, μετοπώρου δ᾽ ἁβρὸν
    Ἴακχον.[127]

21. huius oraculi vim, numinis nominisque interpretationem, qua Liber pater et sol ΙΑΩ significatur, exsecutus est Cornelius Labeo in libro cui titulus est De oraculo Apollinis Clarii. 22. item Orpheus, Liberum atque Solem unum esse deum eundemque demonstrans, de ornatu vestituque eius in sacris Liberalibus ita scribit:

ταῦτά τε πάντα τελεῖν ἦρι[128] σκευῇ πυκάσαντα
σῶμα θεοῦ μίμημα περικλύτου ἡελίοιο·
πρῶτα μὲν οὖν φλογέαις ἐναλίγκιον ἀκτίνεσσιν
πέπλον φοινίκεον πυρὶ εἴκελον[129] ἀμφιβαλέσθαι·
αὐτὰρ ὕπερθε νεβροῖο παναίολον εὐρὺ καθάψαι
δέρμα πολύστικτον θηρὸς κατὰ δεξιὸν ὦμον,
ἄστρων δαιδαλέων μίμημ᾽ ἱεροῦ τε πόλοιο.
εἶτα δ᾽ ὕπερθε νεβρῆς χρύσεον ζωστῆρα
    βαλέσθαι,
παμφανόωντα, πέριξ στέρνων φορέειν, μέγα
    σῆμα,
εὐθὺς ὅτ᾽ ἐκ περάτων γαίης φαέθων ἀνορούων
χρυσείαις ἀκτῖσι βάλῃ ῥόον Ὠκεανοῖο,
αὐγὴ δ᾽ ἄσπετος ᾖ, ἀνὰ δὲ δρόσῳ ἀμφιμιγεῖσα

[127] Ἴακχον Jan, cf. Mastandrea 1977, 160–1: ΙΑΩ ω
[128] ἦρι Geel apud Jan: ΕΡΙ β₁F, praviora cett.
[129] εἴκελον ed. Bipont. 1788: ΙΚΕΛΟΝ ω

say that the greatest god of all is Iaô:
Hades in winter, Zeus at the start of spring,
the sun in summer, delicate Iacchos [= Dionysos] in
  the fall.

21. Cornelius Labeo sought out this oracle's meaning, developing an interpretation of the godhead and his name that identifies father Liber and the sun as Iaô, in his book titled *On the Oracle of Apollo of Claros* (fr. 18 Mast.). 22. Similarly, in showing that Liber and the sun are one and the same god, Orpheus describes the god's garments and paraphernalia in the rites of the Liberalia[493] as follows (*PEGr* fr. 538, 541):

In the morning complete all these things, decking out
the god's body as a likeness of the far-famed sun:
first, then, clothe him in a crimson cloak,
flame-like, an image of his blazing rays;
then on top of that fasten from his right shoulder a
  fawn's
broad hide, many-colored, the dappled skin of the
  beast
to represent the intricate stars and the holy vault of
  heaven.
Next place a golden belt on top of the fawn skin,
all radiant, to wear round his chest, a great sign,
just as when he leaps up gleaming from the earth's
  rim
and strikes the flood of Ôkean with his golden rays,
and a glow, indescribable, that mingles with the dew

[493] Cf. 1.4.15n.

μαρμαίρῃ δίνησιν ἑλισσομένη κατὰ κύκλον,
πρόσθε θεοῦ· ζωστὴρ δ' ἄρ' ὑπὸ στέρνων
ἀμετρήτων
φαίνεται Ὠκεανοῦ κύκλος, μέγα θαῦμα ἰδέσθαι.

23. hinc et Vergilius sciens Liberum patrem solem esse et Cererem lunam, qui pariter fertilitatibus glebae et maturandis frugibus vel nocturno temperamento vel diurno calore moderantur, "vestro," ait,

> si munere tellus
> Chaoniam pingui glandem mutavit arista.

24. solem vero terrenae esse fecunditatis auctorem idem poeta profano mox docuit exemplo, cum ait,

> Saepe etiam steriles incendere profuit agros,

et reliqua. si enim hominum commento ignis adhibitus multiplex praestat auxilium, quid adscribendum est aetherio solis calori?

19 'Quae de Libero patre dicta sunt, haec Martem eundem ac solem esse demonstrant: si quidem plerique Liberum cum Marte coniungunt, unum deum esse monstrantes. unde Bacchus Ἐννάλιος cognominatur, quod est inter propria Martis nomina. 2. colitur etiam apud Lacedaemonios simulacrum Liberi patris hasta insigne, non thyrso. sed et cum thyrsum tenet, quid aliud quam latens telum

---

494 Chaonia, an area in NW Epirus, included Dodona (cf. 1.7.28), where oracles were believed to issue from an oak tree sacred to Zeus: "Chaonian" came to refer to oaks in general.

495 E.g., *Il.* 17.211, 18.309, 20.69; ambiguously applied to Dio-

and sparkles as it whirls, round and round, in a circle
before the god: the belt below his boundless chest
appears as the circle of Ôkean, a great wonder to see.

23. Hence Virgil, too, aware that father Liber is the sun
and Ceres the moon, together regulating the earth's fertility and the crops' ripening with the night's mild warmth
and the day's heat, says (*G.* 1.7–8),

> . . . if through your gift the earth
> exchanged the Chaonian acorn for the rich ear of
> grain.[494]

24. The same poet, soon after that passage, showed that
the sun is the source of the earth's fertility by means of an
example drawn from daily life, saying (*G.* 1.84),

> often it has also been of use to set the sterile fields
> afire,

and so on: for if humankind by its devising uses fire to provide aid in many forms, what should we think the sun's
heavenly heat can do?

'My remarks on father Liber also show that Mars is   19
identified with the sun, since most people link Liber to
Mars, showing that they are a single god. That's why Bacchus has the surname *Enyalios* ["warlike"], which is one
of Mars' own names.[495] 2. There's also a cult statue of father Liber among the Lacedaemonians distinguished by a
spear, not a thyrsus (though even when he holds a thyrsus,
is it anything but a disguised spear he carries?). Its tip is

nysos and Ares at *PMGr* fr. 1027b "Bromios [= Dionysos] spear-
carrier Enyalios exulting in the clangor of war father Ares."

gerit? cuius mucro hedera lambente protegitur, quod ostendit vinculo quodam patientiae obligandos impetus belli. habet enim hedera vinciendi obligandique naturam. nec non et calor vini, cuius Liber pater auctor est, saepe homines ad furorem bellicum usque propellit. 3. igitur propter cognatum utriusque effectus calorem Martem ac Liberum unum eundemque deum esse voluerunt. certe Romani utrumque patris appellatione venerantur, alterum Liberum patrem, alterum Marspitrem id est Martem patrem cognominantes. 4. hinc etiam Liber pater bellorum potens probatur, quod eum primum ediderunt auctorem triumphi. cum igitur Liber pater idem ac sol sit, Mars vero idem ac Liber pater, Martem solem esse quis dubitet? 5. Accitani etiam, Hispana gens, simulacrum Martis radiis ornatum maxima religione celebrant, Neton vocantes. 6. et certe ratio naturalis exigit ut di caloris caelestis parentes magis nominibus quam re substantiaque divisi sint: fervorem autem quo animus excandescit excitaturque alias ad iram, alias ad virtutes, non numquam ad temporalis furoris excessum, per quas res etiam bella nascuntur, Martem cognominaverunt; cuius vim poeta exprimendo et similitudini ignis adplicando ait:

μαίνετο δ᾽ ὡς ὅτ᾽ Ἄρης ἐγχέσπαλος ἢ ὀλοὸν
πῦρ.

---

496 Cf. Cornut. p. 60.4–5 and 7.1.22 below.

497 Cf. Varro *Latin Language* 8.33, 49, 9.75, Gell. 5.12.5.

498 Dionysos "invented" the procession (Cornut. p. 61.18–19, Pliny *Natural History* 7.191) when he returned in triumph from conquering India (Val. Max. 3.6.6, Serv. on *A.* 3.125).

499 Cf. Pliny *Natural History* 3.25.

covered with an ivy wreath,[496] which shows that the on-slaught of war should be held in check, as it were, by the bondage of forbearance, for ivy has the natural capacity to bind and hold in check. Wine's heat, too, for which father Liber is the source, often drives men to the frenzy of war. 3. Because their characteristic actions derive from kindred kinds of heat, men have claimed that Mars and Liber are one and the same god. The Romans, certainly, worship both under the description of "father," calling one "father Liber," the other "Marspiter,"[497] that is, "father Mars." 4. Father Liber is also shown to be a god of war, because they have claimed that he is the originator of the triumphal procession.[498] Since father Liber is the same as the sun, and Mars is the same as father Liber, who would doubt that Mars is the sun? 5. The Accitani, a people of Spain,[499] have a very important cult in which they worship a statue of Mars decorated with the sun's rays, calling him Neton. 6. And of course natural science requires us to believe that the gods who are the sources of heavenly heat are distinct in their names rather than in their essential substance: so the boiling heat that sets the mind ablaze and stirs it now to anger, now to deeds of valor, sometimes, too, to wild acts of temporary madness—all these being the causes of wars—they named "Mars," whose force the poet expressed through the simile of fire, saying (*Il.* 15.605):

he was raging like Ares spear-brandisher or like
    destroying fire.

in summa pronuntiandum est effectum solis, de quo fervor animorum, de quo calor sanguinis excitatur, Martem vocari.

7. 'Vt vero Mercurius sol probetur, superius edocta suffragio sunt. eundem enim esse Apollinem atque Mercurium vel hinc apparet, quod apud multas gentes stella Mercurii ad Apollinis nomen refertur et quod Apollo Musis praesidet, Mercurius sermonem, quod est Musarum munus, impertit. 8. praeter hoc quoque Mercurium pro sole censeri multa documenta sunt. primum quod simulacra Mercurii pennatis alis adornantur, quae res monstrat solis velocitatem. 9. nam quia mentis potentem Mercurium credimus appellatumque ita intellegimus ἀπὸ τοῦ ἑρμηνεύειν, et sol mundi mens est, summa est autem velocitas mentis, ut ait Homerus,

ὡς εἰ πτερὸν ἠὲ νόημα,

ideo pennis Mercurius quasi ipsa natura solis ornatur. 10. hoc argumentum Aegyptii lucidius absolvunt, ipsius solis simulacra pennata fingentes, quibus color apud illos non unus est. alterum enim caerulea specie, alterum clara fingunt. ex his clarum superum et caeruleum inferum vocant, inferi autem nomen soli datur, cum in inferiore hemisphaerio, id est hiemalibus signis, cursum suum peragit,

---

500 Cf. [Arist.] *On the Universe* 2 392a26–27.

501 Cf. 1.17.5n.   502 Cf. Cornut. p. 22.3–5, John Lydus *On the Months* 4.76 fin.   503 "Bright" and "dark" perhaps echo imagery found in the "Litany of Re": "Homage to thee, Re, supreme power, . . . Dark Face. . . . Homage to thee, Re, supreme power, . . . who judges the gods as Blazing One. . . . O Re in the West, placed into the earth, he who gives light to those of the

In short, we must affirm that the action of the sun that stirs us, making our minds boil and our blood run hot, is called Mars.

7. 'A proof that Mercury is the sun is supported by what I've said so far. The fact that many nations refer to the planet Mercury with the name of Apollo makes plain that Apollo is the same as Mercury,[500] as does the fact that Apollo is in charge of the Muses and Mercury gives us speech, which is the gift of the Muses. 8. There is much evidence besides that Mercury is judged to be the sun. First, there's the fact that images of Mercury are equipped with feathered wings, representing the speed of the sun. 9. For since we believe that Mercury is the god of thought and understand that he takes his name from "interpreting" [*hermêneuein*],[501] and since the sun is the mind of the cosmic order, while nothing is swifter than the mind,[502] as Homer says (*Od.* 7.36),

as if a winged thing or a thought,

Mercury is equipped with wings, as if with the sun's very nature. 10. The Egyptians provide more straightforward proof in fashioning winged images of the sun in more than one color, one dark, one bright.[503] They call the bright one "of the upper world," the dark one "of the lower world": the latter name is given to the sun when it follows its course in the lower hemisphere—that is, through the signs of the zodiac in winter—the former, when it makes its circuit

Netherworld!" (Piankoff 1964, 27, 29). For the descent into the abyss of Aten, the solar disk, and his rebirth, cf. Michalowski 1969, p. 414 pl. 578–79, 582, 584–85; for the winged solar disk, cf. Lange and Hirmer 1968, color pl. XVII, XLIII.

superi, cum partem zodiaci ambit aestivam. 11. eadem circa Mercurium sub alia fabula fictio est, cum inter superos
et inferos deos administer ac nuntius aestimatur. 12. Argiphontes praeterea cognominatur non quod Argum pere-
merit, quem ferunt per ambitum capitis multorum oculorum luminibus ornatum custodisse Iunonis imperio Inachi
filiam Io, eius deae paelicem, conversam in bovis formam:
sed sub huius modi fabula Argus est caelum stellarum luce
distinctum, quibus inesse quaedam species caelestium videtur oculorum. 13. caelum autem Argum vocari placuit a
candore et velocitate, παρὰ το λευκὸν καὶ ταχύ. et videtur
terram desuper observare, quam Aegyptii hieroglyphicis
litteris cum significare volunt, ponunt bovis figuram. is
ergo ambitus caeli stellarum luminibus ornatus tunc aestimatur enectus a Mercurio, cum sol diurno tempore ob-
scurando sidera veluti enecat, vi luminis sui conspectum
eorum auferendo mortalibus.

14. 'Pleraque etiam simulacra Mercurii quadrato statu
figurantur, solo capite insignita et virilibus erectis, quae
figura significat solem mundi esse caput et rerum satorem,
omnemque vim eius non in quodam divisorum ministerio
membrorum, sed in sola mente consistere, cuius sedes in

---

504 E.g., *Il.* 2.103 and often; with M.'s preferred derivation
cf. Cornut. p. 21.11–15, Hesych. A.7037, Elias *Comm. on Arist.
Categ.* p. 140.30–32, *Etym. Gud.* A p.186.2–3, Eustath. *Comm.
Od.* 1:192.11–12.   505 The form of the story told most elabo-
rately at Ov. *Met.* 1.588–746.   506 Cf. Hesych. A.7037.

507 There is no "hieroglyph" of this sort: M. or his source perhaps refers to the goddess Hathor, daughter of the sun-god Re,
who was represented as a cow (Lange and Hirmer 1968, pl. 146–
47), or as a woman with cow's horns (ibid. pl. 39), with a solar disk
inset between the horns (exx. at Rome: Roullet 1972, p. 129–30).

through the zodiac's summer segment. 11. The same tale is told of Mercury in a different form, when he is conceived as an attendant carrying messages between the gods below and the gods above. 12. He is, furthermore, called Argiphontes,[504] not because he killed Argus, who (the story goes) was equipped with many eyes all around his head and was therefore ordered by Juno to keep watch over Io, daughter of Inachus, whom Juno turned into a cow because she was her rival for Jupiter's affections;[505] but rather according to a version of the story in which Argus is the sky above, marked out by the light of stars that look like heavenly eyes. 13. It was decided that heaven be called Argus [Gk. *argos* = 'white'] because it is white (*leukon*) and swift (*tachy*)[506] and seems to keep watch upon the earth from above: when the Egyptians wish to represent the earth in hieroglyphics, they use the figure of a cow.[507] That heavenly circuit, then, with its starlight, is conceived of as slain by Mercury when the sun in the daytime blots out the stars and, as it were, slays them, removing them from mortal sight with its own strong light.

14. 'Very often, too, images of Mercury are fashioned with a square base, showing only the god's head and erect penis,[508] a figure signifying that the sun is the head of the cosmic order and world's begetter, and that all his strength does not somehow serve a set of different limbs but is concentrated in thought alone, which has its seat in the head.

---

[508] Cf. Hdt. 2.51, Cic. *On the Nature of the Gods* 3.56, Cornut. p. 23.11–22, Paus. 6.26.5, Plotin. *Enn*. 3.6.19, Mart. Cap. 2.102, Eustath. *Comm. Il*. 4:546.10–13, *LIMC* 5,1:300–6, 374–78, 5.2:199–216.

capite est. 15. quattuor latera eadem ratione finguntur qua et tetrachordum Mercurio creditur attributum. quippe significat hic numerus vel totidem plagas mundi vel quattuor vices temporum quibus annus includitur, vel quod duobus aequinoctiis duobusque solstitiis zodiaci ratio distincta est, ut lyra Apollinis chordarum septem tot caelestium sphaerarum motus praestat intellegi, quibus solem moderatorem natura constituit. 16. in Mercurio solem coli etiam ex caduceo claret, quod Aegyptii in specie draconum maris et feminae coniunctorum figuraverunt Mercurio consecrandum. hi dracones parte media voluminis sui in vicem nodo quem vocant Herculis obligantur, primaeque partes eorum, reflexae in circulum, pressis osculis ambitum circuli iungunt, et post nodum caudae revocantur ad capulum caducei ornanturque alis ex eadem capuli parte nascentibus. 17. argumentum caducei ad genituram quoque hominum, quae genesis appellatur, Aegyptii protendunt, deos praestites homini nascenti, quattuor adesse memorantes, Δαίμονα Τύχην Ἔρωτα Ἀνάγκην, et duo

---

509 Hermes' invention of the lyre is the first episode of the *Homeric Hymn to Hermes* (24–54, where the instrument has 7 strings); no consistent distinction is drawn between a 4-string lyre of Hermes and a 7-string lyre of Apollo, though invention of the former is ascribed to Hermes, of the latter to Apollo, at Σ Pind. *P.* hypoth. a (cf. Paus. 5.14.8 with 9.5.8–9), and Apollo's 7-string lyre is associated with the Pleiades or the "seven planets" (= sun, moon, and five known planets, the "heavenly spheres" here mentioned) at Eratosth. *Catast.* 1.24R, Σ Vat. Dionys. Thr. *GG* 1,3:198.1–6, cf. Philo *On the Craftsmanship of the Universe* 126; note also that the 4th day of the month was Hermes' day, the 7th Apollo's (cf. West on Hes. *Works and Days* 770–71). On the music produced by the heavenly spheres' motion, cf. 1.22.7n.

15. The square figure's four sides are fashioned according to the same principle that attributes the four-stringed lyre to Mercury. Indeed, this number signifies the four quarters of the world, or the four seasons that define the year, or the two equinoxes and two solstices that articulate the system of the zodiac, just as Apollo's seven-stringed lyre represents the seven motions of the heavenly spheres.[509] 16. That the sun is worshipped in Mercury's guise is also apparent from his wand, the caduceus, which the Egyptians fashioned in the shape of two intertwined serpents, male and female, and consecrated to Mercury.[510] These serpents are bound together at the middle by the so-called knot of Hercules;[511] their heads and necks, curving round in a circle, are joined in a kiss to complete the circle; and below the knot their tails rejoin the caduceus' hilt and are equipped with wings that sprout from the same part of the wand. 17. The Egyptians also use the caduceus' significance to explain people's horoscope ("genesis" it's called), saying that four gods attend a human being as it's born, Deity [*Daimôn*], Chance [*Tykhê*], Love [*Erôs*], and Necessity

[510] Cf. Soph. fr. 701 (*TrGF* 4:484), Cornut. p. 22.18–21, Athenag. *Embassy* 20.3, Hygin. *Astron.* 2.7.2, Serv. on *A.* 8.138, John Lydus *On the Months* 1.22, *LIMC* 5,2:271ff., esp. 273 (no. 918a), 276 (no. 942b, 946a), 281 (no. 964), 282 (no. 978a), 283 (no. 985).

[511] Athenag. ibid. ("the so-called *Hêrakleôtikon hamma*"), cf. Pliny *Natural History* 28.64 on its use as a surgical ligature (directions for tying it at Orib. *Coll. Med.* 48.8, if *Hêrakleôtikon* there is derived directly from *Hêraklês*); also used of the knot that secured a Roman bride's belt, to be undone by her husband (Paul. Fest. p. 55.13–18).

priores solem ac lunam intellegi volunt quod sol auctor spiritus caloris ac luminis humanae vitae genitor et custos est
et ideo nascentis Δαίμων (id est deus) creditur, luna Τύχη,
quia corporum praesul est quae fortuitorum varietate iac-
tantur; Amor osculo significatur, Necessitas nodo. 18. cur
pennae adiciantur iam superius absolutum est. ad huius
modi argumenta draconum praecipue volumen electum
est propter iter utriusque sideris flexuosum.

20   'Hinc est quod simulacris et Aesculapii et Salutis draco
subiungitur, quod hi ad solis naturam lunaeque referuntur.
et est Aesculapius vis salubris de substantia solis subve-
niens animis corporibusque mortalium. Salus autem naturae lunaris effectus est quo corpora animantum iuvantur
salutifero firmata temperamento. 2. ideo ergo simulacris
eorum iunguntur figurae draconum, quia praestant ut humana corpora velut infirmitatis pelle deposita ad pristinum
revirescant vigorem, ut revirescunt dracones per annos
singulos pelle senectutis exuta. propterea et ad ipsum solem species draconis refertur, quia sol semper velut a quadam imae depressionis senecta in altitudinem suam ut in
robur revertitur iuventutis. 3. esse autem draconem inter
praecipua solis argumenta etiam nominis fictione mon-

512 The quartet is central to ancient astrology: cf. Vettius
Valens *Anthol.* 4.11, Paul. Alex. *Elements of Astrology* p. 49 Boer,
Hephaestion *Astrology* 1:254.2–4.

513 Cf. Paul. Alex. ibid., DServ. on *A.* 4.242.

514 Cf. Cornut. p. 70.7–12; by specifying "beneath" M. seems
to refer esp. to images of the god seated, e.g., *LIMC* 2,2:638 (no.
63), 639 (no. 65, 67), 641 (no. 86). A serpent, taken to be the in-
carnation of Aesculapius (Asclepius), was brought from the cult
center of Epidaurus when an epidemic caused the god to be introduced to Rome in 291 BCE (cf. esp. Ov. *Met.* 15.622–745).

[*Anangkê*]:[512] the first two they mean to be regarded as the sun and the moon,[513] because the sun, as the source of breath, warmth, and light, is the begetter and guardian of human life and so is believed to be the *Daimôn*, or deity, of the one being born; whereas the moon is *Tychê*, because she is in charge of our bodies, which are buffeted by various chance circumstances. Love is signified by a kiss, Necessity by a knot. 18. Why wings are added has already been explained. The serpents' coils were chosen for this sort of symbolism because both sun and moon have a course.

'This is the reason why a serpent is placed beneath the image of Aesculapius[514] and of Salus ["Well-being"], which are related to the nature of the sun and the moon. Aesculapius is the health-giving strength that comes upon mortal minds and bodies from the substance of the sun; Salus, by contrast, is the action of the moon's nature that supports the bodies of living creatures and strengthens them with its health-giving balance. 2. Figures of serpents are joined to their images, then, because they insure that human bodies are rejuvenated and regain their original vigor, as though by shedding their old skin of infirmity, just as serpents are rejuvenated from one year to the next by shedding the skin of old age. For that reason, too, the serpent's likeness is related to the sun himself, because the sun always returns from the old age, as it were, of its nadir and regains its acme, as thought restored to robust youth. 3. That the serpent [*draco*] is among the chief symbols of the sun is shown by the way its name is formed from 20

The temple of Salus on the Quirinal was dedicated by C. Iunius Bubulcus in 302 (Livy 9. 43. 5, 10. 1. 9, *LTUR* 4: 229–30).

SATURNALIA

stratur, quod sit nuncupatus ἀπὸ τοῦ δέρκειν id est videre.
nam ferunt hunc serpentem acie acutissima et pervigili naturam sideris huius imitari atque ideo aedium adytorum
oraculorum thesaurorum custodiam draconibus adsignari.
4. Aesculapium vero eundem esse atque Apollinem non
solum hinc probatur quod ex illo natus creditur, sed quod
ei et vis divinationis adiungitur. nam Apollodorus in libris quibus titulus est Περὶ θεῶν scribit quod Aesculapius
divinationibus et auguriis praesit. 5. nec mirum, si quidem medicinae atque divinationum consociatae sunt dis-
ciplinae. nam medicus vel commoda vel incommoda in
corpore futura praenoscit, sicut ait Hippocrates oportere
medicum dicere de aegro, τά τε παρεόντα καὶ τὰ προγε-
γονότα καὶ τὰ μέλλοντα ἔσεσθαι, id est,

> quae sint, quae fuerint, quae mox ventura
>   sequentur.[130]

quod congruit divinationibus quae sciunt

> τά τ᾽ ἐόντα τά τ᾽ ἐσσόμενα πρό τ᾽ ἐόντα.

6. 'Sed nec Hercules a substantia solis alienus est:
quippe Hercules ea est solis potestas quae humano generi
virtutem ad similitudinem praestat deorum. nec aestimes
Alcmena apud Thebas Boeotias[131] natum solum vel primum Herculem nuncupatum: immo post multos atque
postremus ille hac appellatione dignatus est honoratusque
hoc nomine quia nimia fortitudine meruit nomen dei

130 sequentur] trahantur *Verg.*
131 Boeotias *ed. Ven. 1513:* boetias ω

270

derkein, that is, "to see":[515] for they say that this serpent imitates this star's nature with very sharp and always wakeful glance, and that serpents are made to guard temples, shrines, oracles, and treasuries on that account. 4. That Aesculapius is the same as the sun is proved not only by the fact that he is believed to be the sun's offspring but also because he has the power of divination. Apollodorus, in his books titled *On the Gods*, writes (no. 244 fr. 116 *FGrH*) that Aesculapius is in charge of prophecies and auguries. 5. And that is not surprising, seeing that the disciplines of medicine and divination are closely allied: a physician foresees both the good states and the bad that a body will experience, just as Hippocrates says (*Progn*. 1) that a physician must tell about a sick person "the things that are and were before and those that are going to be," that is (*G.* 4.393),

> the things that are, that were, and that soon will come to follow.

And that squares with prophecies, which know (*Il.* 1.70)

> the things that are, that will be, and that were before.

6. 'But neither does Hercules lack a share in the sun's substance: in fact, Hercules is the power of the sun that provides a godlike valor to the human race. Nor should you suppose that the one born to Alcmena in Boeotian Thebes was the only or first man named Hercules: rather, he was the last in a long line to be dignified with the appellation and was honored with this name because by superhu-

[515] Cf. Paul. Fest. p. 59.9–13, John Lydus *On the Months* 4.6; the etymology is correct.

virtutem regentis. 7. ceterum deus Hercules religiose quidem et apud Tyron colitur, verum sacratissima et augustis-
sima Aegyptii eum religione venerantur ultraque memoriam, quae apud illos retro longissima est, ut carentem
initio colunt. 8. ipse creditur et Gigantas interemisse cum
caelo propugnaret quasi virtus deorum. Gigantas autem
quid aliud fuisse credendum est quam hominum quandam
impiam gentem deos negantem et ideo aestimatam deos
pellere de caelesti sede voluisse? 9. horum pedes in draconum volumina desinebant, quod significat nihil eos rec-
tum, nihil superum cogitasse, totius vitae eorum gressu
atque processu in inferna mergente. ab hac gente sol poenas debitas vi pestiferi caloris exegit. 10. et re vera Herculem solem esse vel ex nomine claret. Ἡρακλῆς enim quid
aliud est nisi Ἥρας (id est aeris) κλέος? quae porro alia aeris gloria est nisi solis illuminatio, cuius recessu profundi-
tate occulitur tenebrarum? 11. praeterea sacrorum admi-
nistrationes apud Aegyptios multiplici actu multiplicem
dei adserunt potestatem, significantes Herculem hunc
esse τὸν ἐν πᾶσι καὶ διὰ πάντων ἥλιον. 12. ex re quoque

516 Cf. Cic. *On the Nature of the Gods* 3.42.

517 "Egyptian Hercules" (= Melqart): cf. Hdt. 2.44, Paus.
10.13.8, Arrian *Alexander's Anabasis* 2.16.2, Philost. *Life of Apollonius* 3.32.

518 Cf. Ephorus fr. 34 (no. 70 *FGrH*), Diod. Sic. 1.24.2,
[Apollod.] *Library* 1.38.

519 Cf. esp. the frieze of the Great Altar of Zeus at Pergamum:
LIMC 4,2:112–13, with, e.g., ibid. 117, 154–56.

520 Cf. John Lydus *On the Months* 4.67.

521 Cf. Diod. Sic. 1.24.4, Orion *Etym.* H p. 69.8, *Etym. Gud.* H

man strength he gained the title as patron god of valor.[516]
7. Now, the god Hercules is paid cult with all due observance even in Tyre; but it's the Egyptians who worship him
with observances that are most holy and august, and their
cult extends back beyond the reach of memory—which
among them goes very far back indeed—as though it has
always existed.[517] 8. He himself is believed to have slain the
Giants, too, when he seemed to embody the valor of the
gods in defending heaven.[518] But what should we suppose
the Giants were, if not some impious nation of men who
denied the gods and were therefore thought to have aimed
at driving the gods from their seat in heaven? 9. The Giants' feet ended in serpents' coils,[519] which symbolizes that
their thoughts were in no way upright and godlike, that at
every step and stage of their lives they were sinking into
the world below. From this nation the sun exacted the penalty they owed with a blast of pestilential heat. 10. And
in fact even Hercules' name makes it plain as day that
he is the sun.[520] For what is *Hêraclês* other than "Hera's
[*Hêras*]"—that is, the air's—"glory [*kleos*]"?[521] And what,
furthermore, is the air's glory if not the light of the sun, at
whose withdrawal the heavens are hidden in deep shadow?
11. Moreover, the way the Egyptians perform his sacred
rites with many different actions shows that the god's
power is also multiple, signifying that Hercules is "the sun
in all and through all."[522] 12. No trivial evidence is gath-

p. 247.49ff., Eustath. *Comm. Il.* 2:102, *Etym. Mag.* p. 435.20,
Suda H.476. Hera/Juno = the air, see 1.15.20n.

[522] The phrase appears to echo Paul *Letter to the Ephesians*
4:6 "One God and the Father of all, who is over all and through all
and in all."

alibi terrarum gesta argumentum non vile colligitur. nam Theron rex Hispaniae citerioris cum ad expugnandum Herculis templum ageretur furore instructus exercitu navium, Gaditani ex adverso venerunt provecti navibus longis commissoque proelio adhuc aequo Marte consistente pugna, subito in fugam versae sunt regiae naves simulque improviso igne correptae conflagraverunt. paucissimi qui superfuerant hostium capti indicaverunt apparuisse sibi leones proris Gaditanae classis superstantes ac subito suas naves immissis radiis, quales in Solis capite pinguntur, exustas.

13. 'Eidem Aegypto adiacens civitas, quae conditorem Alexandrum Macedonem gloriatur, Sarapin atque Isin cultu paene attonitae venerationis observat. omnem tamen illam venerationem soli se sub illius nomine testatur impendere, vel dum calathum capiti eius infigunt vel dum simulacro signum tricipitis animantis adiungunt. 14. quod exprimit medio eodemque maximo capite leonis effigiem, dextra parte caput canis exoritur mansueta specie blandientis, pars vero laeva cervicis rapacis lupi capite finitur easque formas animalium draco conectit volumine suo, capite redeunte ad dei dexteram qua compescitur monstrum. 15. ergo leonis capite monstratur praesens tempus,

---

523 On the Phoenician cult of Hercules/Melqart at Gades, site of the "Pillars of Hercules," cf. Pomp. Mela 3.46, Dionys. Perieg. *Description of the World* 451–54, Philost. *Life of Apollonius* 2.33; acc. to Euseb. *Preparation for the Gospel* 3.11.25, he was identified with the sun by Porphyry. The incident recounted here is otherwise unknown.

524 The mourning of Isis, the goddess of generation and nurturing, brought her brother-husband Osiris back to life when

ered from the god's actions elsewhere in the world, too:[523] when Theron, king of nearer Spain, was driven by madness to attack Hercules' sacred precinct and assembled a fleet, the people of Gades sailed out to meet him on long ships, and when the battle that was joined was still being fought by both sides on an equal footing, the king's ships suddenly turned to flee and at the same time unexpectedly caught fire and burned. When the very few enemy to survive were captured, they said that they had seen lions standing on the prows of the ships from Gades and that their own ships were suddenly scorched by rays that came down upon them, like the rays depicted on the sun's head.

13. 'The city bordering on Egypt, which boasts of Alexander of Macedon as its founder, worships Sarapis and Isis with an almost crazed veneration.[524] Yet the city gives evidence that it is really offering up that worship to the sun under Sarapis' name, when it sets a basket atop his head or joins to his image the statue of a three-headed creature:[525] 14. its middle head—the largest—has the appearance of a lion; on the right the head of a dog rears up, tame and fawning; and the left part of the neck ends in the head of a rapacious wolf. A serpent with its coils binds these figures together, while its head returns to the god's right hand, which keeps the monster at bay. 15. The lion's head, then, points to the present time, poised for action, powerful and

he was murdered by his brother Set, cf. 1.21.11. On Sarapis cf. 1.7.14n.; with the syncretism here, cf. Mart. Cap. 2.191.

[525] The basket is a regular feature in representations of Sarapis, cf. *LIMC* 7,2:504ff.; for Sarapis with Cerberus, the three-headed hound of the underworld, cf. *LIMC* 7,1:670–71, 689–90.

quia condicio eius inter praeteritum futurumque actu
praesenti valida fervensque est. sed et praeteritum tempus
lupi capite signatur, quod memoria rerum transactarum
rapitur et aufertur. item canis blandientis effigies futuri
temporis designat eventum, de quo nobis spes, licet incer-
ta, blanditur. tempora autem cui nisi proprio famularentur
auctori? cuius vertex insignitus calatho et altitudinem sideris monstrat et potentiam capacitatis ostendit, quia in
eum omnia terrena redeunt dum inmisso calore rapiuntur.
16. accipe nunc quid de sole vel Sarapi pronuntietur oraculo. nam Sarapis, quem Aegyptii deum maximum prodiderunt, oratus a Nicocreonte Cypriorum rege quis deorun
haberetur, his versibus sollicitam religionem regis in-
struxit:

17. εἰμὶ θεὸς τοιός δὲ μαθεῖν, οἷόν κ' ἐγὼ εἴπω·
οὐράνιος κόσμος κεφαλή, γαστὴρ δὲ θάλασσα,
γαῖα δέ μοι πόδες εἰσί, τὰ δ' οὔατ' ἐν αἰθέρι
κεῖται,
ὄμμα δὲ τηλαυγὲς λαμπρὸν φάος ἠελίοιο

18. ex his apparet Sarapis et solis unam et individuam esse
naturam. Isis iuncta religione celebratur, quae est vel terra
vel natura rerum subiacens soli. hinc est quod continuatis
uberibus corpus deae omne densetur, quia vel terrae vel
rerum naturae altu nutritur universitas.

21   'Adonin quoque solem esse non dubitabitur inspecta
religione Assyriorum, apud quos Veneris Aphacitidis[132] et

132 Aphacitidis Selden (De Dis Syriis Synt. II, c. 3, p. 278
[1672], coll. Zos. 1.58.1): Architidis ω

urgent, between the past and the future, while the wolf's head signifies time past, because the memory of bygone events is snatched up and carried off; similarly, the image of the fawning dog represents future events, which hope— uncertain though it is—presents to us with winning aspect. But whom do these times serve save the one who is their source? The basket that adorns his head points to both the lofty position of the star and its capacious power, since all earthbound things return to it, carried off by the heat it lets loose. 16. Now hear what the oracle declares about the sun, or Sarapis. For when Sarapis, whom the Egyptians declared the greatest god, was asked by king Nicocreon of Cyprus which of the gods he was, he calmed the king's religious scruples with these verses (*Anth. Gr.* App. c. 6 no. 186, 3:501 Cougny = *PEGr* Orphica fr. 861):

17. What sort of god I am learn as I instruct you:
the array of heaven is my head, the sea my belly,
the earth my feet, my ears rest in the ether,
my far-gleaming eye is the bright light of the sun.

18. From this it is clear that Sarapis is the single and undivided nature of the soul. Isis is worshipped in a kindred cult as either earth or the natural order subject to the sun.[526] That is why the goddess' entire body is thick with an unbroken series of breasts:[527] the whole of the earth or natural order gains its sustenance from her.

'You will not doubt that Adonis, too, is the sun[528] once   21
you've considered the beliefs of the Assyrians, who once

---

[526] Cf. Plut. *Mor.* 363D, Serv. on *A.* 8.696.

[527] This is the form of the Artemis of Ephesus: *LIMC* 2,1:755– 63, 2,2: 564–73.   [528] Cf. Mart. Cap. 2.192.

Adonis maxima olim veneratio viguit, quam nunc Phoenices tenent. nam physici terrae superius hemisphaerium, cuius partem incolimus, Veneris appellatione coluerunt, inferius vero hemisphaerium terrae Proserpinam vocaverunt. 2. ergo apud Assyrios sive Phoenicas lugens inducitur dea, quod sol, annuo gressu per duodecim signorum ordinem pergens, partem quoque hemisphaerii inferioris ingreditur, quia de duodecim signis zodiaci sex superiora, sex inferiora censentur. 3. et cum est in inferioribus et ideo dies breviores facit, lugere creditur dea, tamquam sole raptu mortis temporalis amisso et a Proserpina retento, quam numen terrae inferioris circuli et antipodum diximus. rursumque Adonin redditum Veneri credi volunt cum sol, evictis sex signis inferioris ordinis, incipit nostri circuli lustrare hemisphaerium cum incremento luminis et dierum. 4. ab apro autem tradunt interemptum Adonin, hiemis imaginem in hoc animale fingentes, quod aper hispidus et asper gaudet locis umidis lutosis pruinaque contectis proprieque hiemali fructu pascitur glande. ergo hiems veluti vulnus est solis quae et lucem eius nobis minuit et calorem, quod utrumque animantibus accidit morte. 5. simulacrum huius deae in monte Libano fingitur capite obnupto, specie tristi, faciem manu laeva intra

---

[529] I.e., Aphrodite of Aphaca, cf. §5n.

[530] With §§1–4 compare Lucian *On the Syrian Goddess* 6, on the rites of Adonis in the temple of "Aphrodite" (Ba'alat Gebal) in Byblos (Phoenicia), with Lightfoot 2003, 305–26.

[531] Cf. 1.19.10   [532] Cf. [Apollod.] *Library* 3.184–85, Ov. *Met.* 10.724–39, Cornut. p. 55.2–4, Euseb. *Preparation for the Gospel* 3.11.9, Hippol. *Refutation of all Heresies* 5.7.11–12, [Nonnus] *Mythological Scholia* 5.38, Σ Theoc. 3.48.

had a vigorous cult of Venus Aphacitis[529] and Adonis, now
maintained by the Phoenicians.[530] For the physical scientists paid cult to the earth's upper hemisphere—the part
we inhabit—under the name of Venus, while they called
the lower hemisphere Proserpina. 2. Among the Assyrians
or Phoenicians, then, the goddess is brought in grieving,
because the sun, in making its annual progress through the
twelve signs in sequence, enters the lower hemisphere too,
six of the zodiac's signs being considered upper signs, six of
them lower.[531] 3. And when he is among the lower signs
and therefore makes the days shorter, the goddess is believed to mourn, as though the sun has been for a time
snatched away by death and is being kept by Proserpina,[532]
who I have said is the divinity of the earth's lower zone and
the people who dwell there. They believe that Adonis is
again restored to Venus when the sun overcomes the six
lower signs and begins to illuminate our zone's hemisphere
with lengthening days. 4. They say, however, that Adonis
was killed by a boar, using that animal to represent the winter, because the boar, being shaggy and rough, delights in
places that are damp, muddy, and covered with frost, and it
forages for acorns, the quintessential produce of winter.
Winter, then, is in a sense a wound inflicted on the sun,
since it robs us of light and heat, a loss deadly to living
things. 5. On Mount Lebanon they fashion an image of
Venus[533] with veiled head, sad expression, resting her face

[533] This is the "Aphrodite" of Aphaca, on whom cf. Lucian *On
the Syrian Goddess* 9, with Lightfoot 2003, 328–31: for the imagery of the "mourning Venus," cf. *LIMC* 3,1:1078, 3,2:739 (no.1),
and Lightfoot ibid. 329 and fig. 30.

amictum sustinens; lacrimae visione conspicientium ma-
nare creduntur. quae imago, praeter quod lugentis est ut
diximus deae, terrae quoque hiemalis est, quo tempore
obnupta nubibus sole viduata stupet, fontesque veluti
terrae oculi uberius manant, agrique interim suo cultu vi-
dui maestam faciem sui monstrant. 6. sed cum sol emersit
ab inferioribus partibus terrae vernalisque aequinoctii
transgreditur fines augendo diem, tunc est Venus laeta et
pulchra: virent arva segetibus, prata herbis, arbores foliis.
ideo maiores nostri Aprilem mensem Veneri dicaverunt.

7. 'Similiter Phryges, fabulis et sacrorum administratio-
nibus immutatis, circa Matrem Deum et Attinem eadem
intellegi praestant. 8. quis enim ambigat Matrem Deum
terram haberi? haec dea leonibus vehitur, validis impetu
atque fervore animalibus, quae natura caeli est, cuius am-
bitu aer continetur qui vehit terram. 9. solem vero sub nomine Attinis ornant fistula et virga. fistula ordinem spiritus
inaequalis ostendit, quia venti, in quibus nulla aequalitas
est, propriam sumunt de sole substantiam; virga potestatem solis adserit qui cuncta moderatur. 10. praecipuam autem solis in his caerimoniis verti rationem hinc etiam potest colligi, quod ritu eorum catabasi finita simulationeque
luctus peracta, celebratur laetitiae exordium a. d. octavum

---

534 Cf. 1.12.8–11.   535 For Attis, another reflex of the
"dying god" figure, and the cult of the Great Mother of the Gods
(Cybêlê) cf. Lucr. 2.600–60, Catull. 63, Ov. *F.* 4.221–44, Paus.
7.17.10–12, Arnob. 5.5–17.   536 Cf. Varro *Divine Antiquities*
fr. 64, 268, Arnob. 3.32.2–3, Aug. *City of God* 7.24.

537 Cf. *LIMC* 8,2:511, 514–16.   538 Cf. 1.23.20.

539 Images of Attis with a Pan's-pipe and/or shepherd's crook
are common: e.g., *LIMC* 3,2:18–19, 21, 24–25, 33, 37, 43. With
the syncretism here, cf. Mart. Cap. 2.192.

on her left hand behind her veil; her tears flow (they believe) when people look upon her. Beyond the fact that it represents a grieving goddess, as I said, this image also represents the earth in winter, when it is veiled by clouds, bereft of the sun, and paralyzed, when the springs that are, as it were, the earth's eyes flow more copiously, and when the fields, untilled and unadorned, are the picture of depression. 6. But when the sun has emerged from the lower regions of the earth, passes the boundary of the vernal equinox, and makes the days longer, then Venus is glad and fair: the plowed fields grow green with crops, the meadows with grasses, the trees with leaves. That is why our ancestors dedicated April to Venus.[534]

7. 'In like fashion the Phrygians, who have kept unchanged the performance of their rites and the tales attached to them, allow us to understand the Mother of the Gods and Attis along the same lines.[535] 8. For surely no one doubts that the Mother of the Gods is thought to be the earth:[536] the goddess is carried along by lions,[537] animals whose powerful, hot-blooded attacks capture the nature of heaven, whose sphere embraces the air that carries the earth.[538] 9. They outfit the sun, under the name of Attis, with a pipe and a rod:[539] the pipe represents a sequence of uneven breaths, because the winds, which have nothing even about them, take their substance from the sun; the rod shows the power of the sun, which regulates all things. 10. That these rites are chiefly to be interpreted as concerned with the sun can be gathered also from the fact that when (according to their custom) his descent to the underworld has been completed and they have acted out a period of mourning, the time of rejoicing begins on the eighth day before the Kalends of April [March 25], which

Kalendas Apriles. quem diem Hilaria appellant, quo primum tempore sol diem longiorem nocte protendit.

11. 'Idem sub diversis nominibus religionis effectus est apud Aegyptios cum Isis Osirin luget. nec in occulto est neque aliud esse Osirin quam solem, nec Isin aliud esse quam terram (ut diximus) naturamve rerum, eademque ratio quae circa Adonin et Attinem vertitur in Aegyptia quoque religione luctum et laetitiam vicibus annuae administrationis alternat. 12. hunc Osirin Aegyptii ut solem esse adserant, quotiens hieroglyphicis litteris suis exprimere volunt, insculpunt sceptron inque eo speciem oculi exprimunt, et hoc signo Osirin monstrant, significantes hunc deum solem esse regalique potestate sublimem cuncta despicere, quia solem Iovis oculum appellat antiquitas. 13. apud eosdem Apollo, qui est sol, Horus vocatur, ex quo et horae viginti quattuor quibus dies noxque conficitur nomen acceperunt et quattuor tempora quibus annuus orbis impletur ὧραι[133] vocantur.

14. 'Idem Aegyptii volentes ipsius solis nomine dicare simulacrum figuravere raso capite sed dextra parte crine remanente. servatus crinis docet solem naturae rerum numquam esse in operto, dempti autem capilli residente

---

[133] ὧραι Jan: horae ω

---

[540] The "Feast of Gladness," on 25 March, was part of the spring festival of the Great Mother, marking the resurrection of Attis: cf. Julian *Oration* 5.168D, *CIL* 1² p.313.

[541] Cf. 1.20.18.

[542] Cf. 1.23.9; on Osiris, cf. Plut. *Mor.* 354F-355A, 371E, Euseb. *Preparation for the Gospel* 1.9.2. M. seems to describe a standard hieroglyph of the sun: a small circle within a larger one

282

they call the Hilaria,[540] the first occasion when the sun makes the day longer than the night.

11. 'Though the names are different, the same religious expression occurs among the Egyptians when Isis mourns Osiris. It is obvious that Osiris is nothing other than the sun, Isis nothing other than the earth (as I've said)[541] or the natural order, and the same interpretation that is applicable to Adonis and Attis can be applied to the Egyptian rites: grief and joy alternate with the changing conduct of the year. 12. To make plain that this Osiris is the sun, the Egyptians carve a scepter whenever they want to represent him in hieroglyphics: on the scepter they set the image of an eye and with this symbol signify Osiris, showing that this god is the sun and that he looks down on all things with kingly power from on high, as the ancients called the sun the eye of Jupiter.[542] 13. The Egyptians also call Apollo— that is, the sun—Horus,[543] who gave his name to both the twenty-four hours [horae] that a day and night comprise and the four seasons [Gk. hôrai] that complete the year's cycle.[544]

14. 'When these same Egyptians wanted to dedicate an image under the name of the sun itself, they fashioned it with a shaved head, but kept the hair on the right side:[545] the hair that was kept symbolizes that that the sun is never concealed from the natural order, while the hair that was

(which could appear to be an eye) atop a vertical stroke (the "scepter" in M.'s description).

[543] Cf. Hdt. 2.156, Diod. Sic. 1.25.7, Plut. Mor. 355F, 375F, John Lydus On the Months 2.5; for the sun as the eye of Horus, see Plut. Mor. 372B.   [544] Cf. Cens. 19.6.

[545] This appears to be a fiction.

radice monstrant hoc sidus etiam tempore quo non visitur a nobis rursum emergendi, uti capillos, habere substantiam. 15. eodem argumento significatur et tempus quo angusta lux est cum velut abrasis incrementis angustaque manente extantia, ad minimum diei sol pervenit spatium, quod veteres appellavere brumale solstitium, brumam a brevitate dierum cognominantes, id est βραχὺ ἦμαρ. ex quibus latebris vel angustiis rursus emergens, ad aestivum hemisphaerium tamquam enascens in augmenta porrigitur et tunc ad regnum suum pervenisse iam creditur. 16. propterea Aegyptii animal in zodiaco consecravere ea caeli parte qua maxime annuo cursu sol valido effervet calore Leonisque inibi signum domicilium solis appellant quia id animal videtur ex natura solis substantiam ducere, 17. primum quia impetu et calore praestat animalia uti praestat sol sidera, validusque est leo pectore et priore corporis parte ac degenerat posterioribus membris, aeque solis vis prima parte diei ad meridiem increscit, vel prima parte anni a vere in aestatem, mox elanguescens deducitur vel ad occasum, qui diei, vel ad hiemem, quae anni pars videtur esse posterior. idemque oculis patentibus atque igneis cernitur semper, ut sol patenti igneoque oculo terram conspectu perpetuo atque infatigabili cernit.

18. 'Nec solus Leo sed signa quoque universa zodiaci ad naturam solis iure referuntur. et ut ab Ariete incipiam,

---

546 Cf. Varro *Latin Language* 6.8, *LALE* 85; the etymology (*bruma* < *brevissima*, "shortest [day]") is correct.

547 Cf. Aratus *CCAG* 5,4:166.6–7, Aelian *On the Nature of Animals* 12.7, Sex. Emp. *Against the Professors* 5.34, Vettius Valens *Anthol.* 1.2, Paul. Alex. *Elements of Astrology* p. 5.6–7; the sun is in Leo 23 July–22 August.

removed—with the roots yet remaining—signifies that this star retains its essence even when we cannot see it. 15. The same symbol also signifies the point at which the light is confined, when the growth, as it were, has been shorn away, leaving only the stubble, and the sun reaches the shortest day, which the ancients called the "brumal" solstice, calling it "bruma" from the shortness [*brevitas*] of the days,[546] or in Greek *brachy hêmar*. When the sun emerges again from its narrow confines and is born again, so to speak, into the hemisphere of summer, it makes the days longer and is then believed to have come into its true domain. 16. For that reason the Egyptians consecrated an animal among the signs of the zodiac in that part of the heavens where the sun burns hottest in its yearly course, and there they call the sign of Leo the house of the sun, because that animal seems to derive its essence from the nature of the sun:[547] 17. first, because in its hot-blooded aggression it surpasses other animals as the sun surpasses the other stars; second, because the lion's strength resides in its chest and forequarters, while its hindquarters do not rise to the same standard, just as the sun's strength, in the first part of the day, increases toward noon—or, in the first part of the year, from spring to summer—and then soon fades, as sunset approaches in the latter part of the day or as the sun rides lower in the sky toward winter, the latter part of the year. The lion is also seen to have wide-open, fiery eyes, as the sun looks upon the earth with its open, fiery eye in one long, untiring gaze.

18. 'And it is not just Leo but all the signs of the zodiac that are rightly understood in relation to the sun's nature. To start from the Ram [Aries], its agreement with the sun

magna illi concordia est: nam is per menses sex hibernos si-
nistro incubat lateri, ab aequinoctio verno supra dextrum
latus, sicut et sol ab eodem tempore dextrum hemisphaerium, reliquo ambit sinistrum. 19. ideo et Ammonem,
quem deum solem occidentem Libyes existimant, arietinis
cornibus fingunt, quibus maxime id animal valet sicut sol
radiis. nam et apud Graecos ἀπὸ τοῦ κάρα κρίος appellatur.

20. 'Taurum vero ad solem referri multiplici ratione Ae-
gyptius cultus ostendit, vel quia apud Heliupolim taurum
soli consecratum, quem Mneuin[134] cognominant, maxime
colunt, vel quia bos Apis in civitate Memphi solis instar ex-
cipitur, vel quia in oppido Hermunthi magnifico Apollinis
templo consecratum soli colunt taurum, Buchin[135] cognominantes, insignem miraculis convenientibus naturae
solis. 21. nam et per singulas horas mutare colores adfirma-

---

[134] Mneuin *Selden* (*De diis Syris, Synt. I, c. 4, p. 138* [1672]):
neuton ω
[135] Buchin (*i.e.,* Βοῦχιν) *Spiegelberg* (*APF* 1 [1901] 339–42):
Bacin ω

---

[548] The astrological year begins with Aries, the start of which
coincides with the vernal equinox. With the following allegory cf.
Aelian *On the Nature of Animals* 10.18
[549] "Right" and "left" = north and south from the perspective
of someone facing west to follow the sun's course, cf. 1.17.48.
[550] Ammon, the chief god of Egyptian Thebes, ultimately
identified with the sun god Re (cf. Mart. Cap. 2.192); the Greeks
equated him with Zeus by the 5th cent. BCE, and from the same
period on he is commonly represented with ram's horns (*LIMC*
1,2:534–54): cf. Hdt. 2.42.1, 4.181.2, Eur. fr. 955h (*TGrF* 5,2:958),

is plain:[548] it lies upon its left side during the six winter months and on its right starting with the vernal equinox, just as the sun makes its circuit of the hemisphere on the right starting from the same point, the hemisphere on the left the rest of the time.[549] 19. For that reason they also represent Ammon, the god the Libyans regard as the setting sun, with ram's horns,[550] which are the heart of that animal's power as the rays are of the sun's; note too that the Greeks call the ram *krios* from the word for "head" [*kara*].[551]

20. 'Egyptian cult practice shows that the Bull [Taurus] has a manifold relation to the sun: because in Heliupolis they especially worship a bull called Mnevis, which is consecrated to the sun;[552] or because the Apis bull in the city of Memphis[553] is welcomed as the likeness of the sun; or because in the town of Hermunthis, in a splendid temple of Apollo, they pay cult to a bull they call Bouchis, which is consecrated to the sun and distinguished by miraculous qualities appropriate to the sun's nature.[554] 21. For it is said to change color from one hour to the next and has a shaggy

Diod. Sic. 3.73.1, Paus. 8.32.1, Arnob. 6.12, (D)Serv. on *A.* 4.196, Mart. Cap. 2.157.

[551] Surely a slip for "horn" = Gk. *keras*.

[552] Cf. Hecat. Abder. fr. 25.1353 (no. 264 *FGrH*), Manetho fr. 8 (*FHG* 2), Diod. Sic. 1.84.4, Strabo 17.1.22, 27, Plut. *Mor.* 364C, Aelian *On the Nature of Animals* 11.11, Porph. *On Statues* 10.87, with Michalowski 1969, p. 406 pl. 517, 519. Heliopolis ("Sun-city" < *Per-Re*, "City of Re," the sun god) was on the Nile Delta, about 10 km NE of mod. Cairo; cf. 1.23.10.

[553] Cf. Hdt. 3.27, Pliny *Natural History* 8.184–85, Solin. 1.32.

[554] Bouchis was evidently assimilated to the sun god Re (Spiegelberg 1901).

tur et hirsutus setis dicitur in adversum nascentibus contra naturam omnium animalium. unde habetur velut imago solis in adversam mundi partem nitentis.

22. 'Gemini autem, qui alternis mortibus vivere creduntur, quid aliud nisi solem unum eundemque significant, modo descendentem in ima mundi, modo mundi in summam altitudinem resurgentem?

23. 'Cancer obliquo gressu quid aliud nisi iter solis ostendit, qui viam numquam rectam sed per illam semper meare sortitus est,

obliquus qua se signorum verteret ordo?

maximeque in illo signo sol a cursu supero incipit obliquus inferiora iam petere. de Leone iam supra dictum est.

24. 'Virgo autem, quae manu aristam refert, quid aliud quam δύναμις ἡλιακή quae fructibus curat? et ideo Iustitia creditur quae sola facit nascentes fructus ad usus hominum pervenire.

25. 'Scorpius totus, in quo Libra est, naturam solis imaginatur, qui hieme torpescit et transacta hac aculeum rursus erigit vi sua, nullum natura damnum ex hiberno torpore perpessa.

---

555 I.e., the sun moves counter to the rotation of the celestial sphere in which the fixed stars are set: see *Commentary* 1.18.

556 On the alternating deaths of the Twins = Castor and Pollux cf. *Od.* 11.299–304, Pind. *N.* 10.87–88, with *A.* 6.121–22 (quoted at 4.5.2), Ov. *F.* 5.715–20, Sex. Emp. *Against the Astrologers* 9.37, Lact. *Divine Institutes* 1.10.5, John Lydus *On the Months* 4.17.

557 Cf. 1.17.31n. and 1.17.63.

558 I.e., the sun enters Cancer (22 June–22 July) at the summer solstice: 1.17.26n.

coat of bristles that grow opposite to the direction naturally found in all other animals: hence it is regarded as being like the sun, which casts its light in the direction opposite to that of the heavens.[555]

22. 'As for the Twins [Gemini], who are believed to take turns living and dying,[556] what do they symbolize if not the very same sun, which now descends to the depths of cosmos, now rises back up to its summit?

23. 'What else does the Crab [Cancer] represent with its slantwise gait but the path of the sun,[557] which never follows a straight path but is fated always to wander along (*G*. 1.239)

where the constellations' slanting sequence spins?

It is precisely in the Crab that the sun begins to turn from its upper course and make for the lower on a slanting path.[558] I've already spoken about the Lion [Leo] above.[559]

24. 'The Maiden [Virgo], who carries an ear of grain in her hand, is none other than the *dynamis hêliakê* ["power of the sun"] that cares for the fruits of the earth: for that reason she is identified with Justice,[560] who alone causes those fruits to sprout and come forth for the benefit of men.

25. 'The Scorpion as a whole, which includes the Scale [Libra], is the very image of the sun's nature: it becomes inert in winter and, once winter is past, again has the strength to raise its telson, its nature having suffered no loss from its winter retirement.

[559] 1.21.16–17.   [560] Cf. Eratosth. *Catast*. 1.9 (interpreting Hes. *Works and Days* 256 astrologically), Arat. *Phaen*. 133–36, Vettius Valens *Anthol*. 1.2.

26. 'Sagittarius qui omnium zodiaci domiciliorum imus atque postremus est, ideo ex homine in feram per membra posteriora degenerat, quasi postremis partibus suis a superis in inferna detrusus; sagittam tamen iacit quod indicat tunc quoque universorum constare vitam radio solis vel ab ima parte venientis. Capricornus ab infernis partibus ad supera solem reducens, caprae naturam videtur imitari, quae dum pascitur ab imis partibus semper prominentium scopulorum alta deposcit.

27. 'Aquarius nonne ipsam vim solis ostendit? unde enim imber caderet in terras nisi solis calor ad supera traheret umorem, cuius refusio pluvialis est copia? In ultimo ordine zodiaci Pisces locati sunt, quos consecravit soli non aliqua naturae suae imaginatio ut cetera, sed ostentatio potentiae sideris, a quo vita non solum aeriis terrenisque animalibus datur, sed illis quoque quorum conversatio aquis mersa velut a conspectu solis exulat. tanta est vis solis ut abstrusa quoque penetrando vivificet.

22   'Et ut ad solis multiplicem potestatem revolvatur oratio, Nemesis quae contra superbiam colitur quid aliud est quam solis potestas, cuius ista natura est ut fulgentia obscuret et conspectui auferat, quaeque sunt in obscuro inluminet offeratque conspectui!

---

561 Sc. because the sun passes out of Sagittarius (23 Nov.–22 Dec.) at the winter solstice.

562 Cf. 1.17.63.

563 Perhaps originally a chthonian goddess, Nemesis was the complement of Aidôs ("Shame"), personifying the spirit of righteous indignation and retribution; she was commonly represented as a winged figure with reins and a scale (*LIMC* 6,1:735–36 with, e.g., 6,2:441 [no. 1563]).

26. 'The Archer [Sagittarius], lowest and last of all the houses in the zodiac,[561] turns from a human being into a beast in its hindquarters, as if those hind parts shoved it down from the upper regions to the lower; yet it shoots an arrow, which shows that the life of every single creature depends on the ray of the sun even when it emerges from the lowest regions. The Goat's Horn [Capricornus], which starts to lead the sun back from the lower regions to the upper, seems to imitate a goat's nature: while grazing, it always seeks the heights of overhanging crags instead of the low-lying pastures.[562]

27. 'Doesn't the Water-carrier [Aquarius] display the sun's very essence? For how does rain come to fall upon the earth save through the heat of the sun, which draws up the moisture that pours back down in abundant showers? The Fish [Pisces] occupy the last place in the zodiac's sequence: they are consecrated to the sun not by some figurative interpretation of their nature, as with the rest of the signs, but because they directly display the sun's power, which gives life not just to creatures of the air and the land but also to those that spend their time submerged in the water, as though exiled from the sight of the sun. So great is the sun's power that it reaches down even to beings that are hidden away and quickens them with life.

'Now, to let my discourse circle back to the manifold 22 power of the sun: surely Nemesis, who is worshipped as the antidote to arrogance,[563] is nothing other than the power of the sun, seeing that it's her nature to obscure the brilliant and take them from our sight, and contrarily to throw light on the obscure and present them to our sight.

2. 'Pan ipse, quem vocant Inuum, sub hoc habitu quo cernitur solem se esse prudentioribus permittit intellegi. 3. hunc deum Arcades colunt appellantes τὸν τῆς ὕλης κύριον, non silvarum dominum sed universae substantiae materialis dominatorem significari volentes, cuius materiae vis universorum corporum, seu illa divina sive terrena sint, componit essentiam. 4. ergo Inui cornua barbaeque prolixa demissio naturam lucis ostendunt, qua sol et ambitum caeli superioris inluminat et inferiora conlustrat, unde Homerus de eo ait,

> ὤρνυθ᾽, ἵν᾽ ἀθανάτοισι φόως φέροι ἠδὲ
> βροτοῖσιν.

quid fistula vel virga significent superius in habitu Attinis expressimus. 5. quod in caprae pedes desinit, haec argumenti ratio est, quia materia, quae in omnem substantiam sole dispensante porrigitur, divinis de se corporibus effectis in terrae finitur elementum. 6. ad huius igitur extremitatis signum pedes huius animalis electi sunt, quod et terrenum esset et tamen semper peteret alta pascendo, sicut sol, vel cum radios superne demittit in terras vel cum se recolligit, in montibus visitur. 7. huius Inui amor et deliciae Ἠχώ creditur nullius oculis obnoxia, quod significat har-

---

564 Inuus was a rustic god variously identified with Pan, as here (cf. Livy 1.5.3, Serv. on A. 6.775), Faunus (Serv. ibid.), or Silvanus (Anon. *Origin of the Roman Nation* 4.6); his name allegedly derived "from 'entering' [*ineundo*, sc. in a sexual sense] all animals indiscriminately, whence he is also called Incubo" (Serv. ibid.).

565 Gk. ὕλη = "woods" and, secondarily, "raw material/matter," hence M.'s following remarks; cf. *Comm.* 1.12.11.

2. 'Pan himself, whom they call Inuus,[564] allows the more perceptive among us to understand that in the character he presents to us, he is the sun. 3. The Arcadians worship this god under the title "lord of the *hylê*,"[565] by which they mean not "lord of the woods" but "master of all matter": the power of this matter is essential to the composition of all bodies, whether divine or earthly. 4. The horns of Inuus, then, and his long beard point to the nature of light, by which the sun both shines on the circle of heaven above and lights the regions below, causing Homer to say of him (*Il.* 11.2 = 19.2 = *Od.* 5.2):

he rose up to bring light to gods and mortals.

I've already made plain the meaning of the pipe or rod in discussing Attis' appearance.[566] 5. That his legs end in goat's hooves symbolizes the fact that matter, which the sun distributes so that it penetrates the essence of all things, produces the bodies of the gods and then ends up providing the earth's basic substance. 6. The goat's feet were chosen to symbolize this end-point because it is of the earth and yet always seeks the heights as it grazes,[567] just as the sun is seen shining on the mountains, whether it is sending down its rays upon the earth from above or is gathering itself to rise. 7. Inuus is believed to love his darling Echo,[568] whom none can see: this symbolizes the heav-

[566] Cf. 1.21.9.
[567] Cf. 1.17.63, on Capricorn.
[568] Cf. Lucian *Twice Accused* 12, Philost. *Images* 2.11.2, Eutolmius Schol. *Anth. Gr.* 6.87, Procop. *Decl.* 1.29, 3.27, 4.45, Nonnus *Dionys.* 32.276–80.

moniam caeli, quae soli amica est quasi sphaerarum omnium de quibus nascitur moderatori nec tamen potest nostris umquam sensibus deprehendi.

8. 'Saturnus ipse, qui auctor est temporum et ideo a Graecis immutata littera Κρόνος quasi Χρόνος vocatur, quid aliud nisi sol intellegendus est cum tradatur ordo elementorum temporum numerositate distinctus, luce patefactus, nexus aeternitate conductus, visione discretus, quae omnia actum solis ostendunt?

23   'Nec ipse Iuppiter rex deorum naturam solis videtur excedere, sed eundem esse Iovem ac solem claris docetur indiciis. nam cum ait Homerus,

> Ζεὺς γὰρ ἐς Ὠκεανὸν μετ᾽ ἀμύμονας Αἰθιοπῆας
> χθιζὸν[136] ἔβη μετὰ[137] δαῖτα, θεοὶ δ᾽ ἅμα πάντες
>   ἕποντο,
> δωδεκάτῃ δέ τοι αὖθις[138] ἐλεύσεται Οὐλυμπόνδε,

2. Iovis appellatione solem intellegi Cornificius scribit, cui unda Oceani velut dapes ministrat. ideo enim, sicut et Posidonius et Cleanthes adfirmant, solis meatus a plaga quae

---

[136] χθιζὸν] χθιζὸς Hom.   [137] μετὰ ω, codd. plerique Hom.: κατὰ Aristarch., Arist. Byz., et al.
[138] αὖθις] αὖτις Hom.

---

569 Acc. to a theory that might go back to Pythagoras, the movements of the sun, moon, and 5 known planets (1.19.15n.) produced the "music of the spheres," a sound harmoniously modulated by the intervals among the heavenly bodies: cf., e.g., Aristotle *On the Heavens* 2.9 290b12ff. (criticizing the theory), Cic. *On the Nature of the Gods* 3.27 (Pease ad loc. gives a catalog of other discussions), and esp. *On the Commonwealth* 6.18 with M.'s

ens' harmony, which is beloved of the sun, who governs all
the spheres from which this harmony arises, though it can
never be perceived by our senses.[569]

8. 'Saturn himself is the source of time and so is called
by the Greeks (with the change of one letter) not *Khronos*
but *Kronos*:[570] how can he not be recognized as the sun,
when an order of the elements is passed down that is defined by units of time, revealed by the light, held together
by an eternal bond, and distinguished by our sight, all of
which display the sun's effects?

'Nor does Jupiter himself, the king of the gods, seem   23
superior to the sun's nature; rather, there are clear indica-
tions to show that Jupiter and the sun are the same. When
Homer says (*Il.* 1.423–25),[571]

> For yesterday Zeus went to Ôkean, for a feast
> with the blameless Ethiopians, and all the gods
>   followed,
> but again on the twelfth day he will come to
>   Olympus,

2. Cornificius writes (fr. 6 *GRF* 1:476) that "Jupiter" [i.e.,
Zeus] means the sun, for whom the water of Ocean lays a
feast, in a sense. Accordingly, as both Posidonius (fr. 118
E.-K.[2])[572] and Cleanthes (fr. 501 *SVF* 1:112) affirm, the

---

Comm. 2.1.2ff. We cannot hear or distinguish this music because
it has been in our ears since birth (thus the theorists criticized by
Aristotle) or because the sound is too great for the human ear to
take in (*Comm.* 2.4.14).

[570] Cf. 1.8.6.   [571] Cf. Eustath. *Comm. Il.* 1:197.1–5.

[572] It is unlikely that the fragment as quoted reflects Posidonius' views (see Kidd's comm., 2,1:458–60).

usta dicitur non recedit, quia sub ipsa currit Oceanus qui terram et ambit et dividit, omnium autem physicorum adsertione constat calorem umore nutriri. 3. nam quod ait θεοὶ δ' ἅμα πάντες ἕποντο, sidera intelleguntur, quae cum eo ad occasus ortusque cotidiano impetu caeli feruntur eodemque aluntur umore. θεοὺς enim dicunt sidera et stellas ἀπὸ τοῦ θέειν, id est τρέχειν, quod semper in cursu sint, ἢ ἀπὸ τοῦ θεωρεῖσθαι. 4. addit poeta δωδεκάτῃ δέ τοι αὖθις, non dierum sed horarum significans numerum, quibus referuntur ad hemisphaerii superioris exortum. 5. intellectum nostrum in eandem sententiam ducunt etiam de Timaeo Platonis haec verba: ὁ μὲν δὴ μέγας ἡγεμὼν ἐν οὐρανῷ Ζεὺς ἐλαύνων πτηνὸν ἅρμα πρῶτος πορεύεται, διακοσμῶν πάντα καὶ ἐπιμελούμενος· τῷ δὲ ἕπεται στρατιὰ θεῶν καὶ δαιμόνων κατὰ ἔνδεκα μέρη κεκοσμημένη. μένει δὲ Ἑστία ἐν θεῶν οἴκῳ μόνη. his enim verbis magnum in caelo ducem solem vult sub appellatione Iovis intellegi, alato curru velocitatem sideris monstrans. 6. nam quia in quocumque signo fuerit praestat omnia signa et sidera signorumque praestites deos, videtur cunctos deos ducatu praeire ornando cuncta ordinandoque atque ideo velut exercitum eius ceteros deos haberi per undecim[139] signorum partes distributos, quia ipse duo-

---

[139] undecim *Jan*: duodecim ω

---

[573] On the doctrine of the five "zones" that comprise the earth's surface, two frigid, two temperate, and one parched, cf. Cic. *On the Commonwealth* 6.20–22 with M.'s *Comm.* 2.6, and *Comm.* 2.9 on the role of Ocean. [574] Cf. Pl. *Cratylus* 397D2–4, Cornut. p. 2.13–16, Clem. Alex. *Protreptic* 2.26.1, *Epimer. Hom.* 1.483(a1), *Etym. Gud.* Θ p. 258.57–59, 269.6–10, Eustath. *Comm. Il.* 1:246.16, 685:24, 686.5–6.

sun's journey does not depart from the so-called "parched" zone, under which Ocean runs, circling the earth and marking its limits;[573] and the physical scientists universally hold that heat is fed by moisture. 3. As for the fact that Homer says, "and all the gods followed along," he means the constellations, which are borne along with the sun to the west and the east by the daily movement of the heavens, and are fed by the same moisture. For they call the constellations and stars *theoi* ["gods"] from *thëein* ["run"], because they are always in motion, or from *theôreisthai* ["be observed"].[574] 4. The poet adds "but again on the twelfth" to indicate the number of hours, not days, the time it takes them to come back and rise in the upper hemisphere. 5. The following words from Plato's *Timaeus* (*Phaedr.* 246E4–247A1) lead us to think along the same lines: "Zeus, heaven's great guide, drives his winged chariot and leads the way, ordering and taking thought for all things; and the host of gods and divine powers follows after him arranged in eleven divisions. Only Hestia stays behind in the gods' dwelling." With these words he intends it to be understood that the sun is "heaven's great leader," here called "Jupiter" [i.e., Zeus], while the "winged chariot" points to the sun's speed.[575] 6. Because the sun, in whatever sign he happens to be, is superior to all signs and constellations and to the gods that are the signs' guardians,[576] he seems to go before all the gods as their leader, arranging and setting all things in order, and the rest of the gods, like an army, seem to be distributed among eleven of the signs,

575 Cf. Eustath. *Comm. Il.* 1:523:21–23, *Comm. Od.* 2:11.14–15, similarly interpreting Pl. *Phaedr.* 246E4–5.
576 Each sign of the zodiac was the house of a specific god, e.g., Scorpio of Mars and Libra of Venus, 1.12.11.

decimi signi, in quocumque signo fuerit, locum occupat.
7. nomen autem daemonum cum deorum appellatione co-
niungit, aut quia di sunt δαήμονες, id est scientes futuri,
aut ut Posidonius scribit in libris quibus titulus est Περὶ
ἡρώων καὶ δαιμόνων quia ex aetheria substantia parta
atque divisa qualitas illis est, sive ἀπὸ τοῦ δαιομένου, id est
καιομένου, seu ἀπὸ τοῦ δαιομένου, hoc est μεριζομένου.
8. quod autem addit μένει δὲ Ἑστία ἐν θεῶν οἴκῳ μόνη,
significat quia haec sola, quam terram esse accipimus, ma-
net immobilis intra domum deorum, id est intra mundum,
ut ait Euripides,

κ αὶ Γαῖα μῆτερ· Ἑστίαν δέ σ' οἱ σοφοὶ
βροτῶν καλοῦσιν ἡμένην ἐν αἰθέρι.

9. hinc quoque ostenditur quid de sole et Iove sit sentien-
dum cum alibi dicitur,

πάντα ἰδὼν Διὸς ὀφθαλμὸς καὶ πάντα νοήσας,

et alibi,

Ἥλιος θ', ὃς πάντ' ἐφορᾷς καὶ πάντ' ἐπακούεις,

unde utrumque constat una potestate censendum.
10. ᾽Assyrii quoque solem sub nomine Iovis, quem Δία

577 Cf. Pl. *Crat.* 398B, Plotin. *Enn.* 6.7.6, Lact. *Divine Institutes* 2.14.6, Serv. on *A.* 3.111, Aug. *City of God* 9.20, Mart. Cap.
2.154, Hesych. Δ.73, Σ D *Il.* 1.222, *Epimer. Hom.* 1.222.
578 Cf. Dion. Hal. 2.66.3, Ov. *F.* 6.267, Arnob. 3.32.2, Aug.
City of God 7.16, Hermias *Schol. Phaedr.* p. 135.29ff.
579 Heliupolis ("Sun-city") = Baalbek in the Bekaa Valley of
Syria (for "Assyria" cf. 1.17.66n.); Zeus/Jupiter here = Baal. On

because he himself in whatever sign he happens to be, fills the place of the twelfth sign. 7. He mentions "divine powers" [*daimones*] along with the gods, either because they are *daêmones*, that is, seers,[577] or—as Posidonius writes (fr. 24 E.-K.[2]) in his books titled *On Heroes and Divine Powers*—because their essence is created and apportioned from the substance of ether, being called *daimones* from the verb *daiein* that means "set alight" or from the verb *daiein* that means "apportion." 8. The added thought that "Only Hestia [goddess of the hearth] stays behind in the gods' dwelling" means that only this god, whom we take to be the earth,[578] remains unmoved within the gods' dwelling, that is, the cosmic order, as Euripides says (fr. 944 *TGrF* 5,2:938):

> and mother Earth: the wise among mortals
> call you Hestia, sitting still in the ether.

9. Another statement makes plain what we should think about the sun and Jupiter (Hes. *Op.* 267):

> the eye of Zeus that sees all and apprehends all,

and again (*Il.* 3.277),

> and the Sun, you who watch over all and overhear all,

which establishes that they should be thought to have the same power.

10. 'The Assyrians too, in the city called Heliupolis,[579]

the following, otherwise unattested story see Lightfoot 2003, 303–5; on §§10–21 see the detailed analysis of Hajjar 1977, 2:442–57.

Ἡλιουπολίτην cognominant, maximis caerimoniis celebrant in civitate quae Heliupolis nuncupatur. eius dei simulacrum sumptum est de oppido Aegypti quod et ipsum
Heliupolis[140] appellatur, regnante apud Aegyptios Sene-
mure seu idem Senepos nomine fuit, perlatumque est primum in eam per Opiam legatum Deloboris regis Assyriorum sacerdotesque Aegyptios quorum princeps fuit
Partemetis diuque habitum apud Assyrios postea Heliu-
polin commigravit. 11. cur ita factum quaque ratione Aegypto profectum in haec loca ubi nunc est postea venerit,
rituque Assyrio magis quam Aegyptio colatur, dicere su-
persedi, quia ad praesentem non attinet causam. 12. hunc
vero eundem Iovem solemque esse cum ex ipso sacrorum
ritu tum ex habitu dinoscitur. simulacrum enim aureum
specie imberbi instat dextera elevata cum flagro in aurigae
modum; laeva tenet fulmen et spicas, quae cuncta Iovis so-
lisque consociatam potentiam monstrant. 13. huius templi
religio etiam divinatione praepollet, quae ad Apollinis potestatem refertur, qui idem atque sol est. vehitur enim
simulacrum dei Heliupolitani ferculo, uti vehuntur in
pompa ludorum circensium deorum simulacra, et subeunt
plerumque provinciae proceres raso capite, longi temporis
castimonia puri, ferunturque divino spiritu, non suo arbitrio sed quo deus propellit vehentes, ut videmus apud

---

[140] Heliu- . . . Heliu- *Willis*: helio- . . . helio- ω

---

[580] On Egyptian Heliupolis, cf. 1.21.20n.

[581] The whip and ears of grain are the standard accoutrements
of the Hadad/Zeus of Heliupolis: cf. Hajjar 1985, 63–69. There
was a beardless statue of Zeus at Olympia (*LIMC* 8,1:325–26), but

worship the sun with very great ceremony under the name of Jupiter, whom they call "Zeus of Heliupolis." The god's image was taken from an Egyptian town that is itself also called Heliupolis,[580] when Senemuris ruled Egypt (or perhaps he was named Senepos), and was first brought to Heliupolis by Opias, a lieutenant of the Assyrian king Delobor, and by Egyptian priests led by Partemetis; after the Assyrians had held it for a long time, it was transferred to Heliupolis. 11. Why that happened, how it left Egypt and later came to the place where it now is, why it is paid cult in the Assyrian, not Egyptian, manner—all this I've thought it superfluous to relate, since it has no bearing on the topic at hand. 12. That this Jupiter is the same as the sun is evident both from the very nature of his cult and from his appearance. For his statue is of gold, beardless, with its right hand raised and holding a whip, like a charioteer, its left hand holding a lightning bolt and ears of grain, all of which point to the conjoined power of Jupiter and the sun.[581] 13. Divination, too, plays a preponderant role in the temple's cult, and that is related to the power of Apollo, who is identified with the sun. The image of the god of Heliupolis is carried on a litter, like the images of the gods in the procession at our Circus Games,[582] and the leading men of the province usually bear the load, their heads shaved, their bodies kept ritually pure by long sexual abstinence: they are borne along by the god's spirit, carrying the image not where they choose but where the god moves

this was very much the exception, and ears of grain were similarly uncommon (*LIMC* 8,1:357, 367).

[582] I.e., at the Roman Games (*ludi Romani*), 5–19 Sept.: cf. Dion. Hal. 7.72.1, Suet. *Aug.* 16.3, with 1.6.15 above.

Antium promoveri simulacra Fortunarum ad danda responsa.

14. 'Consulunt hunc deum et absentes missis diplomatibus consignatis, rescribitque ordine ad ea quae consultatione addita continentur. sic et imperator Traianus initurus ex ea provincia Parthiam cum exercitu, constantissimae religionis hortantibus amicis, qui maxima huiusce numinis ceperant experimenta, ut de eventu consuleret rei coeptae, egit Romano consilio, prius explorando fidem religionis, ne forte fraus subesset humana; et primum misit signatos codicillos ad quos sibi rescribi vellet. 15. deus iussit adferri chartam eamque signari puram et mitti, stupentibus sacerdotibus ad eius modi factum. ignorabant quippe condicionem codicillorum. hos cum maxima admiratione Traianus excepit, quod ipse quoque puris tabellis cum deo egisset. 16. tunc aliis codicillis conscriptis signatisque consuluit an Romam perpetrato bello rediturus esset. vitem centurialem deus ex muneribus in aede dedicatis deferri iussit divisamque in partes sudario condi ac proinde ferri. exitus rei obitu Traiani apparuit ossibus Romam relatis. nam fragmentis species reliquiarum, vitis argumento casus futuri tempus ostensum est.

17. 'Et ne sermo per singulorum nomina deorum vage-

---

583 The procedure matches that of the oracle of Apollo/Nebo at Hieropolis (1.17.66n.) described at Lucian *On the Syrian Goddess* 36; cf. Lightfoot 2003, 464–66, 469, and Hajjar 1977, 2:449, for sim. procedures elsewhere.

584 Antium (mod. Anzio) lay on the coast ca. 53 km south of Rome: its two sister goddesses of Fortune were renowned, cf. Hor. *Odes* 1.35.1 (with Porphyrio), Martial 5.1.3–4, Suet. *Cal.* 57.3, Fronto *On Orations* 6.

302

them,[583] as we see the images of Fortune brought out at Antium[584] to give oracular responses.

14. 'People make inquiries of this god even from a distance by sending sealed tablets, and the god replies to the questions in writing, one after the other. So, too, when the emperor Trajan was going to invade Parthia from Syria and friends of his—men of unswerving piety who had put the divinity to very stringent tests—were urging him to ask it about the expedition's outcome, he adopted a very Roman strategy, testing the ritual's reliability lest some deception of human origin chanced to lurk. So first he sent sealed tablets, to which he sought a written reply. 15. The god ordered a sheet of papyrus to be fetched and then had it sealed, with nothing written on it, and sent off, leaving the priests astonished at the god's action. Of course, they didn't know the state of the tablets: Trajan received what the god had sent with great wonder, since he himself had used blank tablets in his dealings with the god. 16. So another set of tablets were written up and sealed, with this question: would he conclude the war and return to Rome? The god had a centurion's staff fetched from among the offerings dedicated in the temple and ordered that it be cut up, its parts put in a napkin and sent right off to Trajan. The outcome became apparent when Trajan died and his bones were brought back to Rome:[585] his remains were like the pieces of the staff, a symbol that revealed a time of misfortune to come.

17. 'To keep my discourse from meandering from this

[585] Trajan died of a stroke while returning from Parthia in August 117 CE.

tur, accipe quid Assyrii de potentia solis opinentur. deo
enim, quem summum maximumque venerantur, Adad nomen dederunt. eius nominis interpretatio significat unus
unus. 18. hunc ergo ut potentissimum adorant deum sed
subiungunt eidem deam nomine Adargatin omnemque
potestatem cunctarum rerum his duobus attribuunt, solem terramque intellegentes, nec multitudine nominum
enuntiantes divisam eorum per omnes species potestatem,
sed argumentis quibus ornantur significantes multiplicem
praestantiam duplicis numinis. 19. ipsa autem argumenta
solis rationem loquuntur. namque simulacrum Adad insigne cernitur radiis inclinatis, quibus monstratur vim caeli
in radiis esse solis qui demittuntur in terram. Adargatidis[141] simulacrum sursum versum reclinatis radiis insigne
est monstrando radiorum vi superne missorum enasci
quaecumque terra progenerat. 20. sub eodem simulacro
species leonum sunt, eadem ratione terram esse monstrantes qua Phryges finxere Matrem Deum id est terram
leonibus vehi.

[141] Adargatidis *Jan*: Adargadis α, -gidis β

---

[586] The Mesopotamian god of weather and fertility, Adad
(East Semitic) or Hadad (West Semitic), was Hellenized as Zeus:
cf. Lucian *On the Syrian Goddess* 31 ("the one they call Zeus by
another name" = the Hadad of Hieropolis/Bambykê: cf. Hajjar
1985, 359); among Latin authors he is otherwise mentioned only
by Pliny (*Natural History* 37.186). The same interpretation of
his name, based on the Syriac word for "one" (*had*), was known
to M.'s younger contemporary Proclus (*Commentary on Plato's
Parmenides* p. 60).

[587] The goddess Adargatis (or Atargatis: Pliny *Natural History*
5.81), Lucian's "Syrian goddess," was worshipped at Heliupolis/

god's name to that, let me tell you what the Assyrians think of the sun's power. To the god whom they revere as the highest and greatest they gave the name "Adad," which can be translated as "one one."[586] 18. This god, then, they worship as most powerful, but they give him as a consort the goddess named Adargatis[587] and ascribe all power over all things to this pair, whom they understand to be the sun and the earth; nor do they distinguish all the different manifestations of their power, giving each a different name, but they use the symbols with which they are adorned to signify the many-sided excellence of the two-fold godhead. 19. The symbols themselves, moreover, provide an account of the sun: the image of Adad is distinguished by rays angled downward, making plain that heaven's power is in the rays of the sun that are sent down to earth; the image of Adargatis is distinguished by rays angled upward, making plain that all the things the earth produces come to be thanks to the power of the rays sent from above.[588] 20. Under Adargatis, too, there are images of lions,[589] showing that she is the earth in the same way that the Phrygians fashioned the Mother God, which is to say, the earth, being drawn by lions.[590]

Baalbek with Adad: with §§18–20 compare Lucian *On the Syrian Goddess* 31–32 (the cult statues of "Hera" and "Zeus"), with Lightfoot 2003, 434–47; for the goddess' iconography cf. *LIMC* 3,2:263–66, 4,2:210 (no. 12), Lightfoot figs. 10, 36, Hajjar 1985, 136–57.   [588] The radiate imagery is not attested in the material evidence for either deity: cf. Hajjar 1985, 135, Lightfoot 2003, 436, 440–41.   [589] See Hajjar 1977, 2 fig. 80–81, Lightfoot 2003, 19–21, 362 fig. 31.

[590] Cf. 1.21.8.

21. 'Postremo potentiam solis ad omnium potestatum summitatem referri indicant theologi, qui in sacris hoc brevissima precatione demonstrant dicentes, Ἥλιε παντοκράτορ, κόσμου πνεῦμα, κόσμου δύναμις, κόσμου φῶς. 22. solem esse omnia et Orpheus testatur his versibus:

κέκλυθι τηλεπόρου δίνης ἑλικαύγεα¹⁴² κύκλον
οὐρανίαις στροφάλιγξι περίδρομον αἰὲν ἑλίσσων,
ἀγλαὲ¹⁴³ Ζεῦ Διόνυσε, πάτερ πόντου, πάτερ αἴης,
Ἥλιε παγγενέτορ πανταίολε¹⁴⁴ χρυσεοφεγγές.'

24   Hic cum Praetextatus fecisset loquendi finem, omnes in eum adfixis vultibus admirationem stupore prodebant. dein laudare hic memoriam, ille doctrinam, cuncti religionem, adfirmantes hunc esse unum arcanae deorum naturae conscium qui solus divina et adsequi animo et eloqui posset ingenio. 2. inter haec Evangelus, 'equidem,' inquit, 'miror potuisse tantorum potestatem numinum comprehendi; verum quod Mantuanum nostrum ad singula, cum de divinis sermo est, testem citatis, gratiosius est quam ut iudicio fieri putetur. 3. an ego credam quod ille, cum diceret "Liber et alma Ceres" pro sole ac luna, non hoc in alterius poetae imitationem posuit, ita dici audiens, cur tamen diceretur ignorans? 4. nisi forte, ut Graeci omnia sua in im-

---

¹⁴² ἑλικ- ed. Basil. 1535: ΕΛΚ- ω
¹⁴³ ἀγλαὲ ed. Ven. 1472: ΑΓΑΑ ω
¹⁴⁴ Πὰν αἰόλε Gesner

21. 'Finally, those who discourse on the gods show that the sun's power is reckoned as the totality of all powers, a point they make plain in their rites by this very brief prayer: "Sun the ruler of all, breath of the universe, power of the universe, light of the universe." 22. In the following verses Orpheus, too, bears witness that the sun is all things (*PEGr* fr. 539 I):

> Hear, you who ever make your orb with its circling
> rays
> whirl round in heavenly eddies, traveling far in its
> circuit,
> splendid Zeus, Dionysus, father of sea, father of
> earth,
> Sun who begets all, all radiant, shining like gold.'

Here, as Praetextatus finished speaking, all had their 24 eyes fixed upon him, with looks that made plain their astonishment and wonder. Then this one began to praise his memory, that one his learning, all of them his piety, swearing that *here* was the one man who knew the gods' secret nature, the only man with the intellect to grasp things divine and the ability to expound them. 2. Amid all this Evangelus said, 'I for my part am impressed that the power of such great divinities could be thus comprehended; but that you call our friend from Mantua as witness to this detail and that, when matters divine are the subject—that should be thought more a display of favoritism than of good judgment. 3. Or am I to believe that when he says "Liber and nurturing Ceres" (*G.* 1.7), meaning "sun and moon," he's not doing it out of imitation of some other poet, hearing the words spoken but without a clue as to why? 4. Unless, perhaps, just like the Greeks, who puff

mensum tollunt, nos quoque etiam poetas nostros volumus
philosophari, cum ipse Tullius, qui non minus professus
est philosophandi studium quam loquendi, quotiens aut
de natura deorum aut de fato aut de divinatione disputat
gloriam quam oratione conflavit incondita rerum relatione
minuat.'

5. Tum Symmachus: 'De Cicerone, Evangele, qui con-
viciis impenetrabilis est, post videbimus; nunc quia cum
Marone nobis negotium est, respondeas volo utrum
poetae huius opera instituendis tantum pueris idonea iudi-
ces, an alia illis altiora inesse fatearis. videris enim mihi ita
adhuc Vergilianos habere versus qualiter eos pueri magistris praelegentibus canebamus.'

6. 'Immo pueri cum essemus, Symmache, sine iudicio
mirabamur, inspicere autem vitia nec per magistros nec
per aetatem licebat. quae tamen non pudenter quisquam
negabit, cum ipse confessus sit. qui enim moriens poema
suum legavit igni, quid nisi famae suae vulnera posteritati
subtrahenda curavit? 7. nec immerito. erubuit quippe de
se futura iudicia, si legeretur petitio deae precantis filio
arma a marito cui soli nupserat nec ex eo prolem susce-
pisse se noverat, vel si mille alia multum pudenda seu in
verbis modo Graecis modo barbaris seu in ipsa disposi-
tione operis deprehenderentur.'

---

591 Evangelus refers by title to the three works on religious
questions that Cicero wrote in 45–44 BCE.

592 If this refers to a subsequent discussion in *Sat.*, it presumably looks ahead to Symmachus' discussion of rhetoric (lost with
the start of the dialogue's third day, cf. Introd. §4).

593 So Gell. 17.10.7, Donatus *Life of Virgil* 37–41; the latter reports Augustus' countermanding of the request.

594 The embarrassment is addressed by Serv. on *A.* 8.373.

their accomplishments up out of all proportion, we too want to claim that even our poets are philosophers, when Tully himself, who claimed to be a student of philosophy no less than of speech, squanders what glory he accumulated with his oratory thanks to the half-baked account he provides the moment he speaks on the nature of the gods, or on fate, or on divination.'[591]

5. Then Symmachus said, 'As for Cicero, who shrugs off insults—we'll see about him later, Evangelus.[592] Right now Maro is our concern: so tell me, please, do you think his works are fit only for teaching boys, or do you admit that they have a deeper content? For you seem to me still to think of Virgil's verses the way we did as boys, when we chanted them out for our teachers when they lectured.'

6. 'Not at all, Symmachus: when we were boys we admired the verses without judging them, and neither our teachers nor our stage in life allowed us to take a good look at the faults. Yet no one can brazenly deny they're there, seeing that he himself acknowledged them: why did he bequeath his own poem to the flames on his death bed,[593] if not to make sure that the damage to his reputation would be concealed from later generations? 7. And right he was: obviously he blushed to think of posterity's verdict, if they read of the goddess pleading with her husband to make arms for her son (*A.* 8.370–86)—the only husband she'd had, and she well knew she'd had no children by him![594]— or if they caught out the thousands of other deeply embarrassing flaws, whether in his choice of words—now Greek, now barbarous[595]—or in the very organization of the work.'

[595] Virgil's use of Greek and other non-Latin words is discussed favorably at 6.4.17–23.

8. Cumque adhuc dicentem omnes exhorruissent, subtexuit Symmachus: 'haec est quidem, Evangele, Maronis
gloria ut nullius laudibus crescat, nullius vituperatione mi-
nuatur, verum ista quae proscindis defendere quilibet potest ex plebeia grammaticorum cohorte, ne Servio nostro,
qui priscos, ut mea fert opinio, praeceptores doctrina
praestat, in excusandis talibus quaeratur iniuria. sed quaero utrum cum poetica tibi in tanto poeta displicuerit, nervi
tamen oratorii, qui in eodem validissimi sunt, placere videantur?'

9. Haec verba primum Evangeli risus excepit. deinde
subiecit: 'id hercle restat denique, ut et oratorem Vergi-
lium renuntietis: nec mirum cum et ad philosophos eum
ambitus vester paulo ante provexerit!'

10. 'Si in hac opinione es,' inquit Symmachus, 'ut Maro
tibi nihil nisi poeticum sensissse aestimetur, licet hoc
quoque eidem nomen invideris, audi quid de operis sui
multiplici doctrina ipse pronuntiet. ipsius enim Maronis
epistula, qua compellat Augustum, ita incipit: 11. "ego
vero frequentes a te litteras accipio"; et infra, "de Aenea
quidem meo, si mehercle iam dignum auribus haberem
tuis, libenter mitterem, sed tanta inchoata res est ut paene
vitio mentis tantum opus ingressus mihi videar, cum prae-
sertim, ut scis, alia quoque studia ad id opus multoque po-
tiora impertiar." 12. nec his Vergilii verbis copia rerum dis-
sonat, quam plerique omnes litteratores pedibus inlotis
praetereunt, tamquam nihil ultra verborum explanatio-

---

596 Lit. "with unwashed feet": a proverb more common in
Greek (e.g., Lucian *Demonax* 4, *Teacher of Public Speaking* 14,
Pseudologistês 4, Euseb. *Church History* 10.4.39) than in Latin
(Gell. 1.9.8, 17.5.14), explained as being applied to "those who ig-

8. When they had all shuddered with repugnance while he was still speaking, Symmachus followed up by saying: 'Such is Maro's glory, Evangelus, that no man's praise makes it greater, and no man's attacks make it less. As for those points you pick at, anyone from the common run of grammarians could fend off your criticisms—not to insult our friend Servius, who I think more learned than the teachers of old, by having him make excuses for such things. But tell me: granted that you take no pleasure in the great poet's poetry, does his oratorical muscle, which he also has in abundance, seem to meet your standard?'

9. Evangelus first laughed in response, then added: 'My god, so that's what's left—for you all to declare Virgil an orator too! No wonder, given that your flattery just now promoted him to the philosophers' ranks!'

10. 'If you think,' said Symmachus, 'that Maro's mind ran to nothing but poetry—though you begrudge him the name of poet too—listen to what he himself says about the many-sided learning his work entailed, in a letter that Maro himself addressed to Augustus. 11. It starts off, "I've received a number of letters from you," and a bit further on says, "As for my Aeneas, I swear, if I had something worthy of your ears, I'd gladly send him to you, but the thing I've begun is on such a massive scale that I almost think I was crazy to have started such a grand project, especially since, as you know, I'm devoting other, much more valuable sorts of learning to it too." 12. Nor does the poem's abundant variety put the lie to Virgil's words, though practically all the schoolteachers pass it by with unseemly haste,[596] as though a grammarian were allowed to know

norantly undertake certain tasks and actions" (Zenob. *Epitome* 1.95).

nem liceat nosse grammatico. ita sibi belli isti homines certos scientiae fines et velut quaedam pomeria et effata posuerunt, ultra quae si quis egredi audeat, introspexisse in aedem deae a qua mares absterrentur existimandus sit. 13. sed nos quos crassa Minerva dedecet non patiamur abstrusa esse adyta sacri poematis sed arcanorum sensuum investigato aditu doctorum cultu celebranda praebeamus reclusa penetralia. 14. et ne videar velle omnia unus amplecti, spondeo violentissima inventa vel sensa rhetoricae in Vergiliano me opere demonstraturum, Eusebio autem, oratorum eloquentissimo, non praeripio de oratoria apud Maronem arte tractatum, quem et doctrina et docendi usu melius exsequetur. reliquos omnes qui adestis impense precatus sim, ut quid vestrum quisque praecipuum sibi adnotaverit de Maronis ingenio, velut ex symbola conferamus.' 15. mirum in modum alacritatem omnibus qui aderant haec verba pepererunt, et adsurgens quisque in desiderium alios audiendi non vidit et se in idem munus vocandum. itaque hortatu mutuo concitati in adsensum facile ac libenter animati sunt intuentesque omnes Praetextatum orabant ut iudicium suum primus aperiret, ceteris per ordinem quem casus sedendi fecerat secuturis.

16. Et Vettius: 'equidem inter omnia quibus eminet laus Maronis hoc adsiduus lector admiror, quia doctissime ius pontificium tamquam hoc professus in multa et varia

---

597 I.e., the Good Goddess, discussed at 1.12.21–29, from whose rites men were barred.   598 Eusebius' remarks occupy all of the surviving remnant of Book 4 and the first chapter of Book 5; but since part of his discussion and all of Symmachus' remarks are lost, it is difficult to say exactly how M. distinguished Virgil's rhetorical skills from his oratorical skills.

only how to parse. That's how those fine fellows have fixed limits to their own expertise, like some sort of sacred boundary that the augurs have defined, and if anyone should dare set foot beyond it, he must be judged to have peered into the shrine of the goddess from whom men must keep far off.[597] 13. But we should have a finer understanding: let's not allow this sacred poem's inner sancta to be concealed, but instead let's trace the path to its secret meanings and fling open its inmost shrine so that it's available to the worship of the learned. 14. And lest I seem to claim all topics for myself, I undertake to make plain the rhetorical skill of Virgil's oeuvre—its most forceful conceits and expressions—though I do not want to deprive Eusebius, the most eloquent of speakers, of the chance to treat Maro's oratorical skill, since he will be better suited by both his scholarship and his teaching.[598] Let me also earnestly ask the rest of you who are gathered here to contribute remarks on whatever aspect of Maro's genius has chiefly claimed your attention, like an offering to a communal banquet.' 15. All present fell in with this suggestion with remarkable speed, as each one rose to say how much he'd like to hear the others, not realizing that he too would be called on to contribute. So by urging each other eagerly on, they reached an easy and happy consensus; then turning to Praetextatus, they all asked him to reveal his preference first, with the rest to follow in order according to where they happened to be sitting.

16. Vettius then said, 'Among all of Maro's supremely praiseworthy aspects, my constant reading causes me to marvel at this: in many different places in his work he observed pontifical law as knowledgeably as he would if he

operis sui parte servavit et, si tantae dissertationi sermo
non cesserit, promitto fore ut Vergilius noster pontifex
maximus adseratur.'

17. Post hunc Flavianus, 'apud poetam nostrum,' inquit, 'tantam scientiam iuris auguralis invenio ut si aliarum
disciplinarum doctrina destitueretur, haec illum vel sola
professio sublimaret.'

18. Eustathius deinde, 'maxime,' inquit, 'praedicarem
quanta de Graecis cautus et tamquam aliud agens modo
artifici dissimulatione, modo professa imitatione transtule-
rit, ni me maior admiratio de astrologia totaque philosophia teneret, quam parcus et sobrius operi suo nusquam
reprehendendus aspersit.'

19. Rufius[145] Albinus alterum fovens Praetextati latus
iuxtaque eum Caecina Albinus, ambo vetustatis adfectatio-
nem in Vergilio praedicabant, alter in versibus, Caecina in
verbis.

20. Avienus, 'non adsumam mihi,' ait, 'ut unam aliquam
de Vergilianis virtutibus audeam praedicare, sed audiendo
quaecumque dicetis, si quid vel de his mihi videbitur vel
iam dudum legenti adnotandum visum est, opportunius

---

145 Rufius *Marinone*: Furius ω (*haec nomina archetypon
deinceps semper confundit, quod posthac tacebo: v. Marinone*[2] *p.
61*)

---

599 I.e., he will be shown to be supremely knowledgeable in
pontifical lore (Book 3.1–12). The emperor had been supreme
pontiff (head of the college of pontiffs, cf. 1.14.6n.) since Augustus, but the position was held in name only from the time of
Constantine the Great, and the name itself was rejected by Gratian some years before the dramatic date of the dialogue.

had made it his specialty. So if my discourse does not fail to rise to so great a subject, I promise that our Virgil will be shown to be the supreme pontiff.'[599]

17. Following him Flavianus said, 'I find that our poet displays such great knowledge of augural lore that if his learning in the other branches of knowledge were to desert him, his expertise in this field alone would make him preeminent.'

18. Then Eustathius said, 'I'd make special mention of his attentiveness to matters Greek, and how he made his borrowings now artfully disguised—as though intent on some other purpose—now expressly imitative,[600] did I not admire still more his knowledge of astrology and of all philosophy, which he sprinkled sparingly and soberly over his work, nowhere leaving himself open to criticism.'[601]

19. Rufius Albinus, seated right next to Praetextatus, and Caecina Albinus beside him both drew particular attention to how Virgil strove to achieve an air of antiquity, the one pointing to his versification, the other his diction.[602]

20. Avienus said, 'I'll not claim to be so bold as to single out any one of Virgil's virtues, but if anything occurs to me while I hear you speak on your chosen topics, or if I've spotted something noteworthy in my reading before now, I'll produce it as the occasion prompts—but don't forget to

[600] As Eustathius does in fact do in Book 5.2–22.

[601] Flavianus' and Eustathius' accounts on the morning of the second day have been lost in the large lacuna between Book 2 and Book 3.

[602] Book 6.1–3 and 6.4–5, respectively.

proferam: modo memineritis a Servio nostro exigendum ut quidquid obscurum videbitur quasi litteratorum omnium longe maximus palam faciat.'

21. His dictis et universo coetui complacitis Praetextatus cum in se conversa omnium ora vidisset, 'philosophia,' inquit, 'quod unicum est munus deorum et disciplina disciplinarum, honoranda est anteloquio, unde meminerit Eustathius primum sibi locum ad disserendum omni alia professione cedente concessum. huic tu, mi Flaviane, succedes ut et auditu vestro recreer et aliquanto silentio instaurem vires loquendi.'

22. Inter haec servilis moderator obsequii, cui cura vel adolendi Penates vel struendi penum et domesticorum actuum ministros regendi, admonet dominum familiam pro sollemnitate annui moris epulatam. 23. hoc enim festo religiosae domus prius famulos instructis tamquam ad usum domini dapibus honorant, et ita demum patribus familias mensae apparatus novatur. insinuat igitur praesul famulitii cenae tempus et dominos iam vocare. 24. tum Praetextatus: 'reservandus igitur est Vergilius noster ad meliorem partem diei, ut mane novum inspiciendo per ordinem carmini destinemus. nunc hora nos admonet ut honore vestro haec mensa dignetur. sed Eustathius et post hunc Nicomachus meminerint crastina dissertatione servari sibi anteloquii functionem.' 25. et Flavianus: 'ex placita iam vos lege convenio, ut sequenti die Penates mei beari se tanti

---

603 Book 6.6–9.

604 The description imitates A. 1.703–4, on the household of Dido.

605 Cf. 1.10.22, 1.12.7.

606 Cf. 1.17.34.

demand of our friend Servius that he clarify anything that appears obscure,[603] since he is by far the greatest of all teachers.'

21. When these remarks had found agreement all around, and Praetextatus noticed that everyone was looking at him, he said, 'Philosophy—that singular gift of the gods and the discipline of disciplines—should have the honor of being treated first: accordingly, let Eustathius keep in mind that all the other topics are giving way and granting him the opportunity to speak first. Then you, my dear Flavianus, will follow him, so that I can both be refreshed by hearing you and regain my powers of speech by keeping silent for a bit.'

22. In the midst of these remarks the slave in charge of the other slaves, who was responsible for burning incense before the Penates and maintaining the storeroom[604] and keeping the domestic staff in line, let his master know that the slaves had had their celebratory feast according to the annual custom. 23. For during this holiday observant households do their slaves the honor of allowing them to dine first, as though on a meal prepared for their master,[605] with the table being set anew for the heads of household only after they have finished: then the chief slave lets the masters know that it is time to dine. 24. Then Praetextatus said: 'Our dear Virgil must be held over to a more suitable portion of the day: let's appoint "the new morning"[606] for examining the poem, one topic after the other. Now the hour reminds me that this table is to be honored by your presence. But let Eustathius, and Flavianus after him, bear in mind that the job of leading off tomorrow's discussion is reserved for them.' 25. To which Flavianus replied: 'I want to bring you all together according to the

coetus hospitio glorientur.' his cum omnes adsensi essent, ad cenam alio aliud de his quae inter se contulerant reminiscente adprobanteque cum magna alacritate animi concesserunt.[146]

---

[146] *post* concesserunt *nihil subscriptum sed spatium relictum in* αςC (LIB. II. D[m]), *spat. om.* Mπ, EXPLICIT LIBER .I. SATVRNALIORVM. INCIPIT SECVNDVS P, MACROBII (AMBROSII *add.* F) THEODOSII VIRI ILLVSTRIS (INL R) SATVRNALIORVM LIBER PRIMVS EXPLICIT FELICITER RF, MACROBII THEODOSII VIRI INL SATVRNALIORVM LIBER SECVNDVS AC[m] (Secundus Liber F[m], *man. rec.*)

principle we've agreed on, so that on the following day my household gods might boast that they have been blessed by so great a company.' When everyone agreed to this, they withdrew to their meal with great enthusiasm, each recalling and praising a different aspect of their earlier discussions.

LIBER SECVNDVS[1]

1   Hic ubi modestus edendi modus cessare fecit castimoniam
ferculorum, et convivialis laetitia minusculis poculis orie-
batur, Avienus ait, 'bene ac sapienter Maro noster tumul-
tuosum et sobrium uno eodemque versu descripsit sub
paucorum verborum immutatione convivium. nam ubi
sub apparatu regio procedere solet luxus ad strepitum,
"postquam prima" inquit "quies epulis . . . ," at cum heroes
castigatis dapibus adsidunt, non reducit quietem, quia nec
praecessit tumultus, sed "postquam exempta fames epulis
. . . " 2. nostrum hoc convivium, quod et heroici saeculi pu-
dicitiam et nostri conduxit elegantiam, in quo splendor sobrius et diligens parsimonia, Agathonis convivio vel post
magniloquentiam Platonis non componere tantum sed nec
praeferre dubitaverim. 3. nam ipse rex mensae nec in moribus Socrate minor et in re publica philosopho efficacior;
ceteri qui adestis eminentiores estis ad studia virtutum,
quam ut poetis comicis et Alcibiadi, qui tantum fuit fortis
ad crimina, aliisque quibus frequens illud convivium fuit
vos quisquam aestimet comparandos.'

1 *add*. PAC^m, *inscript. caret* ω

---

[1] Afternoon, 17 December.   [2] The occasion is the feast
that Dido gives for Aeneas and his men at the end of *A*. 1; Servius
ad loc. offers a similar interpretation.

BOOK TWO[1]

When their modest style of dining had brought the simple   1
sequence of courses to a close and festive good cheer was
arising from their small cups of wine, Avienus said, 'Wisely
and well did our Maro describe the uproarious feast and
the sober sort with a small change of wording in one and
the same verse: given that indulgence tends to turn noisy at
a royal display, he writes, "After the first lull in the dining
. . . "(A. 1. 723),[2] whereas when the heroes sit down to their
restrained dinner, the poet doesn't reintroduce a "lull"—
since no uproar preceded—but writes, "After dining removed their hunger . . . " (A. 1. 216). 2. I would not hesitate, not just to compare, but even to prefer this banquet of
ours—combining the modesty of the heroic age with the
elegance of our own, an occasion of sober brilliance and
careful thrift—to the banquet of Agathon, for all of Plato's
fine talk.[3] 3. For the lord of our table is no less a man than
Socrates in his character, and more effective in public life
than the philosopher; the rest of you who are present are
too distinguished in your pursuit of the virtues for anyone
to think you comparable to comic poets[4] and Alcibiades—
brave only when it came to mischief—and the others who
thronged that banquet.'

---

[3] Cf. 1.1.3.   [4] An invidious plural, Aristophanes being
the only comic poet to figure in Plato's *Symposium*.

4. 'Bona verba quaeso,' Praetextatus ait, 'circa reverentiam tantum Socraticae maiestatis. nam reliquis, qui in illo fuere symposio, haec lumina quis non praeponenda consentiat? sed quorsum tibi, Aviene, hoc tendit exemplum?' 5. 'quia sub illorum,' inquit, 'supercilio non defuit qui psaltriam intromitti peteret, ut puella ex industria supra naturam mollior canora dulcedine et saltationis lubrico exerceret inlecebris philosophantes. 6. illic hoc fieri temptatum est, ut Agathonis victoria celebraretur, nos honorem dei cuius hoc festum est nullo admixtu voluptatis augemus. neque ego sum nescius vos nec tristitiam nec nubilum vultum in bonis ducere nec Crassum illum quem Cicero auctore Lucilio semel in vita risisse scribit magnopere mirari.'

7. Ad haec cum Praetextatus diceret ludicras voluptates nec suis Penatibus adsuetas nec ante coetum tam serium producendas, excepit Symmachus: 8. 'quia "Saturnalibus optimo dierum," ut ait Veronensis poeta, nec voluptas nobis ut Stoicis tamquam hostis repudianda est nec ut Epicureis summum bonum in voluptate ponendum, excogitemus alacritatem lascivia carentem—et, ni fallor, inveni, ut iocos veterum ac nobilium virorum edecumatos ex mul-

---

5 *bona verba quaeso*, lit. "I ask for good words/words of good omen": borrowed from Ter. *Andria* 205, the phrase belongs to the realm of sacrifice, which should be free from ill-omened speech, cf. Tibull. 2.2.1, Ov. *F.* 1.72.

6 Cf. Pl. *Symp.* 176E, 212D.

7 M. Licinius Crassus, nicknamed Agelastus ("Laughless"), grandfather of the triumvir: Cic. *On the Boundaries of Good and Evil* 5.92, *Tusculan Disputations* 3.31 (in both places citing Lucilius, fr. 1316), cf. Pliny *Natural History* 7.79 (~ Solin. 1.72), Fronto *To Antoninus Pius on Eloquence* 4.8, Jerome *Epist.* 7.5, Amm. Marc. 26.9.11.

4. 'Please, mind what you say,'[5] Praetextatus rejoined, 'at least as concerns the respect owed Socrates' greatness. As for the other guests at that symposium, yes, who would not think that the lights of our age here gathered are superior to them? But what's the point of this comparison, Avienus?' 5. 'My point is that even among that haughty lot there was still one who wanted a woman brought in to play the harp,[6] so that the girl—made up to be more voluptuous than nature intended—would charm them with her sweet singing and lewd dancing while they philosophized. 6. Agathon's victory celebration was the occasion where that sort of thing was tried, whereas we seek to increase the honor of the god whose feast this is while keeping well clear of sensuality—though I'm perfectly aware that you all do not count as goods either gloom or a cloudy visage, and do not much admire the famous Crassus, who according to Cicero (following Lucilius) laughed just once in his life.'[7]

7. When in response Praetextatus said that pleasures of the comic stage did not keep company with his household gods and should not be introduced into so serious a gathering, Symmachus replied, 8. 'Since

on the Saturnalia, best of days,

as the poet of Verona says (Catull. 14.15), we shouldn't reject pleasure as though it were an enemy, like the Stoics, nor count pleasure the highest good, like the Epicureans, let's think of something fun that's also proper—wait, I think I've got it: let's take turns telling choice jokes that a

tiiugis libris relatione mutua proferamus. 9. haec nobis sit
litterata laetitia et docta cavillatio vicem planipedis et subulonis[2] impudica et praetextata[3] verba iacientis [ad pudo-
rem ac modestiam versus imitata].[4] 10. haec res et cura et
studio digna veteribus visa est. et iam primum animadver-
to duos quos eloquentissimos antiqua aetas tulit, comicum
Plautum et oratorem Tullium, eos ambos etiam ad iocorum venustatem ceteris praestitisse. 11. Plautus quidem
ea re clarus fuit ut post mortem eius comoediae, quae in-
certae ferebantur, Plautinae tamen esse de iocorum copia
noscerentur. 12. Cicero autem quantum in ea re valuerit
quis ignorat qui vel liberti eius libros quos is de iocis patro-
ni composuit (quos quidam ipsius putant esse) legere curavit? quis item nescit consularem eum scurram ab inimicis
appellari solitum? quod in oratione etiam sua Vatinius posuit. 13. atque ego, ni longum esset, referrem in quibus
causis, cum nocentissimos reos tueretur, victoriam iocis
adeptus sit, ut ecce pro L. Flacco, quem repetundarum
reum ioci opportunitate de manifestissimis criminibus
exemit. is iocus in oratione non extat, mihi ex libro Furii

2 subulonis *Marcilius*: sab- ω

3 praetextata S: -texta ω

4 ad . . . imitata *pro glossemate damn. Timpanaro, Gnomon
1964, 792*

8 Beyond the books referred to below, note the collections of
dicta made by Julius Caesar (Cic. *Fam.* 9.16.4, Suet. *Jul.* 56.7), C.
Trebonius (Cic. *Fam.* 15.21.2), the grammarian Melissus (Suet.
Gramm. 21), and the jurist A. Cascellius (*Dig.* 1.2.2.45, cf. 2.6.1
below).

range of different books attribute to noble men of old.[8]
9. Let this literate enjoyment and learned banter of ours
substitute for the barefoot dancer and the coarse clown
who spews shameless indecencies. 10. The ancients
thought humor worthy of careful study: to start with, I note
that two of the most eloquent men of old, the comic writer
Plautus and the orator Tully, were both second to none in
the charm of their jokes. 11. Indeed, Plautus was so famous
for this that after his death comedies circulating with no
sure indication of authorship were recognized as Plautine
from their abundant jokes.[9] 12. As for Cicero, no one could
be unaware of his mastery in this area if he's bothered to
read the books his freedman compiled of his former master's jokes (though some think the jokes are the freedman's).[10] Similarly, who doesn't know that his enemies
used to call him "the consular wag"? In fact, Vatinius even
used the phrase in a speech.[11] 13. And if it wouldn't take
too long, I'd tell you about the cases in which he was defending clients who were dead guilty but nonetheless got
them off with his jokes: take the case of Lucius Flaccus, for
example, whom Cicero got off with a timely joke when he
was on trial for extortion and his crimes were as plain as
black and white—the joke isn't found in the speech itself,

[9] Cf. Gell. 3.3.3, citing Varro for applying a criterion very like
this to identify authentic scripts of Plautus.

[10] Cf. Quint. 6.3.3–5, Plut. *Cic.* 25–27; the freedman in question was Cicero's secretary M. Tullius Tiro.

[11] When P. Vatinius appeared as a witness against a man
Cicero was defending in March 56, Cicero attacked him and his
testimony in the surviving invective, *Against Vatinius*; cf. 2.3.5n.

Bibaculi[5] notus est et inter alia eius dicta celebratur.
14. sed in hoc verbum non casu incidi, volens feci. iocos
enim hoc genus veteres nostri dicta dicebant. testis idem
Cicero qui in libro epistularum ad Cornelium Nepotem
secundo sic ait: "itaque nostri, cum omnia quae dixissemus
dicta essent, quae facete et breviter et acute locuti essemus, ea proprio nomine appellari dicta voluerunt." haec
Cicero. Novius vero Pomponiusque iocos non raro dicteria
nominant. 15. Marcus etiam Cato ille Censorius argute io-
cari solitus est. horum nos ab invidia muniret auctoritas,
etiam si nostris cavillaremur, at cum veteribus dicta referamus, ipsa utique auctorum dignitate defendimur. si ergo
probatis inventum, agite quod cuique de dictis talibus in
mentem veniet vicissim memoriam nostram excitando referamus.' 16. placuit universis laetitiae excogitata sobrie-
tas, et ut Praetextatus incipiendo auctoritatem de exemplo
praeberet hortati sunt.

2   Tum ille: 'dictum volo hostis referre, sed victi et cuius
memoria instaurat Romanorum triumphos. Hannibal Car-
thaginiensis apud regem Antiochum profugus facetissime

5 Furii Bibaculi *ed. Lugd. 1538 in marg.*: fusii (fufii β) viva-
culi ω

---

12 Otherwise unknown, unless it is the learned miscellany
Pliny the elder cites under the title *Lucubrations* (*Natural History*
pr. 24). The speech *pro Flacco*, involving a charge of extortion
against a provincial governor, is only partially extant today, as it evidently was already in the time of M. or his source: the "saying" to
which M. refers cannot be identified.

13 Lit. "our people" (*nostri*), which suggests that Cicero was
drawing a contrast with Greek usage: cf. the practice in the dia-

but I learned of it from Furius Bibaculus' book,[12] and it's among his celebrated sayings. 14. I use the word "sayings" [*dicta*] not by chance but intentionally, since our ancestors used that term for jokes of this sort, as Cicero himself attests in Book 2 of his letters to Cornelius Nepos (fr. II.1): "And so, though all the things we say [*dicere*] are 'things said' [*dicta*], we Romans[13] wished to reserve the name *dicta* for things said with wit, brevity, and point." That's Cicero; but Novius and Pomponius often call jokes "*jeux de* speech."[14] 15. Marcus Cato, the great Censor, also used to engage in jests.[15] Thanks to the authority of such men people could not begrudge us our jokes, even if we were to indulge our own line of banter; but since we trace these witticisms back to the ancients, the high standing of those authors certainly provides us with cover. If you approve what I've come up with, then, let's all recount such *dicta* as come to mind, so that each of us primes the others' memory as we go.' 16. The staid entertainment Symmachus had devised was agreeable to all, and they urged Praetextatus to lend the authority of his example by starting things off.

He then said: 'I want to recount the witticism of an enemy—but one we beat, one whose memory makes the Romans' triumphs live again: Hannibal of Carthage, who engaged in some witty raillery as an exile at the court of   2

logue of having a Latin-speaker, in conversation with a Greek, refer to Virgil as "our poet," Homer as "your poet" (e.g., 5.3.16) or vice versa (e.g., 5.2.16).

[14] *dicteria*, a hybrid word formed from a Latin root (*dict-*) and Greek suffix (*-êrion*).   [15] Cf. Cic. *On the Orator* 2.271, *On Appropriate Actions* 1.104, Plut. *Cato the Elder* 25.2 (with the witticisms gathered ibid. 8).

cavillatus est. 2. ea cavillatio huiusce modi fuit. ostende-
bat Antiochus in campo copias ingentes quas bellum populo Romano facturus comparaverat convertebatque[6] exercitum insignibus argenteis et aureis florentem, inducebat
etiam currus cum falcibus et elephantos cum turribus
equitatumque frenis et ephippiis monilibus ac faleris prae-
fulgentem. atque ibi rex contemplatione tanti ac tam or-
nati exercitus gloriabundus Hannibalem aspicit et, "pu-
tasne," inquit, "satis esse Romanis haec omnia?" 3. tunc
Poenus eludens ignaviam imbelliamque militum cius pre-
tiose armatorum, "plane," inquit, "satis esse credo Romanis haec, et si avarissimi sunt." nihil prorsum neque tam
lepide neque tam acerbe dici potest. rex de numero exercitus sui ac de aestimanda aequiperatione quaesiverat,
respondit Hannibal de praeda.'

4. Flavianus subiecit: 'sacrificium apud veteres fuit
quod vocabatur "propter viam." in eo mos erat ut si quid ex
epulis superfuisset, igne consumeretur. hinc[7] Catonis iocus est. namque Albidium quendam, qui bona sua come-
disset et novissime domum quae ei reliqua erat incendio
perdidisset, propter viam fecisse dicebat: quod comesse
non potuerit, id combussisse.'

5. Symmachus deinde, 'mater M. Bruti Servilia cum
pretiosum aere parvo fundum abstulisset a Caesare subi-
ciente hastae bona civium, non effugit dictum tale Cicero-

[6] contuebaturque *Madvig adv. crit. 3, 250*
[7] hinc *ed. Colon. 1521*: hic ω

[16] Hannibal was forced by his political enemies to flee to the
Seleucid king Antiochus III in 195 BCE. §§2–3 are based on Gell.
5.5.

king Antiochus.[16] 2. It goes like this. On a parade ground Antiochus was showing off the vast army he had assembled to wage war with Rome, having the host turn this way and that, so that the field seemed to blossom with their gold and silver insignia. He even brought on chariots that had wheels equipped with scythes, and turreted elephants, and cavalry with gleaming bridles and collars and trappings. Exulting at the sight of such a large and well-equipped army, the king looked at Hannibal and asked, "Do you think all this is enough for the Romans?" 3. Mocking the unwarlike and supine soldiery the king had outfitted at such great expense, the Carthaginian replied, "Oh yes, I think this is enough for the Romans, even though they are very, very greedy." I can't imagine a more amusing and more cutting remark: asked by the king to evaluate the army's size and equipage, Hannibal replied by speaking of it as booty.'

4. Flavianus followed up: 'There was a sacrifice that the ancients used to call a "for-the-road," in which they burned any leftovers from a feast.[17] This gave Cato the material for a joke: when a certain Albidius had eaten up his estate and then lost his house—the only thing left to him—in a fire, Cato said that he had performed a for-the-road: what he couldn't eat up, he burned.'

5. Then Symmachus said, 'When Caesar was auctioning off citizens' goods, Servilia, Marcus Brutus' mother, got a valuable estate at a low price—but not without becoming the target of the following witticism of Cicero's: "Oh

---

[17] For the ritual cf. Fest. p. 254.12–14, Plaut. *Rudens* 148–50, Laberius 87–88.

nis "et quidem[8] quo melius emptum sciatis, comparavit
Servilia hunc fundum tertia deducta." filia autem Serviliae
erat Iunia Tertia eademque C. Cassii uxor, lasciviente dic-
tatore tam in matrem quam in puellam. tunc luxuriam se-
nis adulteri civitas subinde rumoribus iocisque carpebat,
ut mala non tantum seria forent.'

6. Post hunc Caecina Albinus: 'Plancus in iudicio forte
amici, cum molestum testem destruere vellet, interrogavit, quia sutorem sciebat, quo artificio se tueretur. ille ur-
bane respondit: "gallam subigo." sutorium hoc habetur
instrumentum, quod non infacete in adulterii exprobrationem ambiguitate convertit. nam Plancus in Maevia Galla
nupta male audiebat.'

7. Secutus est Rufius Albinus: 'post Mutinensem fugam quaerentibus quid ageret Antonius, respondisse fami-
liaris eius ferebatur: "quod canis in Aegypto: bibit et fugit."
quando in illis regionibus constat canes raptu crocodilo-
rum exterritos currere et bibere.'

8. Eustathius deinde: 'Publi‹li›us[9] Mucium in primis
malivolum cum vidisset solito tristiorem, "aut Mucio," inquit, "nescio quid incommodi accessit aut nescio cui aliquid
boni." 9. Inde Avienus: 'Faustus Sullae filius cum soror
eius eodem tempore duo moechos haberet, Fulvium fullo-

8 et quidem O[1] (*ut vid.*): equidem ω
9 Publilius *Holford-Strevens*: Publius ω

---

18 The anecdote, set after the defeat of the senatorial forces at
Pharsalus in 48 BCE, is told at Suet. *Jul.* 50.2, though without the
Republican point of view implied by M.'s ref. to Rome's "misery";
the key verb, *deducere*, can mean both "deduct" and "escort'
19 I.e., Plancus was reputed to be a cuckold thanks to Galla's
adultery.

yes, the bargain was even better: Servilia got the estate with a third taken off'—the point being that Junia Tertia ["the Third"] was Servilia's daughter and the wife of Gaius Cassius, and that the dictator was carrying on with both the mother and the daughter. The old adulterer's wanton behavior was constant fodder for the city's gossip and jokes, giving it some amusement in its misery.'[18]

6. After Symmachus, Caecina Albinus said: 'When Plancus happened to be defending a friend in court and wanted to undermine a troublesome witness, he asked him (knowing him to be a shoemaker) what craft he practiced to support himself. The man replied smoothly, "I grind the gall-nut [*galla*]," referring to a thing shoemakers use, which he wittily exploited to cast a reference to adultery in Plancus' face: for Plancus' reputation was suffering because of Maevia Galla, to whom he was married.'[19]

7. Rufius Albinus then followed: 'When people were asking what Antony was doing after the rout at Mutina [43 BCE], a friend of his is said to have replied: "What a dog does in Egypt: drink and run"—it being well known that in those parts dogs drink and run for fear of being snatched by the crocodiles.'[20]

8. Next Eustathius: 'When Publilius saw that Mucius, one of the most spiteful people going, was looking sadder than usual, he said, "Either Mucius has had a bit of bad luck, or someone else has had a bit of good." 9. Then Avienus: 'When Sulla's daughter, Fausta, was carrying on affairs with two men at the same time, a launderer's son

[20] Cf. Pliny *Natural History* 8.148, Aelian *Historical Miscellany* 1.4 (~ *On the Nature of Animals* 6.53).

nis filium et Pompeium cognomine Maculam, "miror," inquit, "sororem meam habere maculam cum fullonem habeat."'

10. Hic Evangelus: 'apud L. Mallium, qui optimus pictor Romae habebatur, Servilius Geminus forte cenabat cumque filios eius deformes vidisset, "non similiter," inquit "Malli, fingis et pingis." et Mallius, "in tenebris enim fingo," inquit, "luce pingo."'

11. Eusebius deinde, 'Demosthenes,' inquit, 'excitatus ad Laidis famam, cuius formam tunc Graecia mirabatur, accessit ut et ipse famoso amore potiretur. qui ubi dimidium talentum unius pretium noctis audivit, discessit hoc dicto: "οὐκ ἀγοράζω τοσούτου μετανοῆσαι."'

12. Inter haec cum Servius ordine se vocante per verecundiam sileret, 'omnes nos,' inquit Evangelus, 'impudentes, grammatice, pronuntias, si tacere talia vis videri tuitione[10] pudoris, unde neque tuum nec Dysarii aut Hori supercilium liberum erit a superbiae nota, ni Praetextatum et nos velitis imitari.' 13. tunc Servius, postquam magis silentium erubescendum vidit, ad libertatem se similis relationis animavit. 'M'.,'[11] inquit, 'Otacilius[12] Pitholaus, cum Caninius Rebilus[13] uno tantum die consul fuisset, dixit, "ante flamines, nunc consules diales

---

[10] tuitione G: tuitonem ω

[11] M'. *Lewis* (*recte, nisi Macrob. ipse erravit*): M. ω

[12] Otacilius *ed. Paris. 1585*: votacilius ω, Voltacilius *Marinone*[2]

[13] Caninius Rebilus *Willis* (C- Revilus *ed. Ven. 1528*, C-Rivilius *ed. Colon. 1521*): maius (gaius β) servilius ω

---

[21] The painter is otherwise unknown; several Servilii Gemini

named Fulvius and Pompeius Macula, her brother, Faustus, said, "I'm surprised my sister has a stain [*macula*] when she has a launderer."'

10. Hereupon Evangelus said: 'Servilius Geminus happened to be dining at the home of Lucius Mallius, then considered the best painter in Rome, when he saw Mallius' two ugly sons: "You don't make children," he said, "the way you make pictures." "That," said Mallius, "is because I make children in the dark, pictures in the light."'[21]

11. Next, Eusebius said, 'Demosthenes' interest was piqued by the fame of Laïs, whose beauty then had all Greece agog, so he approached her with the aim of enjoying her notorious charms himself. When he heard that she charged half a talent[22] for a single night, he departed with the remark, "That's too high a price to pay for regret."'[23]

12. When it came Servius' turn and he kept silent out of shyness, Evangelus said, 'You declare us all shameless, school-teacher, if you want to appear to keep silent as a way of safeguarding your own sense of shame: neither your haughtiness nor that of Dysarius or Horus will escape being branded as arrogance if you do not choose to imitate Praetextatus and the rest of us.' 13. Seeing that silence was more embarrassing than speech, Servius nerved himself to take the liberty of telling a similar story: "When Caninius Rebilus held the consulship for only a single day [31 December 45 BCE], Manius Otacilius Pitholaus said, "Before this we've had 'daylight priests,' now we have day-

were politically prominent in the 2nd half of the 3rd cent. BCE, including the consuls of 252 and 248, 217, and 203.

[22] 1/2 talent (of silver) = just under 13 kg, cf. 1.5.14n.

[23] §11 is based on Gell. 1.8.5–6 (citing Sotion's *Cornucopia*).

fiunt."' 14. nec Dysarius ultra exprobrationem taciturnitatis expectans ait . . .

15. Post hunc Horus quoque, 'adfero ad vos,' inquit, 'δίστιχον Platonis, quo ille adulescens luserit cum tragoediis quoque eadem aetate praeluderet:

τὴν ψυχὴν Ἀγάθωνα φιλῶν ἐπὶ χείλεσιν ἔσχον·
ἦλθε γὰρ ἡ τλήμων ὡς διαβησομένη.'

16. Orta ex his laetitia et omnibus in censorium risum remissis ac retractantibus quae a singulis antiquae festivitatis sapore prolata sunt, Symmachus ait, 'hos Platonis versiculos, quorum magis venustatem[14] an brevitatem mireris incertum est, legisse memini in Latinum tanto latius versos quanto solet nostra quam Graecorum lingua brevior et angustior aestimari. 17. et ut opinor haec verba sunt:

> Dum semiulco savio
> meum puellum savior
> dulcemque florem spiritus
> duco ex aperto tramite,
> 5   anima[15] aegra et saucia
> cucurrit ad labias mihi
> rictumque[16] in oris pervium

[14] venustatem R[1]: vetust- ω

[15] anima] *metri causa* animula *Carrio,* anima mea *Hertz, alii alia*

[16] rictumque δ: rectumque ω

---

[24] Cf. 7.3.10 for the same joke with a different attribution, and 2.3.6 for further jokes at Caninius' expense. The "daylight priest"

light consuls.'"[24] 14. Dysarius did not wait to be scolded for his silence but said, . . .

15. After Dysarius Horus said, 'I give you a couplet by Plato, a *jeu d'esprit* of his youth, when he also tried his hand at tragedy (*Anth. Gr.* 5.78):[25]

As I kissed Agathon, I caught my soul on my lips:
  it meant, poor thing, to go over to him.'

16. These anecdotes gave rise to much merriment, as they all relaxed in sober-sided laughter and thought back on the contributions each one had made, so redolent of old-fashioned good cheer. Symmachus said, 'One doesn't know which to admire more, the charm of those verses or their concision. But I remember reading a Latin version of them—rather longer than the original, inasmuch as Latin is generally thought to be more a modest and limited language than Greek.[26] 17. It goes like this, I believe (p. 348 *FPL*[3], cf. *FLP*[2] pp. 395–96):

While kissing my boy
with half-parted lips,
drawing his breath's sweet
bloom from its open course,
my poor wounded soul   5
raced up to my lips and
strained to leap across

(*flamen Dialis*) was the priest of Diespiter (= Jupiter), "father [*pater*] daylight [*dies*]" (cf. 1.15.14); on the *flamines*, 1.10.15n.

[25] §15–17 are based on Gell. 19.11. For Plato's youthful experimentation cf. Diogenes Laertius 3.5.

[26] I.e., as a lexically impoverished language (cf. Lucr. 1.139, 1.832 ~ 3.260, Pliny *Epist*. 4.18.2) Latin must use more words to convey any given idea; cf. 5.3.2.

et labra pueri mollia
rimata itineri[17] transitus
10   ut transiliret[18] nititur.
tum si morae quid plusculae
fuisset in coetu osculi,
amoris igne percita
transisset et me linqueret,
15   et mira prorsum res foret[19]
ut ad me fierem[20] mortuus,
ad puerum[21] intus viverem.

3   'Sed miror omnes vos ioca tacuisse Ciceronis, in quibus facundissimus ut in omnibus fuit, et, si videtur, ut aedituus responsa numinis sui praedicat ita ego quae memoria suggesserit refero dicta Ciceronis.'

2. tum omnibus ad audiendum erectis ille sic incipit: 'M. Cicero cum apud Damasippum cenaret et ille mediocri vino posito diceret, "bibite Falernum hoc, annorum quadraginta est." "bene," inquit, "aetatem fert." 3. Idem cum Lentulum generum suum, exiguae staturae[22] hominem, longo gladio adcinctum vidisset: "quis," inquit, "generum meum ad gladium adligavit?" 4. Nec Q. Ciceroni fratri circa similem mordacitatem pepercit. nam cum in ea

17 itineri *ed. Colon. 1521, Gell.*: itiner ω

18 transiliret *ed. Colon. 1521, Gell.*: transire ω, vi transilire *Havet crit. verb. 130*

19 foret *ed. Colon. 1521*: fieret ω (*haud dubie ex sequenti* fierem), moveret *Gell.*

20 ut ad me fierem (*sic et Gell.*)] ut fierem ad me *L. Müller*

21 puerum (*sic et Gell.*)] puerulum *Bücheler*, puerum at *Meurs*, puerum ut *Scaliger*

22 staturae XA²C²: naturae ω

to the passage of the boy's
parted mouth and soft lips.
If we had lingered a moment more   10
in the union of our kiss,
then—roused by love's fire—
it would have passed over and left me:
a strange thing that would be,   15
leaving me dead to myself
but alive to the boy, within him.

'But I'm surprised that you all haven't mentioned   3
Cicero's jests, which found him as fluent as he was in all
manner of speech: if you'd like, I'm ready to recount the
witticisms that I've recalled, like a temple-warden an-
nouncing the oracles of his god.'

2. When they showed themselves to be an eager audience, he began as follows: 'When Marcus Cicero was
dining with Damasippus and his host served an undistinguished wine, saying, "Drink this forty-year old Falern-
ian,"[27] Cicero replied. "It wears its age well" (*dicta* 10).
3. Seeing his son-in-law Lentulus,[28] a short fellow, girt with
a long sword, Cicero asked, "Who tied my son-in-law to a
sword?" (*dicta* 12). 4. Nor did his biting wit spare his
brother, Quintus, in a similar connection: when in the

[27] One of the premier Roman wines, produced in the *ager
Falernus* of northern Campania.

[28] I.e., P. Cornelius Dolabella, who was adopted by a plebeian
Lentulus in 47 BCE so that he could stand for the tribunate; he
divorced Tullia the following year.

SATURNALIA

provincia quam ille rexerat vidisset clipeatam imaginem
eius ingentibus lineamentis usque ad pectus ex more
pictam—erat autem Quintus ipse staturae parvae—ait,
"frater meus dimidius maior est quam totus."

5. 'In consulatu Vatinii, quem paucis diebus gessit, no-
tabilis Ciceronis urbanitas circumferebatur. "magnum os-
tentum," inquit, "anno Vatinii factum est, quod illo consule
nec bruma nec ver nec aestas nec autumnus fuit." querenti
deinde Vatinio quod gravatus esset domum ad se infirma-
tum venire, respondit, "volui in consulatu tuo venire, sed
nox me comprehendit." ulcisci autem se Cicero videbatur,
ut qui respondisse sibi Vatinium meminerat, cum umeris
se rei publicae de exilio reportatum gloriaretur, "Unde
ergo tibi varices?"

6. 'Caninius quoque Rebilus, qui uno die, ut iam Servius rettulit, consul fuit, rostra cum ascendisset, pariter
honorem iniit consulatus et eieravit: quod Cicero omni
gaudens occasione urbanitatis increpuit, "λόγῳ θεω-
ρητός²³ est Caninius consul," et deinde, "hoc consecutus
est Rebilus, ut quaereretur quibus consulibus consul fue-

²³ λόγῳ θεωρητός *scripsi*: ΛΟΓΟΘΕΩΡΗΤΟϹ ω

---

²⁹ Quintus governed the province of Asia in 61–58 BCE; if the
story is true, Cicero would have seen the bust when he passed
through the province on his way to govern Cilicia (51–50 BCE).

³⁰ Vatinius was made consul in December 47 BCE, the last
month of the consular year. The remarks Cicero allegedly made
then presuppose the enmity exemplified by their clash nine years
earlier (2.1.12n.), though they had by that time been reconciled,
and Vatinius tried to help Cicero when he was seeking Caesar's
permission to return to Rome after the battle of Pharsalus in 48.

province Quintus had governed[29] Cicero saw his portrait
bust, armed with a round shield and drawn larger than
life in the usual head-to-chest fashion, Cicero said—since
Quintus himself was rather short—"Half of my brother is
bigger than the whole" (*dicta* 5).

5. 'In Vatinius' consulship,[30] which he held for only a
few days, one of Cicero's noteworthy *mots* was in circulation: "A great marvel," he said, "came to pass in the year
of Vatinius, when there was neither winter nor spring nor
summer nor fall while he was consul." When Vatinius
complained that Cicero had found it a bother to pay him a
sick-call at his home, Cicero replied, "I wanted to come
during your consulship, but nightfall overtook me" (*dicta*
31–32).[31] Cicero appeared to be getting his own back,
since he recalled that when he boasted how he had been
borne back from exile on the shoulders of the commonwealth, Vatinius had said, "How did you get those varicose
veins, then?"[32]

6. 'Similarly, Caninius Rebilus was consul for a single
day, as Servius has already recalled:[33] at the same time
he mounted the rostra to enter his office, he swore the
oath that's customary at the end of a consul's term. Cicero,
who never let an opportunity for a witticism pass, gave
him the raspberry: "Caninius is a consul *entièrement
théorique*," he said, then, "Rebilus brought it about that

[31] Cf. Plut. *Jul.* 58.1 (applying the joke to Caninius Rebilus, cf.
§6 below and 7.3.10).   [32] Cf. Quint. 11.3.143, Cassius Dio
46.18.2; the jibe perhaps alludes not just to the unsightliness of
varicose veins but also to the belief that they caused impotence
([Arist.] *Problems* 4.20 878b-879a). Cicero was in exile March 58–
August 57 BCE.   [33] 2.2.13; cf. Tac. *Hist.* 3.37

rit." dicere praeterea non destitit: "vigilantem habemus consulem Caninium, qui in consulatu suo somnum non vidit."

7. 'Pompeius Ciceronis facetiarum impatiens fuit. cuius haec dicta ferebantur: "ego vero quem fugiam habeo, quem sequar non habeo." sed et cum ad Pompeium venisset, dicentibus sero eum venisse respondit, "minime sero veni, nam nihil hic paratum video." 8. deinde interroganti Pompeio ubi gener eius Dolabella esset, respondit, "cum socero tuo." et cum donasset Pompeius transfugam civitate Romana, "o hominem bellum!" inquit, "Gallis civitatem promittit alienam, qui nobis nostram non potest reddere." propter quae merito videbatur dixisse Pompeius: "cupio ad hostes Cicero transeat ut nos timeat."

9. 'In Caesarem quoque mordacitas Ciceronis dentes suos strinxit. nam primum post victoriam Caesaris interrogatus cur in electione partis errasset, respondit, "praecinctura me decepit," iocatus in Caesarem, qui ita toga praecingebatur ut trahendo laciniam velut mollis incederet, adeo ut Sulla tamquam providus dixerit Pompeio, "cave

---

34 In the first joke Cicero uses a Gk. phrase, *logô theôrêtos* ("perceptible by reason alone"), applied to an entity whose existence cannot be empirically verified. The second joke turns on the Roman dating formula that used the two ordinary consuls' names to identify a calendar year (cf. §5 "in the year of Vatinius"), and on the fact that Rebilus' consulship was the last day of the calendar year, between two consular years.

35 Cf. Cic. *Fam.* 7.30.1.

36 Cf. Cic. *Att.* 8.7.2 = Quint. 6.3.109, Plut. *Cic.* 37.3, *Mor.* 205C.

37 After the outbreak of civil war in January 49 BCE Cicero was torn between staying in Italy and following Pompey, who crossed

people had to ask themselves, in whose consulship was he consul?"[34] Nor did he forbear from adding, "We have a watchful consul in Caninius: he didn't see a moment's sleep during his term" (*dicta* 22–24).[35]

7. 'Pompey had no patience for Cicero's barbs, which included the following: "I know whom to flee, but I don't know whom to follow";[36] and when he finally joined Pompey, "I certainly didn't arrive late, since I see no preparations have been made";[37] 8. then, when Pompey asked where his son-in-law Dolabella was, Cicero answered, "With your father-in-law";[38] and when Pompey had given Roman citizenship to someone who had crossed over from Caesar's side, Cicero said, "What a fine fellow! He offers Gauls a citizenship that isn't theirs but can't restore our own to us."[39] All of which suggests that he had earned Pompey's comment, "I want Cicero to cross over to the enemy, so that he'll have us to fear" (*dicta* 18–21).[40]

9. Cicero's biting wit bared its teeth against Caesar too. First, when asked after Caesar's victory how he'd come to choose the wrong side, "The drape of his toga fooled me":[41] he was mocking Caesar because he wore his toga draped so that its hem dragged like a train and his walk looked effeminate, which had even caused Sulla to tell

over from Brundisium to Greece in March. He joined the Pompeians in June.

[38] Cf. Plut. *Mor.* 205C-D; Pompey had been married to Caesar's daughter, Julia, in 59–54 BCE.

[39] Cf. the story of the two Allobroges at Caes. *Civil War* 3.59.1ff.

[40] Cf. Quint. 6.3.111.

[41] Cf. Cass. Dio 43.43.4

tibi illum puerum male praecinctum." 10. deinde cum Laberius in fine ludorum anulo aureo honoratus a Caesare e
vestigio in quattuordecim ad spectandum[24] transiit, violato
ordine et cum detrectatus est eques Romanus et comminus remissus, ait Cicero praetereunti Laberio et sedile
quaerenti, "recepissem te nisi anguste sederem," simul et
illum respuens et in novum senatum iocatus, cuius numerum Caesar supra fas auxerat. nec impune. respondit enim
Laberius, "mirum si anguste sedes qui soles duabus sellis
sedere," exprobrata levitate Ciceroni, qua inmerito optimus civis male audiebat. 11. idem Cicero alias facilitatem
Caesaris in adlegendo senatu inrisit palam. nam cum ab
hospite suo P. Mallio rogaretur ut decurionatum privigno
eius expediret adsistente frequentia dixit: "Romae, si vis,
habebit; Pompeiis difficile est." 12. nec intra haec eius
mordacitas stetit: quippe ab Androne quodam Laodiceno
salutatus, cum causam adventus requisisset comperis-

---

[24] spectandum J[2]CUS: expec- ω

---

[42] Cf. Suet. *Jul.* 45.3, Cass. Dio ibid.

[43] The occasion was Caesar's Victory Games in Sept. 46 BCE,
cf. Suet. *Jul.* 39.2, with Cic. *Fam.* 12.18.2. By acquiescing in Caesar's request to appear on the stage (see 2.7.2–8), Laberius placed
himself in the category of actors—persons of diminished social
standing (cf. 3.14.11n.)—thereby forfeiting his status as a Roman
knight; Caesar's gift of the gold ring symbolized its restitution.
The knights would have been affronted by the disrespect entailed
in Laberius' shedding his rank for cash (2.7.2) and in Caesar's
casual restoration of it. On the knights privileged seating, see
3.14.12n.: even if we assume that Laberius passed Cicero in the
orchestra, where senators sat, on his way to the knights' rows, the

Pompey, prophetically, "Watch out for that badly draped boy."[42] 10. At some time after that, Caesar honored Laberius with a knight's gold ring at the end of the games. Laberius immediately went to watch from the fourteen rows reserved for knights, the order he had affronted both when he was stripped of the rank and when he was restored in their presence:[43] as Laberius passed, in search of a seat, Cicero said, "I'd make room for you if the seating weren't so cramped," simultaneously spurning Laberius and mocking the new senate that Caesar had enlarged beyond the sanctioned limit.[44] Nor did he get away with it: "Odd that you're cramped," Laberius replied, "given that you usually occupy two seats,"[45] as a reproof of the political inconstancy that gossip unjustly imputed to that best of citizens. 11. On another occasion, too, Cicero openly mocked Caesar's nonchalance in adding new members to the senate: when he was asked by his host Publius Mallius to help clear the way for his stepson to gain a decurionate,[46] Cicero said, before a throng of witnesses: "He'll get it at Rome, if you like; at Pompeii, not so easy" (*dicta* 2–4). 12. Nor was his bite limited to these remarks: on receiving the customary morning greeting from a certain Andro of Laodicea, he asked the man how he came to be in Rome;

premise of the following repartee is rather obscure (there probably has been some confusion on M.'s part).

[44] By rewarding supporters with membership in the senate, Caesar increased its size from ca. 600 to ca. 900.

[45] The jest appears also at Sen. *Contr.* 7.3.9 and is repeated by M. at 7.3.8. [46] Decurions were the town councilors of Roman colonies and municipalities; their position was analogous to that of senators at Rome.

setque—nam ille se legatum de libertate patriae ad Caesarem venisse respondit—ita expressit publicam servitutem:
"ἐὰν ἐπιτύχῃς, καὶ περὶ ἡμῶν πρέσβευσον."

13. 'Vigebat in eo excedens iocos et seria mordacitas, ut
hoc est ex epistula ad C. Cassium dictatoris violatorem:
"vellem idibus Martiis me ad cenam invitasses, profecto
reliquiarum nihil fuisset. nunc me reliquiae vestrae exer-
cent." idem Cicero de Pisone genero et de M. Lepido lepi-
dissime cavillatus est—'

14. Dicente adhuc Symmacho et, ut videbatur, plura
dicturo intercedens Avienus, ut fieri in sermonibus convi-
valibus solet, 'nec Augustus,' inquit, 'Caesar in huius modi
dicacitate quoquam minor et fortasse nec Tullio, et, si volentibus vobis erit, aliqua eius quae memoria suggesserit
relaturus sum.' 15. et Horus: 'permitte, Aviene, Symmachus explicet de his quos iam nominaverat dicta Ciceronis,
et opportunius quae de Augusto vis referre succedent.'
16. reticente Avieno Symmachus: 'Cicero, inquam, cum
Piso gener eius mollius incederet, filia autem concitatius,
ait filiae "ambula tamquam vir," et cum M. Lepidus in senatu dixisset patribus conscriptis . . . , Tullius ait, "ego non
tanti fecissem ὁμοιόπτωτον." sed perge, Aviene, ne ultra
te dicturientem retardem.'

---

[47] More appropriate, presumably, because M. Aemilius Lepidus was the future Augustus' colleague in the Triumvirate established in November 43 BCE.   [48] Or perhaps "Walk like a
man," the noun used, *vir*, being capable of denoting both.

[49] The word Cicero used, *homoioptôton*, denotes a figure of
speech in which words with the same grammatical case-ending
(*ptôsis*) are used in parallel clauses: the loss of Lepidus' remark
leaves his point opaque.

and when he found out—for Andro replied that he had come on an embassy to Caesar, to secure his homeland's freedom—Cicero's reply alluded to Rome's servitude: "if you succeed, please intercede for us too" (*dicta* 1).

13. 'The vigor of his mordant wit wasn't limited to jests but could be deadly serious too, as this example shows, from a letter to Gaius Cassius, Caesar's murderer (*Fam.* 12.4.1): "I wish you had invited me to the banquet on the Ides of March: there certainly wouldn't have been any leftovers. Now those leftovers are proving to be a pain." Cicero also made a very pleasant joke about his son-in-law Piso and Marcus Lepidus . . . '

14. As Symmachus was still speaking and, it appeared, intending to speak some more, Avienus interrupted—as often happens in table-talk—and said, 'In this kind of cut-and-thrust, Caesar Augustus was second to no one, perhaps not even to Cicero: if you'd like, I'll recount some of his witticisms that I recall.' 15. To which Horus said, 'Avienus, let Symmachus finish reporting Cicero's witticisms about the men he mentioned, and the account you want to give about Augustus will make a more appropriate sequel.'[47] 16. As Avienus fell silent, Symmachus went on: 'As I was saying, since Cicero's son-in-law, Piso, had a rather effeminate gait, while his daughter had a more vigorous stride, Cicero said to his daughter, "Walk like your husband";[48] and when Marcus Lepidus told the conscript fathers in the senate, ". . .," Tully said, "I wouldn't have made so much out of a *ressemblance de cas*" (*dicta* 15–16).[49] But go on, Avienus, don't let me keep you when you're dying to speak.'

4   Et ille: 'Augustus, inquam, Caesar adfectavit iocos, salvo tamen maiestatis pudorisque respectu nec ut caderet in scurram. 2. Aiacem tragoediam scripserat eandemque quod sibi displicuisset deleverat. postea L. Varius[25] tragoediarum scriptor interrogabat eum quid ageret Aiax suus. et ille, "in spongiam," inquit, "incubuit." 3. Idem Augustus cum ei quidam libellum trepidus offerret et modo proferret manum modo retraheret, "putas," inquit, "te assem elephanto dare?" 4. Idem cum ab eo Pacuvius Taurus congiarium peteret diceretque iam hoc homines vulgo loqui, non parvam sibi ab illo pecuniam datam: "sed tu," inquit, "noli credere."

5. 'Alium praefectura equitum submotum et insuper salarium postulantem dicentemque: "non lucri causa dari hoc mihi rogo, sed ut iudicio tuo munus videar impetrasse et ita officium deposuisse," hoc dicto repercussit: "tu te accepisse apud omnes adfirma, et ego dedisse me non negabo." 6. Vrbanitas eiusdem innotuit circa Herennium deditum vitiis iuvenem. quem cum castris excedere iussisset et ille supplex hac deprecatione uteretur, "quo modo ad patrias sedes revertar? quid patri meo dicam?," respondit, "dic me tibi displicuisse." 7. Saxo in expeditione percus-

---

[25] Varius *ed. Lugd. Bat. 1597*: graius ω

---

[50] Cf. Suet. *Aug*. 85.2. Seeing that he had been disgraced, the Greek hero Ajax killed himself by falling upon his sword; being dissatisfied with his *Ajax*, Augustus wiped away the ink with a sponge.   [51] Cf. Quint. 6.3.59, Suet. *Aug*. 53.2

[52] Perhaps the Sex. Pacuvius Taurus attested as plebeian aedile of unspecified date (Pliny *Natural History* 34.22).

[53] Cf. Quint. 6.3.64.

346

Avienus began: 'Jests, as I said, were something of a   4
passion for Caesar Augustus, though of course he retained
a proper regard for his high standing and sense of decency, to avoid descending to the level of a wag. 2. He had
written a tragedy, the *Ajax*, and then erased it all because
he didn't like it. When the tragic poet Lucius Varius asked
him how his Ajax was faring, Augustus said, "He's fallen on
his sponge" (*dicta* 49 Malc.).[50] 3. When someone was hesi-
tantly offering him a petition, now extending his hand, now
taking it back, Augustus said, "Do you think you're giving a
penny to an elephant?" (*dicta* 8 Malc.).[51] 4. When Pacuvius Taurus[52] was asking for a bit of largesse and told him
that people were already saying Augustus had given him a
large cash gift, the latter said, "But don't you believe them"
(*dicta* 50 Malc.).

5. 'When he removed another man from his cavalry
command, the fellow had the nerve to ask for his stipend,
saying, "The money isn't the object, but I want it to appear
that you found me up to the task, so that I resigned my
commission voluntarily," Augustus slapped him down by
replying, "You just tell everyone you received it, and I
won't deny that I gave it" (*dicta* 51 Malc.). 6. A witticism
of his gained notoriety in connection with Herennius, a
young man sunk in vice: when Augustus ordered him out
of his camp, the young man threw himself on Augustus'
mercy, saying, "How can I return home? What will I tell
my father?" Augustus replied, "Tell him I displeased you"
(*dicta* 10 Malc.).[53] 7. When a soldier was struck by a rock

sum ac notabili cicatrice in fronte deformem, nimium tamen sua opera iactantem sic leniter castigavit: "at tu cum fugies," inquit, "numquam post te respexeris." 8. Galbae, cuius informe gibbo erat corpus, agenti apud se causam et frequenter dicenti, "corrige in me siquid reprehendis," respondit, "ego te monere possum, corrigere non possum."

9. 'Cum multi Severo Cassio accusante absolverentur, et architectus fori Augusti expectationem operis diu traheret, ita iocatus est: "vellem Cassius et meum forum accuset." 10. Vettius cum monumentum patris exarasset, ait Augustus, "hoc est vere monumentum patris colere." 11. Cum audisset inter pueros quos in Syria Herodes rex Iudaeorum intra bimatum iussit interfici filium quoque eius occisum, ait, "melius est Herodis porcum esse quam filium." 12. Idem Augustus, quia Mecenatem suum noverat stilo esse remisso, molli et dissoluto, talem se in epistulis quas ad eum scribebat saepius exhibebat et contra castigationem loquendi, quam alias ille scribendo servabat, in epistula ad Maecenatem familiari plura in iocos effusa subtexuit: "vale mel gentium[26] †meculle†,[27] ebur ex Etru-

---

26 mel gentium] mi ebenum *Jahn* (*Hermes* 2 [1867]: 247)
27 meculle Nβ, melcule DP²G: Medulliae *Turnebus*

---

54 Cf. Quint. 6.3.75 (ascribed to a C. Caesar of the early 1st cent. BCE, prob. Strabo Vopiscus, a noted wit).

55 The temple of Mars the Avenger, the centerpiece of Augustus' forum, was vowed before the battle of Philippi in 42 BCE and dedicated 40 years later. The joke turns on the verb *absolvi*, which can mean both "be acquitted" and "be completed."

on campaign, gaining a conspicuous scar on his forehead, then made too much of his efforts, Augustus gently reproved him by saying, "Mind, when you run away in future, never look behind you" (*dicta* 52 Malc.).[54] 8. When Galba, whose body was deformed by a hump on his back, was pleading a case before him and kept saying, "Set me straight if you find any fault," Augustus said, "I can advise you, but I cannot set you straight" (*dicta* 53 Malc.).

9. 'When many people whom Cassius Severus prosecuted were being acquitted, at the same time that the architect of Augustus' forum was dragging out the operation, Augustus joked, "I wish Cassius would prosecute my forum too"[55] (*dicta* 54 Malc.). 10. When Vettius had plowed under his father's memorial stone, Augustus remarked, "Now that's what I call cultivating your father's memory" (*dicta* 55 Malc.). 11. On hearing that the son of Herod, king of the Jews, had been slain when Herod ordered that all boys in Syria under the age of two be killed, Augustus said, "It's better to be Herod's pig than his son" (*dicta* 56 Malc.).[56] 12. Because he knew that Maecenas had a free-and-easy writing style given to extravagance and effeminacy, he often adopted the same character in the letters he wrote to him, the opposite of the austere style he otherwise cultivated in his writing. So he rounded off a personal letter to Maecenas with the following jocular effusion (*epist.* fr. 32 Malc.): "Farewell, my honey of all the world, . . . my

[56] On this witticism, certainly apocryphal in its present form, see Introd. §1 ad fin.

ria, lasar Arretinum, adamas Supernas, Tiberinum marga-
ritum, Cilniorum²⁸ smaragde, iaspi figulorum,²⁹ berulle
Porsenae, carbunculum †habeas†,³⁰ ἵνα συντέμω πάντα,
ἄλλαγμα³¹ moecharum."

13. 'Exceptus est a quodam cena satis parca et quasi co-
tidiana; nam paene nulli se invitanti negabat. post epulum
igitur inops ac sine ullo apparatu discedens vale dicenti
hoc tantum insusurravit: "non putabam me tibi tam fami-
liarem." 14. Cum de Tyriae purpurae quam emi iusse-
rat obscuritate quereretur, dicente venditore, "erige altius et suspice," his usus est salibus: "quid? ego, ut me
populus Romanus dicat bene cultum, in solario ambu-
laturus sum?" 15. Nomenculatori suo, de cuius oblivione
querebatur, dicenti, "numquid ad forum mandas?," "accipe," inquit, "commendaticias, quia illic neminem nosti."

²⁸ Cilniorum *ed. Paris. 1585*: cilneorum ω
²⁹ figulorum] Iguvinorum *Jahn*
³⁰ habeas] Hadriae *Jahn*   ³¹ ἄλλαγμα *Morgan*: μάλαγμα
ω (μαλάγματα *ed. Ven. 1472*)

---

57 Lasar, a pungent resin extracted from the silphium plant
of Cyrene (Egypt), was a medicament counted "among the out-
standing gifts of nature" (Pliny *Natural History* 22.101), to the extent that the plant was harvested to extinction.

58 The places named have no natural connection with the precious substances Augustus associates with them; the point, presumably, is that pearls from the Tiber (e.g.) would be all the more
precious for their rarity. "Cilnii" and "Porsenna," like "Etruria"
and "Arretium," glance at Maecenas' Etrurian background: the
Cilnii were a great family of Arretium, perhaps related to Maecenas on his mother's side (Tac. *Ann.* 6.11 mistakenly applies the
name Cilnius to Maecenas himself); Lars Porsenna, the king of

ivory of Etruria, lasar of Arretium,[57] diamond of the Adriatic, pearl of the Tiber, emerald of the Cilnii, potters' jasper, beryl of Porsenna, carbuncle . . .—*bref*—the sluts' *récompense*."[58]

13. 'After being entertained by some fellow with a spare and undistinguished meal (for he almost never turned down an invitation), he set out for home, without bodyguard or entourage, and whispered in his host's ear as he was saying goodbye, "I didn't think that I was such a close friend of yours" (*dicta* 57 Malc.). 14. When he was complaining about the dull color of some Tyrian purple he had ordered, and the merchant said, "Hold it up higher in the light and look at it," he wittily replied, "You mean I need to stroll about on my balcony so the Roman people can say I'm well dressed?" (*dicta* 58 Malc.)[59] 15. He had a naming-slave[60] whose forgetfulness gave him cause to complain: when the man asked, "Is there anything for me to take to the forum?," Augustus said, "Here, take some letters of introduction, since you know no one there" (*dicta* 59 Malc.).

Clusium, tried to compel the Romans to reinstate Tarquin the Proud after his expulsion. The connection of potters (the MSS' *figulorum*) with jasper is obscure, and Jahn's *Iguviorum* ("of the [Umbrian] Iguvii") has found favor with editors. If *allagma* (for the MSS' *malagma*, "poultice") is correct at the end of the catalog, the point is that Maecenas embodies all the precious gifts that a mistress could hope to be given. Augustus perhaps was glancing at one of Maecenas' own poems, addressed to Horace, which mentions emeralds, beryls, pearls, and jasper (fr. 2 *FPL*[3]).

[59] Contrast Augustus' preference for home-spun garments reported at Suet. *Aug.* 73.1.

[60] I.e., a slave responsible for murmuring in his master's ear the names of people he chanced to meet.

16. Vatinio in prima sua aetate eleganter insultavit. contusus[32] ille podagra volebat tamen videri discussisse iam vitium et ⟨cottidie⟩[33] mille passus ambulare se gloriabatur. cui Caesar, "non miror," inquit, "dies aliquanto sunt longiores." 17. Relata ad se magnitudine aeris alieni quam quidam eques Romanus dum vixit excedentem ducenties celaverat, culcitam emi cubicularem in eius auctione sibi iussit et praeceptum mirantibus hanc rationem reddidit: "habenda est ad somnum culcita in qua ille, cum tantum deberet, dormire potuit." 18. Non est intermittendus sermo eius quem Catonis honori dedit. venit forte in domum in qua Cato habitaverat, dein Strabone in adulationem Caesaris male existimante de pervicacia Catonis ait, "quisquis praesentem statum civitatis commutari non volet et civis et vir bonus est." satis serio et Catonem laudavit et sibi, nequis adfectaret res novare, consuluit.

19. 'Soleo in Augusto magis mirari quos pertulit iocos quam ipse quos protulit, quia maior est patientiae quam facundiae laus, maxime cum aequanimiter aliqua etiam iocis mordaciora pertulerit. 20. cuiusdam provincialis iocus asper innotuit. intraverat Romam simillimus Caesari et in se omnium ora converterat. Augustus perduci ad se hominem iussit visumque hoc modo interrogavit: "dic mihi, adulescens, fuit aliquando mater tua Romae?" negavit ille, nec contentus adiecit: "sed pater meus saepe."

---

[32] contusus *ed. Bipont. 1788*: -fusus ω

[33] cottidie *suppl. Fraenkel* (*apud Timpanaro Gnomon 1964, 792*)

---

[61] Cf. Quint. 6.3.77 (ascribing the insult to Cicero), with 2.3.5 above.

16. When still quite young, he offered Vatinius this choice bit of mockery: though the latter was sore with the gout, he wanted to appear to have shaken off the disorder and so was boasting that he was walking a mile each day: "I'm not surprised," Caesar said, "seeing that the days are getting a bit longer" (*dicta* 60 Malc.).[61] 17. When he learned of the huge debt that a certain Roman knight had concealed while he was alive—more than 20,000,000 sesterces!—he ordered that a pillow from the man's bedroom be purchased at the estate-auction and, when people were surprised at the command, explained, "I have to sleep on the pillow that man was able to sleep on when he was so deep in debt" (*dicta* 61 Malc.). 18. I shouldn't pass over the compliment that he paid Cato: when he happened on the house where Cato had lived and, to flatter Caesar, Strabo made a disparaging remark about Cato's obstinacy, Caesar said, "Whoever does not wish the existing constitution to be changed is a good man and a good citizen" (*dicta* 62 Malc.). A remark meant in earnest, to be sure, in praise of Cato, and in his own self-interest, to discourage anyone from attempting revolution.

19. 'I am often struck more by the jests Augustus put up with than by those he made, since forbearance is more praiseworthy than glibness—especially given that he put up with some remarks whose bite went beyond jesting. 20. An edged barb on the part of a provincial gained a certain notoriety. When the man came to Rome he caused everyone to stare, because he was the spit and image of Caesar: Augustus ordered that the fellow be brought to him and asked him, "Tell me, young man, was your mother ever in Rome?" Not content with a simple "no," the man added, "But my father was, any number of times."

21. Temporibus triumviralibus Pollio, cum Fescenninos in eum Augustus scripsisset, ait, "at ego taceo. non est enim facile in eum scribere qui potest proscribere." 22. Curtius eques Romanus deliciis diffluens,[34] cum macrum turdum sumpsisset in convivio Caesaris, interrogavit an mittere liceret. responderat princeps, "quidni liceat?" ille per fenestram statim misit. 23. Aes alienum Augustus cuiusdam senatoris cari sibi non rogatus exsolverat numerato quadragies. at ille pro gratiarum actione hoc solum ei scripsit: "mihi nihil?" 24. Solebat Licinus[35] libertus eius inchoanti opera patrono magnas pecunias conferre; quem morem secutus centum promisit per libellum in quo virgulae superductae pars ultra pecuniae defectionem protendebatur, vacante infra loco. Caesar occasione usus priori alterum centum[36] sua manu iunxit, spatio diligenter expleto et affectata litterae similitudine, geminatamque accepit summam, dissimulante liberto, qui postea coepto alio opere leniter factum suum Caesari obiecit libello tali dato: "confero tibi, domine, ad novi operis impensam quod videbitur."

[34] diff- *ed. Colon. 1521*: def- ω
[35] Licinus *Marinone²*: -nius ω
[36] centum *scripsi*: centies ω

---

[62] Fescennine verse, properly so called, was ribald poetry sung at weddings, with insults directed at the groom; the latter element presumably explains the extended use here, where invective poetry seems to be meant (for Augustus' talent in this vein, cf. Martial 11.20). Pollio used the verbs *scribere* ("write") and *proscribere* ("record publicly in writing/post"), the latter referring to the "proscriptions" of 43–42 BCE, when the Triumvirs posted the names of those declared to be public enemies.

[63] The knight in question might well be the Curtius Postumus known from Cicero's correspondence, a follower of Caesar and

21. When in the triumviral period Augustus had written some Fescinnine verses aimed at Pollio, the latter said, "But I'll keep my peace: it's not easy to have a war of words with a man who can sign your death warrant."[62] 22. When Curtius, a Roman knight and extreme voluptuary, picked up a scrawny thrush at one of Caesar's banquets, he asked if he'd be permitted to send it back: when the emperor replied, "Of course," he straightway threw it out the window.[63] 23. Unprompted, Augustus settled the debts of a certain senator whom he liked, to the tune of 4,000,000 sesterces: by way of thanks, the man wrote only, "Nothing for me?" 24. Whenever Augustus was beginning a new project, his freedman Licinus[64] made a large cash contribution. In line with that custom he promised 100,000 sesterces in a note in which part of the superscript bar extended beyond the number specifying the amount, leaving an empty space beneath:[65] Caesar took the opportunity to add another hundred thousand in his own hand, carefully filling the space and making the writing match, and he received the doubled amount. The freedman said nothing, but the next time Caesar began a project he offered a gentle reproach for what had been done by writing a note that read, "My lord, to the expense of the new project I contribute what you think right."

later Octavian who probably also = the Postumus who received Horace *Odes* 2.14 (cf. White 1995).

[64] C. Julius Licinus was a freedman of Julius Caesar: Augustus used him as a procurator in Gaul, then pardoned him when he used his position to amass the great fortune alluded to here (Suet. *Aug.* 67.1, Cassius Dio 54.21).

[65] Multiples of 1,000 were expressed by placing a horizontal bar over the relevant number: $100{,}000 = 100 \times 1{,}000 = \overline{\mathrm{C}}$.

25. 'Mira etiam censoris Augusti et laudata patientia. corripiebatur eques Romanus a principe tamquam minuisset facultates suas, at ille se multiplicasse coram probavit. mox eidem obiecit quod ad contrahendum matrimonium legibus non paruisset. ille uxorem sibi et tres esse liberos dixit. tum adiecit: "posthac, Caesar, cum de honestis hominibus inquiris, honestis mandato." 26. etiam militis non libertatem tantum sed et temeritatem tulit. in quadam villa inquietas noctes agebat, rumpente somnum eius crebro noctuae cantu. prendendam curavit noctuam miles aucupii peritus et spe ingentis praemii pertulit. laudato imperator mille nummos dari iussit. ille ausus est dicere, "malo vivat," avemque dimisit. quis non miratus est non offenso Caesare abisse militem contumacem? 27. Veteranus cum die sibi dicto periclitaretur, accessit in publico ad Caesarem rogavitque ut sibi adesset. ille advocatum quem ex comitatu suo elegerat sine mora dedit commendavitque ei litigatorem. exclamavit ingenti voce veteranus, "at non ego, Caesar, periclitante te Actiaco bello vicarium quaesivi, sed pro te ipse pugnavi," detexitque impressas cicatrices. erubuit Caesar venitque in advocationem, ut qui vereretur non superbus tantum sed etiam ingratus videri.

---

66 Augustus was never censor but recorded completing the census—which would entail reviewing citizens' financial resources—in 28 BCE (when he was consul), 8 BCE and 14 CE (with consular *imperium*: *Res Gestae* 8.2–4); Cassius Dio also reports a census in 11 BCE (54.35.1) and one of wealthier citizens in Italy in 4 CE (55.13.4–6).

67 I.e., he satisfied the marriage laws (the *lex Iulia* of 18 BCE, supplemented by the *lex Papia-Poppaea* of 9 CE) that penalized celibacy and rewarded the production of three living children.

25. 'As censor Augustus displayed a striking and praise-worthy forbearance.[66] He was upbraiding a Roman knight for having squandered his resources, but the man demonstrated in his presence that he had actually increased them. Soon after he reproached the same man for not obeying the laws prescribing marriage, but the man said he had a wife and three children,[67] and added, "From now on, Caesar, give honorable men the job of investigating honorable men." 26. In the case of a soldier, he tolerated speech that was not merely free but brazen: when he was passing some restless nights at a villa where an owl's hooting was disturbing his sleep, a soldier who was also a skilled bird-catcher caught the bird and brought it to Augustus, expecting a huge reward. The emperor praised him and ordered that he be given 1,000 sesterces—at which point the soldier dared to say, "I'd rather see it live," and let the bird go. Who could not amazed that Caesar took no offense and let the defiant soldier off scot-free? 27. When an army veteran was facing a trial and had his court-date set, he approached Caesar in public and asked him to support him at his trial. Caesar immediately chose someone from his entourage to serve as his advocate and introduced the man to the soldier: thereupon the veteran cried out in a loud voice, "But *I* did not look for someone to serve in my place when you were in danger at the battle of Actium [31 BCE]: I fought for you myself," and he uncovered his scars. Caesar blushed and came to support him, for fear of appearing not just arrogant but also ungrateful.[68]

[68] Cf. Cass. Dio 55.4.2.

28. 'Delectatus inter cenam erat symphoniacis Toranii
Flacci mangonis atque eos frumento donaverat, cum in
alia acroamata fuisset nummis liberalis, eosdemque postea
Toranius[37] aeque inter cenam quaerenti Caesari sic excu-
savit: "ad molas sunt."

29. 'Sublimis Actiaca victoria revertebatur. occurrit ei
inter gratulantes corvum tenens, quem instituerat haec dicere: "ave Caesar victor imperator." miratus Caesar officio-
sam avem viginti milibus nummum emit. socius opificis, ad
quem nihil ex illa liberalitate pervenerat, adfirmavit Caesari habere illum et alium corvum, quem ut adferre coge-
retur rogavit. adlatus verba quae didicerat expressit: "ave
victor imperator Antoni." nihil exasperatus satis duxit iu-
bere illum dividere donativum cum contubernali. 30. salutatus similiter a psittaco, emi eum iussit. idem miratus in
pica hanc quoque redemit. exemplum sutorem pauperem
sollicitavit ut corvum institueret ad parem salutationem,
qui impendio exhaustus saepe ad avem non respondentem
dicere solebat, "opera et impensa periit." aliquando tamen corvus coepit dicere dictatam salutationem. hac audi-
ta dum transit Augustus respondit, "satis domi salutato-
rum talium habeo." superfuit corvo memoria, ut et illa
quibus dominum querentem solebat audire subtexeret:
"opera et impensa periit." ad quod Caesar risit emique
avem iussit quanti nullam adhuc emerat.

[37] Toranii . . . Toranius (T(h)oranius *appellatur ap. Plin. NH
7.56, Suet. Aug. 69.1)*] Toron- *bis* ω (turon- *bis* δ), *quod nomen
nusquam invenitur*

---

[69] Normally the privilege of citizens.

28. 'At a banquet he was delighted by the musicians of the slave-dealer Toronius Flaccus and, though he had rewarded other entertainers with cash, he gave these the gift of a grain ration.[69] When he subsequently asked for the same musicians to entertain at another banquet, Toronius offered his regrets, saying, "They're milling the grain."

29. 'When he was returning to Rome on top of the world after his victory at Actium, one of those who ran to congratulate him was holding a raven that he had taught to say, "Hail Caesar, the victorious commander." Marveling at the dutiful bird, Caesar bought it for 20,000 sesterces. The trainer's confederate, who had gained nothing from this generous act, swore to Caesar that the man had another raven, too, which Caesar asked to be shown. When it was brought out it spoke the words it had been taught: "Hail the victorious commander, Antony." Nothing fazed, Caesar thought it sufficient that the trainer divide the gift with his mate. 30. When he was similarly greeted by a parrot, he ordered its purchase and, admiring a magpie with the same skill, he bought it too. Seeing this, a poor shoemaker was moved to teach a raven to give the same salute: but after he'd spent his last penny on the bird—which remained mute—he kept saying, over and over, "My effort and my money, down the drain." At length, however, the raven began to repeat the greeting it was taught; but when Augustus heard it as he was passing by, he said in response, "I have greeters of that sort in abundance at home." The raven still remembered hearing his master's complaint, and so ended by saying, "My effort and my money, down the drain." That made Caesar laugh, so he had the bird purchased at a price higher than all the rest.

31. 'Solebat descendenti a Palatio Caesari honorificum aliquod epigramma porrigere Graeculus. id cum frustra saepe fecisset rursusque eum idem facturum vidisset Augustus, breve sua manu in charta exaravit Graecum epigramma, pergenti deinde ad se obviam misit. ille legendo laudare, mirari tam voce quam vultu cumque accessisset ad sellam, demissa in fundam pauperem manu paucos denarios protulit quos principi daret, adiectus hic sermo, νὴ τὴν σὴν τύχην, Σεβαστέ, εἰ πλέον εἶχον, πλέον ⟨ἂν⟩[38] ἐδίδουν. secuto omnium risu dispensatorem Caesar vocavit et sestertia centum milia numerare Graeculo iussit.

5   'Vultis aliqua et filiae eius Iuliae dicta referamus? sed si garrulus non putabor, volo de moribus feminae pauca praemittere, ni quisquam vestrum habeat seria et discenda quae proferat.' hortantibusque omnibus ut coepto insisteret, ita de Iulia orsus est: 2. 'annum agebat tricesimum et octavum, tempus aetatis, si mens sana superesset, vergentis in senium, sed indulgentia tam fortunae quam patris abutebatur, cum alioquin litterarum amor multaque eruditio, quod in illa domo facile erat, praeterea mitis humanitas minimeque saevus animus ingentem feminae gratiam conciliarent, mirantibus qui vitia noscebant tantam pariter diversitatem. 3. non semel praeceperat pater, temperato

---

[38] ἂν suppl. Holford-Strevens

---

[70] Site of the palace complex that Augustus constructed.

[71] Lit. "[I swear] by your *tykhê*, Augustus," invoking the great man's personal "[good] fortune" (Lat. *fortuna*, Gk. *tykhê*), which later became a standard component of the emperor's divinized traits.

[72] The account begins, oddly, with 2 BCE, the year of Julia's

31. 'Whenever Caesar came down to the forum from the Palatine,[70] some little Greek would offer him an epigram in his honor. When the man had done this a number of times, to no effect, and Augustus saw that he was about to do it again, he quickly wrote out an epigram in Greek on a papyrus sheet and sent it to the man who was coming toward him. On reading it, the man began to express his wonder and admiration with his words and his expression; then approaching Caesar's seat he put his hand into his wretched purse and took out a few coins to give the emperor, adding, "I swear, Augustus[71]—if I had more, I'd give more." After all the bystanders had laughed, Caesar ordered his steward to count out 100,000 sesterces for the little Greek.

'Would you like me also to relate some witticisms of his 5 daughter Julia? If I'll not be thought a windbag, though, I'd like to first say a few words about the woman's character— unless someone has some serious remarks to make for our edification.' When they all urged him to press on with his plan, he began to speak about Julia in these terms: 2. 'She was thirty-seven,[72] a point in life when—if you have any sense left—you know you're no longer young, but she was abusing her standing as fortune's darling, and her father's, though in other respects she gained a great deal of credit for her love of literature and extensive learning (attainments not hard to come by in that household), and her kindness, fellow-feeling, and lack of cruelty besides: those familiar with her vices could only wonder at the evenly matched contrast. 3. More than once her father told her, in

banishment to the island Pandateria for her alleged multiple adulteries, an event unremarked in what follows.

tamen inter indulgentiam gravitatemque sermone, moderaretur profusos cultus perspicuosque comitatus. idem cum ad nepotum turbam similitudinemque respexerat qua repraesentabatur Agrippa, dubitare de pudicitia filiae erubescebat. 4. inde blandiebatur sibi Augustus laetum in filia animum usque ad speciem procacitatis sed reatu liberum, et talem fuisse apud maiores Claudiam credere audebat. itaque inter amicos dixit duas habere se filias delicatas, quas necesse haberet ferre, rem publicam et Iuliam.

5. Venerat ad eum licentiore vestitu et oculos offenderat patris tacentis. mutavit cultus sui postera die morem et laetum patrem affectata severitate complexa est. at ille qui pridie dolorem suum continuerat, gaudium continere non potuit et, "quantum hic," ait, "in filia Augusti probabilior est cultus?" non defuit patrocinio suo Iulia his verbis: "hodie enim me patris oculis ornavi, heri viri." 6. Notum et illud. averterant in se populum in spectaculo gladiatorum Livia et Iulia comitatus dissimilitudine: quippe cingentibus Liviam gravibus viris, haec iuventutis et quidem luxuriosae grege circumsedebatur. admonuit pater scripto, videret quantum inter duas principes feminas interesset. eleganter illa rescripsit: "et hi mecum senes fient."

---

73 Julia and Agrippa had five children before the latter's death in 12 BCE; her other two marriages, to her cousin M. Claudius Marcellus (in 25 BCE) and the future emperor Tiberius (in 11 BCE), were childless.

74 I.e., Claudia Quinta, a matron of questionable reputation who proved her good character when the Great Mother was brought to Rome in 204 BCE: after the barge carrying the goddess' cult-stone ran aground in the Tiber, Claudia prayed to the goddess for a sign to establish her good name, then effortlessly pulled the barge free (e.g., Ov. *F.* 4.305–28; for a version to similar effect, minus the miraculous element, Livy 29.14.12).

tones that balanced indulgence and strictness, that she should be less extravagant in her dress and adornments and in her eye-catching entourage; and yet when he saw his crowd of grandchildren and their resemblance to Agrippa,[73] he was ashamed of doubting his daughter's fidelity. 4. And so Augustus deluded himself with the thought that his daughter's high spirits gave the appearance of license but were innocent in fact, and he dared to believe that Claudia of old had been just like that:[74] he told his friends that he had two spoiled daughters—the commonwealth and Julia—and he would just have to put up with them (*dicta* 63 Malc.).

5. 'She came to him dressed suggestively, and the sight offended her father, though he said nothing. The next day she changed her style of dress and, trying to look serious, gave her pleased father a hug. Though he had been able to conceal his unhappiness the day before, he couldn't conceal his joy now, and said, "Isn't this style of dress so much more becoming in the daughter of Augustus?" But she was not at a loss for words in her own defense: "Yes, because today I dressed to please my father; yesterday I dressed to please my husband" (*dicta* 64 Malc.). 6. The following incident became notorious too. At a set of gladiatorial contests the very different entourages of Livia and Julia caught the people's attention, with men of weight and standing gathered around Livia, while Julia was surrounded by a gaggle of youths of decidedly dandified appearance. Her father slipped her a note pointing out the difference between the two first ladies—to which she nicely wrote back, "These young men will grow old with me, too."

7. 'Eadem Iulia mature habere coeperat canos, quos legere secrete solebat. subitus interventus patris aliquando oppressit ornatrices. dissimulavit Augustus deprehensis super vestem earum canis, et aliis sermonibus tempore extracto induxit aetatis mentionem interrogavitque filiam utrum post aliquot annos cana esse mallet an calva; et cum illa respondisset, "ego, pater, cana esse malo," sic illi mendacium obiecit: "quid ergo istae te calvam tam cito faciunt?" 8. Item cum gravem amicum audisset Iulia suadentem melius facturam[39] si se composuisset ad exemplar paternae frugalitatis, ait, "ille obliviscitur Caesarem se esse, ego memini me Caesaris filiam."

9. 'Cumque conscii flagitiorum mirarentur quo modo similes Agrippae filios pareret, quae tam vulgo potestatem corporis sui faceret, ait, "numquam enim nisi navi plena tollo vectorem." 10. Simile dictum Popilliae[40] Marci filiae, quae miranti cuidam quid esset quapropter aliae bestiae numquam marem desiderarent nisi cum praegnantes vellent fieri, respondit, "bestiae enim sunt."

6   'Sed ut a feminis ad viros et a lascivis iocis ad honestos revertar, Cascellius[41] iuris consultus urbanitatis mirae libertatisque habebatur, praecipue tamen is iocus eius innotuit. lapidatus a populo Vatinius cum gladiatorium munus ederet obtinuerat ut aediles edicerent, nequis in hare-

---

[39] facturam R²AC: futuram ω (*om.* P)
[40] Popilliae] Populiae ω (*quod nomen fere nusquam invenitur*)
[41] Cascellius *ed. Paris. 1585*: caecilius ω (*recte infra*)

---

[75] This is perhaps the "Paulla Popillia, Marcus' daughter," who was the wife of Gnaeus Piso, conspirator against Julius Caesar and cos. suff. 23 (a suggestion I owe to J. D. Morgan: cf. *IG* 7.305, Syme 1986, 368–69).

7. 'Julia was getting prematurely gray and took to plucking her gray hair in secret. One day her father surprised her hairdressers with his arrival, and they stopped their work. Pretending not to notice the gray hairs on their garments, Augustus chatted about some other topics for a while before steering the conversation around to the topic of age, then asked his daughter whether—some years hence—she would rather be bald or gray: when she replied, "I, father, would prefer to be gray," he reproved her fib by saying, "Then why are these women trying so hard to make you bald?" (*dicta* 65 Malc.) 8. When a friend of strict views tried to persuade Julia that she'd do better to conform herself to the model of her father's sober habits, she said, "He forgets that he is Caesar, but I remember that I am Caesar's daughter."

9. 'When people aware of her outrageous behavior expressed surprise that her sons looked just like Agrippa, though she had been so free in letting others enjoy her charms, she said, "I take on a passenger only when the ship's hold is full." 10. Compare the *mot* of Marcus Popillius' daughter:[75] when someone wondered why other animals sought a male of the species only when they wished to become pregnant, she replied, "Because they're animals."

'But to turn from women back to men, and from naughty jokes to decent ones, the legal expert Cascellius was generally considered a man of marvelous wit and candor, though this jest gained particular notoriety: when the people stoned Vatinius while he was giving a gladiatorial show,[76] he got the aediles to issue a decree that only fruit

[76] Gladiatorial games given by Vatinius were mocked by Cicero in a speech delivered in March 56 BCE (*Sest.* 134–35).

nam nisi pomum misisse vellet. forte his diebus Cascellius
consultus a quodam an nux pinea pomum esset respondit,
"si in Vatinium missurus est, pomum est." 2. Mercatori
deinde, quem ad modum cum socio navem divideret interroganti, respondisse traditur, "navem si dividis, nec tu
nec socius habebitis." 3. In Galbam eloquentia clarum sed
quem habitus, ut supra dixi, corporis destruebat M. Lollii
vox circumferebatur: "ingenium Galbae male habitat."
4. In eundem Galbam Orbilius grammaticus acerbius inrisit. prodierat Orbilius in reum testis. quem Galba ut
confunderet dissimulata professione eius interrogavit,
"quid artium facis?" respondit: "in sole gibbos soleo fricare." 5. L. Caecilius, cum C. Caesar aliis qui secum pila
lusitabant centena sestertia, illi uni quinquaginta dari iussisset, "quid? ego," inquit, "una manu ludo?"

6. 'Cum iratus esse P. Clodius D. Laberio[42] diceretur
quod ei mimum petenti non dedisset, "quid amplius," inquit, "mihi facturus es, nisi ut Dyrrhachium eam et re-
deam?," ludens ad Ciceronis exilium.

---

[42] Laberio F[m]: valerio ω

---

[77] Cf. Quint. 6.3.87.   [78] Cf. 2.4.8
[79] Contrast the judgment that the deformity of Vatinius' body
rivaled the baseness of his mind (Vell. 2.69.4).

[80] Cf. Suet. *Gramm.* 9.5 (also involving Orbilius, though
the butt is a Varro Murena and the punch line is different). The
verb *fricare*, here translated "drub" (cf. Pl. *Pseud.* 1190), literally
means "rub/chafe/massage"; "alfresco" (*in sole*) because trials
were held out of doors.   [81] Perhaps 56 BCE, when Clodius
was one of the curule aediles, responsible for the Games of the
Great Mother (4–10 April) and Roman Games (5–13 September),

366

was to be thrown in the arena; when someone happened to ask Cascellius at about the same time whether in his opinion a pine cone was a fruit, he said, "If a person is going to throw it at Vatinius, it's a fruit." 2. When a merchant asked him how he should divide a ship with his partner, he is said to have replied, "If you divide the ship, neither you nor your partner will have it."[77] 3. A witticism of Marcus Lollius circulated at the expense of Galba, who was renowned for his eloquence, though the deformity I've remarked[78] detracted from the effect: "Galba's genius inhabits a hovel."[79] 4. Galba was also mocked quite harshly by the grammarian Orbilius, when he appeared in court as a witness against Galba's client: when Galba, to disconcert him, pretended not to know his profession and asked, "What's your line of work?," Orbilius replied, "I give hunchbacks an alfresco drubbing."[80] 5. When Gaius Caesar gave 100,000 sesterces to the men who were playing ball with him but ordered that 50,000 be given to Lucius Caecilius, the latter said, "Why? Am I playing with one hand?"

6. 'When Publius Clodius was said to be in a snit with Decimus Laberius because he didn't comply with Clodius' request for a mime script,[81] Laberius said, "What are you going to do to me? Make me go to Dyrrachium and come back?," alluding to Cicero's exile.[82]

at which theatrical productions were mounted, although the earthy comedy known as "mime" is otherwise attested only for the festival of Flora (28 April–3 May) overseen by the plebeian aediles.   [82] When Cicero was in exile (cf. 2.3.5) he spent the period November 58–August 57 BCE in Dyrrachium (mod. Durrës, Albania) on the coast of Epirus.

7 'Sed quia et paulo ante Aurelius Symmachus et ego
nunc Laberii fecimus mentionem, si aliqua huius atque
Publilii[43] dicta referemus, videbimur et adhibendi convivio mimos vitasse lasciviam et tamen celebritatem quam
cum adsunt illi excitare pollicentur imitari. 2. Laberium
asperae libertatis equitem Romanum Caesar quingentis
milibus invitavit ut prodiret in scaenam et ipse ageret mimos quos scriptitabat. sed potestas non solum si invitet sed
et si supplicet cogit, unde se et Laberius a Caesare coac-
tum in prologo testatur his versibus:

> 3. Necessitas, cuius cursus transversi impetum
> voluerunt multi effugere, pauci potuerunt,
> quo me detrusti[44] paene extremis sensibus?
> quem nulla ambitio, nulla umquam largitio,
> 5 nullus timor, vis nulla, nulla auctoritas
> movere potuit in iuventa de statu,
> ecce in senecta ut facile labefecit loco
> viri excellentis mente clemente edita
> summissa placide blandiloquens oratio?
> 10 et enim ipsi di negare cui nil potuerunt,
> hominem me denegare quis posset pati?
> ego[45] bis tricenis annis actis sine nota
> eques Romanus ⟨e⟩[46] Lare egressus meo

43 Publilii NP2: Publii DP1Tβ
44 detrusti *Scaliger*: detrusit ω
45 ego *ed. Ven. 1513*: ergo ω
46 e *Fruterius (epist. ad Muretum)*, ex *Scaliger*, om. ω

---

83 Cf. 2.3.10 and 2.6.5; all concern the same episode, set in 46
BCE.

'But since both Aurelius Symmachus, a little earlier,   7
and I just now mentioned Laberius,[83] if we relate some of
his witticisms, and those of Publilius too, we'll avoid the
lewdness entailed in actually bringing mimes into our banquet while imitating the high spirits that their presence
promises to arouse. 2. Caesar offered Laberius, a Roman
knight whose candor gave no quarter, 500,000 sesterces
to appear onstage and perform the mimes that he used
to write.[84] But since supreme power has the force of compulsion whether it extends an invitation or even pleads,
Laberius too felt Caesar's compulsion, as he bears witness
in these verses from the prologue (140–166):[85]

3. O Necessity, whose blind-side assaults many
have sought to avoid—most to no avail—
where have you made me fall, when I'm nearly
breathing my last? No ambition, no largesse,
no fear, no force, no man's prestige could   5
make me shift my stance when I was young:
now that I'm old, do you see how easily I'm
undone by the invitation—humble and mild—
that issues from the merciful mind
of the man who towers above us? Of course,   10
for me to say "no" to the man the very gods
have denied nothing—would that not be outrageous?
I—who have passed twice thirty years with not a
    mark

[84] On the consequences of appearing onstage—the premise of
the following actions—see 2.3.10n.
[85] §§2–3 are probably based on Gell. 8.15, of which only the
summary heading now survives.

domum revertar mimus. nimirum hoc die
15 uno plus vixi mihi quam vivendum fuit.
    Fortuna immoderata in bono aeque atque in malo,
    si tibi erat libitum litterarum laudibus
    florens[47] cacumen nostrae famae frangere,
    cur cum vigebam membris praeviridantibus,
20 satis facere populo et tali cum poteram viro,
    non flexilem me[48] concurvasti ut carperes?
    nuncine[49] me deicis? quo? quid ad scaenam adfero?
    decorem formae an dignitatem corporis,
    animi virtutem an vocis iucundae sonum?
25 ut hedera serpens vires arboreas necat,
    ita me vetustas amplexu annorum enecat.
    sepulcri similis nihil nisi nomen retineo.

4. 'In ipsa quoque actione subinde se, qua poterat, ulcis-
cebatur, inducto habitu Syri qui velut flagris caesus praeri-
pientique se similis exclamabat,

porro, Quirites, libertatem perdimus,

et paulo post adiecit,

necesse est multos timeat quem multi timent.

---

[47] florens *Lipsius*: floris ω

[48] flexilem me *Bücheler*: flexibilem me ω, me flexibilem *Muretus*

[49] nuncine *Schneidewin*: nunc ω

---

[86] Cf. Cic. *On Appropriate Actions* 2.24, Sen. *On Anger* 2.11.3,

against my name—left my household gods a Roman
    knight
to return to them—a mime. Surely today   15
I've lived one day longer than I ought.
O Fortune, who know no mean in good and bad
    alike,
if it was your pleasure to break me at the pinnacle,
in the full bloom of the fame I'd won by my glory in
    letters,
why did you not make me bow down, to destroy my
    pliant self,   20
when I still had the vigor of limbs in their prime,
when I could put on a proper show for the people
    and the great man?
Now you cast me down? Why? What do I bring to the
    stage?
The beauty and dignity of a well-formed body,
the mind's wit or a sweet-sounding voice?   25
As ivy destroys the vital force of trees by creeping
    'round them,
so long passage of years is killing me.
Like a tomb, I keep nothing but my name.

4. 'In the performance itself that followed he also took
his revenge as he could, putting on the costume of a Syrian
who had been whipped and was trying to escape, crying
out (172),

From this moment on, citizens, we lose our freedom

and adding a little later (139):

He whom many fear must needs fear many.[86]

5. 'Quo dicto universitas populi ad solum Caesarem oculos et ora convertit, notantes impotentiam eius hac dicacitate lapidatam. ob haec in Publilium[50] vertit favorem.

6. 'Is Publilius natione Syrus cum puer ad patronum domini esset adductus, promeruit eum non minus salibus et ingenio quam forma. nam forte cum ille servum suum hydropicum iacentem in area vidisset increpuissetque quid in sole faceret, respondit, "aquam calefacit." ioculari deinde super cena exorta quaestione quodnam esset molestum otium, aliud alio opinante, ille "podagrici pedes" dixit. 7. ob haec et alia manu missus et maiore cura cruditus, cum mimos componeret ingentique adsensu in Italiae oppidis agere coepisset, productus Romae per Caesaris ludos omnes qui tunc scripta et operas suas in scaenam locaverant provocavit ut singuli secum posita in vicem materia pro tempore contenderent. nec ullo recusante superavit omnes, in quis et Laberium. 8. unde Caesar adridens hoc modo pronuntiavit:

favente tibi me victus es, Laberi, a Syro;

statimque Publilio palmam et Laberio anulum aureum cum quingentis sestertiis dedit. tunc Publilius[51] ad Laberium recedentem ait,

quicum contendisti scriptor, hunc spectator subleva.

[50] Publilium D²PṣK: Publium ω
[51] Publilius DP: Publius ω

---

[87] Dropsy (= edema) is a swelling of the soft tissues caused by the accumulation of excess water.
[88] Cf. 2.3.10, Cic. *Fam.* 12.18.2.
[89] For the significance of the award, cf. 2.3.10 n.

5. 'At that the people turned as one to look at Caesar alone, making plain that this caustic remark had scored a direct hit on his high-handedness, and this caused him to shift his support to Publilius.

6. 'Publilius, a Syrian by birth, was brought to his master's patron as a boy and won him over by his wit and talent as much as by his beauty: for when the patron happened to see a slave of his who suffered from dropsy lying in the courtyard, he scolded him, asking what he thought he was doing out there in the sun—and Publilius said, "He's heating water."[87] And when the question arose over dinner as to what counted as a disagreeable way of taking one's ease, with now one man, now another venturing an opinion, he said, "Having the gout." 7. By such displays of wit he earned his freedom and received a superior education. When he was composing and performing mimes and his shows had begun to find great favor in the towns of Italy, he took the stage at Rome during Caesar's games[88] and challenged all those who had hired out their scripts or acting skills to compete with him in improvised performances, one on one, taking turns setting the themes. They all took up the challenge, and they all lost, including Laberius. 8. Thereupon Caesar declared with a laugh:

> Though I'm your fan, Laberius, you were beaten by
>   the Syrian;

and at once he awarded the palm of victory to Publilius and a gold ring[89] with 500,000 sesterces to Laberius. Then Publilius said to Laberius, as he withdrew,

> Support as a spectator the man with whom you competed as a writer.

9. sed et Laberius sequenti statim commissione mimo
novo interiecit hos versus:

> Non possunt primi esse omnes omni in tempore.
> summum ad gradum cum claritatis veneris,
> consistes aegre et citius quam ascendas cades.[52]
> cecidi ego, cadet qui sequitur: laus est publica.

10. 'Publilii autem sententiae feruntur lepidae et ad
communem usum accommodatissimae, ex quibus has fere
memini singulis versibus circumscriptas:

11. Beneficium dando accepit qui digno dedit.
> feras, non culpes, quod mutari non potest.
> cui plus licet quam par est, plus vult quam licet.
> comes facundus in via pro vehiculo est.
> frugalitas miseria est rumoris boni.
> heredis fletus sub persona risus est.
> furor fit laesa saepius patientia.
> improbe Neptunum accusat, qui iterum naufragium
>   facit.
> nimium altercando veritas amittitur.
> pars benefici[53] est, quod petitur si cito[54] neges.

---

[52] cades *Florilegium Gallicum* (*Muñoz Jiménez RHT n.s. 3*
[2008]: 101): decidas ω
[53] benefici V[1]: -ficii ω
[54] cito ω: belle *Syrus*, velle *codd. Gell.*

---

[90] Cf. Gell. 17.14.4.

9. But at the very next set of games Laberius inserted these verses in a new mime (167–70):

> All men cannot come out first each time.
> When you've reached the highest step on fame's
>   ladder,
> you'll find it hard to keep your footing and fall more
>   quickly than you rise:
> I fell, and so will the one who follows: fame belongs
>   to no one man.

10. 'There are in circulation, moreover, Publilius' pointed sayings, which are very handy for general application: here are the examples I remember, one-liners all:[90]

11. A person who does a favor for a worthy man
    receives one in the doing. (B 12)
You should endure what can't be changed, not
    complain about it. (F 11)
A person allowed more than is fair wants more than
    he's allowed. (C 46)
On a journey a pleasant companion is as good as a
    ride. (C 17)
Sobriety is the unhappy burden of a good reputation.
    (F 28)
A weeping heir is laughing beneath his mask. (H 19)
Forbearance too often abused becomes rage. (F 13)
A person who's shipwrecked twice has no right to
    blame Neptune. (I 63)
The truth gets lost in excessive bickering. (N 40)
It's at least half a favor to turn down a request
    promptly. (P 20)

ita amicum habeas, posse ut fieri[55] hunc inimicum
  putes.
veterem ferendo iniuriam invites novam.
numquam periclum sine periclo vincitur.

12. 'Sed quia semel ingressus sum scaenam loquendo,
nec Pylades histrio nobis omittendus est, qui clarus in
opere suo fuit temporibus Augusti et Hylam discipulum
usque ad aequalitatis contentionem eruditione provexit.
13. populus deinde inter utriusque suffragia divisus est, et
cum canticum quoddam saltaret Hylas cuius clausula erat
τὸν μέγαν Ἀγαμέμνονα, sublimem ingentemque Hylas
velut metiebatur. non tulit Pylades et exclamavit e cavea:
σὺ μακρὸν οὐ μέγαν ποιεῖς. 14. tunc eum populus coegit
idem saltare canticum cumque ad locum venisset quem re-
prehenderat, expressit cogitantem, nihil magis ratus magno duci convenire quam pro omnibus cogitare. 15. saltabat
Hylas Oedipodem, et Pylades hac voce securitatem saltan-
tis castigavit: σὺ βλέπεις. 16. cum in Herculem furentem
prodisset et non nullis incessum histrioni convenientem
non servare videretur, deposita persona ridentes increpuit:
μωροί, μαινόμενον ὀρχοῦμαι. 17. hac fabula et sagittas ie-
cit in populum. eandem personam cum iussu Augusti in

---

[55] fieri ω, *Gell.*: facile fieri *Syrus*

---

[91] As performers in the "pantomime," Pylades and Hylas
wordlessly danced stories, typically from Greek tragedy, accompanied by music and a chorus; it was an art form distinct from the
earthier, often bawdy "mimes" of the sort written by Laberius and
Publilius.
[92] I.e., we are to understand that this is the blind Oedipus,
whose hesitant movements Hylas failed to represent.

Treat a friend as you would were you to imagine his
    becoming your enemy. (I 16)
By putting up with an old wrong you invite a fresh
    one. (V 16)
Danger is never overcome without danger. (N 7)

12. 'But having once mounted the stage in giving my account, I shouldn't omit the actor Pylades, who flourished in
the Augustan age and brought his follower Hylas so far
along in his art that they competed on an equal footing.[91]
13. The people then divided its support between the two,
and when Hylas was dancing to some song whose conclud-
ing rhythm contained the phrase "the great Agamemnon,"
Hylas measured out his stature to give the impression of
someone massive and grand: Pylades lost his patience and
called out from the audience, "You're making him big,
not great!" 14. Then the audience made him dance the
same piece again, and when he reached the passage that
Pylades had criticized, he adopted the posture of one engaged in reflection, judging that taking thought for all was
the thing most appropriate for a great general. 15. When
Hylas was dancing the character of Oedipus, Pylades criticized his nonchalance with the remark, "You're peek-
ing."[92] 16. When Pylades acted the part of the insane Hercules and some thought he wasn't maintaining the gait appropriate to an actor, he took his mask off and scolded the
people who were laughing by saying, "Idiots! I'm dancing a
madman!" 17. In the same play he shot an arrow into the
audience; and when he was acting Hercules at Augustus'
behest in his dining hall, he aimed his bow and shot some

triclinio ageret, et intendit arcum et spicula immisit. nec indignatus est Caesar eodem se loco Pyladi quo populum Romanum fuisse. 18. hic quia ferebatur mutasse rudis illius saltationis ritum, quae apud maiores viguit, et venustam induxisse novitatem, interrogatus ab Augusto quae saltationi contulisset, respondit,

αὐλῶν συρίγγων τ᾽ ἐνοπὴν ὅμαδόν τ᾽ ἀνθρώπων.

19. idem cum propter populi seditionem pro contentione inter se Hylamque habita concitatam indignationem excepisset Augusti, respondit, "καὶ ἀχαριστεῖς, βασιλεῦ· ἔασον αὐτοὺς περὶ ἡμᾶς ἀσχολεῖσθαι."'

8   His dictis et excitata laetitia cum in Avieno memoria florida et amoenitas laudaretur ingenii, mensas secundas minister admovit. 2. et Flavianus: 'multi, ut aestimo, in hoc a Varrone dissentiunt, qui in illa lepidissima satura Menippea, quae inscribitur Nescis quid vesper vehat, de secunda mensa placentas removit: sed quaeso dicas, Caecina, verba ipsa Varronis, si tibi beneficio memoriae tenacioris haeserunt.' 3. et Albinus, 'locus,' inquit, 'Varronis quem referri a me imperas, in his fere verbis est: "bellaria ea maxime sunt mellita quae mellita non sunt: dulcibus enim cum πέψει societas infida." significant autem bellaria omne mensae secundae genus. nam quae πέμματα Graeci vel τραγήματα dixerunt, ea veteres nostri appellavere bellaria; vina quoque dulciora est invenire in comoediis antiquioribus hoc vocabulo dictaque ea Liberi bellaria.'

---

93 I.e., the audience could not only see the scene represented but virtually experience it as though it were fully present.

94 Cf. Cass. Dio 54.17.4 (a similar anecdote involving Pylades and the mime Bathyllus, the favorite of Maecenas).

arrows—and Augustus thought it only fair to find himself
in the same position, vis-à-vis Pylades, as the Roman people had been. 18. Since Pylades was said to have changed
the old style of dancing that had had its heyday with our ancestors and to have introduced a new and charming style,
he was asked by Augustus what contribution he had made
to dance and answered (*Il.* 10.13):

the sound of pipes and flutes and the din of men.[93]

19. When his competition with Hylas provoked a riot, he
replied to Augustus' outrage with the comment: "You're
being ungrateful indeed, your highness: let them be dis-
tracted by us."[94]

Delighted by these remarks the company set about   8
praising Avienus' powers of memory and pleasing wit, as a
slave brought in dessert.[95] 2. Flavianus said, 'I imagine
many people disagree with Varro, who banned cakes from
dessert in that wonderfully captivating Menippean satire
of his called *You Know Not What the Evening Will Bring*
(fr. 333 Cèbe): but Caecina, your memory's better—please
give us the exact quotation.'[96] 3. Caecina Albinus replied,
'The passage in Varro that you want me to relate goes very
much like this (fr. 341 Cèbe): "Those treats are sweet-
est that have not been sweetened: for sweets don't reliably make common cause with good digestion." "Treats"
is the term our ancestors used to denote every sort of
dessert—what the Greeks called "cakes" [*pemmata*] or
"sweetmeats" [*tragêmata*]; you can also find this label applied to the sweeter varieties of wine in the older comedies, where they're called "Liber's treats."'

---

[95] Evening, 17 December.
[96] §§2–3 are based on Gell. 13.11.1, 6–7.

4. Et Evangelus: 'agite antequam surgendum nobis sit, vino indulgeamus, quod decreti Platonici auctoritate faciemus, qui aestimavit fomitem esse quendam et ignitabulum[56] ingenii virtutisque, si mens et corpus hominis vino flagret.' 5. Tunc Eustathius: 'quid agis,' inquit, 'Euangele? an Platonem aestimas haurienda passim vina suasisse et non magis inter minuta pocula iucundiorem liberalioremque invitationem, quae fieret sub quibusdam quasi arbitris et magistris conviviorum sobriis, non improbasse? et hoc est quod in primo et secundo de legibus non inutile viris esse decernit. 6. nam et modicis honestisque inter bibendum remissionibus refici integrarique animos ad instauranda sobrietatis officia existimavit redditosque sensim laetiores ad intentiones rursus capessendas fieri habiliores; et simul, siqui penitus in his adfectionum cupiditatumque errores inessent quos celaret alioquin[57] pudor reverens, ea omnia sine gravi periculo libertate per vinum data detegi et ad corrigendum medendumque fieri opportuniora. 7. atque hoc etiam Plato ibidem dicit, non defugiendas[58] esse huiusce modi exercitationes adversum propulsandam vini violentiam, neque ullum umquam continentem prorsum aut temperantem satis fideliter visum esse cui vita non inter ipsa errorum pericula et in mediis voluptatum inlecebris explorata sit. 8. nam cui libentiae gratiaeque omnes conviviorum incognitae sint, quique illarum omnino expers sit, si eum forte ad partici-

56 incitabulum δ, *Gell.*
57 alioqui β, aliqui *Gell.*
58 def- *Gell.*: diff- ω

97 Cf. Pl. *Laws* 672A-D. §§4–9 are based on Gell. 15.2.3–8

4. Then Evangelus said, 'Come now, before it's time to leave the table, let's have a nice round or two of wine, sanctioned by the pronouncement of Plato, who judged that if a person's mind and body burn with wine, it provides the kindling and the spark of wit and courage.'[97] 5. Then Eustathius said, 'What are you up to, Evangelus? Do you really suppose that Plato urged us to guzzle wine as we please, instead of approving a more pleasant and decent call to drink, with modest servings supervised by what might be called sober "arbiters" or "masters" of the carouse? *That* is what he says is expedient for men, in Books 1 and 2 of *Laws*. 6. For he thought that the modest and respectable forms of relaxation provided by drink restore our minds and make them whole again, so that we can resume the duties proper to sobriety:[98] as our good cheer is gradually restored, we become more fit to concentrate again on our projects. At the same time, if people are subject to character faults and misconceived desires that a modest circumspection otherwise keeps hidden, they're all uncovered without serious risk by the release that wine brings and so become more available to correction and healing. 7. In the same passage Plato adds that we shouldn't avoid opportunities of this sort, to train ourselves in combating the powerful effects of wine, and that no one has ever been reliably shown to be so self-controlled and balanced that his way of life would not be challenged by being faced with errors' perils and pleasures' snares.[99] 8. A man who does not know the delights and allurements of the banquet and has not partaken of them (Plato says) is beguiled and taken

[98] Cf. Pl. *Laws* 637B-641D.
[99] Cf. Pl. *Laws* 647E-648E.

pandas huius modi voluptates aut voluntas tulerit aut casus
induxerit aut necessitas impulerit, mox deleniri et capi
neque mentem eius animumque consistere. 9. congre-
diendum igitur et tamquam in acie quadam cum volupta-
riis rebus cumque ista vini licentia comminus decernen-
dum, ut adversus eas non fuga nec absentia simus tuti, sed
vigore animi et constanti praesentia moderatoque usu
temperantiam continentiamque tueamur; et calefacto simul refotoque animo, si quid in eo vel frigidae tristitiae vel
torpentis verecundiae fuerit diluamus.

10. 'Sed quia voluptatum fecimus mentionem, docet
Aristoteles a quibus voluptatibus sit cavendum. quinque
enim sunt hominum sensus, quos Graeci αἰσθήσεις appellant, per quos voluptas animo aut corpori quaeri videtur, tactus gustus odoratus visus auditus. 11. ex his omnibus voluptas quae immodice capitur ea turpis atque
improba est. sed enim quae nimia ex gustu atque tactu
est, ea igitur gemina[59] voluptas, sicut sapientes viri censuerunt, omnium rerum foedissima est eosque maxime
qui sese duabus istis voluptatibus dediderunt gravissimi
vitii vocabulis Graeci appellaverunt vel ἀκρατεῖς vel
ἀκολάστους, nos eos vel incontinentes dicimus vel intem-
perantes. 12. istas autem voluptates duas, gustus atque tactus, id est cibi et veneris, solas hominibus communes videmus esse cum beluis, et idcirco in pecudum ferorumque
animalium numero habetur quisquis est his ferarum

[59] igitur gemina *om. Gell.*

captive, his mind and its thoughts find no stable place to stand, if choice or chance or compulsion causes him to become acquainted with such pleasures. 9. As in battle, then, we have to square up to the enemy—pleasures and indulgence in wine—and fight them at close quarters, so that we fortify ourselves against them not by flight or evasion but by relying on mental exertion, unswerving resolution, and moderate indulgence to preserve our balance and self-restraint. That way, when our mind has been warmed and refreshed at once, we may wash away whatever element there was in it of chill despondency and supine diffidence.

10. 'But since the topic of pleasure has come up, Aristotle teaches us[100] which pleasures we have to guard against. Human beings have five senses, which the Greeks call *aisthêseis*, and these—touch, taste, smell, sight, hearing—are the pathways by which the body and mind seek pleasure. 11. Pleasure derived immoderately from all these senses is base and wicked, but excessive pleasure derived from taste and touch—a compound pleasure, as wise men have judged it—is the most disgusting of all: to those, especially, who surrendered to these pleasures the Greeks applied the terms for the most serious of vices, calling them *akratês* or *akolastoi*, or as we say, "incontinent" or "uncontrolled." 12. We understand that the two pleasures of taste and touch—that is, food and sex—are the only ones that human beings share with the beasts, and that's why anyone wholly in the grip of these pleasure is counted among the animals of the fields and the wilds; all other

---

[100] Beyond the quotation in §14, cf. Arist. *Nicomachean Ethics* 3.10–12 1117b-1119b, 7.7 1150a-b, *Eudemian Ethics* 3.2 1230a-1231b. §§10–16 are based on Gell. 19.2.1–8.

voluptatibus occupatus; ceterae ex tribus aliis sensibus
proficiscentes hominum tantum propriae sunt. 13. verba
super hac re Aristotelis philosophi in medium proferam, ut
quid de his infamibus voluptatibus tam clarus atque incli-
tus vir sentiat publicetur:

14. Διὰ τί οἱ[60] κατὰ τὴν τῆς ἁφῆς ἢ γεύσεως ἡδο-
νὴν ἐγγινομένην ἐὰν[61] ὑπερβάλωσιν,[62] ἀκρατεῖς
λέγονται; οἵ τε γὰρ περὶ τὰ ἀφροδίσια ἀκόλαστοι
τοιοῦτοι, οἵ τε περὶ τὰς τῆς τροφῆς ἀπολαύσεις.
τῶν δὲ κατὰ τὴν τροφὴν ἀπ' ἐνίων μὲν ἐν τῇ γλώτ-
τῃ τὸ ἡδύ, ἀπ' ἐνίων δὲ ἐν τῷ λάρυγγι, διὸ καὶ
Φιλόξενος γεράνου λάρυγγα[63] εὔχετο ἔχειν·[64] ἢ
διὰ τὸ τὰς ἀπὸ τούτων γιγνομένας ἡδονὰς κοινὰς
εἶναι ἡμῖν καὶ τοῖς ἄλλοις ζῴοις, ἅτε δὲ οὐσῶν
κοινῶν αἰσχρὰν εἶναι τὴν ὑποταγήν, αὐτίκα[65]
τὸν[66] ὑπὸ τούτων ἡττώμενον ψέγομεν καὶ ἀκρατῆ
καὶ ἀκόλαστον λέγομεν διὰ τὸ ὑπὸ τῶν χειρίστων
ἡδονῶν ἡττᾶσθαι· οὐσῶν δὲ τῶν αἰσθήσεων πέντε
τὰ[67] ἄλλα ζῷα ἀπὸ δύο μόνων[68] ἥδεται, κατὰ δὲ
τὰς ἄλλας ἢ ὅλως οὐχ ἥδεται ἢ κατὰ συμβεβηκὸς
τοῦτο πάσχει.

[60] τί οἱ ed. Colon. 1521, Gell.: ΤΟΙ ω
[61] ἐγγινομένην ἐὰν ω (γιγνομένην ἐὰν Gell): οὗ ἂν Arist.
[62] ὑπερβάλωσιν ω, Gell.: -βάλωσιν Arist.
[63] λάρυγγα ω, Gell.: φάρυγγα Arist.
[64] post ἔχειν om. οἱ δὲ κατὰ τὴν ὄψιν καὶ τὴν ἀκοὴν οὐκέτι ω,
Gell.
[65] ἅτε δὲ ... αὐτίκα ω: ἅτε οὖν οὖσαι κοιναὶ ἀτιμόταταί εἰσι

pleasures, which derive from the three remaining senses, are peculiar to human beings. 13. I'll quote the words of the philosopher Aristotle on this topic, so that we may share the sentiments of so brilliant and famous a man concerning these disgraceful pleasures (*Probl.* 28 949b–950a):

14. Why are people who go to excess in pursuing the pleasure of touch or taste called "incontinent" [*akratês*]? For people who lack control in matters of sex are of that sort, and those who lack control in the enjoyment derived from food. Of those concerning food, the sweetness derived from some things is perceived by the tongue, from others, by the throat, and that is why Philoxenus prayed to have "a crane's throat."[101] Or else it is because we share the pleasures derived from these sources with other animals, and since subjection to these shared pleasures is shameful, we do not hesitate to reproach the person overcome by them and call him "incontinent" and "uncontrolled," because he is overcome by the worst pleasures: for other animals derive pleasure from only two of the five existing senses and are either wholly insensible to pleasure from the other three or experience it only contingently.

[101] Because it is long (the Greeks did not know giraffes).

καὶ μάλιστα ἢ μόναι ἐπονείδιστοι, ὥστε [ὥς Gell.] Arist., Gell., ed. Colon. 1521

66 τὸν W²: ΤΟ ω

67 τὰ ω, Gell.: τά τε Arist.

68 μόνων Pβ₁, Arist.: -νον N (om. DGβ₂), codd. Gell., ed. Ven. 1472; post μόνων om. τῶν προειρημένων ω, codd. Gell.

15. quis igitur habens aliquid humani pudoris voluptatibus istis duabus, coeundi atque comedendi, quae homini cum sue atque asino communes sunt, gratuletur? 16. Socrates quidem dicebat multos homines propterea velle vivere ut ederent et biberent, se bibere atque esse ut viveret. Hippocrates autem, divina vir scientia, de coitu Venerio ita existimabat, partem esse quandam morbi taeterrimi quem nostri comitialem dixerunt. namque ipsius verba haec traduntur: τὴν συνουσίαν εἶναι μικρὰν ἐπιληψίαν . . .[69]

[69] *nihil subscriptum sed spatium relictum in* αLC (2–3 *lin.* αL, 13–14 *litt.* C), MACROBII THEODOSII VC ET INL CONVIVIORVM PRIMI DIEI SATVRNALIORUM EXPLICIT β

15. Will anyone with a shred of human decency, then, exult in those two pleasure, of sexual intercourse and gluttony, which human beings share with swine and asses? 16. Indeed, Socrates used to say that many people wish to live so they might eat and drink, whereas he ate and drank so that he might live.[102] Hippocrates, a man of godlike understanding, thought that sexual intercourse has something in common with the utterly repulsive illness we call the "comitial disease":[103] his words, as they've been handed down, are, "Intercourse is a small seizure"[104] . . .

[102] Cf. Muson. Ruf. p. 102.9–11, Plut. *Mor.* 21E, Gell. 19.2.7, Athen. 158F, Diog. Laert. 2.34, Stob. 3.17.21.

[103] I.e., epilepsy, so called because if anyone suffered a seizure during a voting assembly (*comitia*), the assembly had to be suspended and the voting postponed.

[104] The formulation, absent from Hippocrates' extant writings, is otherwise attributed to Democritus (Clem. Alex. *Paedagogue* 1.94, Galen 17,1:521, Stob. 3.6.28) or Eryximachus (Stob. 3.6.44).